CHILDREN OF THE JAPANESE STATE

Children of the Japanese State

The Changing Role of Child Protection Institutions in Contemporary Japan

ROGER GOODMAN

To Ito,
with best wishes and many
thanks for all your help,
Roger
16. Oct. 2000

OXFORD
UNIVERSITY PRESS

OXFORD

UNIVERSITY PRESS

Great Clarendon Street, Oxford OX2 6DP

Oxford University Press is a department of the University of Oxford.
It furthers the University's objective of excellence in research, scholarship,
and education by publishing worldwide in

Oxford New York

Athens Auckland Bangkok Bogotá Buenos Aires Calcutta Cape Town
Chennai Dar es Salaam Delhi Florence Hong Kong Istanbul Karachi
Kuala Lumpur Madrid Melbourne Mexico City Mumbai Nairobi Paris
São Paulo Shanghai Singapore Taipei Tokyo Toronto Warsaw

with associated companies in Berlin Ibadan

Oxford is a registered trade mark of Oxford University Press in the UK
and in certain other countries
Published in the United States by Oxford University Press Inc., New York

© Roger Goodman 2000

The moral rights of the author have been asserted
Database right Oxford University Press (maker)

First published 2000

British Library Cataloguing in Publication Data

Data available

Library of Congress Cataloging in Publication Data

Data applied for

ISBN 0-19-823421-X
ISBN 0-19-823422-8 pbk

1 3 5 7 9 10 8 6 4 2

Typeset in Minion by J&L Composition Ltd, Filey, North Yorkshire

Printed in Great Britain on acid-free paper by
Biddles Ltd., Guildford and King's Lynn

For my Parents

ACKNOWLEDGEMENTS

This book has been a long time in preparation and has incurred numerous debts along the way. It is a pleasure to be able to acknowledge some of these here, although I do not wish in any way to hold anyone else responsible for the conclusions I have drawn.

As David Berridge (Berridge and Brodie, 1998: 25), the leading ethnographer of children's homes in the UK, has written in his most recent book, 'in-depth studies of children's homes must be among the most sensitive and potentially threatening areas of social inquiry'. My greatest thanks, therefore, must go to the successive heads, staff, children, and families of the *yōgoshisetsu* (children's home) which I have called 'Kodomo Gakuen' for their openness and friendliness at all times. The heads more than anyone helped me to try and understand not only the way in which Japanese children's homes operate but also the cultural, historical, and sociological context from which they have emerged. I am only too aware that I must often have been a further burden on overworked and overtired staff and I hope that my admiration for their efforts comes through in the text. The children in the home were a constant source of delight and surprise to me. In the course of researching this project, I have frequently worried about the ethics of gaining intellectual capital from the experience of children who have often been through great trauma. If, however, my writing about these experiences can help inform the practice and ideas of child welfare specialists, and thereby improve the quality of care offered to other children, either inside or outside Japan, then I believe this project will have been worthwhile. I hope sincerely that everyone at Kodomo Gakuen—the head, children, and staff—feel on reading this text that I have represented fairly the world of *yōgoshisetsu* to which they introduced me.

I must thank the heads and staff of a large number of other welfare institutions for children throughout Japan as well as in the UK. As is common anthropological practice, I have not identified clearly any of the institutions I visited nor any of the staff who guided me. I hope, however, that those who helped me will recognize themselves and feel their ideas are reflected accurately, and I am very grateful to them for all their help.

Similarly, I have not identified many other individuals – from senior government officials to former heads of homes to former residents of homes – who gave up their time and shared many of their feelings with me on a range of sensitive topics. One individual, however, whom I would like to thank by name is Tokumasu Kōji who, at the time I started on this research, was working for Kōdansha Shuppansha. It was he who convinced me, when I indeed had other research plans, to undertake this project, and it was he who made the original introductions and encouraged me to ask difficult questions, inspired in part by the fact that he himself, as an undergraduate student, had done his own study of *yōgoshisetsu* in the mid-1970s.

The other source of inspiration for this project has been my partner Carolyn Dodd, who, as a social worker (latterly manager) in a Children and Families Team in the UK, would sometimes ask me what would happen in Japan with the type of cases that she was dealing with on a daily basis. In almost all cases, I neither knew the answer to her questions nor could find anything in the literature that could supply it for me. As an anthropologist of Japan, I was naturally stimulated to try and find out for myself. Carolyn accompanied me to Japan both in 1991—when, half-way through the original fieldwork on which this book is based, our first son, Sam, was born—and in 1998/9. During this second visit, Carolyn, as part of her own research project, was attached to a Child Guidance Centre in Osaka; Sam attended a local elementary school and our second son, Joe, attended a local day-care centre (*hoikuen*). To a very great extent, all of their experiences have added to the texture of the account that follows, and I, of course, thank them with all my love, while also hoping that these experiences have been ones that they have enjoyed and will treasure.

The nature of academic work these days is such that the opportunity for one person to engage in long-term overseas fieldwork inevitably means that colleagues have to shoulder extra burdens. I would like to thank here, therefore, my former colleagues in the Department of Sociology and the Contemporary Japan Centre at the University of Essex, where I worked until 1993, and my current colleagues in the Institute of Social and Cultural Anthropology and the Nissan Institute of Japanese Studies in Oxford. At the same time, I would like to thank those institutions and scholars who offered me a base while I was doing my fieldwork in Japan. In 1991 I was based at the Compartment of Social Anthropology at Hitotsubashi University in Tokyo and in 1998/9 at the National Museum of Ethnology in Osaka. I would particularly like to thank Nagashima Nobuhiro and Nakamaki Hirochika, who were my respective sponsors, as well as the many other individuals at both institutions who both befriended and helped me and my family. In 1991 my research was supported by a grant from the Japan Society for the Promotion of Science, and in 1998/9 by the Japanese Ministry of Education to whom, again, thanks and acknowledgements are due.

In the course of writing up, I have incurred so many debts that it is impossible to list them all by name. In particular, though, I have become indebted to Tsuzaki Tetsuo of Bukkyō University, with whom I have been involved in a long dialogue about the relative merits of Japanese and British child welfare programmes since we first met, by chance, at a conference in 1991. We have not always agreed in these discussions, but he has unfailingly been kind enough to correct my basic errors and to bring to my attention relevant works without ever insisting that I should necessarily see things exactly the way that he does. This to me is the basis of true scholarly communication.

Others whom I must mention for help far beyond the call of academic duty include Eyal Ben-Ari, Mike Cowin, Deguchi Akira, Ronald Dore, David Gough, Hayashi Hiroyasu, Hino Katsumi, Higuchi Norio, Hiraoka Koichi, Isono Fujiko, Ito Yone, Iwasaki Nobuko, Kosaka Kazuo, Matsubara Yasuo, Minemoto Koji, Ian Neary, Sakamoto Takeshi, Takei Emiko, Tokumasu Satomi, Yoshida Tsuneo, Yui Kiyomitsu, and the staff of the Kodomo Mirai Zaidan (The Foundation for Children's Future). I owe a special debt to Ito Peng, with whom I undertook a joint project on East Asian welfare (published in Gøsta Esping-Andersen (ed.), *Welfare States in Transition*, London: Sage, 1996) that greatly broadened my general understanding of social welfare in Japan.

It is a commonplace for academics to thank their students as a body for their intellectual input. In this case, however, I must single out three students in particular from whose work I have benefited directly: Kirstie Sobue, who wrote an undergraduate thesis on *yōgoshisetsu* at the University of Cambridge in 1992 (and whom I taught briefly as a graduate student at the University of Essex a few years later); Kelly Hagan, whose undergraduate thesis on *yōgoshisetsu* I supervised at the University of Oxford in 1993–4; and Karen Aarre, also based in Oxford, whose master's and doctoral theses on children's homes in Portugal I also supervised. The insights that all three managed to glean, as young, single females working full-time in the homes they studied, have added enormously to my own understanding of the worlds of those who work in children's homes.

One further aspect of the nature of the current academic world is the pressure to publish work, often before one is completely sure about its conclusions. Sections of Chapter 7 have been published in Joy Hendry (ed.), *Interpreting Japanese Society* (London: Routledge, 1998) and sections of Chapter 2 in Goodman, White, and Kwon (eds.), *The East Asian Welfare Model: Welfare Orientalism and the State* (London: Routledge, 1998). I would like to acknowledge the help I received from Joy Hendry, Huck-ju Kwon, and the late Gordon White in writing these chapters.

Finally, I am very grateful to the very large number of people who have been involved in turning this manuscript into print. In particular, thanks are due to Anne Ashby, Jane Baker, Rachael Hutchinson, Dorothy McCarthy, Janet Moth, Ozawa Chikako, and Andrew Schuller. As with all those whose help I acknowledge, however, I wish to absolve them of any blame for faults and mistakes which remain in the text. I alone am responsible for these.

I dedicate this book to my parents, with love and gratitude.

R.J.G.

Oxford, April 2000

CONTENTS

LIST OF TABLES

LIST OF FIGURES

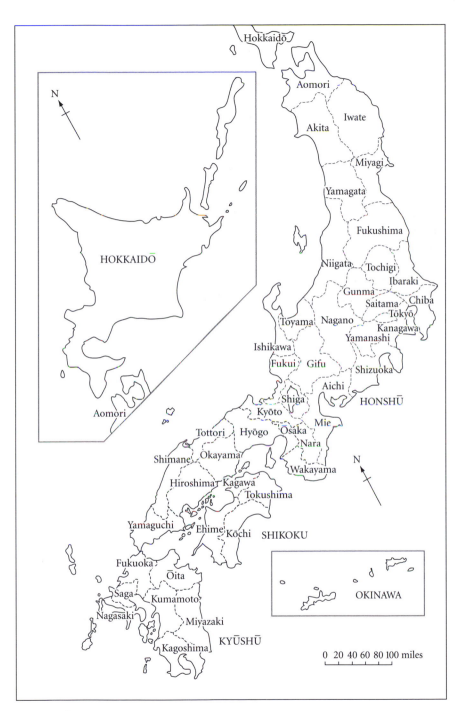

Japan: Prefectures

LIST OF ABBREVIATIONS FOR NEWSPAPERS AND REPORTS CITED IN THE TEXT

Where newspapers and annual reports are referred to only once or twice the full title is given in the text. When articles and reports are bylined, the name of the author is also included, e.g. Hino, *AS*, 3 June 1998; Sakuraya, *KH*, 1996: 105.

AS	*Asahi Shinbun* (Asahi newspaper)
DY	*Daily Yomiuri*
JIC	*Japan: An International Comparison*, produced annually by the Keizai Kōhō Centre (Japan Institute for Social and Economic Affairs)
JT	*Japan Times*
JTW	*Japan Times Weekly* (changed to fortnightly from 1999)
KH	*Kodomo Hakusho* (White Paper on Children, produced annually by the Nihon Kodomo wo Mamorukai)
KK	*Kenkyū Kaigi* (Zenkoku Yōgoshisetsuchō Kenkyū Kaigi, annual research report of the research meeting of the heads of all *yōgoshisetsu* which was first held in 1946, hence no. 50 refers to 1996)
KSH	*Kōsei Hakusho* (Annual Report on Health and Welfare, produced by the Ministry of Health and Welfare)
MMJF	*Me de Miru Jidō Fukushi* (Graphs and Charts on Japan's Child Welfare Services, produced annually by Kodomo Mirai Zaidan)
MS	*Mainichi Shinbun* (Mainichi newspaper)
NTN	*Nihon Tōkei Nenkan* (Japanese Statistical Yearbook)
YnJ	*Yōgojidōra no Jittai* (survey of children in care undertaken every five years by the Ministry of Health and Welfare since 1977. The full results of the survey carried out in March 1998 have not been published as of April 2000, but it has been possible to incorporate some preliminary results from the survey in the text
YS	*Yomiuri Shinbun* (Yomiuri newspaper)
YSI	*Yōgoshisetsu Ichiran* (annual register of all homes—including their quotas, staff size, and foundation dates—produced annually by the Yōgoshisetsu Kyōgikai)
Ysno30nen	Yōgoshisetsu no Sanjūnen (thirtieth anniversary history of *yōgoshisetsu*, published in 1977 by the Yōgoshisetsu Kyōgikai)
Ysno40nen	Yōgoshisetsu no Yonjūnen (fortieth anniversary history of *yōgoshisetsu*, published in 1987 by the Yōgoshisetsu Kyōgikai)

A NOTE TO THE READER

All Japanese names are given in the Japanese fashion with the family name first. In continuation of what has thus far been a rather lonely campaign, I have not followed the standard romanization for words in the Japanese language which have been taken from Western languages, i.e. *Enzeru Puran* (for Angel Plan) or *gurūpu hōmu* (for group home). This is to avoid unnecessarily confusing people who do not know Japanese and who might be interested in the number of such Western loanwords which figure in the discussions about child welfare in Japan. As a result, such Western loanwords are romanized (i.e. written in the roman alphabet) in their original form, but italicized, e.g. *Angel Plan*; *group home.*

For the translation of Japanese social welfare terms, I have generally followed Nakamura, Kojima, and Thompson (1981).

Macrons have been used to mark long vowels in Japanese, except in the case of well-known places such as Osaka, Tokyo, and Kyoto.

All monetary values are expressed in yen when discussing financial issues in Japan since translations into pounds or dollars are rendered almost meaningless by the rapidly changing exchange rate between the countries. For the purposes of comparison, however, £1 was around ¥170 in 1991 and ¥165 in early 2000; $1 about ¥150 in 1991 and ¥105 in early 2000.

1

Introduction

THE STUDY OF SOCIAL EXCLUSION IN JAPAN

This book is a study in Japan of what it has become fashionable in Britain to call the 'socially excluded' or the 'underclass', namely the sector of the society which is so far removed from the political and economic levers of power that it has virtually no say in the way that it is treated. It seeks to answer the question of what happens to such people in Japanese society and why.

As many of the new academics of social exclusion in Britain have discovered, it is not always easy to define those who are 'socially excluded'. In Japan, where there has been a marked tendency in the post-war period to minimize class, regional, and other differences, such definitions can be even more difficult. Much of the work on social exclusion in Japan has concentrated on Japan's minority groups—Ainu, Okinawans, *zainichi-Kankokujin* (Japanese-Koreans), atom-bomb victims, *burakumin* (former untouchables)—who have faced considerable discrimination in the post-war period. All these groups, however, have been able to mobilize politically and hence their status has gradually improved in recent years (see Weiner, 1997). More recent work has focused on Japan's day-labourers, who live in flop-houses in Tokyo, Osaka, and Yokohama (Fowler, 1996; Stevens, 1997). While such individuals may live on the very fringes of Japanese society, however, some scholars (see Gill, forthcoming) suggest that, in some cases, their detachment from society may include elements of escape, as well as exclusion.

In the mid-1980s I decided that the best way to study social exclusion in Japanese society would be through the study of children who, through no fault of their own, were pushed to the margins of society. Children, by definition, are at a remove from the levers of economic and political power and hence, I thought, the way that they were treated would shed interesting light on Japanese social values. This approach, however, proved highly problematic.

First, I undertook a study of Japanese children who had lived overseas and then returned to Japan (known in Japanese as *kikokushijo*). In the early 1980s such children were widely described as Japan's newest minority group who were being stigmatized on return to Japan as a result of their contamination by the outside world and seemed to present an excellent example of a socially excluded group. As I eventually discovered, however (Goodman, 1990), the parents of *kikokushijo* were from a very upper-middle-class sector of Japanese society—doctors, academics, journalists, diplomats, and businessmen—who were determined that their hard-earned social status was not going to be jeopardized in the case of their children by the fact that they had gone overseas in the service of their country. Their powerful lobbying of the government brought about the development of special educational services, a special university entrance system, and company employment quotas which did not exist for any other group, and their skilful linking through the mass media of *kikokushijo* with the buzzword of internationalization led to their children being seen (often unrealistically) as the sole possessors of skills that were needed to take Japan into the twenty-first century. The *kikokushijo* in the 1980s therefore may have been a 'minority group' in terms of their numbers, but they were certainly not a 'marginal group' in terms of their economic and political power.

Next, in the early 1990s, I began a study of schools for children with a handicap (*yōgogakkō*). It has often been said that those with a handicap in Japan are strongly discriminated against, in part because their families wish them to be kept invisible to avoid upsetting the marriage chances of relatives. This project, however, was short-lived mainly because of the rapid realization that anyone can have a handicapped child, and that when parents with political and economic power have handicapped children they will use that power to protect the best interests of their children.[1]

As so often in anthropological research, it was serendipity that led me to turn my attention to the institutions which are the focus of this book. A former informant in the school where I had done research on *kikokushijo* told me how twenty years earlier he had worked in an institution in west Tokyo and had come across a section of Japanese society about which he had previously known nothing. He wrote his graduation thesis on the institution (Tokumasa, 1974) and had kept in contact with it over the years. If I really wanted to understand how Japanese society treated its most vulnerable members, he suggested, then I should study such institutions which were for children whose parents cannot, will not, or are not allowed to look after them. In Japanese these institutions are known as *jidō yōgoshisetsu*, or more simply *yōgoshisetsu*.

The word *yōgoshisetsu* is not easy to translate and indeed for this reason alone I will use it regularly throughout this account. For the purposes of euphony, however, at times it will be necessary to use an English equivalent. The problem is which English equivalent to use. In part this is difficult because there is a difference between American and British English over what to call institutions for children whose parents do not care for them. When, in the mid-1990s, there was a heated debate in the United States about the usefulness of such institutions—following the suggestion of Newt Gingrich, then Speaker of the House, that they might be a way to deal with the growing problem of broken families in the US—they were referred to as 'orphanages' (McKenzie, 1999). Even though *yōgoshisetsu* are often introduced in Japan as *mae no kojiin* ('what used to be called orphanages'), few children in equivalent institutions in Britain, or in the United States, or, as we shall see, in Japan are actually orphans, and hence the term is somewhat misleading. In Britain, similar institutions are generally called 'children's homes', although the fact that an increasingly large proportion of residents are teenagers and hence hardly 'children' is also misleading but probably closer to the Japanese sense of the meaning of *yōgoshisetsu*. Indeed, in April 1998 the word *jidō*, meaning 'child' or 'children', was officially appended to *yōgoshisetsu* and hence their name can be literally translated as 'child protection institutions'. When I do not use the Japanese term, therefore, I have decided to refer to *yōgoshisetsu* as 'children's homes' or just 'homes', or sometimes as 'institutions', which reflects the fact that they tend to be much larger than their British counterparts.[2]

My former informant offered to introduce me to the head of the home where he had previously worked. The head was sympathetic to my new research proposal and in turn introduced me to the head of another *yōgoshisetsu* very near to where I was living in west Tokyo. This home—which I have decided to call Kodomo Gakuen (literally, 'children's campus'), since this gives a better indication of the size of the home than Kodomoen, meaning children's home, which was the other name I considered using—was well known in Japan and often received foreign, as well as Japanese, visitors and researchers. In some ways, it was a showcase home, and indeed the day before I visited it for the first time there were articles in several of the national daily newspapers about a new programme the home was running (for single-father families who required temporary care for their children) and a few days after my first visit a thirty-minute documentary programme about the home was broadcast on Tokyo television. The head of Kodomo Gakuen invited me to come to the home to teach English to the staff and the children, and in return he agreed to endeavour to explain to me how Japan's system of child welfare worked.

Over an eight-month period in 1991 I visited Kodomo Gakuen regularly, sometimes to teach English, sometimes to participate in activities in the home. I was also introduced to and visited several other homes in the Tokyo area as well as attending conferences and meetings on child welfare and interviewing policy-makers and academics in the field. I quickly became convinced that the children in the homes (sometimes known in Japanese as *yōgoshisetsuji*) were not only a minority group in terms of numbers but also a marginal group in terms of access to economic and political power. Where their experience differed most noticeably from that of the *kikokushijo* and the children in the *yōgogakkō* was that their parents did not look after their interests. In many cases, the parents of the children had simply disappeared. In other cases, contact with the children had been minimal. Even when *yōgoshisetsu* had made positive efforts to maintain contact with the parents, parents had never formed any type of group to act on behalf of their children. It is largely for these reasons that there is virtually no parental voice in the account that follows.

The following account is meant neither to criticize nor endorse the current system of child protection in Japan, but sets out as far as possible simply to describe it and set it in a social and historical context.[3] There are a number of reasons why I am keen to take this approach. First, there is virtually nothing written in

English, not only on the child welfare services but indeed on personal social services in Japan in general.[4] It is of course true that there is no literature in English about the system of personal social services of many societies, but the absence of such material in the case of Japan must be by some way the most significant. Not only does Japan have the world's second-largest economy, but it also has: the world's highest figures for longevity; the lowest rates of infant mortality; rates of divorce between one-quarter and one-third those of northern European and North American societies; by far the lowest rate of illegitimate births (less than 1 per cent) and of lone-parent families of all OECD societies; probably the world's most highly educated and literate population; the lowest rates for serious crimes in the OECD, and, between 1985 and 1995, a juvenile crime rate that declined significantly. Moreover, it has maintained all these figures in the face of trends which might have been expected to take it in the opposite direction over the past forty years: continual urbanization, rapid nuclearization of the family, the world's most rapidly ageing population, and—during the 1990s—its worst and longest recession during the post-war period, during which the economy actually contracted and the official rate of unemployment almost doubled. At the same time—and for some foreign observers most interesting of all—throughout the post-war period, Japan has had a much lower proportion of direct government spending on social welfare than most of its OECD competitors.

Given the above facts, it is small wonder that over the past twenty-five years, since the beginning of the so-called 'Japanese economic miracle', there have been periodic calls in other OECD countries facing rapidly rising welfare bills and increasing social problems to look at Japan's welfare system as a possible model for welfare reform (see Goodman, forthcoming). Yet there has been precious little for Western commentators and policy-makers to draw on in their examination of the Japanese welfare system. While this has allowed them sometimes to project on to Japan an idealized version of what they would like a welfare society to be (essentially, cheap and effective)—a process that Gordon White and I have elsewhere called 'welfare orientalism' (see White and Goodman, 1998)—it has rarely led to informed debate about the Japanese welfare system and its possible implications for the welfare systems of other societies. It is intended, therefore, that the detailed account of the child welfare system that follows will illuminate many of the discussions about Japanese social welfare provision, and also allow policy-makers and practitioners outside Japan to view their own practices in the light of another, very different, system.

The second reason why this account concentrates on describing how the child protection system operates in Japan is that the system has been in such a state of flux over the past few years. When I returned to Japan in 1998, this time to Osaka for a year, I quickly discovered that much had changed, and was currently changing, in the world of child welfare since my original fieldwork seven years earlier. Also many trends that I had scarcely been aware of when I had done my first project had become the source of major debate and discussion. Indeed, as I caught up with what had happened at Kodomo Gakuen during these years and visited institutions which I had not been to before, I began to revise some of my earlier thoughts about the situation of *yōgoshisetsu* in particular and child welfare in general in Japanese society. While I cannot pretend that this diachronic approach was planned—and indeed, such planning is an increasingly rare luxury in the academic world, where there is growing pressure for swift publication—the result is that what follows is enriched in three important ways. It offers a far more dynamic sense of the world of social welfare and the debates within it than the synchronic and rather oversimplified view with which I returned from my original fieldwork. It presents a greater sense of the variation in social work practice in Japan, particularly between the Kantō area around Tokyo and the Kansai area around Osaka. Finally, it offers a fuller picture of the relationship between the different parts of the child welfare system. This last point is largely because my knowledge of the way *jidōsōdanjo* (child consultation centres) operate in the Kansai area of Japan was greatly informed by the fact that my partner Carolyn Dodd, herself a social work manager in England, was able to shadow a worker from a *jidōsōdanjo* in Osaka over several weeks in the winter of 1998/9 while I was carrying out interviews and visiting institutions elsewhere.

CHILD PROTECTION IN COMPARATIVE PERSPECTIVE

Many scholars have recognized that the study of child protection is also the study of social attitudes towards children and families. Lorraine Fox Harding (1991: 3–4), for example, has written about children in Britain:

While it is true that the formal child care machinery of the state only involves a minority of children . . . the role of the state—in providing care for children as an alternative to parental care, in intervening between parent and child in various ways, and in prescribing certain rules surrounding childhood—can tell us much about childhood in society and how children are perceived and treated.

In the case of Japan, however, the issue of welfare provision for children has particular pertinence since, as it is often pointed out, the country has very few natural resources other than its children. Children are often described as *kuni no takara* (the country's jewels) and investment in, and the socialization and treatment of, the young is seen by some as potentially the single most important area of social policy.

The obvious differences between societies, however, do not mean that comparison of their child protection systems is impossible. Indeed, while the changes and developments that take place in different countries reflect different beliefs, ideologies, and traditions, it is possible to summarize most of the issues which underlie child protection quite succinctly, as I hope the following comparison of the current situation in Japan and the UK in the 1990s shows.[5]

State Care versus Familial Care[6]

When children come to the attention of the state as lacking in care, is it thought to be better for them no longer to live with their natural families, who are manifesting problems in caring for them, or for them to remain as far as possible in those families with the state supporting the families to look after them?

It would appear that proportionally far fewer children in Japan come into the care of the state than in the UK. According to Kamizono (1999), while, in 1992, in England (with 13 million children under 18 years old) there were around 54,400 children in the care of the local authorities (0.4 per cent of all children), in Japan (with an under-18 population of 30.79 million) there were around 31,000 (0.1 per cent of the child population) in roughly equivalent types of welfare facilities or foster-families.[7] On the other hand, the absolute number of children in protective care in Japan has remained relatively stable over the past forty years, while in most other OECD countries it has dropped dramatically in line with a drop in birth rates and changes in child welfare policy. In Britain, for example, the total number of children in the care of the state dropped from 92,300 in 1981 to 53,700 in 1998 (Hayden *et al.*, 1999: 36).

Compulsory Placement versus Voluntary Placement

Is it better for children placed in institutions to be placed there by the state (which will thereby take responsibility for their well-being) or voluntarily by their parents (who will retain the right to resume their care at any time)?

In the UK in 1998 the courts were involved in over 30 per cent of cases when children came into care (Hayden *et al.*, 1999: 53). In Japan the courts are very rarely involved in placing children in care; during the whole of 1997, only three children were placed in *yōgoshisetsu* on court orders (JTW, 15 Nov. 1999).

Professional Field Social Workers versus Local Government Bureaucrats

Should placements in child welfare institutions be made by officials who are specialists in child social welfare—even if these are not considered particularly high-status jobs or there is a danger of them becoming, in the expression of Richan and Mendelsohn (1973), an 'unloved profession'—or by high-status local government bureaucrats, who may have little or no experience of child welfare?[8]

In the UK the placement of children in care has largely been overseen by professionally qualified social workers who are charged with monitoring the level of care children receive once they have been placed in residential or foster homes or allowed to stay with their families on court orders. Japan has never developed a system of professional social work, and relies on a combination of local government bureaucrats and locally based volunteers to monitor the welfare of children in need of protection.

Institutional Care versus Pseudo-Familial Care

If the natural parents or extended family are unavailable or unable to look after the child, is it better for the child to be placed in a residential institution or for a pseudo-family (such as a foster-family or adoptive family) to be found?

When children do come into care in Japan, there is comparatively a much higher reliance on residential care than in the UK. Very little use is made of alternative forms of care such as fostering. Of children officially 'in care' in the UK, the number actually living in children's homes has steadily decreased to around 15 per cent; in Japan the comparable figure in the late 1980s is around 90 per cent, and has been increasing in recent years.[9]

Public Institutions versus Private Institutions

Should child welfare institutions and fostering agencies be operated by public agencies and staffed by public employees or by private organizations which can charge the state for the services they offer?

In Japan, over 90 per cent of *yōgoshisetsu* are private (*minkan shisetsu*) and private institutions and organizations have led the way in the development of child protection institutions since the end of the nineteenth century. In the UK, while private charities such as Dr Barnardo's played an important role in the development of orphanages, the state has taken responsibility for the care of needy children since Parliament enacted the Poor Law Act in 1601. Today about 30 per cent of children's homes are private (Kahan, 1994: 12), though they receive public money for the services they provide in the same way that *yōgoshisetsu* receive public funds through what is known as the *sochi seido* placement system.[10]

Uniform Institutions versus Diverse Institutions

Should child welfare institutions be closely regulated to ensure maximum homogeneity and equality of care for all children who come into care or should they be allowed to develop their own individual characteristics so that children can be placed in the institution that most closely meets their needs and avoid what Maxwell (1999: 263) calls the 'cookie-cutter effect'?

In the UK, residential units for children in care have become increasingly specialized so that it is almost, as Sinclair and Gibbs (1998) and Berridge and Brodie (1998) describe, impossible to classify them other than as individual units offering their own distinctive programmes to meet the needs of certain special groups of children in the general population. The job of field social workers in local government Children and Families teams is largely to seek out the most appropriate placement for children who come into the care of the local authority and to try to obtain a place for them and secure the money to finance that place. In Japan there is very little individual therapeutic treatment available, and it is still the norm to treat the children in *yōgoshisetsu* in a much more uniform manner.

Large versus Small Institutions

Should institutions be large enough to be able to work on economies of scale which prevent the child welfare sector becoming a drain on the public purse (and the cause of public complaint) or should they be operated on as small a scale as possible in an attempt to replicate 'real' family life?

According to a House of Commons report (1998: pp. vii–x), children's homes in England today house on average less than five children and are often hard to distinguish from private residences in their size and furnishings; in Japan, the average size of homes is still over fifty children, and the buildings in which children live tend to be large and conspicuous.[11]

Family Rehabilitation versus Stability of Institutions

Should institutions aim at rehabilitation of the child into the family or the foster family (which will be able to offer more individual attention even if such placements may periodically break down) or should they invest their efforts in providing a long-term stable environment for the child in an institution where they can put down roots, feel secure, and which they know will always be there for them even after they have left?

In the UK, placements of children in residential care must be reviewed at least every six months in order to avoid the placement continuing any longer than necessary. Over the past twenty years, stays have become progressively shorter and, according to a survey by Sinclair and Gibbs (1998: 88–9), most are less than six months and the average for 'long-term' stays is just over a year. In Japan, stays have become longer over the past two decades, and the average stay of all children is almost five years.

Specialist Residential Staff versus Generalist Residential Staff

Is it more important that residential staff in institutions are qualified in child welfare and able to offer therapeutic treatment and counselling to the children who come into the institutions or is it better for them to have received a general, high level of education and to have demonstrated a commitment to the field and an ability to offer support and discipline to children in care?

In Japan all full-time residential care staff must have a child-care qualification of some kind, and over 80 per cent will have attended at least two years of tertiary education. According to the Utting Report (Utting, 1991), a survey of twenty local authorities in 1990 found that 70 per cent of child-care staff and 20 per cent of heads of local authority homes in the UK had no professional qualifications. By the end of the decade, almost all heads of homes had social work qualifications, but the situation had changed little in the case of the rest of the care staff (Hayden *et al.*, 1999: 157).

Volunteers versus No Volunteers

Should homes use volunteer staff from the local community to help children with their homework and in other activities, or is the presence of volunteers a reinforcement of the unnatural situation of institutional care, which should aim to be as much like a 'normal' family as possible?

In children's homes in England, staffing levels of at least one member of staff to each child largely obviate the need for volunteers.[12] In Japan, the state has stipulated since 1976 that homes must employ at least one member of staff for every six children it looks after over the age of 6, and volunteers provide an important source of support to the children in residence. Residential care per child per year is, therefore, much cheaper in Japan (possibly as low as ¥3 million or £15,000) compared to the UK (roughly ¥12 million or £60,000, according to Sinclair and Gibbs, 1998: 239).[13]

Charity versus Citizenship

Should homes accept charity in the form of donations, food, clothing, and toys from members of the public or should the state supply such things in sufficient quantity to children who have come into care, though no fault of their own, and have a 'right' to them as 'citizens' of the state?

Berridge and Brodie (1998: 94) report the ambivalence felt in children's homes in England about accepting free tickets to performances because of an association with charity that is seen as potentially demeaning to the self-respect and dignity of the children in the homes. There are very few *yōgoshisetsu* in Japan which do not accept charitable support and many have established sophisticated systems for raising charitable funds.

Separation versus Integration of 'Delinquent' Children

Should children showing signs of delinquent behaviour (which may be the result of difficult family backgrounds) be separated from those who come into care because their families cannot look after them but who have not manifested such behaviours (in case they become influenced by the behaviour of the 'delinquent' children)?

In general, children in *yōgoshisetsu* seem to manifest less delinquent behaviour than children in children's homes. This is largely because children who are considered delinquent or potentially delinquent in Japan are placed in separate institutions (called *kyōgoin*) while in Britain, since the Children and Young Persons Act of 1969, the policy has been to place them in children's homes (Tsuzaki Tetsuo, 1996: 4).[14]

Integration Into the Community versus Avoidance of Stigmatization

Should institutions try to integrate themselves as far as possible into the local community and try to engender in the children in their care a sense of pride in their institution, or should they try to make the institution as inconspicuous as possible for fear of stigmatizing the children who live in it?

Yōgoshisetsu have not been as widely tainted by scandal nor as negatively perceived as have children's homes in several European countries during the past fifteen years (see Colton and Hellinckx, 1993; Madge, 1994; Pringle, 1998). In the US indeed, as the Republican Party discovered to its cost in the mid–1990s, even to appear to endorse such institutions is to risk public opprobrium (McKenzie, 1999). Residential institutions in the US and some European countries have become widely criticized, not only because they are believed to cost more than other alternatives and frequently fail to achieve their objective of rehabilitating children into their families, but also because, through stigmatizing and institutionalizing those who come into care, they are seen to create more problems than they solve. In Japan such criticisms, where they have existed, have been much more muted, and homes have generally enjoyed a more positive public image.

It should be pointed out that *yōgoshisetsu* have much more in common with child protection institutions in some other Western countries, in particular in southern Europe, than they do with those in the UK or the US. Aarre's (1998, 2000) account of a children's home in Portugal suggests considerable similarities with institutions in Japan in terms of size, management, and organization, although not in their relation to the state. As we shall see later when we look at fostering, it may indeed be helpful to think of two systems of child protection in Europe—a northern and a southern one—though, as Aarre (1998) points out, attempts by the European Union to impose a single model may radically alter this in the next few years.

[handwritten margin note: Japanese yōgoshisetsu more like Southern European type]

There is also, as we shall see, considerable variation between *yōgoshisetsu* in Japan. Some *yōgoshisetsu*, for example, seek foster placements and pursue contact with parents much more actively than others; some operate smaller units than others; some hire more specialized staff than others; some prefer to organize children by the same age, while others organize them by different ages. Most interestingly, however, *yōgoshisetsu* appear to be on the verge of radically altering their role in Japanese child welfare. The account that follows is largely an exploration of how and why this change is coming about.

OUTLINE OF THE BOOK

Chapter 2 sets out a context for understanding the child welfare system in Japan in the 1990s by describing the development of the Japanese welfare system more generally. There is a widely disseminated version of the development of welfare which suggests that the modern welfare system is a direct result of patterns of welfare developed from the time of Japan's earliest recorded history. As we shall see, this 'official history' needs to be treated with a certain amount of scepticism since it appears to be as much the 'invention of tradition' as historical fact. Nevertheless, this invented tradition—in particular, the role of Buddhism, Christianity, Confucianism, and the Imperial Family—does have important implications for modern views of child welfare.

The second part of Chapter 2 gives an insight into how personal social services operate in contemporary Japanese society and some of the debates which surround the provision of welfare. In particular, it focuses on the role of the *minsei.jidōiin* system which is described by many as the most characteristically 'Japanese' feature of Japanese welfare provision. In the 1980s, the *minsei.jidōiin* system was substantially reinforced by the establishment of a new system called *shūnin jidōiin*. This development is examined in some detail because it relates directly to the main social welfare issues facing Japan at the end of the 1990s.

Chapter 3 presents an overview of the operation of the child welfare system in the 1990s and examines how the state deals with the situation of single-parent families, delinquent youth, and abandoned babies. It also sets out the historical background of *yōgoshisetsu* and the varied backgrounds of the children who have come into their care at different times during the post-war period. As will be seen, the reasons why children come into care are often extremely complex and rarely reducible to a single cause.

One of the most conspicuous characteristics of the child welfare system at the beginning of the 1990s was how little it seemed to have changed throughout the post-war period. In 1998, however, the first major revision of the 1947 Child Welfare Law was implemented, and this is outlined at the end of Chapter 3 since it sets the scene for many of the debates which are discussed in subsequent chapters.

Chapter 4 describes in some detail the organization, management, and staffing of *yōgoshisetsu*. While there is considerable, and in the context of Japan somewhat surprising, diversity between institutions, there are also a number of important common characteristics among many homes. One of the most interesting of these is the *dōzoku keiei* (same-family management) system of *yōgoshisetsu*, of which Kodomo Gakuen is an example. This system is described in detail both because, for reasons which will become clear later, it is a style of management which is virtually ignored in the Japanese literature on *yōgoshisetsu*, and also because it has important implications for issues of staffing, recruitment, pay, and conditions of those who work in the child welfare field.

Care workers in Japan constitute one of the fastest-growing sectors of the Japanese employment market as the society rapidly ages. For this reason alone, it is important to examine the employment conditions of some such, about whom there is almost no published research in English. It is interesting, for example, to note how few changes have been made in the employment conditions of staff in *yōgoshisetsu* in recent years, despite the many other changes taking place in the child welfare system at the end of the 1990s. There has been no change since 1976 in the maximum number of children per member of staff, and it is hence still common for there to be as many as twelve or thirteen children per member of staff on duty at any one time. It is partly—though it should be emphasized not totally—as a result of this low staff : resident ratio that almost all *yōgoshisetsu* make use of volunteer help, an issue which is also examined in this chapter.

On 1 April 1999 an important change came into force regarding the staffing of *yōgoshisetsu*. This was the introduction in some homes of part-time therapists paid for by central government to work with children who have been abused. While the budget for such therapists remains very small and the number of staff involved will consequently be tiny, the implications of this new development for *yōgoshisetsu* are significant. This new programme illustrates for the first time the acceptance by the state that children in *yōgoshisetsu* are not simply there because of their parents' problems, but also because they themselves may have suffered abuse and are in need of individual help.

Chapter 5 examines how children who come into *yōgoshisetsu*—some of whom will spend much, even all, of their childhood in such institutions—are cared for and socialized. There are significant differences here both between homes at any one point in time and also within homes over time which reflect differing ideological standpoints and provide interesting insights into how Japanese ideas of child socialization and child care have been contested and changed.

Chapter 6 tries to measure the effectiveness of the way *yōgoshisetsu* look after children. This, for obvious reasons, is a highly problematic project, not least because it is very difficult to estimate what would have happened to the same children if they had not come into care. In general, children seem to be well looked after in material and physical terms. There have been some reported cases of abuse within institutions (some by staff of children, some by children of other children), but there is little evidence as yet of what Berridge and Brodie (1998: 10) call the 'series of crises and scandals' afflicting children's homes in the UK over the past fifteen years.

Other ways to measure the 'success' of *yōgoshisetsu* are to look at how children from the institutions fare in the education system and how they manage once they leave the homes. In both cases the evidence is not encouraging. Children from the homes lag far behind their schoolmates educationally, and appear to face considerable problems in society once they leave. In the 1990s, the number of children staying on in the education system increased significantly and the state began to provide better mechanisms to prepare children for leaving care and for supporting them once they had left, but it is a curious—and, in Japan, where statistics are kept on almost everything, probably significant—fact that there are still no official figures either on what happens to residents once they leave the care system, nor how many children currently in care are the children of those who have themselves been in care (known in Japanese as *nisei*).

Chapter 7 looks at two possible alternatives to *yōgoshisetsu*—adoption and fostering. While Japan is not alone among OECD countries in its reliance on residential institutions for children who come into care, it appears to be unusual in that the relative proportion in institutions has been on the rise in recent years, while both the absolute and relative numbers fostered and adopted have been on the decrease. These trends need some explanation since there are long histories of both fostering and adoption in Japan, and there were vigorous attempts by the state to bolster both systems through the introduction of new laws in the late 1980s.

Chapter 8 sets out to describe the new emerging role of *yōgoshisetsu* in Japan, and to explain how this new role developed and why *yōgoshisetsu* did not simply disappear in the 1990s as so many similar institutions did in the US and UK. In some ways, this question is best answered by asking why *yōgoshisetsu* changed so little in the fifty years after 1947 when so much else in Japan changed so radically. To this the simple answer is that there was no pressure—either internally or externally—for them to alter the way they operated.

In the early 1990s, however, *yōgoshisetsu* found themselves for the first time confronted by two serious challenges to their continuing existence: a rapidly declining birth rate (which meant that fewer children would need to be placed in care) and the demands of the UN Convention on the Rights of the Child (which was strongly critical of the practice of institutional care). Despite government attempts to increase the birth rate and protests that the UN Convention imposed a north European or Anglo-Saxon view of children's rights on a very different cultural context, many *yōgoshisetsu* felt that they needed to reform in order to ensure their survival in the new century. At the same time, *yōgoshisetsu* began to find themselves well situated to deal with a new and major social problem that was beginning to emerge in Japan—the 'discovery' that children were being abused in Japanese society. Chapter 8 explores this 'discovery' in some depth: how practices which had previously been considered culturally acceptable were reinterpreted as abusive; how the problem of 'child abuse' was officially defined so that it could be measured and tackled; how the media 'explained' the problem in terms of change in Japanese society; and how the absolute authority of parents over their children came to be questioned. Indeed, as this book was going to press in April 2000, discussion of child abuse dominated the media. Almost daily articles reported on cases of child abuse taking place either in families or in welfare institutions and there was considerable coverage of proposals by the ruling coalition to introduce legislation in May 2000 which would require mandatory reporting of suspicions of abuse; the granting of greater powers to local officials to investigate those suspicions; a more rigorous definition of what constitutes abuse; and a greater use of the power to remove the authority of parents who abuse (see *YS*, 19 Apr. 2000; *AS*, 27 Apr. 2000). In conclusion, Chapter 8 argues that it has been the convergence of these different factors—the 'discovery' of child abuse, pressure from children's rights groups, and the decrease in the fertility rate—which have led to the development of a new and distinctive role for child protection institutions in Japan at the start of the twenty-first century.

2

The Development and Delivery of Welfare in Japan

THE 'ORIGINS' OF WELFARE IN JAPAN

There is a popular and widely disseminated version of the development of social welfare in Japan that begins with the actions, in the sixth century AD, of Shōtoku Taishi (574–622) (see e.g. Amenomori, 1977; JNC–ICSW, 1990; Kōseishō Jidōkateikyoku, 1998; Nagashima, 1996; Nomoto, 1998; Yamaoka, 1998). Shōtoku, Japan's first great state policy-maker, is the man widely credited with bringing Buddhism to Japan, and Buddhism is seen to have been the driving force behind most of the early welfare activities in Japan, including the establishment of the first welfare institute, Shika-no-In, in the compound of Shitennōji Temple in Naniwa (present-day Osaka) in AD 591. Shika-no-In included four different types of welfare and medical institution, including a home (Hidenin) which catered to the poor and the needy. Most commentators describe Hidenin as the first precursor of today's welfare institutions for both the elderly and the young, and also make the point (see e.g. Nomoto, 1998: 19) that the principle behind it and all other early welfare institutions was to provide care only to those who could not look after themselves and who could not otherwise be cared for by their community or family—mainly children under 16 without fathers, and elderly people over 60 without children. This principle, it is said, became formalized in the Taihō Code of AD 702 (Japan's first public assistance programme), which stressed that the welfare of the needy was first the responsibility of the immediate family, then of relatives, then of the community, and, only in the last resort, of the state.

Buddhism is also seen as the driving force behind the actions of the two other figures during the Nara and early Heian periods best known for their welfare activities: Wake no Hiromushi (730–99) and the Buddhist priest Gyōki (668–749) (Nagashima, 1996: 49–5). The figure of Wake no Hiromushi is still portrayed every year at the widely attended Kyoto Jidai Matsuri procession in October, where she is described, in the English-language leaflet accompanying the procession, as a 'woman [who] took care of many orphans, her merciful deeds serv[ing] as the foundation for Japanese orphanages'.

During the late Kamakura and Muromachi periods, Japan split into a series of small, non-unified fiefdoms. The welfare of the needy was placed in the hands of local feudal lords, some of whom are recorded as having provided at least a minimal level of support to those most in need. In general, though, welfare activity in most commentaries is still associated during Japan's Middle Ages with the actions of Buddhist priests such as Chōgen (1128–1206), Eison (1201–90), and Ninshō (1217–1303), the last of whom is credited with the refounding of the Hidenin welfare facility for the poor and needy, including orphaned children. Since such individuals worked without any form of state support, some commentators (e.g. Nomoto, 1998: 37) suggest that they might be seen as the precursors of today's social work volunteers. In almost all accounts, the welfare activities of early Japanese Buddhists are explained in terms of *jihi*, a Buddhist concept derived from two Pali and Sanskrit words meaning 'true brotherly or parental love' and 'compassion, pity, or pathos'. As Nakamura, Kojima, and Thompson (1991: 12) point out: 'The concept of *jihi* is . . . seen as the basic attribute of a person who seeks salvation in Mahayana Buddhist thought (*bosatsu*). An understanding of this word helps one in understanding the development of the welfare movement in Japan.'

An alternative version of the development of welfare institutions in Japan places the Imperial Family at its centre. Such versions (see Tatara, 1975: 12; Tsuji, 1934) point to recorded examples of Imperial welfare activity dating from some 200 years before Shōtoku Taishi as well as to the almshouse purportedly founded by the Empress Kōmyō in the compound of Kokufuji Temple in the eighth century, and suggest that the association of the Imperial Family with welfare activity in Japan has been strong and unbroken ever since (see Checkland, 1994).

The significance that some commentators give to both of these versions of the 'origins' of Japanese welfare needs to be treated with considerable caution. Sally Hastings (1995: 68), for example, suggests that the image of a benevolent emperor caring for his people is actually 'a modern construct' and cautions against taking the accounts of Imperial activities in pre-modern times too literally. It is certainly the case that the image of the Imperial Family in Japan has been carefully cultivated over many centuries (see Large, 1992). Similarly, the connection between the activities of individual Buddhists in the sixth to thirteenth centuries with current welfare activities is very tenuous indeed. Nakura (1995: 31–2), for example, states that, during the Tokugawa period (1603–1868), the shogunate tried to prevent the development of Buddhist social and medical work and to force Buddhist priests to concentrate on funeral and memorial services. Nevertheless, that such 'origin' stories persist is not without present-day significance.

The third element in most historical accounts of the development of welfare facilities and activities in Japan was heralded by the arrival of Francis Xavier (1506–52) and other Christian missionaries from 1549 onwards. These Christians are recorded as having performed many charitable acts alongside their missionary and commercial activities: Xavier was particularly active in organizing welfare activities for the elderly and the orphaned in western Japan, and the Portuguese missionary Luis d'Almeida (1525–83), who arrived in Japan in 1552, set up a famous orphanage in Ōita Prefecture. One common explanation for this missionary activity was their shock—contrary to their otherwise favourable impression of Japan when they arrived—at the abortion and infanticide of unwanted babies in Japan (Kojima, 1986: 124; LaFleur, 1992: 94, 184). This may be one of the earliest examples of differing cultural views over how welfare should best be provided for a population. Demographers have long explained the stable level of the Japanese population over this period of 250 years—while the Chinese population was doubling in size—in terms of the deliberate murder or abandonment of children, euphemistically known as *mabiki* (thinning out). The term is derived from the practice of thinning out rice crops to ensure the best chances of survival of the remaining stalks (see Macfarlane, 1998). This method of family planning was particularly widespread in north-western Japan, where the combination of a harsh climate and a repressive tax system made it difficult for families to survive with more than one or two children to feed. Infanticide was common, and solace, or appeasement of the dead child, was found in buying or making *kokeshi* dolls, which are thin wooden representations of children.[1]

The rationalization of the process of infanticide in the feudal period was both religious and economic. A child younger than 7 had an uncertain life in any case, and could still return to this world even if sent back to the 'other world' to wait a little longer; they were viewed as 'intermediate beings' who had left the other world but were not yet incorporated into this one and, according to Iijima (1987: 4) people talked of killing children as 'sending a child back', and a dead child was given a special non-Buddhist funeral. LaFleur, in his book *Liquid Life* (1992), suggests that the practice—which some commentators suggest may have meant a rate of infanticide of around 40 per cent over the whole population—was not simply born of poverty but was also common in wealthier urban areas, and related to the idea that it was the quality of life of those who were allowed to grow up that was paramount over the quantity of those who survived. In LaFleur's view, *mabiki* should be seen as a positive form of obtaining and maintaining the preferred family size and can be interpreted as a sign of responsible parenting and the love of children rather than the abuse of unwanted infants.[2]

The work of the Christian missionaries was drastically curtailed by the anti-Christian edicts of 1613 and it was stopped altogether with the order for the expulsion of all missionaries in 1639 after less than a century of activity. Nevertheless, they had in this time introduced the concept of Christian welfare work which they could refer back to when Japan was reopened to the outside world at the end of the nineteenth century. Since that time, Christian groups have been one of the main providers of private personal social services until today, despite the fact that the actual number of Christians in Japan has never exceeded 1 per cent of the total population.

In the Tokugawa period, responsibility for social welfare was quite consciously devolved to the family and the community in a system—the *gonin gumi seido* (five-family-unit system) set up in 1643—that was as much about social control as it was about providing aid to those in need. The Tokugawa regime has been characterized as one of the most conservative and feudal 'police states' in recorded history: social mobility was banned (though, as the market economy grew towards the end of the period, this became honoured more often in the breach than the observance) and the mutual responsibility that was built in to the *gonin gumi seido* meant that not only was the community as a whole responsible for the welfare of each individual, but it was also responsible for individuals' actions and punishable for their wrongdoings. Informers for the state authorities were believed to be everywhere, and peer pressure to self-police became the norm (see Sansom, 1962: ch. 11). Hard work and frugality were considered to be the most effective means of avoiding poverty, and this ideology was backed up by the propagation of a strict neo-Confucian moral code which emphasized respect for the status quo.

In many accounts, the *gonin gumi seido* is taken to be the precursor of the wartime *tonarigumi* (neighbourhood associations), 'descendants' of which can still be seen in Japan today in the form of neighbourhood associations, known as *chōnaikai* (see Bestor, 1989). The suggestion that either Tokugawa ideas of neo-Confucianism or the establishment of the *gonin guni seido* had a direct influence on the development of contemporary ideas about welfare provision and delivery, however, needs to be treated with considerable caution. Indeed, where links have been made they may represent the 'reinvention of tradition' as much as historical continuity (Hastings, 1995: 75).

Some *daimyō* during the Tokugawa period attempted periodically to introduce legislation to try and control practices of child murder and abandonment in their domains, either by making them punishable (as in Fukuoka) or by offering money (*yōikuhi*) to help parents bring up their children, as was tried in Sendai and Mito. Significantly, however, no welfare facilities specifically for the care and protection of children were built during this entire period. Indeed, it was only at the very end of the Tokugawa period that a leading agronomist, Satō Nobuhiro (1769–1850), first proposed the establishment of state-run institutions for the poor and the needy. In summary, therefore, the role of the state in the provision of welfare in Tokugawa Japan is perhaps best described in the phrase used by Komatsu (1992) as one of 'peripheral non-responsibility'. Until the Meiji period (1868–1912), there was, as Collick (1988: 205) puts it, a 'long-standing conviction, based on traditional Confucian moral teachings, that the family and the local community were the proper organs for the relief of distress'.

While the standard versions of the early development of welfare in Japan need to be treated with considerable caution for their historical accuracy, they do provide a useful 'legitimization' for, and explanation of, some of the features of more modern forms of welfare provision and delivery and a backdrop to some of the debates about how the current welfare system might be reformed. The Buddhist concept of *jihi* continues to be seen as in opposition to the development of a welfare state based on citizenship and rights. The neo-Confucian ideology of hard work, frugality, and mutual family support that was emphasized in the Tokugawa period is contrasted with individuals receiving support directly from the state.

Christianity is seen by most people in Japan as closely connected with the establishment and running of welfare institutions despite the tiny number of Christians in the Japanese population. The Imperial Family is still perceived to be a major benefactor of welfare activities, in particular child welfare.

THE BEGINNINGS OF ORGANIZED WELFARE

While historians can point to individual examples of social welfare activity at certain points in the pre-modern period in Japan, the majority date the start of the development of a welfare system to the Meiji Restoration of 1868 when, 'Among the . . . declarations issued by the new Meiji government of 1868, can be found one declaring, "Offer compassion for widowers, widows, the lonely, and the maimed" ' (JNC–ICSW, 1988: 9). This proclamation was followed by the beginnings of state legislation but, significantly, this was aimed in the first instance at developing a strong military and navy: a system of disability and retirement allowances for the army in 1871, similar benefits for the navy in 1875, for the police in 1882, and for civilian officials in 1884. As Campbell (1983: 210) says: 'Aid for the general public did not come as quickly'. When it did arrive, as in the Poor Relief Regulation (Jukkyū Kisoku) of 1874, it was, as with most pre-war legislation, a reaction to popular unrest, and in essence constituted only the legal institutionalization of existing feudal systems of community, family, and religious mutual support backed up by minimal state financial aid for those who could not be cared for within the other systems. Social policy throughout the Meiji period was seen more as an instrument to control unrest—very much in the style of Bismarckian policies at the same time in Germany[3]—than the means by which the state sought to provide a minimum standard of living for its citizenry.

The Meiji government followed a strict policy of what, today, would be called *laissez-faire* economics, coupled with an ideology that state intervention was not only unnecessary but might, indeed, prove counter-productive by developing lazy and dependent attitudes in the population as a whole (Hastings, 1995: 18). The one major exception to this pattern was the institutionalization of a comprehensive and compulsory elementary educational system which was seen as the key to Japanese modernization and a means to avoid colonization. In 1875, around 35 per cent of children were receiving elementary education; by 1905, the figure was over 95 per cent.

On the other hand, individual firms began from the 1890s to take on a more major role in providing for the welfare of their workers in order to attract and keep employees. Rodney Clark (1979) provides a good account of how and why this happened. Japan's early industrialization was based around the textile industry. Most of those employed were young girls from poor farming households. They worked in factories where they were placed in the 'care' of older male owners. These girls worked, at best, for very low wages; in many cases they were virtually indentured, especially in northern Japan, where famine meant that parents were forced to 'sell' their daughters to mills where they had to work out their contracts. The work was tedious and unhealthy (there were high rates of both tuberculosis and accidents) and the hours very long—often thirteen or fourteen a day. Foremen, who were paid according to production rates, applied as much pressure as they could. Abuse—of every description—was rife and the workers, in many cases little more than child labourers, had no one to whom they could turn for help.

The first real signs of worker protest were recorded in 1886, but it did not become effective until the 1890s, when employers, in a rapidly expanding market, began to face labour shortages and increasing labour mobility as workers took their new skills to competitors. To remedy this, employers began to improve labour conditions, offering their female workers housing, food and *o-keiko* (training in the traditional arts needed to improve marriage prospects).

When new industries—metalworking and engineering—that involved the employment of an increasingly skilled male labour force came to the fore at the turn of the century, employers made the shift from daily wages to offering career prospects, promotion in return for loyalty, welfare schemes, and bonuses, all as a means of keeping their workers. In the case of both female and male workers—though particularly the latter—employers developed a new rhetoric to legitimate and justify their position. This rhetoric was founded on the idea of the company as family, as a unique Japanese form of occupational grouping that arose naturally out of feudal (Tokugawa) tradition. As Clark (1979: 41) puts it:

The metaphor of the family, besides harking back to Tokugawa tradition, was perfectly adapted to interpret employment practices forced on employers by the labour market. The notion of family-as-firm was also consistent with one of the central political concepts of the Meiji period, a concept widely supposed to have remote historical antecedents, but one which was in fact a new garment of old threads: that the Japanese nation itself was a gigantic family with the emperor at its head. Such a well-connected and plausible doctrine as familism, therefore, was able to assert itself over the brash and contentious theories that might have proceeded from some obvious facts: that there were enormous differences in the way managers and workers were treated [and] that industrial relations were sometimes very bad.

THE *HŌMENIIN* COMMUNITY VOLUNTEERS

It was in the light of further social unrest in the 1910s in Japan, however, that perhaps the most characteristic feature of the contemporary welfare system emerged in the form of the *hōmeniin* system, and it was no coincidence that this took place in the Kansai area which was, in many ways, the centre of Japanese capitalism during the Taishō period (1912–26).[4] Osaka, in particular, was experiencing a great influx of migrants, both from the countryside and also from Korea, as a result of which acute social problems—slums, unemployment, poverty—emerged and social unrest developed. As Tamai (forthcoming) reports, one important civil servant, Ogawa Shigejirō, writing in 1912, wondered whether it might be possible, in order to tackle the problem of poverty, for the local authorities to develop 'a "Japanese" way' that emphasized the importance of the family (especially the wife, who managed the family budget) rather than simply replicating the Western model of poor relief.

Ogawa moved to Osaka in 1913 and set up a study group on social work and social reform. This group examined alternative systems of social welfare provision, including the system of household mutual support in China, the *gonin gumi seido* of feudal Japan, and various models from Germany, Britain, and the USA. When the 'rice riots'—the storming of the government-controlled rice shops in response to sharp rises in the price of rice—broke out in 1918, they were particularly severe and prolonged in Osaka, and it was largely in response to these that Ogawa and the governor of Osaka, Hayashi Ichizō, institutionalized a system of locally appointed, unpaid, volunteers who would advise and help those in poverty.[5] The system was called the *hōmeniin* system: *hōmen* meaning an area of the city designated by the city government as poor; *iin* meaning supervisor.

Tatara (1975: 145–69) describes the *hōmeniin* system as a synthesis of the German Elberfeld programme and the Friendly Visitors of the Charity Organization Society in London. Only the influence of the former was acknowledged by contemporary policy-makers, possibly, as Hastings (1995: 88) suggests, because it too relied on male workers, whereas the British example relied mainly on women. Volunteers were locally based individuals, such as teachers, policemen, pharmacists, and, ironically, rice dealers, who had daily contact with the poor. They could receive no financial payment for their work and were normally responsible for some 200 households in their area. They counselled the poor, sought medical supplies for the sick, and investigated whether individuals were eligible for relief. As Itō (1995) points out, however, the *hōmeniin* system differed from the Elberfeld system in one crucial respect. Although the *hōmeniin* were able to offer financial assistance to individuals from their relief fund (which included subsidies from city and prefectural government), most of their resources came either from money collected from donations or else from the pockets of the *hōmeniin* themselves, and most of their work was advising individuals on how to improve the management of their household budgets (Nomoto, 1998: 92–5). The underlying principle of their work, therefore, was that it was always better to help the poor to be independent of, rather than reliant on, the state.[6]

The role of the *hōmeniin* evolved over the next twenty years and spread throughout Japan (Chūbachi and Taira, 1976: 424): they grew in number and their role changed from one of social control and prevention of social unrest to becoming by 1940 a genuinely courageous and relatively loud (100,000 individuals) voice calling for improved social legislation, while their social control function had largely been taken over by compulsory local neighbourhood associations (the *tonarigumi*). A Poor Relief Law (Kyūgohō) was enacted in 1929 obliging local authorities to provide some level of care for the poor; a Ministry of Welfare was established in 1938; and pensions insurance for various groups was introduced from 1939 so that, as Gould (1993: 36) points out, Japan had already begun to put down the foundation of a welfare state before the Second World War. However, as Japan plunged further and further into what historians call the 'dark valley' (*kurai tani*) of the early 1940s, the roles of the *tonarigumi* and *hōmeniin* became increasingly intertwined as a means of ensuring full co-operation in the war effort.

THE DEVELOPMENT OF SOCIAL WELFARE PROVISION IN THE POST-WAR PERIOD

It would be a mistake to assume that the war had only a negative effect on social development in Japan, since wartime mobilization actually involved some significant egalitarian and communitarian elements which left an important legacy in the post-war period. Following the introduction of the National Mobilization Law (Kokka Sōdōinhō) in 1939, the government, led by the fledgling Welfare Ministry, issued a set of regulations concerning labour relations which, according to some scholars, effectively created the modern Japanese corporation management structure and institutionalized many company welfare practices (Gordon, 1985: 262). During the war too, the health insurance schemes which had first been established on a small scale in the 1920s were expanded to maintain the health of citizens, particularly those of conscription age (Maruo, 1986: 65). Further, according to some commentators, the treatment of *burakumin*—Japan's 'outcaste' class which, despite officially being reclassified as 'new commoners' (*shinheimin*) in the 1870s, continued to be treated as social pariahs during the pre-war period—was improved under the ideology that all Japanese were the children (*sekishi*) of the emperor.

When, however, Japan finally emerged from nearly fourteen years of continuous warfare in 1945, it found itself being run by the American-led occupation forces of General MacArthur. One of MacArthur's first missions was to eradicate the ultra-nationalism of the wartime period and to disseminate the concepts of democracy, liberalism, and citizenship which the Allies had seen themselves fighting to defend. Welfare reforms were very much part of the new culture that the occupying forces wanted to see take root in Japan (see Tatara, 1980). A new Constitution was promulgated in 1946—largely under the guidance of the Americans, though most commentators now agree that it did have the support of the Japanese government—which included the commitment (Article 25) to provide welfare for all Japan's citizens on an equal basis, and not simply to selected, economically productive, elements of the population. This was an enormous undertaking in a country that had been all but totally destroyed, whose infrastructure had been dismantled, with a huge population of widows and orphans and even larger numbers of soldiers and colonists returning from overseas. It was in the light of these difficulties that a US army officer and social administrator, Donald Wilson, recommended that, in the short term at least, despite certain reservations—principally that the judgements of the commissioners tended to be personal rather than objective—the *hōmeniin* system should be maintained (Anderson, 1993: 92; Wilson, 1980: 337–40).

Thus it was that the *hōmeniin* system survived virtually intact the widespread changes brought about during the occupation period. There were no purges nor any extra training; all that changed was its name, from *hōmeniin* to *minseiiin*, so as to distance it from its wartime existence when it was, in the minds of many, more an agency of social control in an ultra-nationalistic state than a provider of social welfare. The term *minseiiin* is generally translated as 'person or persons commissioned to promote and stabilize the life of the people'. Most *minseiiin*, at the time of appointment, were also given the title of *jidōiin* (child welfare offi-cers), specifically charged with looking after the welfare of children within their community, and the full title of the *minseiiin* system incorporates this element (*minsei.jidōiin seido*). The terms of their appointment were modified only slightly from those of the pre-war period, so that:

(*a*) *minseiiin* were to work from a position of equality with those they assisted;
(*b*) they were to be appointed by the Ministry of Health and Welfare (Kōseishō) on the recommendation of local committees;
(*c*) they were to serve three-year terms which could be renewed;
(*d*) they would receive out-of-pocket expenses.

The first of these conditions is particularly significant, since it implies that in the pre-war period their relationship to those they were helping was anything but equal. This was (some say still is) common among those who represented the state in their dealings with individuals and was encapsulated in the still used expression *kanson minpi* (praise the bureaucrat and despise the people).[7] It would appear though that, in the immediate post-war period, there was little change in attitude, not least because the *minseiiin* were, in effect, the only means through which the general public had access to public assistance and were thereby placed in positions of great power and able to generate bonds of debt (*on-gaeshi*) among those who received their help.[8] In 1950 and 1951, however, the system was reformed: new publicly administered welfare offices staffed by paid local govern-ment officials (called '*shakaifukushishuji*'—often translated as 'social workers'[9]) were set up and the *minseiiin* role was officially limited to an advisory capacity. This is a position, as we shall see, that the *minseiiin* system still fills today.

DEVELOPMENT OF THE 'JAPANESE-STYLE WELFARE SOCIETY'

Since 1945 Japan has developed many of the features of a modern welfare state. Starting with the 1947 Workmen's Accident Compensation Insurance Law (Rōdōshō Saigai Hoshō Hokenhō), the Unemployment Insurance Law (Shitsugyō Hokenhō) of 1947, and the Daily Life Security Law (Seikatsu Hogohō) of 1950, which provided a measure of means-tested social assistance, legislation was gradually introduced to ensure that virtually the whole population was covered by some form of health and pensions insurance by the early 1970s, even if benefits were still very low and varied considerably depending upon a person's occupational status.

From the start of the 1970s, public expenditure on social security began to increase rapidly and pensions, health care, and educational levels began to converge with those in west European countries (Gould, 1993: 11–13).[10] In many ways, indeed, Japan could point to some social indicators which seemed to suggest that it was doing better than Western competitors. For example, while in 1960 men and women in the UK could expect to live four and three years longer respectively than their Japanese counterparts, by 1993 these figures had been almost exactly reversed as life expectancy in Japan became the highest in the world (*JIC*, 1996: 13). Moreover, this has been achieved at very low cost compared to most other OECD countries. In education also, it was pointed out, Japanese students consistently came top in international comparative tests in science and mathematics, despite the comparatively low proportion of GNP spent on the system (Lynn, 1988: ch. 2).

To some extent the success stories in health care and education were an indication of the precedence that continued to be given to these areas over personal social services, a pattern that to some extent has defined the development of the modern welfare system in Japan—welfare provision as an investment in the population rather than as a safety net. According to some critics of the state's approach to welfare, this pattern represents an underlying philosophy that has not changed substantially since the Meiji period, despite the attempts of American reformers during the American occupation (1945–52) to introduce a more idealistic model of a welfare system being first and foremost a means to support the weakest members of society (see Adachi, forthcoming). Hence, while Article 25 stipulates the government's obligation to ensure a minimum standard of living for all citizens, the Japanese Supreme Court has historically interpreted this statement as 'an expression of the state's political and ethical obligation'— what Burks (1985: 41) calls a 'program clause'—and has entrusted actual policy-making on social security to the judgement of the government legislature and administration in relation to other demands, as in the pre-war period (JNC–ICSW, 1988, 1990). During the period between 1955 and 1975, the government kept expenditure on social welfare relative to national income stable at around 2 per cent of the GNP (Bronfenbrenner and Yasuba, 1987), and many commentators felt that the lack of social welfare outlay was compensated by a high household savings rate of between 13 and 20 per cent, as families were 'forced' to save against an uncertain future (Tabata, 1990). Against this, however, it must be pointed out that Japan's GNP was beginning to grow very rapidly, and also that it did not need to spend nearly as much as many of its OECD counterparts on juvenile delinquency, drug rehabilitation, teenage or single mothers, and broken families, simply because these social problems were so relatively small in comparison. Similarly, Japan until the late 1990s had had virtually no call on unemployment benefits. Indeed, according to many commentators, full employment was a main plank of post-war social policy. In many ways, therefore, Japanese policy-makers' emphasis on preventing people from falling into poverty through investment in education, health, employment, and a set of universal benefits could be termed a success.

The defining moment in the post-war history of welfare in Japan, however, came in the late 1960s and early 1970s. In the 1967 Lower House election, the Liberal Democratic Party (LDP) gained less than 50 per cent of the vote for the first time since it came into existence in 1955. This fact, combined with growing calls for welfare reforms and the emergence of the ebullient Tanaka Kakuei as the party's main strategic thinker determined to leave his mark on post-war Japanese society, led to the designation of 1973 as *fukushi gannen* (Year One of the Welfare Era). A series of plans was proposed; according to some commentators, if all had been initiated Japan today would have a system with more generous benefits and higher contributions than even the most welfare-oriented of European nations. The welfare budget immediately began to grow.

A worse date for *fukushi gannen*, however, could not have been chosen. The year 1973 saw the first oil shock, a shock that was greater in Japan, which relied completely on imported oil to drive its export economy, than anywhere else. Economic growth rates dropped by 50 to 70 per cent; unemployment trebled between 1975 and 1985. Neither had been calculated for in the welfare budget. The plan for the development of a Western-style welfare system went into rapid reverse and in its place there emerged a model that came to be known as the 'Japanese-style welfare society' (*Nihongata shakai fukushi shakai*).[11] As Watanuki (1986: 265) says, 'the idea of a Japanese-style welfare society [was] rather confused', but, essentially, instead of the move towards the state taking on the major burden of social welfare, it expected this role to be played by the three social institutions of the family, community, and company, and for government expenditure on social security to be maintained at a lower level than in a Western 'welfare state'. Indeed, as Harada (1998: 198–202) points out, the model was called a 'welfare society' as opposed to a 'welfare state' to emphasize that people should not come to depend on the state but on self-help, communal solidarity, the family (generally a euphemism for women), and the firm.

The presentation of the Japanese-style welfare society took two distinct forms.

On the one hand, there developed in Japan during the 1970s a powerful negative rhetoric against the Western-style welfare state which, only five or ten years earlier, had been held up as a model to emulate. This critique focused in particular on the British welfare system, both because Britain was accepted in Japan to be the birthplace of the first fully developed welfare state and because Britain in the early 1970s was going through a phase of economic stagnation, severe strife in the arena of industrial relations, and a variety of apparently intractable social problems. In much of the literature in Japan, a connection was made between these social and economic problems and a highly developed welfare state that created a 'dependency culture', and the phenomenon, along with other things, was labelled the 'British disease' (*Eikoku-byō*) (see Shinkawa and Pempel, 1996: 305–12; Takahashi, 1997a: 136–9, 151). During the late 1970s, similar expressions were used about other European countries such as Italy and France (*Italia-byō*; *France-byō*), as their economies stagnated and that of Japan continued to grow. The Nordic, particularly Scandinavian, model of cradle-to-grave welfare was particularly sharply attacked (*Hokuō fukushi kokka-byō*) and it became common in Japanese social welfare debates to refer to it simply in the context of *hanmen kyōshi* (a model to avoid).[12]

On the other hand, although many of the ideas espoused by the proponents of the new welfare policy in the late 1970s and the 1980s were not unique to Japan—indeed, it could be argued that the assault on the dependency culture, and the back-to-basics emphasis on family values and family responsibility were also pure Thatcherism—these ideas were cloaked in Japan with an aura of 'Japaneseness' as a 'natural' outgrowth of Japanese 'traditional' and 'historical' practices which both served to legitimate them and reduce opposition. The development of company welfare could be explained by the fact that many of Japan's large companies, such as Mitsui (see Roberts, 1973), had developed out of family businesses which had been set up in the Tokugawa period. The idea of mutual community support was buttressed by reference to the *gonin gumi seido* and their links with modern-day organizations such as the 'neighbourhood association' (*tonari-gumi*) (see Bestor, 1989). Finally, in the case of women providing welfare support, it was argued that there was a long 'tradition' of a 'natural' division of labour along gender lines in Japan and that women 'willingly' accepted the responsibility for the private and domestic sphere while men worked in the public, extra-domestic arena. The view that Japan's welfare system should be built on these 'traditional' cultural practices was espoused by a large number of the country's leading thinkers during the 1970s, such as Murakami Yasusuke, Rōyama Shōichi, and Sakamoto Jirō (Takahashi, 1997a: 144).[13]

As the 1970s progressed, therefore, despite some of the ambiguities in its meaning, indeed perhaps in part because of these ambiguities, the term *Nihongata shakai fukushi* (Japanese-style welfare) became increasingly utilized by senior politicians such as prime ministers Ōhira and Miki to describe the form of social welfare they wanted to institute in Japan.[14] The term rapidly gained such common currency that the reversal of the previous plan to build up the welfare state (known in Japanese as *fukushi minaoshi*) met with very little public resistance. In part, this was because (unlike in other countries where state welfare benefits were reduced or abolished in the 1970s and early 1980s) there was no organized resistance from unions in Japan. Unions, being company-based and not national, were essentially interested only in maintaining the benefits they had already secured for the full-time, permanent employees in the companies they represented. These benefits were not under threat and indeed continued to grow as the economy expanded in the 1980s (Hiwatari, 1993; Tabata, 1990). Nor should the role of the media be underestimated. Through a content analysis of magazine articles, Takegawa (1988: 242) discovered that while up to 1975 all articles on welfare took either a positive or a neutral stance, from 1976 onwards the vast majority (around 95 per cent in his sample) took a negative position. Equally significant was government campaigning against welfare, which was felt by many to be a major deterrent to genuine welfare claimants and to lie behind the unreasonable processing of welfare claims by local-government officials (see Asahi Shinbun Japan Access, 1992).[15] Rudd (1994: 17) argues that the state was particularly successful in attaching a sense of stigma to the receipt of welfare rights. But perhaps the main reason for the general acceptance of the idea of Japanese-style welfare was the use by its proponents of symbols of Japanese tradition and national character, such as the strength of the family and the community, that chimed in particular with the growth of national confidence in Japan in the 1970s and 1980s.

This positive view of Japanese welfare reached its zenith in English with the publication of Harvard Professor Ezra Vogel's provocative *Japan as Number One: Lessons for America* (1980). Vogel wrote about the lessons to be gained from the Japanese model which offered 'security without entitlement'. Entitlements had been kept low; there had developed a minimal sense of rights; and the government—or rather the bureaucracy—had been left with the responsibility to effect the most equitable distribution of the nation's wealth. Japanese-style welfare necessitated a minimal bureaucracy (about 10 per cent of its American equivalent), thus keeping taxation low and preventing the development of what Ivan Illich (1977) had recently described as 'welfare professionalism'—professionals and bureaucrats who have created systems to serve their own rather than their clients' needs. Instead, Japan preferred to rely on a large number of voluntary, unpaid workers supervised by a small number of bureaucrats—especially in areas such as social work and probation. These high-status volunteers, *minsei.jidōiin*, represented for Vogel the key figures in the provision of Japanese-style welfare.

THE *MINSEI.JIDŌIIN* SYSTEM IN CONTEMPORARY JAPAN

Today, the *minsei.jidōiin* system is still the main form of direct personal social service provision. The officers are appointed on renewable three-year contracts and on the basis that they have lived in their designated area 'for a long time', have a clear understanding of its social situation, and display enthusiasm for carrying out the promotion of social welfare. While they are called volunteers, they do received a small amount of compensation in the form of 'travel expenses'(around ¥100,000 a year) though this is rarely adequate to compensate for phone bills and actual travel.

The profile of the *minsei.jidōiin* makes interesting reading. Unusually for social work (which in most capitalist societies is a 'female' occupation) until very recently the majority of *minsei.jidōiin* have been male. In the pre-war period, almost all *hōmeniin* were male. It was a major change when 9 per cent (11,812) of the *minsei.jidōiin* appointed in the immediate post-war period were women. This proportion increased to 22 per cent by 1956 (Tatara, 1975: 416–17); 32 per cent in 1971 and finally 50 per cent in 1995 (*Fukushi Shinbun* (Welfare News), 12 Oct. 1998). Over the same period, however, the average age of *minsei.jidōiin* has increased: in 1974, 71 per cent were between the ages of 50 and 70 and 7 per cent were over 70; by 1986, 83 per cent were between 50 and 70 with 7 per cent over 70 (Gould, 1993: 52). The overall average age is today around 60, but since in some communities *minsei.jidōiin* have to retire at 75 (there is no national stipulation on this), this means that in other communities the average age must be much higher. Certainly, some *minsei.jidōiin* are in their eighties.

Each *minsei.jidōiin* gives on average about ninety days of service a year and makes around 120 household visits. As a result, it is no surprise that over 40 per cent give as their occupation 'unemployed' which generally means that they are either retired or else are full-time housewives, probably with grown-up children. Fifty-five per cent of the work of *minsei.jidōiin* is with the elderly, 20 per cent with those in poverty, 10 per cent with the handicapped, 6 per cent with children, and 3 per cent with single-parent families (*Fukushi Shinbun*, 12 Oct. 1998).

The real significance of *minsei.jidōiin*, however, lies in their numbers. These have increased continuously—in the last decade alone by nearly 20 per cent—until today there are around 197,000; by law, there should be, and evidence suggests that there is, one *minsei.jidōiin* for every 120 families in the countryside and one for every 270 in cities. Against this figure, there are for the whole of Japan a mere 18,000 paid local government welfare officials (*shakaifukushishuji*).[16]

Since they are so few in number, the caseload of each individual *shakaifukushishuji* is enormous and hence they are unable to undertake much family-support work by themselves, and are rarely able even to offer a second counselling session. The paid *shakaifukushishuji*, therefore, are forced to draw on the services of the *minsei.jidōiin* in order to maintain some control over their caseloads and, in many cases, it is the *minsei.jidōiin* who undertake household and individual visits while the local government bureaucrats issue the grants, arrange home helps, and make placements in institutions.

Feelings about the *minsei.jidōiin* system have been somewhat ambivalent throughout the post-war period. Wordsworth (1968: 74–5), a Canadian social

worker visiting Japan in the 1960s, concludes her comments on the topic by citing a Japanese source from 1958 reflecting what remains a common view in some
areas today:

The use of volunteers is a vexatious question . . . On the one hand there is a tradition of
using volunteers in very useful ways. On the other hand, those who are most concerned
with raising professional standards are also most critical of the use of untrained volunteers
and concerned that 'Volunteers workers . . . are popularly regarded and depended on as if
they were well-qualified case workers or group workers'.

These differing views of the *minsei.jidōiin* are worth exploring in greater detail
since they mirror many of the wider debates about welfare delivery in Japan. In
the most detailed ethnographic account in English of the *minsei.jidōiin* system in
contemporary Japan, *Changing Japanese Suburbia* (1991), Eyal Ben-Ari suggests
that it presents a model example of the Japanese concept of community care: it
generates a great degree of self-help and self-reliance; the role of the family is central; and close control is kept on spending. In short, it props up rather than
replaces the role of the family and the local community in the provision of social
welfare.

Ben-Ari gives a detailed and vivid account of the perspective *minsei.jidōiin*
have on their own work and, by shadowing and talking with them, he demonstrates what they see as the advantages of their way of operating. They are senior
members of their local communities, respected for their maturity and judgement—what Takahashi and Hashimoto (1997: 311) call 'using their wisdom and
experience' to help others—and with a genuine interest in the welfare of local
families and competent to give advice on how people can manage their lives better. It is quite clear also that they consider it an honour to be called on to talk with
and visit needy people in their community, and indeed *minsei.jidōiin* are often
characterized as *chiiki no meishi* (local worthies). In particular, Ben-Ari emphasizes the ability of *minsei.jidōiin* to understand the lives and problems of those in
their neighbourhoods simply because they are part of, and have long been part of,
those same neighbourhoods. This is in stark contrast to the case of many professional social workers in other industrialized countries, who live outside the communities in which they work, visit them during the day, and then withdraw to
their own communities.[17] A typical household visit involves a cup of tea and a
general discussion, often unconnected directly with welfare issues but allowing
the development of a deeper relationship, a luxury that few professional social
welfare workers would be able to justify to their employers. *Minsei.jidōiin*, indeed,
estimate that over 40 per cent of their workload consists of such social visits
(*KSH*, 1997: 347).

To some extent, the role of the *minsei.jidōiin* in Japan appears to be a good
example of the general acceptance of the authority of representatives of the state
in what might in the UK or US be considered the private domain of the family.
The best-known example of this role is the local police box (*kōban*) found in

every Japanese neighbourhood. Local policemen are full members of the community where they work; they know the local families, what they do, and where
they work, and they are seen, in an idealized fashion anyway, as providing protection for the community rather than as policers of it (Ames, 1981; Bayley,
1976). Ben-Ari argues much the same case for the *minsei.jidōiin*. He describes
them as 'watchdogs' who act as a pressure group on behalf of the local community. They are treated with respect by the officials in the city halls, not least
because of the recognition that they are working voluntarily and without pay.[18]

Ben-Ari's positive view of the *minsei.jidōiin* is based very much on their own
perspective on their work; those who are recipients of their 'services', however, do
not always provide such a positive assessment of their role. Of course, just as the
vast majority of people in all developed societies do not come into contact with
front-line social workers and hence are often unsure of their exact role, so in
Japan, although many people know about *minsei.jidōiin*, they tend to be very
vague about what it is exactly that they do. There remain those, however, who still
sees *minsei.jidōiin* as enforcers of conservative moral codes of conduct rather
than as advocates for the weakest members of society. Certainly, this is the view
of some of those with whom the *minsei.jidōiin* come into contact. Peng (1995), in
her study of single mothers in Japanese society, and Takahashi and Hashimoto
(1997: 308), in their overview of the *minsei.jidōiin* system, clearly demonstrate the
friction that can exist between a young, single mother struggling to retain her
independence and an elderly, generally male, untrained *minsei.jidōiin* who is trying to 'help' her.[19] More significantly, Soeda (1990) estimates that less than 25 per
cent of low-income families take up their entitlement to welfare benefits. If *min-
sei.jidōiin* represent a pressure group on behalf of the members of the local community, then at one level, clearly, the system is not working.[20] One reason given by
critics of the system is simply that, contrary to what 'traditional' practice might
lead one to expect, many individuals do not like to discuss their problems with
their neighbours and would rather suffer in silence (Nakano, 1998: 373–5).

It is clear also that, although the role of *minsei.jidōiin* has evolved and matured
over the past five decades, their individual motivations for the post have not
always been as pure as simply performing their 'civic duty'. Certainly, as Dore
(1958: 70) has pointed out, in the immediate post-war period when they directly
controlled access to state funds, many *minsei.jidōiin* used their positions to
launch political careers, exchanging their ability to obtain funds for the promise
of future votes. It is telling, perhaps, that *minsei.jidōiin*—in combination with
left-wing groups which were concerned about government interference—were
behind successful attempts in 1951 to block government proposals to introduce
professional social workers, arguing that these would simply be duplicating the
work they were already doing (Anderson, 1993: 93). As Ben-Ari (1991) points
out, the power of *minsei.jidōiin* today to abuse the system in the same way is dramatically reduced since individuals have direct access, if they can manage it, to
local government welfare offices and, in any case, *minsei.jidōiin* can generally only

make recommendations on funding and not actual grants themselves. Nevertheless, it still remains the case that *minsei.jidōiin* retain a level of access to audiences
and officials that is denied ordinary citizens. Many *minsei.jidōiin* sit, for example,
on local government social welfare councils (*shakai fukushi kyōgikai*).

The quasi-official, semi-voluntary role of *minsei.jidōiin* is therefore not an
uncontroversial one. It is particularly significant, therefore, that in the mid-1990s
the government decided to expand and reinvigorate the *minsei.jidōiin* system
with the establishment of a new category of welfare volunteers called *shūnin
jidōiin* who were to specialize in cases involving children (see Zenkoku Shakai
Fukushi Kyōgikai Minseibu, 1997). Largely the idea of a senior official in
Kōseishō, the new system sought to reactivate the work of *minsei.jidōiin* in the
area of child welfare since so much of their focus had moved to working with the
elderly in recent years. The recruitment of *shūnin jidōiin* was set at one to every
thirteen to nineteen *minsei.jidōiin* (depending on the area in which they were to
operate) and, as of 1997, almost 14,500 had been appointed (Matsubara, 1997).
In their profile, *shūnin jidōiin* differ significantly from *minsei.jidōiin*: their average age is just under 51 (though if, as with the *minsei.jidōiin*, their three-year
appointments are constantly renewed this will quickly rise) and 76 per cent of
them are women (*KH*, 1998: 430).

It is too early to say whether and how the new system will prove effective—
there are occasional reports of tensions between *shūnin jidōiin* and *minsei.jidōiin*
and between both groups and workers in the local government child guidance
centres (*jidōsōdanjo*) who, in some areas, are not at all keen to call on their services—but what is perhaps most interesting is that such a system should be established at all fifty years after it was decided only reluctantly to allow the
continuation of the *minsei.jidōiin* system as a short-term measure while Japan
recovered from the aftermath of the Second World War. The reasons behind the
establishment of the *shūnin jidōiin* system relate indirectly to the major welfare
issue confronting Japan at the end of the 1990s, an issue that indeed lies behind
most of the welfare reforms in the country during the 1990s—the fact that Japan
is rapidly becoming the world's oldest known human population.

There are any number of ways to illustrate Japan's ageing society, most of
which are by now only too familiar to the Japanese public. If we accept the standard definition of 'aged' as those who are 64 and over, the proportion of the aged
in Japan will change from 4.9 per cent in 1950[21] to 14.5 per cent in 1995, to a projected 25.5 per cent in 2020 (the US by contrast is projected to change only from
12.5 per cent in 1995 to 16.1 per cent in 2020). The proportion of those who are
75 or over will rise even more dramatically, from 1.3 per cent in 1950, to 5.7 per
cent in 1995, to a projected 12.5 per cent in 2020 (Harada, 1998: 176). Or alternatively, it took Japan just twenty-four years to go from a society with 7 per cent
of the population officially defined as aged (1970) to 14 per cent (1994), a demographic shift that took seventy years in the US and 130 years in France; and it will
take Japan only twenty-two years to change from a society with 10 per cent of the

population defined as 'aged' to one with 20 per cent, a transition that it is estimated will take fifty to sixty years in countries such as Italy, Germany, Holland,
and Sweden.

There are two unconnected reasons for the ageing of Japan's population, both
of which require government attention. On the one hand, as we saw earlier,
people in Japan are living longer than anywhere else in the world. Average life
expectancy at birth has increased from just over 50 for men and just under 54 for
women in 1947 to 79 for men and almost 83 for women in 1999. To reach 100 in
Japan is no longer exceptional.

At the same time as longevity has increased, the number of children being
born in Japan has declined dramatically. The total fertility rate (the average
number of children that women are expected to bear during their childbearing
years) has dropped from 5.24 in 1920 to 4.32 in 1949 (the first post-war baby
boom when 2.7 million babies were born), to 2.14 in 1973 (the second post-
war baby boom when 2.09 million babies were born), to 1.57 in 1989 (when
only 1.25 million babies were born). At this point, the Japanese government
decided for the first time to raise public consciousness about the potentially
calamitous effects of such a low birth rate in what the media dubbed the '1.57
shock'.[22]

It should be pointed out that Japan's fertility rate in 1989 was not in fact
uniquely low. Those of Italy and West Germany at the end of the 1980s were even
lower, and those of Britain, France, and the US were not much higher; all were
below the official rate of 2.1 which demographers give as the fertility rate needed
for a society to remain at a constant population. It was the combination of the
decline in the fertility rate with rapidly increasing longevity, plus the fact that
Japan, unlike many other OECD countries, had no plans for nor history of immi-
grant labour—despite the appearance for the first time in the post-war period of
some foreign workers at the end of the 'bubble economy' in the late 1980s—that
led to the sense that Japan faced a demographic crisis. This was perhaps expressed
most vividly in the realization that, while in 1950 there were over twelve people
in Japan of (potentially) working age (15–64) for each aged person, in 1990 there
were only 5.7, and in 2025 there would only be 2.4. Further, as Kwon (1999: 11)
points out, there is very low (and still declining) financial support for the elderly
in Japan by their own children (15.6 per cent of their total income in 1981; 9 per
cent in 1988) compared to some other East Asian societies (Korea, 44.3 per cent
in 1994; Taiwan, 53.2 per cent in 1994). Hence the comparatively high reliance of
Japan's elderly on state pensions (already over 50 per cent of their total income
package at the end of the 1980s) will mean that the working population will have
to transfer much more of its wealth to the elderly if the current system of inter-
generational, pay-as-you-go pension payments persists. Against this, of course, it
should be pointed out that the fact that there will be fewer young people to support means that the overall dependency rate (the so-called 'productive population' of those between the ages of 15 and 64 divided by those under 15 and over

64) will be virtually the same (1.5 workers per dependent) in 2020 as in 1950 (Ferries, 1996: 229).

It was in the light of the above 'discovery' that, in the 1990s, the Japanese government set about seriously trying to develop welfare programmes to support its aged and ageing population.[23] While 60 per cent of those over 64 in Japan continue to live with at least one adult of a younger generation (compared to around 8 per cent in the UK and 14 per cent in the US), the government recognized that this meant a large and growing proportion of aged who did not do so—72 per cent had lived with an adult of a younger generation in 1980—hence it had to significantly increase the provision of home helps, day care, and short-stay community centres and nursing homes. This it did through its *Gold Plan* of 1990, and the demand for such services proved so overwhelming (and the plan itself so conscientiously implemented) that an enlarged *New Gold Plan* had to be introduced in 1994.

It should be pointed out that not only did the *Gold Plan* mean an enormous increase in government welfare expenditure—at both the national and local levels—but it also involved the destigmatization of the elderly receiving 'welfare' (*fukushi*) by renaming such services as 'care' (*kaihō*). The success of the programme also suggested that when such forms of care were available, Japanese families were only too happy to allow the state a role in caring for their aged members.

In order to tackle the problem of the declining fertility rate, the government introduced what it called the *Angel Plan* in 1994 to encourage women to have more children by making it easier to have a family while continuing to work. The plan involved a ten-year programme, starting in 1995, to increase day nurseries, drop-in care for non-working mothers, centres to care for sick children, after-school care centres, and counselling centres for parents with child-care problems (Boling 1998: 177). At the same time, it sought to remove the stigma from a mother who worked and replace it with the idea that the state should support such women to ensure they could have a full career and bring up their families. Unlike the *Gold Plan*, the *Angel Plan* was beset by problems from the moment it was set up, and failed to reach many of its targets as the economy stagnated and many local governments were reluctant to implement its provisions in full, in part because so much of their expenditure was already committed to the *Gold Plan*.[24]

While the establishment of the *shūnin jidōiin* system in 1996 was not directly part of the *Angel Plan*, it must be seen as closely connected to it. On the one hand, more and more of the attention of the *minsei.jidōiin* was being taken up with dealing with the problems of the aged in their communities, and they had increasingly little time to devote to children, as the *jidōiin* element of their name implied they should. On the other hand, the government recognized the importance of giving support to families with children as a means of encouraging an increase in the fertility rate, but did not have the financial means to carry out all the plans it desired. The development of a new type of volunteer social work commissioner who would specialize in working with children was one way of dealing with both problems. At the same time, commissioners could be selected who were perhaps more suitable for working with families with young children than some of the older, male, *minsei.jidōiin*.

The establishment of the *shūnin jidōiin* system was also another example of what Maruo (1986: 68, 76) calls 'Japan's distinctive welfare mix' that draws upon non-state as well as state resources in the provision of welfare and lies somewhere between 'the pure welfare state model, as advocated by European social democrats, and the pure market model, as advocated by Anglo-American economic liberals'. Maruo suggests that people rely in Japan on non-state welfare because they prefer to call on the family and community, though this is somewhat belied by the fact that when the state does provide non-stigmatizing welfare—such as through the *Gold* and *Angel* plans—take-up rates are very high. Nevertheless, there is no doubt that families do provide more welfare support in Japan than in either North American or north European societies. Indeed, as Shinkawa and Pempel (1996) point out, income in Japan is perceived much more in terms of households than individuals, and as long as there is one main breadwinner in a household—and throughout the recession of the 1990s strenuous efforts were often made not to lay off male workers with families to support—it will be unlikely to quality for welfare support even if elderly or female members of the household find themselves without a job.[25] Social policy in Japan continues to concentrate on social investment in education, health, employment, and universal benefits designed to prevent families falling into poverty; when they do fall, programmes such as the semi-official, quasi-voluntary *minsei.jidōiin* provide cheap, front-line support within the local community.

Japan's mixed economy of welfare may be, as Maruo suggests, distinctive, but its development has been a piecemeal operation perhaps best characterized by Lee's (1987: 247) expression as 'social instrumentalism', a highly pragmatic response to immediate political and economic demands as much as, if not more than, the result of historical continuities and cultural traditions. As the next chapter shows, the development of child welfare in Japan has been similarly piecemeal and pragmatic.

3

The Delivery and Development of Child Protection in Japan

Every year, in Japan as in every other advanced industrial society, a small proportion of children come into the care of the state because their parents either cannot or will not look after them to a level which society, in the form of the state, expects. In the case of Japan, the state is represented by the Children and Families Bureau which in 1964 emerged from the Children's Bureau which had been set up in 1946 within the Ministry of Health and Welfare (Kōseishō). To this day, the Bureau retains jurisdiction over the whole system of child welfare in Japan. It is responsible for the overall planning and budget for child welfare as well as for supervising and offering guidance to local administrative organizations and child welfare institutions. Prefectures and the large so-called 'designated' cities in Japan have local responsibility for enacting the policies of the central government with advice from the Child Welfare Councils (Jidō Fukushi Shingikai) or the Child Welfare Subcommittees of their local Social Welfare Councils (Shakai Fukushi Shingikai).

The key post-war legislation for child welfare services in Japan was the new Japanese Constitution of 1946 (which guaranteed the provision of welfare to all Japanese citizens on an equal basis), the Child Welfare Law (Jidō Fukushihō) of 1947 (which provided for child protection, child care, and foster-care systems and laid the foundation for public intervention on behalf of the nation's children), and the Children's Charter (Jidō Kenshō) released on 5 May (Children's Day) 1951 (Article 2 of which stated that 'those children not having homes shall be brought up in an environment having similar advantages'). Together they provided the legislative framework within which child welfare in Japan was carried out virtually unchanged until the first major revision of the Child Welfare Law in 1998, which will be discussed at the end of this chapter.

JIDŌSŌDANJO (CHILD GUIDANCE CENTRES)

The main field agencies within the child welfare system in Japan are the *jidōsōdanjo* (child guidance centres). Every prefecture and designated city in Japan is required by law to set up a *jidōsōdanjo*, and in total there are approximately 175 around the country. The *jidōsōdanjo* were originally set up to provide temporary accommodation and care for children who were found abandoned on the streets at the end of the Second World War (Kashiwame, 1992: 3) and some of them still retain short-stay facilities that can perform this function. Gradually their activities expanded to deal with the problems of juvenile delinquents and disabled children as well as to take care of all children who were without carers, and they became what Kashiwame (1992) calls the 'nucleus' of child welfare activities in Japan. Table 1 gives an indication of the types of consultations which are carried out at the *jidōsōdanjo* throughout Japan. Almost half of all referrals come from families or relatives who are worried about their own children. Many of the remaining cases are passed on by welfare institutions or city officials or are telephone consultations. Only a small proportion of referrals (3.5 per cent) are directly from schools and from medical and nursery facilities (7.5 per cent), both of which are major sources of referral in most European and North American child welfare systems (Tanakajima, *KH*, 1997: 105). Almost no referrals come from children themselves. *Jidōsōdanjo* are, in effect, therefore institutions that give advice about children but not to them.

Over half of the cases dealt with by the *jidōsōdanjo*—and the total number of consultations has changed little over the past thirty-five years—relate to the problems of those with physical and mental disability. Throughout this period, around 10 per cent of referrals have consistently related to consultations concerning the need or possible need for the protective care of children (*yōgosōdan*) and Table 2 shows the reasons given in 1995 for the original approach to the *jidōsōdanjo*. It is from these cases that children who are placed in *yōgoshisetsu* tend to come.

The *jidōsōdanjo* staff include professionals from a number of different fields: physicians, child psychologists, physiotherapists, nursery teachers, clerical staff. The bulk of the work, however, is carried out by the 1,200 or so child welfare officers (*jidōfukushishi*), an important and rather understudied group within the welfare system in Japan (for one of the few descriptions and analyses of the work of *jidōfukushishi*, see Jidōsōdanjo wo Kangaerukai, 1998). It is worth listing the necessary qualifications of the child welfare officers since they play such a crucial part in the system. According to the Child Welfare Law, they are as follows: (*a*) to

TABLE 1. Number and ratio of different types of consultations dealt with by *jidōsōdanjo* in Japan (1998)

Consultation type	No.	%
On child protection (*yōgo sōdan*)	36,819	10.9
On delinquent behaviour	17,669	5.3
On physical and mental disability	177,059	52.7
On child health and other matters	33,813	10.1
On general problems with bringing up and educating children (*yōiku kanren*)	70,881	21.0
Total consultations	**336,241**	**100.0**

Source: YnJ, 2000.

TABLE 2. Reasons for consultations on child protection at *jidōsōdanjo* (1995)

	No. of cases	Proportion (%)
Sickness and disability	5,985	20.1
Disappearance from home	2,243	7.5
Divorce	2,168	7.3
Death	541	1.8
Abandoned child	250	0.8
Family environment (*kazoku kankyō*)	11,491	38.6
[of which abuse cases]	[2,722]	[9.1]
Others	7,110	23.9
Total	**29,788**	**100.0**

Source: adapted from Tanakajima, *KH*, 1997: 105.

have graduated from a school or other institution designated by the Minister of Health and Welfare; or (*b*) to have concluded studies at a university that specialized in psychology, education and/or sociology, or other similar courses (what is known as *sankamoku shikaku*—the three-subject qualification); or (*c*) to be a physician; or (*d*) to have worked in a child welfare operation as a social welfare secretary for two or more years; or (*e*) to be a person to whom (*a*)–(*d*) might apply because they have the requisite academic knowledge and experience required of a child welfare officer (Kashiwame, 1992: 17).

The proportion of staff with these different types of qualifications varies enormously from city to city and prefecture to prefecture, as can be seen in Table 3. In *jidōsōdanjo* in areas such as Yokohama, Osaka, Saitama, Kanagawa, and Niigata, the great majority of staff have specialist social welfare qualifications. As a result, these areas have often been at the forefront of social work practice. In major cities such as Tokyo or Kyoto, however, the majority of the staff in the *jidōsōdanjo* are regular local government officials (*futsū no kōmuin*) who are qualified simply by virtue of the fact that they are doing the job. In the latter case, working in the *jidōsōdanjo* is often of the normal five to three-year job rotation of any local government official and, while it is important to stress that in Japan local government officers still enjoy high social status (and hence come from the most educated sections of the population) and some very talented individuals who perform their jobs extremely professionally end up working in *jidōsōdanjo*, for many of those who work in them this is one of their least popular postings (Masamura and Higuchi, 1996: 42–3).[1]

The workers in the *jidōsōdanjo* either individually or collectively put together a report on, and prepare a plan for, the treatment of each case which is referred to them. They have a range of options from which they can choose. The vast majority (around 90 per cent) of decisions, however, either involve simply offering advice but not taking any follow-up measures or setting up a programme of longer-term advice and counselling ('continuous guidance') (Tochio, 1998: 37). This long-term guidance can be carried out by the *jidōfukushishi* themselves, but their workload does not always allow this.[2] Hence

TABLE 3. Number of staff working in *jidōsōdanjo* with specialist welfare qualifications (1999)

	Heads of *jidōsōdanjo*	Staff members
PREFECTURE		
Hokkaidō	8 (0)	43 (11)
Aomori	3 (0)	16 (0)
Iwate	3 (3)	10 (7)
Miyagi	2 (1)	5 (0)
Akita	1 (0)	4 (0)
Yamagata	2 (0)	12 (5)
Fukushima	3 (1)	20 (1)
Ibaraki	3 (0)	20 (0)
Tochigi	3 (0)	21 (5)
Gunma	3 (0)	18 (0)
Saitama	6 (0)	65 (58)
Chiba	5 (2)	33 (10)
Tokyo	11 (0)	106 (0)
Kanagawa	5 (3)	31 (31)
Niigata	5 (2)	36 (36)
Toyama	2 (2)	9 (9)
Ishikawa	2 (1)	24 (16)
Fukui	2 (1)	10 (10)
Yamanashi	2 (0)	10 (10)
Nagano	5 (0)	17 (17)
Gifu	4 (3)	15 (10)
Shizuoka	4 (3)	32 (11)
Aichi	8 (2)	37 (20)
Mie	5 (4)	19 (0)
Shiga	2 (1)	12 (3)
Kyoto	3 (2)	14 (4)
Osaka	7 (7)	83 (83)
Hyōgo	4 (3)	40 (4)
Nara	2 (1)	8 (0)
Wakayama	2 (0)	12 (11)
Tottori	3 (2)	12 (12)
Shimane	4 (3)	11 (5)
Okayama	3 (3)	16 (16)
Hiroshima	3 (0)	21 (11)
Yamaguchi	4 (1)	16 (2)
Tokushima	1 (0)	8 (0)
Kagawa	1 (1)	12 (12)
Ehime	3 (0)	12 (0)
Kōchi	2 (0)	11 (4)
Fukuoka	4 (1)	18 (10)
Saga	1 (0)	8 (0)
Nagasaki	2 (2)	17 (10)
Kumamoto	2 (1)	12 (2)
Ōita	2 (0)	14 (1)
Miyazaki	3 (3)	10 (3)
Kagoshima	2 (1)	11 (6)
Okinawa	2 (0)	18 (2)

TABLE 3. Continued

	Heads of centre		Staff members	
DESIGNATED CITIES				
Sapporo	1	(0)	16	(7)
Sendai	1	(1)	12	(0)
Chiba City	1	(0)	7	(0)
Kawasaki	2	(0)	19	(13)
Yokohama	3	(3)	21	(21)
Nagoya	1	(0)	18	(0)
Kyoto City	1	(1)	21	(0)
Osaka City	1	(0)	36	(28)
Kōbe	1	(1)	23	(14)
Hiroshima City	1	(1)	9	(1)
Kita Kyūshū	1	(0)	10	(0)
Fukuoka City	1	(0)	8	(0)
Total	174 (67)		1,209 (552)	

Source: *AS*, 7 Feb. 1999.
( ) = those with specialist qualifications (*senmon shoku saiyōsha*)

it is sometimes delegated to the local *minsei.jidōiin* or *shūnin jidōiin* who were discussed in the last chapter.

The remaining 10 per cent of cases dealt with by the *jidōsōdanjo* tend to be more serious and to require more dramatic intervention since it is usually felt in these cases that the child can no longer be left where it is. Technically, according to the Child Welfare Law, only the prefectural and city offices can admit children into welfare facilities and foster placements. In practice, however, the authority for this has been delegated to the *jidōsōdanjo*. In the vast majority of cases, the staff in the *jidōsōdanjo* persuade parents or guardians to place the children voluntarily in welfare institutions. In most cases, this is unproblematic although, as we shall see in Chapter 7, parents tend to be very unwilling to allow their children to be fostered. In other cases, staff in *jidōsōdanjo* have to resort to quite sophisticated (occasionally even rather underhand) techniques in order to persuade unwilling parents and guardians to agree to placements. It is still very unusual, and considered very drastic, for staff to resort to asking the Family Court (*katei saibansho*) to remove the rights of parents or guardians to oppose a placement. There have rarely been more than fifteen children in total in *yōgoshisetsu* at any one time where parental rights have been removed in this way (Konomi, 1996: 141). In any case, it has never been clear whether, even when parents' rights have been removed so that children can be placed in institutions, this actually prevents them from subsequently reclaiming the children whenever they wish.[3]

There are no less than twelve different types of welfare institution prescribed in the Child Welfare Law to which staff in *jidōsōdanjo* can refer children. Most of these are specialized institutions for children with different types of mental and physical disability. There are three types of institution, though, which we need to examine in some detail since they constitute, from the perspective of the *jidōsōdanjo*, those institutions which overlap the most with the *yōgoshisetsu*. These are the homes for mothers and children (*boshiryō*); homes for the training and education of juvenile delinquents (*kyōgoin*); and infant homes (*nyūjiin*).[4]

BOSHIRYŌ (MOTHER AND CHILD HOMES)

As we shall see, many children in welfare institutions in Japan are there because their lone-parent carer has been unable to look after them. However, there are in Japan some measures and institutions which are set up specifically to cater for and try to keep together single-parent families as family units. Most of the available measures are financial in nature. There are systems of tax allowances and income support through the Bereaved Survivor's Pension (for those who are widows) and through the Child-Rearing Allowance (Aid to Dependent Children) systems which are given by both the local and central governments. There are also certain loans and funds such as the Maternal and Child Welfare Loan Fund (Boshi Fukushi Shikin) as provided for under the 1964 Law for the Welfare of Mothers with Dependants and Widows (Boshi oyobi Kafu Fukushihō) which, according to Matsubara (1988), was established to assist single mothers to be economically independent and to provide them with the 'motivation and the will to live'. There are thirteen different types of fund (mostly available either interest-free or at very low interest rates) which are provided variously to help single mothers set up their own businesses, fund their children's education, fund their own vocational training, or pay their housing expenses. The vast proportion of these loans (around 70 per cent) is used for the educational expenses incurred by children after they leave the compulsory education system. Beyond this, lone mothers are given preference in occupational and housing assistance, and prefectural governments may also provide home helps, either at low cost or occasionally free of charge, if a lone mother or one of her children falls sick.

In terms of institutions, the Law for the Welfare of Mothers with Dependants and Widows provides for consultation centres to be set up in all prefectures within the welfare offices (*fukushi jimusho*) of the prefectural or city offices with their own specialist staff. The 1,128 or so staff of these centres, three-quarters of whom are part-time, provide some 470,000 consultations a year, mostly on financial and economic matters (Sōmuchō Seishōnen Taisaku Honbu, 1996: 248). Further, provided for under the same law, there are some seventy-two single-mother welfare centres, which are designed to offer both advice and also short-term vocational training projects for single mothers, and some twenty single-mother respite homes which offer services and play space to lone-mother families either free or at a low cost.

The main service provided by the state for lone-mother families, however, are the *boshiryō*, normally called in English 'mother and child homes'. Tochio (1991: 19) describes these institutions as 'designed to accommodate mothers and children of fatherless families who feel mentally and economically insecure [where] they will come to feel more inclined and eager to achieve self-support and to improve their outlook on life'.

Boshiryō were established immediately after the end of the Second World War for women who had lost their husbands during the wartime period. They reached a peak in 1954 with 654 homes, after which the number declined as more lone-mother families were able to take advantage of the preferential treatment they were entitled to for housing in the rapidly growing public housing sector (Sasaki, 1989).

The main criterion for entry to the *boshiryō* is evidence of financial insecurity. According to a 1985 survey (Matsubara, 1988: 9), 40 per cent of households residing in the homes were recipients of public assistance at a time when the national level was around 1 per cent. Most of the mothers in the homes (80 per cent) also work but, as with other single mothers, their incomes are about one-quarter of the national average (*KH*, 1993: 206–7).

According to Peng (1997: 119), single mothers in Japan are in a difficult situation when it comes to looking after their children. As Ozawa (1991) explains, however, government policy has long been to help them to work and thereby be rehabilitated into the mainstream of society rather than allowing them to come to depend on the state. As a result, in 1990 almost 90 per cent of lone mothers were in work while only 34 per cent of mothers in two-parent families were working.[5] Moreover, because of the highly gendered nature of the Japanese workplace, Japanese women in full-time positions earn around 60 per cent of the equivalent full-time male wage (Brinton, 1993). It is not surprising, therefore, that families headed by lone mothers are the lowest income group of all family types in Japan.

Significantly, whereas in the 1970s the majority of lone mothers were lone mothers as a result of being widowed (61.9 per cent in 1973), by 1993 the vast majority (73.2 per cent) were lone mothers as a result of divorce (*KH*, 1998: 97).[6] While divorced women in Japan had won by the 1990s a major victory by gaining custody of their children in almost three-quarters of all cases (something unthinkable in the pre-war period when children were seen as the property of the father's household),[7] this has been severely tempered by the fact that in 1993 only 15 per cent of divorced lone mothers received any financial support from the fathers of their children (*KSH*, 1998: 78).[8]

In 1998 the 160,000 lone-father families accounted for around 20 per cent of all single-parent families. The situation of course is not any easier for them. Indeed, in some ways, the gendered division of labour makes it even more difficult in that male workers are expected to be available to their employers full-time while their wives look after domestic affairs. Further, Japanese fathers have little experience of domestic affairs and looking after their children. In a 1998 survey, while only 7 per cent of lone mothers reported anxiety about 'household matters' (though 73 per cent felt anxiety about 'economic matters'), the figures for lone fathers were 43 per cent and 29 per cent respectively (*KSH*, 1998: 98). Single fathers are in a cleft stick: they either have to give up their jobs to look after their children or give up their children to keep their jobs (see Hirano *et al.*, 1987; Kasuga, 1989). Few can manage both and, as a result, their average household incomes are about 70 per cent of the national average. Moreover, they are eligible for very few of the benefits available to lone mothers.[9]

Boshiryō are covered by minimum requirements in terms of facilities and space as well as in the provision of nursery and medical care. In 1995 there were some 1906 personnel (80 per cent full-time) working in the 309 *boshiryō* which had 11,245 single mothers and their families, a ratio of just better than 1 : 6. Just under two-thirds of the *boshiryō* are still public, even though the total number of public *boshiryō* has halved over the past thirty years.

As Table 4 shows, today there are around 4,000 households in about 310 *boshiryō* in Japan.[10] One of the most interesting features of these households is that, unlike in the UK where most of the mothers in similar units are admitted as the result of teenage pregnancies, very few are under 20 years old in Japan (in 1987 fewer than 1 per cent) reflecting the very low teenage pregnancy and illegitimacy rates in Japan.[11] Indeed more than half the mothers are in their thirties, suggesting that the separation of couples soon after the birth of their first child is responsible for many lone mothers being in *boshiryō*. The number of children per lone-mother family in the *boshiryō* is slightly higher than the Japanese average: over 50 per cent have two children or more. Around 30 per cent of the children are of pre-school age; 45 per cent are at elementary school (6–12); 17 per cent are at junior high school (13–15) and 7 per cent are over 15 (*KH*, 1993: 206–7).

The overall numbers in *boshiryō* have been declining rapidly over the past forty years, although the proportion of lone-mother families actually doubled in Japan from about 4 per cent of all families with dependants to 8 per cent between 1973 and 1986, largely due to the increasing proportion of mothers gaining custody of their children during this period (Peng, 1997: 115). The decrease in the number of those in the homes has meant that resident families have increasingly been

TABLE 4. Number of households and children in *boshiryō* in Japan (1965–96)

Year	Public *boshiryō*	Private *boshiryō*	Total *boshiryō*	Households	Children
1965	487	134	621	12,768	
1970	405	122	527	10,199	18,429
1975	314	110	424	8,195	16,152
1980	262	107	369	5,210	13,993
1985	239	109	348	5,360	14,753
1990	219	108	327	4,484	11,936
1992	213	109	322	4,397	11,606
1994	207	106	313	4,421	11,573
1996	202	105	307	4,181	11,406

Sources: Jidōsōdanjo wo Kangaeruakai, 1998: 236–7; Kōseishō Jidōkateikyoku, 1998: 289.

those with particularly severe social and economic problems. Families are allowed to stay in *boshiryō* until the youngest child is considered to be sufficiently adult to be independent and, according to a survey from 1987, almost one-quarter of families in *boshiryō* have been there for over five years (*KH*, 1993: 207).

KYŌGOIN (EDUCATIONAL PROTECTIVE FACILITIES)

Kyōgoin are the only institutions for child welfare whose establishment is obligatory for Japan's forty-seven prefectures, and there are currently some fifty-four of them throughout the country. Literally, *kyōgoin* means a facility (*in*) that both educates (*kyō*) and protects (*go*), hence such institutions have come to be known in English rather clumsily as 'homes for the education and training of juvenile delinquents'. All except two are public institutions and—in line with a belief which was prevalent in the early post-war years when the first institutions were set up that juvenile delinquents should be kept away from the temptations of urban life—most of the homes are situated in isolated, rural areas far from the nearest town.

Unlike the juvenile correction centres (*shōnenin*) where young people who have been convicted of crimes are sent, *kyōgoin* are not closed institutions, and indeed much staff time is spent on looking for, and bringing back, children who have absconded, often after visiting their family at weekends or during holiday periods. There is one institution in Japan which offers training for staff to work in *kyōgoin*, but since it has an annual intake of only twenty-five, the vast majority of staff in *kyōgoin* have received no special training and are, as with those at the *jidōsōdanjo*, ordinary public employees who have been posted to the homes to work.[12] Tsuzaki Tetsuo (1996: 9) describes many of these staff as feeling as if they have been passed over for promotion, or in some way disciplined by being posted to such jobs, and he relates this to the occasional reports of excessive use of force by staff on the children in their care.

The *kyōgoin* operate a very strict and tight routine. All of them are residential and most of the children's day is taken up with their academic education (which is based on the mainstream school curriculum) and with training in different types of vocational work such as forestry, farming, woodwork, and pottery. In some of the *kyōgoin*, the children share rooms in cottages run by married couples, which are in the grounds of the institution, but increasingly it has proved difficult to find staff who are willing to do this work (especially when they have young children of their own) and the homes are more likely to be run along the lines of large dormitories. The vast majority of children in the *kyōgoin* are of junior high-school age (13–15), but some 11 per cent are of elementary school age (6–12) and a further 15 per cent are of senior high-school age (16–18), reflecting a policy introduced in 1989 which formalized an arrangement for those who had won places in local senior high schools or had jobs at nearby workplaces to stay on in the *kyōgoin* rather than be moved to more secure units (Yamamoto, 1989: 12).

The ratio of boys to girls in *kyōgoin* has consistently been around 70 : 30 over the past forty years, and the vast majority of placements are of between six and twenty-four months' duration, though with high rates of recidivism and absconding these figures are not easy to interpret (Hanashima, 1994: 10). Ichikawa (1985) argues that the vast majority of children in *kyōgoin* demonstrate standard intellectual ability and that their behaviour and learning problems should mainly be explained by their family circumstances. Indeed the family backgrounds of children in *kyōgoin* are predictably difficult. About 70 per cent are from one-parent families and many of the remaining 30 per cent of children are reported to come from families with severe domestic problems. A 1985 survey cited by Ichikawa suggested that 45 per cent of children came from families with low or unstable incomes. Many of the children are reported as having been deprived of affection in their early years and to have drifted into anti-social behaviour.

The system whereby the children come into the *kyōgoin* is interesting since it overlaps with that for *yōgoshisetsu*. *Kyōgoin* are officially meant for children who have engaged in, or are considered likely to engage in, delinquent behaviour, and to help them overcome their problems. Delinquent or problem children in Japan are dealt with under two separate laws: the Child Welfare Law (Jidō Fukushihō) has responsibility for the welfare of all children under the age of 18, while the Juvenile Law (Shōnenhō) deals with all adolescents between the ages of 14 and 19 as part of the justice system. Whether a child is treated under one or the other of these laws depends not only on their age but also on the approach of the police and the perceived seriousness of the offence. When cases are dealt with by the welfare rather than justice system, it is the *jidōsōdanjo* which must take responsibility for deciding where to place the child in question. Eighty per cent of children in *kyōgoin* are placed there by workers from *jidōsōdanjo* and only 20 per cent by the juvenile courts.

According to Hanashima (1994: 141–3), there used to be considerable interaction between children in *kyōgoin* and those in *yōgoshisetsu*, but it was felt that the former were not a good influence on the latter and it was stopped. The number of children in *kyōgoin* has declined rapidly over the past four decades (see Table 5). The number of institutions, however, has hardly declined at all and the number of places available fell only from 5,846 in 1960 to 4,390 in 1998. As a result the occupancy rate (the number of children in *kyōgoin* against the number of places available) dropped dramatically over this period from 88.9 per cent in 1960 to 38.8 per cent in 1996, though this is far from even across the prefectures: in some prefectures (such as Osaka) the occupancy rate remains as high as 80 per cent, while in others it is as low as 20 per cent.

The overall decline in the number of children in *kyōgoin* can be explained in a variety of ways. In part, it may reflect what Idei (*KH*, 1996) describes as a general

TABLE 5. Number of places available, residents, and occupancy rate in *kyōgoin* (1960–98)

Year	Places available	No. of residents	Occupancy rate (%)
1960	5,846	5,197	88.9
1970	5,538	3,909	70.6
1980	5,304	2,779	52.4
1990	4,893	2,029	41.5
1998	4,390	1,637	37.3

Source: Jidōsōdanjo wo Kangaerukai, 1998: 236–7.

lack of knowledge and understanding about such institutions. In part, it reflects the decline in juvenile delinquency cases (30,000 in 1985; 15,000 in 1995 for example) referred to the *jidōsōdanjo*. In part, it can be explained by the declining number of children within the relevant age group. In part, though, it might be explained, as we shall see later, by the increasing number of children with a history of delinquency who are being placed in *yōgoshisetsu* as opposed to *kyōgoin*.

NYŪJIIN (RESIDENTIAL INFANT-CARE FACILITIES)

Nyūjiin are facilities which are set up to look after infants under 2 years old (*nisai miman*) who for any reason cannot be looked after in their own homes. Their history, as with that of most welfare facilities for children in Japan, began in the immediate post-war period as Japan tried to pull itself together again after the ravages of war. Many children were found abandoned and unwanted. Dower (1999: 62–3) cites a February 1948 report from the Ministry of Welfare which put the number of orphaned and homeless children at 123,510, of which 28,248 had lost parents in air raids, 11,351 had lost parents during the repatriation of Japanese families from the Asian colonies, 2,640 had been abandoned, and an astonishing 81,266 had lost their parents in the turmoil at the end of the war. He denounces the treatment of these children as being like that of cattle—indeed, he says, the method for counting cattle (*ippiki, nihiki*) was also used to count them—and the fact that they were placed in militaristic detention centres where they suffered physical abuse.

In this turmoil, the institutions that were set up to care for unwanted infants were generally funded by overseas charitable foundations such as the American-based private organization LARA (Licenced Agencies for Relief in Asia), the United Nations' Relief and Rehabilitation Administration (UNRRA, later to be called UNICEF) and a variety of private American church organizations. Indeed, according to Saitō (1985: 6), there was no indigenous Japanese charitable support for *nyūjiin* until the 1950s, by which time the number of infant homes had grown to around 120, accommodating close to 3,000 children. As Table 6 shows, as of 1998, there were 115 *nyūjiin* throughout the country with the capacity for 3,698

TABLE 6. Number of homes, places available, residents and occupancy rate in *nyūjiin* (1945–98)

Year	No. of homes	Places available	No. of children	Occupancy rate (%)
1945	19	—	560	—
1947	33	—	704	—
1948	64	—	999	—
1950	97	—	2,077	—
1960	131	3,745	3,123	83.4
1970	126	4,088	3,331	81.5
1980	125	4,230	2,945	69.6
1990	118	3,843	2,599	67.6
1998	115	3,698	2,563	69.3

Source: Jidōsōdanjo wo Kangaerukai, 1998: 236–7; Saitō, 1985: 7.
— Figures not available.

children though housing only 2,563 children. The vast majority of the *nyūjiin* (104) are private institutions and many are attached to *yōgoshisetsu*.

Today *nyūjiin* are normally divided into two types: those which offer a rather hospital-like experience, and those which try to replicate a more or less domestic environment, although with an average capacity of over thirty children this is hard to achieve in any *nyūjiin*, which is largely why similar institutions were closed down in the UK in the 1960s. In the first type, the staff resemble nurses, while in the second they are more like the residential care workers in *yōgoshisetsu*. Across the spectrum, however, staffing levels are roughly equivalent: 3,348 staff (90 per cent full-time) for 2,566 babies and infants, a ratio of 1.3 : 1 (*NTN*, 1998: 644–5).

The reasons for children being admitted to the *nyūjiin*, as for children admitted to *yōgoshisetsu*, provide a reflection of Japan's post-war social history. In the 1940s and 1950s, admissions were mainly due to parental death or major illness, and child abandonment; in the 1960s to parents being too ill—mentally or physically—to look after their children, and to drug abuse, imprisonment, and the abandonment of families by fathers. From the mid-1970s, however, causes were increasingly related to financial problems in families which had got into severe debt.

A 1992 survey (*KH*, 1993: 208–9) breaks the figures for admission down into two main categories: illness of family members which means they cannot look after the child, and other family problems which make child care difficult. The illness of the mother alone accounts for almost one-third of all admissions; the next biggest category is the children of unmarried mothers (*mikon no haha*) or children of extramarital relationships (*kongai shussan*), which together account for 17 per cent of cases. The disappearance of parents and the abandonment by unknown parents of children accounts for a further 14 per cent of the infants in care. While abandonment accounts for a significant number of cases, the figure is perhaps not as large as many in Japan might expect, since probably the most common association of *nyūjiin* in Japan since the 1970s has been with the phenomenon of *coin-locker babies*—children found abandoned in the luggage lockers of railway and bus stations.

In the mid-1990s, however, there suddenly began to appear a new category of children in the *nyūjiin*, especially in large urban areas like Tokyo: children with either one or two foreign parents (see Sakata, *KH*, 1995: 163). This was a category which had scarcely been seen since the end of the American occupation in 1952 and was a result of the sudden influx of foreign workers at the end of the bubble economy of the 1980s and the problems that many of them confronted with the 1990s economic recession. As ever, the intake of *nyūjiin* provided a barometer of wider social events in Japanese society.

YŌGOSHISETSU

The Modern History of the Children's Home in Japan

As we have seen, the provision of social welfare and welfare institutions for all but the most needy was extremely limited throughout Japan before the restoration of the Meiji emperor in 1868. With the beginning of the Meiji period and Japan's drive for modernization in the last third of the nineteenth century, there were the beginnings of state support for needy children. In 1871 a government order granted rice for the upbringing of orphans while another order in 1873 extended this to needy families with more than three children. In general, though, there was little state support for social welfare institutions as welfare policy emphasized the responsibility of the family and the community in caring for society's most needy members.

As a result, the early initiative in constructing a system of welfare institutions in the Meiji period for Japan's needy children had to be taken by individuals and organizations without government support. A short-lived facility (Hita Yōikuen) for children was opened in Ōita Prefecture in Kyūshū in 1869, but closed down in 1873 for financial reasons, and a French nun opened the Wa-Futsu Gakkō in Yokohama in 1872, which cared for a number of Japanese children abandoned as a result of the Boshin civil war which restored the Meiji emperor. Other institutions were established with the support of French missionaries during the late 1870s, and Iwasaki Maki established a home in Nagasaki (Nagashima, 1996: 54).

Historical accounts of the modern children's home in Japan, however, generally begin with the foundation of the Okayama Kojiin (Okayama orphanage) by Ishi'i Jūji (1865–1914) in 1887, branches of which still function today in Takanabe, Miyazaki Prefecture, which was Ishi'i's birthplace.[13] Ishi'i, as a Christian, saw the orphanage as the realization of God's will (Takahashi, 1997b) and his Okayama Kojiin, unfettered by regulation, followed the 'ever-open-door policy' of Dr Barnardo in England, where no destitute child was ever refused admission. It grew quickly after it opened with just four children, and by 1906 it housed 1,200 children with around 200 workers.

The manner in which Ishi'i organized and administered his orphanage is important, since in many ways it set the trend for the subsequent decade as orphanages sprang up in response to the economic and social changes following the Meiji Restoration. Ishi'i's vision of his orphanage was primarily of a Christian family home, in which he and his wife acted as 'parents' to the orphans, combined with an educational institution (*kyōikuin*) where children learnt both academic and vocational skills in a system that he called *jidai kyōikuhō* (period education method). He was keen to distinguish his home from a simple care institution (*yōikuin*) or a reformatory (*kankain*). As a result, in 1896 he set up a primary school within the orphanage, and children in the early days were educated part-time and employed part-time in the two trading houses which Ishi'i had opened in Osaka—one selling rice, the other charcoal—and which, along with overseas and missionary donations, was initially all that supported the home financially. In many ways the home had a very liberal environment: physical punishment was banned; education and one-to-one communication between staff and children were encouraged; and children were organized in small, autonomous 'family-style' groups of around ten children each with their own housekeeper, again imitating the style of Barnardo's homes in England at the time (Takahashi, 1997b: 16). Older children were allowed to stay on in the homes and commute to work from them.

The Okayama Kojiin went through many financial and personal crises. Its future was secured, however, by its endorsement at the beginning of the century by the Meiji emperor himself. Ishi'i was decorated for his services in 1901 and the emperor donated funds to the home in 1902, thus beginning—some argue maintaining—a long relationship between the Imperial Family and child welfare institutions.[14]

In the early years of the Meiji period, Christian (first Catholic and then also Protestant) organizations and individuals dominated welfare activities. The state-sponsored *haibutsu kishaku* (anti-Buddhist) movement made it difficult for Buddhist organizations to get involved in social welfare activities, and the first Buddhist home did not open until 1880 (Yoshida and Uto, 1977: 12).[15] The Sino-Japanese war of 1894–5, however, resulted in such a great increase in the number of orphans and children in need that Christian missionary groups simply could not cope, and Buddhist and other organizations became increasingly active in setting up and running institutions for children (Takiguchi, 1993: 26).

The year 1912 saw the start of the Taishō period, with rapid industrialization and increasing urbanization as people moved from the countryside to the cities to work in factories. It also saw another sharp increase in the number of orphanages and other social welfare facilities, including institutions among the growing overseas Japanese communities, for example on the west coast of the United States (Kuramoto, 1976). It was at this time that the precursor of Kodomo Gakuen was founded when a man took into his care in a house in west Tokyo two children classified as *furyōji* (juvenile delinquents) from an emergency shelter run by the Salvation Army. Over the next few years, he took in more such young people from the juvenile courts and via the probation and parole services before he decided to incorporate his home as a social welfare agency called the Seishin Gakusha in 1925.

The Home Ministry set up a Department of Relief Aid (Kyūgoka) for the first time in 1917 and through the Relief Law (Kyūgohō) enacted in 1929 the state took on the responsibility of caring for poor children (under the age of 13) and orphanages were officially sanctioned as relief institutions (Children and Families Bureau, 1979: 2). This legislation was backed up by the Prevention of Cruelty to Children Law (Jidō Gyakutai Bōshihō) in 1933 and the Mothers' Aid Law (Boshi Hogohō) of 1937. Nevertheless, of the 170 orphanages founded prior to the outbreak of the Pacific War in 1941, only six were administered by public agencies; the rest were all privately established (*YSI*, 1998).

If the Meiji era was the first growth period of the modern children's home, then its second followed straight on from the end of the Pacific War when there were only eighty-six orphanages still operating across the country. For some time, however, the opening of new institutions was complicated by the fact that one of the first actions of the American occupation authorities (SCAP) had been to outlaw the use of state money by or for private religious or charitable foundations (see Nagata, 1968: 193).[16] This came into immediate conflict with the better-known Article 25 of the Constitution, which stated that every citizen had the right to life above a minimum standard of health and culture, and that the state must strive to improve social welfare, social security, and public health in every area. In support of Article 25, the government began for the first time to set up a network of institutions for children in need: *jidōsōdanjo* were created to help with the problem of street children, and new public children's homes were set up in urban areas (Yoneyama, 1997: 34–6). It soon became clear, however, that without further help, financial or institutional, from charitable foundations, there simply were not going to be enough facilities in the immediate post-war period to deal with the large numbers of children in need of care.

In the short term, a number of interim measures were instituted that allowed children to be placed in private institutions. These led to the establishment of fifty-four homes (twelve public and forty-two private) in 1946 alone. The Jidō Fukushihō (Child Welfare Law) was enacted in March 1947, and redefined child welfare as a programme to promote the well-being of all children and not just those in poverty. The law also defined a series of different institutions for child welfare and redefined what until then had been known as orphanages (*kojiin*) as *yōgoshisetsu* (children's homes).[17]

The Child Welfare Law, however, still did not deal with the thorny issue of state funding for private homes. The state continued to pay a fixed sum for the maintenance of children in such homes, but found itself constitutionally unable to contribute to the support of the buildings or other facilities of such homes. The issue was finally resolved in March 1951 by the revision of the Shakai Fukushi

Jigyōhō (Social Welfare Service Law), which defined the scope and nature of all major public and private welfare activities, and which set up (under Article 22) a new type of welfare institution known as a *shakai fukushi hōjin*, literally a social welfare juridical person, which allowed private welfare administrative organizations to provide specific publicly recognized welfare services and to receive public financing for doing so, as long as they agreed to comply with government regulations (Nagata, 1968). In order to become a *shakai fukushi hōjin*, therefore, a home would need to accept the regulation of its staffing, physical plant, and the composition of its Board of Directors (*rijikai*), which could contain only a prescribed number of relatives. Since the *shakai fukushi hōjin* were directly answerable to the Minister of Welfare they were henceforth to be considered on the same basis as public institutions and became eligible for funding of up to 50 per cent of building and administration costs and exempt from corporation and property tax and tax on donations and gifts (JNC–ICSW, 1986: 89–90). Also in 1951, the Children's Charter (Jidō Kenshō) set out the rights of the child and the responsibilities of parents. The idea that children had rights apart from those of their families was a new one that largely reflected the development of discourses on human rights emanating from the fledgling United Nations.

The Seishin Gakusha set up in Tokyo continued as an institution for juvenile delinquents until the war, and was run by the husband of the founder's second daughter. Towards the end of the war he was called up for military service in China, even though he was already 35 years old, and he went, leaving his wife behind to continue running the home with her mother. Of his unit, only he and one other survived; he was arrested and, like many other Japanese soldiers who were caught by the rapidly advancing Soviet troops in the last days of the Pacific War, taken to Siberia as a prisoner. When he returned to Japan in 1947, the Juvenile Law had just been amended and the new Child Welfare Law enacted. Although it was two years since the war had ended, it remained a period of great confusion throughout Japan, and in Tokyo in particular there were still many children without relatives to care for them. Almost immediately, he converted the buildings in west Tokyo—which had just been returned to the family after having been commissioned in the immediate post-war period to be used as a junior high school—into a home for dependent children, and in 1951 the Seishin Gakusha became a *shakai fukushi hōjin* under the new law. However, he was not a well man. He underwent a series of operations for cancer of the oesophagus, and when he eventually died in 1968 his wife took over as the head of Kodomo Gakuen, as the home had become known. She in turn was succeeded by the oldest of their three sons, who was head of the home at the time that I first visited in 1991, the year that it celebrated its official fortieth anniversary, although it could trace back its history nearly twice as long.

Kodomo Gakuen was situated near one of the largest American bases in west Tokyo, and in the early years many of the children in homes were the illegitimate result of unions between Japanese women and members of the American occupying forces. These mixed-race children (*konketsuji*) faced severe discrimination in Japanese society; indeed, one *yōgoshisetsu*, the Elizabeth Saunders Home, was set up specifically to provide them with a refuge. In the 1960s, in order to give such children a fresh start, many were moved from a country which did not want to remember them to a plantation in tropical Brazil (see Hemphill, 1980).[18]

In line with government policy and the demands of the new Constitution for the state to provide care to those who required it, the number of public homes continued to grow until the mid-1950s, by which time there were some 110 homes catering to 7,600 children. Private homes, however, grew even faster as a variety of new charitable and religious groups moved in to the sector. Most of these new homes had an overseas Christian basis and were the product of the efforts of a new wave of missionaries who arrived in Japan with the occupation forces in the immediate post-war period. Others, however, were the work of Japanese new religious movements, such as Seichō no Ie and Tenrikyō, whose support base and finances flourished in the post-war period after years of pre-war and wartime suppression (see Kisala, 1992). Others were opened by more traditional Buddhist organizations, which needed to demonstrate their social commitment as their traditional followers began to turn away from them to the new religions.[19] Others were the result of the desire of single individuals and families to do something in the face of the poverty they could see around them. All of them were encouraged in their efforts by local governments, which could see that setting up such institutions privately might be both more effective and cheaper than through public funds. As Table 7 shows, by 1955 there were some 418 private homes.

In total in 1955 there were 528 *yōgoshisetsu* offering places to almost 33,000 children. In the following forty years the number of homes scarcely changed, so that in 1995 there was exactly the same number of homes, though with almost

TABLE 7. Number of *yōgoshisetsu*, number of children in *yōgoshisetsu*, and birth rate in Japan (1955–96)

Year	No. of homes			No. of children			Birth rate per 1,000 (live births in millions)
	Private	Public	Total	Private	Public	Total	
1955	418	110	528	25,272	7,672	32,944	19.4 (1.82)
1965	462	88	550	27,258	5,728	32,986	18.6 (1.82)
1975	450	75	525	26,893	3,191	30,084	17.1 (1.90)
1980	474	57	531	27,601	3,186	30,787	13.6 (1.58)
1988	484	54	538	26,875	2,720	29,595	10.8 (1.31)
1990	481	52	533	25,121	2,302	27,423	10.0 (1.22)
1992	478	52	530	24,187	2,170	26,357	9.8 (1.22)
1995	478	50	528	23,858	1,883	25,741	9.6 (1.19)
1996	477	50	527	24,151	1,861	26,012	9.7 (1.17)

Sources: *Ysno30nen*, 1976: 313; *KH*, 1998; *NTN*, various years; *MMJF*, 1998: 5.

7,000 fewer children. Over this forty-year period, however, the number of public homes more than halved (from 110 to fifty) while the number of private homes continued to increase; the proportion of children resident in public homes declined from over 23 per cent to just 7 per cent.[20] The other point of interest illustrated in Table 7 is that the relatively consistent number of children in the homes must be seen against a backdrop of a rapidly decreasing birth rate: the numbers of children under the age of 15 in Japan in 1955, 1984, and 1993 were 30.1 million, 26.5 million, and 20.8 million respectively (Preston and Kono, 1988: 278; *JIC*, 1995: 8). Between 1975 and 1995, the number of live births in Japan dropped by 37.3 per cent, while the number of children in *yōgoshisetsu* went down by only 14.4 per cent.

As Table 8 shows, 10 per cent of today's *yōgoshisetsu* can trace their origins back to the Meiji period (1868–1912) and 34 per cent predate 1947 when the word *yōgoshisetsu* was first officially used. Only 2 per cent have been founded since 1980. *Yōgoshisetsu*, therefore, are regarded by many as the modern Japanese welfare institutions with the longest history, older even than old people's homes, and, as is often the case in Japan, with this long history comes high social status. Individual *yōgoshisetsu*, especially private ones, are acutely aware of their individual histories and, especially when they can show that that history is long, will expend a considerable degree of effort in maintaining and disseminating information on

TABLE 8. Foundation dates of current *yōgoshisetsu* (1998) N = 520

1873—1	1909—1	1937— 2	1961—7
1881—2	1910—1	1938— 2	1962—7
1882—1	1911—2	1939— 2	1963—4
1884—1	1912—2	1940— 1	1964—2
1886—1	1913—1	1941— 3	1965—1
1887—3	1915—1	1942— 2	1966—3
1890—2	1916—3	1943— 1	1967—2
1891—5	1918—1	1944— 3	1968—1
1892—1	1919—1	1945—16	1970—1
1893—2	1921—1	1946—42	1971—1
1895—1	1923—6	1947—20	1972—2
1896—1	1924—1	1948—35	1973—3
1897—2	1925—4	1949—41	1974—1
1898—1	1926—2	1950—34	1975—2
1899—1	1927—1	1951—27	1976—3
1900—2	1928—3	1952—25	1977—1
1901—5	1929—4	1953—20	1978—4
1902—3	1930—2	1954—14	1979—5
1903—1	1931—2	1955—23	1980—4
1904—1	1932—2	1956—13	1981—3
1905—3	1933—2	1957—11	1982—1
1906—3	1934—7	1958— 4	1983—1
1907—7	1935—2	1959— 8	1984—1
1908—1	1936—2	1960— 3	1985—4

Source: Derived from *YSI*, Mar. 1998.

it. They will celebrate all anniversaries and especially observe decennial occasions, often with the publication of a new history of the home. While these histories provide interesting social commentary on the years over which the institutions have operated, they also play an important political role in reconstructing a past which reflects well on the institution and sets out the need for its continuation.

Patterns of Admission to Yōgoshisetsu

Under Article 41 of the Child Welfare Law of 1947, *yōgoshisetsu* are defined as institutions (*shisetsu*) for the placement of children, excluding infants, who are either without guardians, or are being mistreated, or are otherwise in need of protective care (*yōgo*).

The term *yōgoshisetsu*, therefore, has been in use in Japan for more than fifty years. It is, however, still not recognized or understood by most Japanese.[21] The most common reaction is to confuse it with *yōgogakkō*, which are facilities for children with a handicap, and indeed this confusion may in part explain why those who are, or who have been, in *yōgoshisetsu* are afraid to reveal the fact, lest people think they have some kind of mental or physical disability. The confusion is understandable, since both words use the same Chinese characters for *yōgo*, which have the sense of care and protection, whereas *shisetsu* refers to any type of welfare or educational institution. For this reason, I have frequently had the experience of being corrected when talking and writing about *yōgoshisetsu* and, like most of those who actually work in such institutions, have had to explain them by the expression *yōgoshisetsu wa mae no kojiin desu* (*yōgoshisetsu* are what used to be called orphanages).

This modern association of *yōgoshisetsu* with orphanages is unfortunate for two reasons. First, the image of orphanages as grim (*kurai*) institutions continues to this day in Japan, and indeed one organization, in trying to praise contemporary *yōgoshisetsu*, differentiates them from orphanages while at the same time explaining what they do in terms of them.[22]

Secondly, it is unfortunate because only a small percentage of children in *yōgoshisetsu* are actually known to be orphans. In 1992, of the 26,357 children in *yōgoshisetsu*, 86.9 per cent were living with either a parent (*ryōshin*) or a step-parent (*kataoya*) at the time that they entered the home (*KH*, 1995: 167). In the case of many others, the fact that the parent was not there did not necessarily mean that they had died, only that they had disappeared and left their children behind. It is important, therefore, as staff sometimes comment, to distinguish between cases where there are no parents (*ryōshin ga nai*) and cases where parents are not there (*ryōshin ga inai*). In the case of only around 0.5 per cent of the children in homes are both parents known to be dead (*YnJ*, 1990: 55).

The Changing Background of Children in Yōgoshisetsu

One of the first points that staff in *yōgoshisetsu* feel that they need to make to visitors is that the children in the homes are not there through any fault or problem of their own but because of the problems which their parents have. As the volumes put out by the Yōgoshisetsu Kyōgikai (Association of Yōgoshisetsu) entitled *Nakumonoka* (I Am Not Going to Cry) suggest, the reasons why children have come into care over the last forty years are a direct reflection of the underside of Japan's post-war development.[23] For example, into the early 1960s there was still widespread poverty and low wages. Many workers were forced to move around the country looking for seasonal work (a practice known as *dekasegi*), and frequently they could not send enough money home to support their children. By the late 1970s, however, Japan had the lowest unemployment rate in the industrial world, rapidly rising incomes, and a fast-improving quality of life. Consumerism was rife—everyone wanted the three Cs of a cooler, car, and colour television—and many barely legal loan companies, known as *sarakin*, were set up to provide people with the wherewithal to purchase such commodities. Many families took on more then they could afford and were stung by the very high interest rates and strong-arm tactics of these loan companies, which often had connections with organized crime groups such as the *yakuza*. The category of 'missing parent' during this period often referred to a parent or guardian simply disappearing so as to avoid these 'loan-sharks' and in the process leaving their children behind.

In the late 1980s Japan actually had severe labour shortages and allowed, for the first time in its history, the introduction of foreign workers to fill these jobs. This in turn created a new category in *yōgoshisetsu* of the children of foreign residents, as well as mixed-race children who had, as mentioned earlier, hardly been seen in homes for the previous thirty years. The collapse of the 1980s bubble economy and the recession of the 1990s also saw the emergence of a new reason for children to be placed in homes—bankruptcy (*hasan*)—as many families found their assets did not cover their outgoings. In this last example, as so often, the reasons for children to be admitted to *yōgoshisetsu* gave an accurate and early barometer reading of a major change in Japanese society.

When one looks at the background of individual families with children in *yōgoshisetsu*, some of the above trends are made even clearer. Table 9 lays out the primary reasons given for children being placed in homes, and shows how these recorded reasons have changed over the past thirty years. By the early 1960s the typical intake of the children's homes had stabilized and was very different from that in the immediate post-war period when almost 90 per cent of children in homes had no recorded parent. Since that time, probably the most consistent underlying reason for children to be placed in *yōgoshisetsu* has been because they were from single-parent families. As we have seen, *boshiryō* provide a measure of support to keep together lone-mother families, but there are only two lone-father

TABLE 9. Primary reported reason for children to be admitted to *yōgoshisetsu* in Japan (1961–92) (%)

	1961	1970	1977	1983	1987	1992
Total child numbers	34,890	30,933	31,540	32,040	29,553	26,725
Death of a parent	21.5	13.1	10.9	9.6	7.5	4.7
Abuse	0.4	2.5	2.4	2.4	2.9	3.5
Divorce or separation	17.4	14.8	19.6	21.0	20.1	13.0
Child abandoned	5.0	1.6	1.0	1.0	1.3	1.0
Missing parent	18.0	27.5	28.7	28.4	26.3	18.5
Parent in prison	4.3	3.0	3.7	3.8	4.7	4.1
Parent in hospital	16.2	15.7	12.9	12.8	11.5	11.3
Parent at work	3.3	1.8	1.0	0.7	1.1	11.1
Negligence	5.7	4.7	4.5	5.6	6.3	7.2
Other/unclear	8.2	9.7	8.4	7.2	11.6	4.5
Parent mentally ill	—	5.6	5.1	5.5	5.2	5.6
Parental discord	—	—	1.8	2.0	1.5	1.6
Refusal to care	—	—	—	—	—	4.2
Bankruptcy	—	—	—	—	—	3.5
Problem with control	—	—	—	—	—	6.2
	100.0	100.0	100.0	100.0	100.0	100.0

Source: *MMJF*, 1990: 55; *KH*, 1994: 133.

— = Category not used.

Note: The results of a survey carried out in 1998 had not been published at the time this book went to press.

dormitories (*fushiryō*) in the whole of Japan and hence many fathers either have to give up their jobs to look after their children or give up their children to keep their job. Significantly therefore, almost exactly half of those who came in to homes directly from their families had been living only with their fathers and, in recent years, one of the main provisions of children's homes has been to deal with the issue of father-headed lone-parent families which is not dealt with elsewhere in Japanese society (*YnJ*, 1990: 19). In some cases single fathers move to live near *yōgoshisetsu*, place their children in the homes during the week, and care for them at weekends. Since 1992, they have been able to use the homes to look after their children in the evenings while they are at work (what is known as *twilight stay*), which explains in part the dramatic increase between 1987 and 1992 in the number of children for whom the main reason given for their placement in a *yōgoshisetsu* is that their parent is working.

It is no surprise that children in *yōgoshisetsu* come from the poorest sections of Japanese society. The average income of their families, as far as surveys can ascertain, is about 25 per cent that of the national average (*YnJ*, 1990: 23). A Tokyo survey of children in care carried out in 1988 showed that, at the time they were admitted to care, 33 per cent of children were living with families that were receiving benefits, when the national average was 0.75 per cent (i.e. 44 times the national average); almost all guardians were living in rented apartments, guest houses, or welfare institutions (60 per cent of Japanese lived in their own homes); more than 13 per cent were unemployed (when unemployment was virtually nil), and the vast majority of the rest were doing manual labouring jobs; and many (15.9 per cent of men) were reported as addicted to gambling, drugs, and alcohol (Kuraoka, 1992: 162, 189).

Furthermore, the educational achievement of the parents of children in homes was very poor by national standards. A 1979 survey suggested that 12.9 per cent of parents had not finished compulsory schooling and a further 66.9 per cent had left the education system as soon as they could, at the age of 15. Even 3.8 per cent of those who had continued in the education system had dropped out before completing the next stage (Kuraoka, 1992: 191). In comparison, by the late 1970s, over 99 per cent of children in Japan were completing compulsory education up to the age of 15; around 94 per cent were continuing on to non-compulsory secondary high school; and around 35 per cent continued to some form of tertiary education. This contrast between the educational backgrounds of the parents of children in care and the general population is very stark and serves to reconfirm the significance in Japan of the connection between status, wealth, and security, on the one hand, and success in the education system on the other. We will return later to this issue when we examine the educational success of the children in care themselves.

Another feature of the background of children in care in Japan, one quite distinctive from other OECD nations, is the fact that in the case of the vast majority their parents were either married or in stable relationships (*naien kankei*) at the time the children were born. The rate of cohabitation without marriage in Japan is extremely low (1.7 per cent) in comparison with many other OECD countries, and less than 5 per cent of Japanese have ever cohabited (*KSH*, 1998: 56). The illegitimacy rate in Japan is even lower (less than 1 per cent) and actually dropped during the 1980s, though it has shown the slightest of increases since (Akaishi and Yoshioka, 1998). The low illegitimacy rate can be explained in part by a high level of knowledge about contraception among young people in Japan (see White, 1993), in part by the very high abortion rate, although most abortions in Japan are performed on married women whose family has reached the desired size.

The evidence suggests, however, that while many parents of children who end up in *yōgoshisetsu* may be married, they married, by Japanese standards, at a very young age. In a 1981 survey of 2,014 children in homes, 17.2 per cent of mothers had married at under 20 years of age, some as young as 15 (Tanno, 1984: 15), while the average age for marriage for women at that time was over 25 (Ochiai, 1996: 55). Since the average time for the birth of the first child was normally a year after marriage, the age at which the mothers of the children in care first gave birth may have been as much as five to ten years younger than the national average. As Jolivet (1997: 11–12) points out, women in Japan who have their first babies at a much earlier age than the average often find themselves cut off from their former friends and, in her opinion, are liable to face social and psychological problems as there are few support groups for young mothers.

Lack of support groups, of course, also helps explain why children come into care in Japan. It is clear that in many cases where children have come finally into *yōgoshisetsu*, the child has first been placed with other relatives, but that they have not been able to provide the necessary care and the placement has had to end. In other cases where children have come straight into care, the lack of extended family can be explained by the fact that the parents may have moved to urban areas from the countryside and have simply lost contact with their relatives, or the extended family has cut off contact with the parent(s) of the child, perhaps because of an unmarried pregnancy or because they did not approve of their partner. But, and this is a theme to which we will come back later, perhaps the significant point in this regard is that made by Kuraoka (1992: 163), namely that 4.2 per cent of fathers and 10.9 per cent of mothers had themselves been in some form of home—infant, children's, education and training, foster, or mother and baby. Such parents simply may not have an extended family available to whom they could turn for support in times of distress.

Officially, the mental illness or disability of parents accounts for around 5 per cent of children being in care. According to Hasegawa (1980: 114), around 80 per cent of these parents are mothers. Often, he suggests, mental disability or mental health problems may be just one factor leading to divorce and family breakdown which is the final (and recorded) reason for admission. Facts and figures, indeed, while they may give an general picture of trends, do not give a real sense of the more complex stories of how individual children come into care. As a few individual examples can show, reasons for admission are seldom limited to a single cause.[24]

The pre-school child: Yūko (4)

Yūko was the youngest of three children. Her father had problems keeping a job, causing tension in the home, and her mother was on bad terms with the neighbours in the area where they lived. Yūko's mother eventually set fire to the neighbours' house and was put in gaol. The two older girls were placed in the care of an aunt and Yūko was admitted to a *yōgoshisetsu* at the age of 3. It was anticipated that when her mother was released from gaol, she would be able to return home, although her father had not stayed in touch during the time she had been in care.

The kindergarten child: Rika (6)

Rika's father was a member of the *yakuza* (organized crime syndicate), and her mother divorced him soon after Rika's birth and disappeared. He took on parental rights at the time of the divorce and tried for a while to bring her up by himself, but one day he took her to work and simply disappeared. She was placed in a *nyūjiin* at the age of two and moved to a *yōgoshisetsu* at the age of 3. Her mother later traced her in the home and began to visit her there. Subsequently, her father gave up parental rights so that her mother could take her home if she wished, but financial problems prevented her from doing so other than for weekend visits.

Elementary-school children: Jun (8) and Mayu (10)

Jun's father worked as a truck driver and was only at home two or three nights a week. Her mother was addicted to playing *pachinko* (pinball) and gambled away the family allowance. She then began to run up substantial debts by borrowing from high-interest loan companies (*sarakin*). Relations between the parents broke down and Jun's mother divorced her husband by procuring his seal (*hanko*) and using it to 'sign' his agreement on the divorce papers. Although he found out in time to prevent the divorce, Jun's father decided not to appeal. Jun was admitted to a *yōgoshisetsu* at the age of 5, along with his elder brother and younger sister. His father came to visit them fairly regularly.

Mayu's mother had a moderate learning disability and never married but had several children by different men. The children were in care in a number of different *yōgoshisetsu*. Mayu was in a *nyūjiin* from the time she was a baby and spent some time with foster parents, whom she still visited at New Year and in the summer. Mayu believed that her foster parents were her real parents (despite having been told that they were not) and kept photographs of them, with her as a baby, in her room. The home had no contact with Mayu's real mother.

Junior high-school children: Naomi (12) and Teruo (14)

Naomi was the fifth of eight children, and was first in a *yōgoshisetsu* at the age of 3 because her mother suffered a nervous breakdown as a result of the stress of bringing up such a large family. She returned home at the age of 5, but appeared unable to bond with her mother, and her behaviour became increasingly problematic, including running away from home. At 10, she began riding on trains without paying, and a couple of times was found asleep on them and was handed over to the police by the rail authorities. She was readmitted to the same *yōgoshisetsu* at the age of 11. In the home, she showed signs of emotional disturbance in her sometimes anti-social behaviour. She insisted on referring to herself by the male pronoun *boku*, and was finding it very hard to come to terms with the onset of menstruation.

Teruo went to live with his father after the divorce of his parents but was shut out, not fed properly, beaten, and generally abused by him. He began to steal things, ran away and got into trouble with the police and was placed in care at the age of 11. He continued to have trouble with the school authorities for bullying and because of his quick temper, and was also constantly being disciplined by the staff in the *yōgoshisetsu*, for a variety of misdemeanours including going into the girls' rooms at night and touching them on the face and arms. He was receiving counselling for bed-wetting.

The senior high-school child: Miko (16)

Miko's mother married very young and Miko was her second child, the elder daughter being around fifteen years older. Miko's father ran through a large inheritance without paying taxes and got himself into debt. Miko was placed in care at the age of 7 when her parents divorced. Her mother visited occasionally and promised several times that Miko would be able to come and live with her in the near future, but nothing had materialized. Miko had not seen her father since she came to the *yōgoshisetsu*.

The working child: Hajime (16)

Hajime was placed in care at the age of 3 when his divorced father, who had been trying to bring him up alone, fell ill. While at school, he had always been considered a problem child (*mondaiji*), and hence it was decided to allow him to stay on in the home after he left school rather than help him set himself up in an independent apartment. The transfer to work helped him mature enormously, and he became committed to helping the younger children and running the sports training in his free time.

The above sketches illustrate most of the significant factors in how and why children come into care in Japan, and also highlight the variety of problems that their parents have faced: mental illness, debt, unemployment, prison sentences, divorce and separation, gambling addiction, ill health. The case studies also show how inadequate parenting often leads to abuse, either wilful or through neglect. Indeed, it is easy to see that the recorded reason for children coming into care is often simply the final twist in a long downward spiral of events, and there is often an arbitrariness to the category under which a particular child is admitted since few cases are the result of a single problem. For this reason, the apparent trends in admission figures over the past forty years should be treated with some caution.

THE 1998 REFORM OF THE CHILD WELFARE LAW

The Child Welfare Law of 1947 saw some thirty minor modifications over its first five decades. In 1996, however, Kōseishō decided that the time had come for a major review, and on 1 April 1998 the first major reform of the Child Welfare Law was introduced in Japan. The review and the revision covered three main areas—the system for admitting children to day-care nurseries (*hoikuen*); the level of state support for families in general in the community; and the function of child welfare institutions—each of which to some extent overlapped.

The Admission of Children to Day Care

The revision of the system for placing children in day care was seen by many as the most important change brought about by the new law. Indeed, some felt that it was the main reason that the review of the existing law had been set up at all. Now, instead of children being placed in a day-care centre by the local government officers once they had met the standards of needing care and protection (a system known as the *sochi seido*), parents will be able to make their own choice of public day-care centre based on information provided by the local government offices, as long as a place is available and they can first convince the local government office of their need.[25] The cost of day care will no longer be determined solely by parental income, as previously, but by the type and amount of day care parents require. It is hoped that, by introducing a market principle (both in terms of choice and payment) into the system of child care, the institutions, which had previously been characterized by their homogeneity, would become increasingly flexible and imaginative in the way they responded to public demand (Suzuki, 1998: 31).

The Support of Families in the Community

In order to support families in the community, the new law also required the establishment of a new subcommittee of each local Child Welfare Council (Jidō Fukushi Shingikai), consisting of medical, legal, and other experts, to consider the recommendations of the local *jidōsōdanjo* either to place individual children in, or to remove them from, child welfare institutions. It was hoped that, on the one hand, this committee would both bolster the *jidōsōdanjo* and gain an overview of their decisions and, on the other hand, ensure that the interests of the child were fully considered and that the child knew and understood what was being decided.[26] In part this latter element related to the provisions of the UN Convention on the Rights of the Child which Japan had ratified in 1994 and which will be considered in more detail in a later chapter.

At the same time and, according to Tochio (1998: 36–7), owing to the perception that the *jidōsōdanjo* were having trouble in dealing with a growing range of problems affecting children in Japan including an apparently rapid growth in cases of child abuse, the new law institutionalized a system of *toshi jidō katei shien centres* (Urban Child and Family Support Centres).[27] These centres were to supplement and support the work of the *jidōsōdanjo*, the local health centres, the welfare offices (*fukushi jimusho*) and the *minsei.jidōiin* and *shūnin jidōiin* systems, and they were charged with establishing consultation and support systems in urban areas depending on local need and demand. Centres were required to set up a system, both through visiting and via telephone, of: providing consultation around the clock; supporting families (particularly single-parent families) in their homes; and following up cases seen by the *jidōsōdanjo* that were not deemed to require placement in a welfare facility. In the first case, the new centres were expected to take calls not only *about* children but also *from* them: one of the trial centres which was set up in 1994 reported that, of the total of 417 calls it received in the following year, one-third were from children themselves. Perhaps most interesting, however, for the account that follows, was the decision that the new *toshi jidō katei shien centres* should be set up as part of existing child welfare institutions. Of the first twenty-four such centres established, twenty-one were in *yōgoshisetsu*.

The Function of Child Welfare Institutions

While one type of welfare institution, *kyojakuji shisetsu* (homes for physically weak children), was abolished altogether and its buildings reclassified as *yōgoshisetsu*—which brought the number of *yōgoshisetsu* in 1999 to 556—most of the proposed changes in the functions of child welfare institutions that came about as a result of the revision of the Child Welfare Law involved a change in name.[28] *Boshiryō* were renamed *boshi seikatsu shien shisetsu* (institutions to support the lives of single mothers and children) to emphasize the notion that such families should be independent of the state where possible. *Kyōgoin* were henceforth to be called *jidō jiritsu shien shisetsu* (institutions to help children develop their own self-supporting capability) so as to emphasize their nature as supportive rather than correctional institutions. They would in future offer an after-care service and take commuting students (including, for the first time, students who refused to attend school), and students placed in the institutions would be required to attend schools outside and no longer on campus as hitherto.

Yōgoshisetsu were renamed *jidō yōgoshisetsu* (*child* protection institutions, rather than simply protection institutions) and their definition was altered to include the phrase *jiritsu wo shien suru koto* (to support the development of self-reliance). This change was introduced in the light of the significant increase in the number of older children in homes over the previous twenty years and the problems that children from homes were having in the education and employment systems (Takahashi, 1998*b*: 45–7), all issues to which we will return.

The revised law also made a number of other more minor changes to the regulations governing *yōgoshisetsu*, including increasing the minimum amount of space required per child (from 2.4 to 3.3 square metres) and abolishing the use of physical punishment. To some extent, however, it was the issues which were not covered in the new law which are most interesting for understanding the role of *yōgoshisetsu* in contemporary Japan. Unlike the case of placement in *hoikuen*, the local authorities will continue to place children in *yōgoshisetsu* through a *sochi seido*, although the fact that the placements will now be overseen by a new committee may introduce an element of the market into the system. While the minimum space per child might have been changed—fairly easily done since, as we have seen, most homes were already some way under capacity—the maximum number of children per room was left unchanged at fifteen. Perhaps most significantly, though, the new law made no change to the ratio of staff to children, and it did not deal at all with the systems of fostering or adoption. Why these omissions are significant will become clearer in subsequent chapters.

4

The Management and Staffing of *Yōgoshisetsu*

UNIFORMITY AND DIFFERENCE

Much writing on Japanese society has concentrated on the way in which the state, mainly through the Ministry of Education (Monbushō), attempts to standardize the experience of all children from birth onwards so as to support an ideology of adult status in society being the result of hard work during the pre-adult period (a meritocracy) rather than of birth or class background.[1] Uniformity is particularly emphasized in those institutions (hospitals, nurseries, schools) which are directly under the control of central government ministries. These latter have long had a tradition, known as the *shukkō* (transfer) system, of posting officials to work in prefectural government offices to ensure that their directives are followed. Hence it is that almost all children in compulsory education (between the ages of 6 and 15) receive virtually the same diet, read almost exactly the same books, wear very similar clothing, follow an annual cycle of events which hardly varies at all, and work in schools that resemble each other in almost every detail.[2]

At one level, it would appear that Kōseishō is as assiduous in determining and standardizing the experience of children within its ambit as is Monbushō. As we have seen, in the case of *yōgoshisetsu*, for example, it stipulates the minimum staffing levels in such institutions, which have been periodically reviewed and improved (see Table 10). It lays down the minimum amount of bedroom space which must be allocated to each child in an institution (increased from 2.47 to 3.3 square metres in 1998) and the maximum number of children who can be allowed to share one room (fifteen). It determines the maximum number of children a home can accept based on its physical resources—the home's quota (*teiin*)—on the basis of which it has determined how much money the institution will receive.[3] Kōseishō determines the minimum age on admission and the point at which the state will stop providing money for a child in a home.[4]

Despite this regulation, however, and quite unlike the case with the compulsory schooling system, *yōgoshisetsu* in Japan differ from each other quite considerably. This makes it harder to write about *yōgoshisetsu* in general, but also more interesting given the emphasis on uniformity in Japanese society. Unlike schools, for example, *yōgoshisetsu* are not immediately obvious from their appearance. They vary considerably in size, as shown in Table 11. This difference can be seen both within and between prefectures and cities; only in Nagano are all homes of the same size. Over 10 per cent of homes still have capacity for more than 100 children. Figures from 1991 (Table 12) show that Hiroshima had the largest homes

TABLE 10. Changes in the legal minimum staff : child ratio for children in *yōgoshisetsu* (1948–present)

Age	Under 3	3–5	Over 5
1948	10 : 1	10 : 1	10 : 1
1963	5 : 1	10 : 1	10 : 1
1964	5 : 1	9 : 1	9 : 1
1966	5 : 1	8 : 1	8 : 1
1968	5 : 1	7 : 1	8 : 1
1969	5 : 1	6 : 1	8 : 1
1970	3 : 1	6 : 1	8 : 1
1971	3 : 1	5.5 : 1	7.5 : 1
1972	3 : 1	5 : 1	7 : 1
1976	2 : 1	4 : 1	6 : 1

Source: Ōshima, 1990: 106–7.

TABLE 11. Profile of *yōgoshisetsu* by maximum capacity (1998) N = 521

Capacity	No. of *yōgoshisetsu*
<20	1*
<20–9	8
<30–9	65
<40–9	82
<50–9	116
<60–9	77
<70–9	48
<80–9	51
<90–9	16
<100–9	25
<110–19	8
<120–9	9
<130–9	3
<140–9	0
<150–9	3
<160–9	2
<170–9	3
<180–9	1
<190–9	1
<200–9	1
<250–9	1

Source: Derived from YSI, Mar. 1998.
* This is a Tokyo prefectural home which is based in Shizuoka Prefecture.

with, on average, 123 places each, followed by Osaka with 122, although in both places occupancy rates at the time were only 70 per cent. Niigata's homes were on average the smallest, with space for only forty children, though Fukui, with thirty children, actually had the smallest average number of children in residence. Over the whole country, the average *yōgoshisetsu* in the late 1990s had room for around sixty children.

TABLE 12. Prefectures and cities with the largest and smallest average capacities and largest and smallest average number of residents per *yōgoshisetsu*

	Capacity	No. of residents
Largest		
Hiroshima City	123	86
Osaka City	122	86
Fukuoka City	100	81
Smallest		
Niigata	40	32
Saga	43	41
Fukui	45	30
Average	64	53

Source: Derived from *KK*, no. 45, 1991: 218–19.

There are some historical explanations for differences in size. Tsuzaki (1999: 86, 92) suggests that the biggest homes tend to be those which were set up by religious, mainly Christian, organizations and that the heads of such homes have used their large size as an effective means of fundraising (*kifu yūdō*), espe-cially from religious communities and churches outside Japan. Over the past two decades the average size of homes—especially in Tokyo, where 130 is seen, unofficially, as the maximum size for any home—has decreased significantly, in part, as we shall see, through policy, in part through the decrease in the birth rate.

There are also significant differences in the proportion of children in the pop-ulation in different areas who are taken into care. As Table 13 shows, children in Kagoshima and Kōchi appear to be up to six times more likely to be placed in a *yōgoshisetsu* than those in Niigata or Yokohama City. Even assuming that there is some variation in the proportion of children within the population in the four areas, the difference is quite dramatic. Somewhat surprisingly, these differences do not seem to reflect a rural–urban divide although it might be expected that there would be more children in care in city areas where there are greater social problems and fewer extended families to offer support.

To some extent differences may reflect the particular social and economic problems which have affected different regions of Japan at particular periods. As we have seen, in the 1960s there developed a phenomenon (known as *dekasegi*) where many men moved away from rural areas to seek out manual labour in the cities. While this was often on a seasonal rather than a permanent basis, it meant that they often had problems supporting their families back home and many children, as a result, needed to be taken into care. As with all emigration move-ment, the *dekasegi* phenomenon was in part due to pull factors, in part due to push factors, which meant that some areas were affected more than others: exam-ples included the decline and closing of the mining industry in Kyūshū (see Allen, 1994) and in Hokkaidō; the Yokkaichi pollution scandal which led to high rates

TABLE 13. Prefectures and cities with the highest and lowest proportions of children in care per 100,000 residents (1991)

Highest	
Kagoshima	44.40
Kōchi	42.04
Kita-Kyūshū City	39.13
Tokushima	38.07
Miyazaki	36.93
Kōbe City	36.71
Ōita	36.22
Nagasaki	36.01
Kumamoto	35.98
Lowest	
Niigata	6.52
Yokohama City	7.49
Chiba	11.78
Shiga	12.04
Kawasaki	12.58
Toyama	12.98
Yamagata	13.93
Saitama	14.32
Shizuoka	14.82

Source: *KH*, 1993: 218–19.

of unemployment in Mie Prefecture; the massive downsizing in the fishing industry which affected fishing communities all along the Japanese coast.

Some of Japan's minorities may also account for a certain proportion of the regional disparities in the number of children in homes. In the mid-1980s, average salaries in Okinawa which, until 1972, remained an American protectorate and the main site for American troops in Japan, remained around 71 per cent of those in mainland Japan, and unemployment, at 5 per cent, was double the then national average (Katayama, *JT*, 21 July 1985). *Ainu* in Hokkaidō and the *zainichi-Kankokujin* (Japanese-Koreans) and *burakumin* (Japan's former outcaste community), who live mainly in the Kansai area, Hiroshima, and northern Kyūshū, all still face economic problems, although it is difficult to measure if these are related to the number of children in *yōgoshisetsu*. The official line on all minority issues in post-war Japan has been to avoid affirmative action which might delay the disappearance of consciousness of difference which is seen as the prerequisite for discrimination. At the same time, minority rights groups, such as the Buraku Kaihō Undō, have vigorously attacked any organization that has attempted to monitor the minority status of individuals. Hence, apart from the Elizabeth Saunders Home, mentioned briefly in the previous chapter, there have been no *yōgoshisetsu* set up to cater specifically to any minority group, and there are no statistics on the number of children in care from minority groups.

In 1995, when the new religious group Aum Shinrikyō was accused of gassing the Tokyo Underground, some fifty children from Aum's main base near Mount Fuji in Shizuoka Prefecture were also taken into care, in Shizuoka and nearby prefectures. In 1995 also many children who lost family members as a result of the Hanshin earthquake were temporarily placed in *yōgoshisetsu*, a process which briefly gave the homes a national exposure they have rarely experienced.

While there are minimum requirements placed on prefectures and cities by central government in regard to welfare provision, they do, of course, have flexibility in the way they spend local taxes that will allow them to go beyond these minimum levels. Some areas of Japan have been able to subsidize their welfare systems more easily than others. These include areas with many large companies which pay high rates of corporation tax, and areas with gambling facilities such as horse-, bicycle-, or motor-boat racing (*keiba, keirin,* and *kyōtei*), from which taxes are by law channelled to local welfare projects (Nagashima, 1998a).[5]

Perhaps the most conspicuous difference between *yōgoshisetsu* and compulsory educational institutions lies in their architecture. While there are some similarities among those homes founded during the two main periods of building—the early Meiji period and the immediate post-war period—in general homes differ from each other considerably. In part architectural differences reflect size. In many cases they reflect religious foundation; most Christian homes have a chapel funded by overseas donations which children are required to attend regularly. In part they reflect their facilities; as Table 14 shows, some homes have excellent facilities—swimming pools, gymnasiums, libraries—while others have virtually none.[6] Homes of course change over the years. Often there are many years between major building projects and, in terms of facilities, some homes can go from the bottom of the hierarchy to the top with remarkable speed once a large donation has been received.

Within homes too, differences are manifest. In some, all the older children, certainly those of senior high-school age (15 or over), have their own rooms, and younger children reside in small rooms of no more than four children each; in other homes, children live in dormitories of up to fifteen each with virtually no privacy. In some homes, children have their own washrooms and showers attached to their rooms; in others, the only washing facilities are the common bath (*furo*) which boys and girls, younger and older children, must use in shifts. According to the association of *yōgoshisetsu*, a home which consists of several small buildings on a single site, each housing fewer than twenty children, is

TABLE 14. Proportion of *yōgoshisetsu* with facilities they can share with the local community (1993) N = 533

Type of facility	Hall	Library	Nursery	Gym	Sports ground	Pool
Have it	346	363	347	133	414	109
Share it	167	121	76	106	301	39
% who have who share	48	33	22	80	73	36

Source: Sakamoto, 1993a: 43.

known as *shōshasei*; those where all children are housed in a single, large building on several floors are known as *taishasei* (see Jidō Yōgo Kenkyūkai, 1995: 70–1, for examples). In 1998 only about 15 per cent of all homes were *shōshasei* (*YSI*, 1998).[7] The vast majority of children live in large, communal buildings. In part, as we shall see later, this reflects ideology, in part it reflects funding.

Homes also differ in their gender and age ratios. There are at least two homes for boys only and a number (run by Christian orders) which take only girls. Most homes are mixed (as are the vast majority of Japanese schools). Over the whole sector, however, there are proportionally more boys (55 per cent) than girls (45 per cent), and in many homes boys outnumber girls by almost 2 : 1.[8]

The age balance within different homes also varies considerably. As Table 15 shows, the average age of children in homes has been steadily rising over the past fifteen years. This trend has been particularly noticeable among the oldest age group (i.e. those over 15). While the average length of time that children spend in *yōgoshisetsu* has been increasing—from 3.8 years in 1977 to 4.5 years in 1987, when about one in eight children had been in care for over nine years (*YnJ*, 1990: 14, 53, 105)[9]—there is enormous variation between homes. Some homes work hard to get their children placed back with their families or in foster placements, whereas others invest much less effort in such exercises and concentrate on the care they can offer in the home. This is an issue to which we will return later.

Despite the efforts of Kōseishō, then, to maintain some level of homogeneity between different homes, there exist differences in many areas. The result is that children placed in different *yōgoshisetsu* may have a much wider variety of experiences than children within the compulsory education system. Occasionally when, for some reason, siblings are placed in different homes—an increasingly uncommon practice—then the differences between homes become particularly manifest. One former resident of a home in Tokyo described in detail the amazement she felt on first visiting her sister in another home and discovering the vastly superior conditions and better treatment there than in her own home. To her, the

TABLE 15. Changes in the age structure of children in *yōgoshisetsu* (1970–98) (%)

Year (age of children)	1970	1980	1990	1998
0–2	3.9	2.4	2.2	3.3
3–5	16.8	15.2	13.2	15.3
6–8	19.5	21.5	16.7	17.3
9–11	22.9	24.9	20.4	19.7
12–14	26.6	25.5	26.6	23.0
15–17	9.8	9.7	18.6	18.4
Over 18	0.5	0.9	2.3	3.0

Source: *KK*, no. 53, 1999: 202.

assignments seemed totally arbitrary. A senior high-school boy at a meeting for older residents from *yōgoshisetsu* held in Gifu in 1992 made the point that children who are placed in homes do not have the opportunity to visit them even once before they are moved in (Gifuken Jidōfukushi Kyōgikai, 1992: 40).

At the local level, the differences between institutions are tacitly acknowledged. The official line (*tatemae*) of the officials at the prefectural *jidōsōdanjo*, however, has generally been that these differences do not mean that any home is better or worse than any other, only that they are different, and that all homes have their own distinctive characters (*tokuchō*) which mark them out from others. These *tokuchō* were widely recognized—K home was very good at sports, especially marathon running; S home was good at finding fostering and adoptive placements; F home was supportive of older children who came into care; H home imposed few rules and allowed children to express themselves—and it was simply a question of finding the right home within the city or prefecture for that particular child at that particular moment.

While it was officially claimed that all homes had their good points, it was unofficially recognized by all in the welfare world that the quality of care that was offered varied enormously among institutions. In the early 1990s, Kōseishō even graded homes on a supposedly secret scale of eight points (A–H) and provided extra money (up to 3 per cent of a home's total annual income) to those that met its criteria for being 'better', such as having closer relations with the local community. This hierarchy, in most people's estimation, suggested that the top 15 per cent of *yōgoshisetsu* were private (informants always included Kodomo Gakuen in this category, not simply, I believe, because they knew that that was where I was doing my research); that the next 10 per cent of homes were the public homes; and that the remaining private homes accounted for the other 75 per cent of the 530 *yōgoshisetsu* in Japan.[10] In many ways, it is the difference between the public and the private homes which is the most significant and, in order to understand this, we need to explore in some detail how the private homes operate, perceive themselves, and are perceived within the welfare world.

THE OPERATION OF PRIVATE (*MINKAN*) *YŌGOSHISETSU*

The relationship between private homes and central and local government officials is a complex one. On the one hand, as we have seen, the government officials provide funds to private institutions as if they were public ones and in return closely monitor them and expect them to follow the advice that they give. The homes are given regular audits (*kansa*) by government officials, who are treated with considerable signs of respect, as are public officials from the local social welfare offices and *jidōsōdanjo* who are always deferred to as *sensei* (literally, one who goes before). In part this reflects the normal relationship between the public and private sectors in Japan. Ever since the Meiji period, the public sector—which was charged with guiding Japan's modernization and industrialization—has been accorded the higher social status (Amenomori, 1997: 207).

On the other hand, the private homes know that they have far more practical knowledge than government officials about what actually happens to children in care. They sometimes feel that they should be thanked for the service they provide rather than being closely regulated and expected to feel grateful for being allowed to take in children. Indeed, they point out, technically they are not allowed to refuse to take in any children who are sent to them via the public *jidōsōdanjo* unless they are full to capacity. In general, private homes tend to be fiercely protective of their own identities and try to maintain as much independence as possible from local and central government officials. One of the most common ways in which they achieve this is through being part of a set of inter-linked welfare institutions, generally called a *shakai fukushi hōjin*, which gives the head of each of them, often members of the same family, considerably more political clout to resist the local government bureaucrats than if they were to act alone. Kodomo Gakuen is part of one of the strongest such welfare organizations in west Tokyo, and hence makes an interesting case study.

As we have seen, *shakai fukushi hōjin* were a new device set up under a 1951 law that enabled private homes to receive public funds. There is little doubt that those welfare facilities that already catered for the young were those that found it easiest to be accredited as *shakai fukushi hōjin*, and that once homes had received this accreditation they were able to open other welfare facilities. This certainly would appear to have been the case with the Seishin Gakusha Shakai Fukushi Hōjin (or Seishin Gakusha, for short).

Under the umbrella of the new Seishin Gakusha, two nurseries (*hoikuen*)[11] opened in 1949; an old people's home (*yōgorōjin home*)[12] in 1951, a few months before Kodomo Gakuen changed its status officially to a *yōgoshisetsu*; another old people's home (*yōgorōjin home*) in 1955; a third nursery in 1959; a third old people's home (*keihi rōjin home*) in 1963; an old people's clinic (*shinryōjo*) in 1963; a second clinic in 1972; a fourth old people's home (*tokubetsu yōgo rōjin home*) in 1975; an old people's welfare centre (*rōjin fukushi centre*) that opened on the same day; a fifth old people's home (*tokubetsu yōgo rōjin home*) in 1977 and a second old people's welfare centre in the same year; and a fourth nursery in 1979. None of these were small institutions: the nurseries on average had space for 120 children and the old people's homes for ninety elderly people.

The *rijikai* (Board of Directors) of the Seishin Gakusha was an impressively high-status group of individuals in the context of Japanese child welfare. In the immediate post-war years there had been occasions where the members of *rijikai* confused their personal role and interests with those of the organizations they were running, leading to some financial scandals. Hence, in the 1951 Social Welfare Service Law, it was decided to limit the number of members in any *rijikai* who could come from the families that ran the homes. At the Seishin Gakusha in 1991, three members of the *rijikai* worked in its institutions and five were individuals from the local community—the heads of the four most local *jidōsōdanjo* and the former head of the Nihon Shakai Jigyō Daigaku, Japan's most prestigious social welfare college which is based in Tokyo. The others were a representative from the Tokyo City Welfare Office, two management secretaries (*kanji*), and a retired accountant. All of them acted in a voluntary capacity; only the accountant would occasionally be paid if he had to do some work over and above his normal duties.

By 1982 the institutions under the Seishin Gakusha had been organized into four separate branches (see Figure I): the Seishin Gakuen branch, which concentrated on child protection; the Seishin Home branch, which concentrated on residential care for the elderly; the Seishin Hoiku branch, which focused on child-care provision; and the Seishin Yōgo branch, which provided an amalgam of day-care services for the elderly.

The activities of the branches were not in fact quite as clear-cut as Figure I suggests: the Seishin Gakuen branch had a nursery (attended by children from the local community as well as from the home); the Seishin Yōgo branch also had a day-care nursery for children alongside its activities for the elderly. A much clearer way to visualize the background of the different branches is to map them on to the family tree of the five daughters of the founder of the original Seishin Gakusha. One daughter married a university professor and did not stay part of the Seishin Gakusha (although her children subsequently became involved in social welfare activities elsewhere), but the other four daughters and their families each set up their own strands of social work activity under the umbrella of the Seishin Gakusha which led to the structure outlined in Figure I. Of the fourteen heads of the institutions run by the Seishin Gakusha in 1982, only two (those most recently opened) were not run by direct or adopted descendants of its original founder. In 1991 the head of the Seishin Gakusha estimated that around 90 per cent of the descendants of the original founder and their families either had worked, were working, or would be working in social welfare institutions, most of them as part of the organization. While the proportion of the heads of institutions within the Seishin Gakusha coming from the same extended family (*dōzoku*) declined in the 1990s as the organization grew faster than the family,[13] it still represents a classic example of one of the most conspicuous styles of welfare organization in Japan, known as a *dōzoku keiei* (same-family management operation). In 1999 many of the next generation of the family were taking courses and training to work in the increasingly diverse social welfare fields in which the Seishin Gakusha operated.

Dōzoku keiei are well-known organizations in many areas of Japanese society. Hamabata (1990) provides an excellent ethnography of the complex ties and relations among the members of a family-owned manufacturing business in Tokyo. James and Benjamin (1988) discuss the role of the organizations (*gakkō hōjin*) which offer a complete educational service from kindergarten to university and how the members of the founder's family often still occupy the main positions

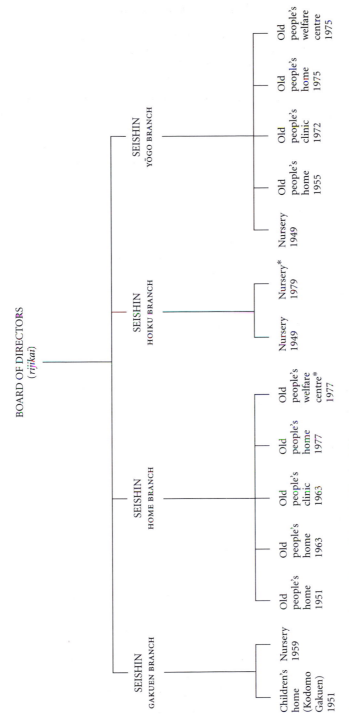

FIG. 1 The Seishin Gakusha Shakai Fukushi Hōjin in 1982

* = Head of institution not part of founder's family.

within these. Virtually nothing, however, has been written, in English or Japanese, about the role of *dōzoku keiei* in the welfare world, although their influence in some areas is very great indeed. In the case of *yōgoshisetsu*, of the 90 per cent of homes which are private (most of which are incorporated as *shakai fukushi hōjin*), some estimates put the number which are *dōzoku keiei* as between 50 and 70 per cent. There are no official figures against which these estimates can be verified and, as we shall see, although several recent heads of the association of *yōgoshisetsu* come from such institutions, the *dōzoku keiei* system of operating homes remains a rather sensitive subject in the world of Japanese child welfare.

At a formal level, the relationship between all the institutions of the Seishin Gakusha does not appear particularly significant. Since financial support is provided by central and local government under specific budget headings with very little room for flexibility, there is little scope for moving money between the institutions. The *rijikai* has some money at its own disposal since, while most contributions that are received from living people tend to go to specific institutions and often for specific projects, it is not unknown for individuals to leave money and property in their wills to a *shakai fukushi hōjin* as a whole. In general, however, this is not a significant amount.

The Seishin Gakusha, however, was able to take advantage of certain economies of scale. The one minibus was used jointly by many of the institutions within the organization, and indeed the head of Kodomo Gakuen once commented that it was government policy to have large organizations (*soshiki*) since they gave a better yield for the money (*jisshū zaigen*) invested in them.[14] There was also considerable interaction between institutions. On the national holiday for old people (Keirō no Hi), the children in Kodomo Gakuen visited the old people's home next door, put on a show for each of the six floors in the home, and presented the old people with something that they had made, such as a name-plate for the room. According to Kaplan *et al.* (1998), this type of inter-generational activity in welfare facilities in Japan (known as *sedaikan kōryū*) is seen by some policy-makers as a potentially important strategy for maintaining cultural continuity in the face of the dramatic demographic changes discussed in Chapter 2 (see also Thang, 1999).

At a more personal level, the relationship between institutions is obviously close in the sense that the heads of most of them come from the same family; they have grown up together and they continue to live and work in close proximity. Husbands and wives often run the same institutions, together with sons and daughters. In 1991 at Kodomo Gakuen, the head's mother and widow of its founder, though very frail, was still technically the home's deputy head (*fuku enchō*) although she was more often referred to as Gakuen no Okāsan (Mother of the Home). His youngest brother, who took over as head in 1992, was the home's senior care worker (*shūnin shidōin*), and his sister ran the Montessori nursery (*hoikuen*) which was in its grounds. His cousin ran the old people's home next door, and his other brother was head of another nursery (*hoikuen*) in the next city.

As far as the staffing of the welfare institutions goes, the *dōzoku keiei* system, based on real kinship relations, has some advantages which mirror those that Japanese companies in general are said to try to recreate through the construction of fictive kinship. Since those who work in welfare institutions have often grown up in those same institutions (as the children of staff), they are imbued with a sense of their values and history. Many wives of heads of homes, for example, seem to work for no, or virtually no, pay alongside their husbands. Certainly, the extra commitment of family members is an explanation one sometimes hears as to why Japanese private institutions are cheaper, more efficient, and more imaginative than public ones.

More generally, the *shakai fukushi hōjin* system is also efficient from the point of view of the state in deciding to whom to grant new licences to open welfare institutions. It is clearly much easier for them to deal with an organization that has a long-standing and respected reputation for setting up and organizing welfare institutions than it is to start from scratch with a completely new organization, the background of which they will need to investigate. As the pressure for new residential welfare institutions builds up with the rapid ageing of Japan's population, so the work of the local and central government welfare organizations is clearly helped by the existence of *shakai fukushi hōjin* of long standing. Since the oldest welfare institutions in Japan are children's homes, albeit in their previous guise as *kojiin* (orphanages), and the biggest call on welfare services in the immediate post-war period, when the new welfare system was set up, was for children, most *shakai fukushi hōjin* were originally founded around the existence of a *yōgoshisetsu* even if today their services tend to be directed much more towards *rōjin homes* (old people's homes) and *hoikuen* (nursery provision for working parents). It is partly for this historical reason that *yōgoshisetsu* have a status in the current welfare system which is out of proportion to the actual number of children for whom they cater. *Shakai fukushi hōjin* that include a *yōgoshisetsu* have generally been in the welfare business for a long time and have built a reputation that the authorities can be sure they will not want to lose by mismanaging any new institution. When the *shakai fukushi hōjin* is run as a *dōzoku keiei*, then the sanction of losing reputation may be even stronger, since, if a lost reputation leads to the closure of an institution or an organization, then the effects on the family's employment in that and subsequent generations will be very severe indeed.

But one seldom reads the above kinds of argument in favour of the *dōzoku keiei* system of social welfare. Indeed, it is an extremely sensitive topic. Some of the reasons for this sensitivity will become clear as we turn to look at the overall system of staffing in *yōgoshisetsu*.

STAFFING

The staff of *yōgoshisetsu* are normally broken down into four separate categories: female residential staff (*hobo*); male residential staff (*jidōshidōin*); office staff (*jimushokuin*), and kitchen staff (*chōriin*). Homes also are required to employ a nutritionist (*eiyōshi*) if they care for forty-one or more children (see Ōshima, 1990: 104).

The fact that homes are required to employ office workers, cooks, and nutritionists is indicative of the size of most institutions that still exist in Japan. Kodomo Gakuen, for example, which could accommodate up to seventy children, employed four secretarial staff to complete the enormous amount of paperwork necessary to meet the auditing requirements of Kōseishō. It had three cooks and one nutritionist as well as two maintenance men who also often doubled up as van drivers. As is typical in Japanese workplaces, there was considerable flexibility of roles and in covering for each other, and all staff, simply by their presence, were involved in child care to some extent. When the home arranged events for the staff, all the full-time ancillary staff were included as much as the full-time residential care workers, and these latter also were often to be found helping in cooking and maintenance work. There were, however, important differences in defined roles, titles, qualifications, and pay scales between the different groups.

Staffing Levels and Hours at Work

As we have seen (Table 10) the minimum child care child : staff ratio is regulated by Kōseishō and has slowly improved over the years. Since 1976 it has stood at 2 : 1 for those under 3; 4 : 1 for those over 3 but still pre-school; and 6 : 1 for those of school age. It is important to understand, however, what these staffing levels mean in actual practice. If, for example, staff in 1991 stuck to the forty-eight hours they were meant to work a week (and as we shall see many worked much longer hours) and if they were equally available during the 168 hours of the week then, at any one time, the child : staff ratio would be 3.5 times these minimum figures: i.e. twenty-one children over the age of 6 to each staff member. In reality, staffing levels are much lower at night when a minimal number of staff are on duty and during the middle of the day in term-time, when most children are away at school and many of the pre-school children attend nurseries either outside or, quite often, inside the homes but staffed separately. In most homes, therefore, the overall ratio was probably closer to ten to thirteen children to each member of care staff at any one time, although, as noted above, other adults would also often be around. As over the past fifteen years children in homes have on average got older—thereby worsening the age-related staff : child ratio—and also demonstrated more severe behavioural problems, there has been a feeling that these minimum staffing levels are inadequate. As a result, in the 1980s some local governments, such as Tokyo and Yokohama, established their own minimum of 5 : 1

Sunday	12.30 – 20.30
Monday	12.30 – 20.30; night duty 20.30 – 06.30
Tuesday	06.30 – 09.30 and 16.30 – 20.30
Wednesday	09.30 – 12.30; 15.10 – 20.30; night duty 20.30 – 06.30
Thursday	06.30 – 14.30
Friday	Day off
Saturday	12.30 – 12.30

Total hours: 63hrs. 20mins. Note that these were minimum hours; they did not allow, for example, for the important handover meetings which took place each morning between night and day staff.

Fig. II One variant of a week's schedule of a *jidōshidōin* at Kodomo Gakuen in 1991/2

for children over 6 rather than the national standard of 6 : 1 (Ōshima, 1990: 105, 108). At Kodomo Gakuen in 1999, there were twenty-two child-care workers for seventy children (a ratio of 1 : 3.2), which was considerably better than the national average of 1 : 3.6 (7,332 child-care staff for 26,759 children).

Even in Kodomo Gakuen, though, the staff worked long and irregular hours, as the timetable for one male *jidōshidōin* in Figure II shows. Technically, by excluding the night duties (*shukuchoku*), this timetable was considered to total 47 hrs. 20 min., and individual workers' timetables varied weekly, so that on average they should not have worked more than forty-two hours per week over the whole year. The length, or the sense of the length, of the week was therefore closely related to the experience of the *shukuchoku*, which most male staff did twice a week. In theory, the *shukuchoku* was voluntary overtime on top of normal work, but it was difficult for male staff to refuse to do it. It was rarely restful. As one care worker in a home with thirty residents of senior high-school age pointed out, there was rarely any time of the night when all of them could be assumed to be asleep, and hence the night duty rarely involved any sleep for the staff.

In reality, staff sometimes found themselves working many more hours than scheduled in their timetable. Those who lived on site especially were often called upon to help out during their so-called off hours. At the same time, of course, unlike with school teachers, there were no periods during the year when the home was completely empty.[15] According to Kuraoka (1992: 196), staff in a survey of seven private homes worked on average 3,400 hours a year.[16]

SALARIES, PAY, AND CONDITIONS

Long hours do not translate into high basic salaries for residential child-care workers. Pay scales vary by age and experience and probably are slightly lower

than the average for those with similar academic qualifications, unlike for example those for teachers, which are probably slightly higher.[17] However, while
there are few overtime payments, there is an extra payment for each *shukuchoku*
(night duty) which can add up to an extra 10 per cent to the pay slip each month.
Further, like all those who work for large companies or local government in
Japan, staff receive twice-yearly bonuses which add up to 5.3 months' worth of
salary (or over 30 per cent of their total annual salary).

There are also certain non-salary financial advantages to be gained from working in *yōgoshisetsu*. For those working in big cities like Tokyo, living on site in
highly subsidized accommodation, as was the case for about half of the staff at
Kodomo Gakuen, is a major boon. In the early 1990s when rents reached their
height in post-war Tokyo, rooms for single staff at Kodomo Gakuen cost as little
as one-fifth their price on the open market, and the best family apartments in the
newest block were around one-third of their market value. Equally importantly,
those who rented this accommodation did not have to pay the non-refundable
reikin (key money) of either two or three months' salary demanded by most land-
lords every time the renting contract was renewed (every two to five years); nor a
two-month deposit; nor a month's commission to an estate agent; nor even to pay
their first month's rent in advance of moving in. Further, when staff ate with the
children while on duty, they did so at a highly subsidized charge which was taken
from their pay packet. Overall, therefore, residential care staff probably receive an
income package that is roughly equivalent to those with similar qualifications in
other professions, though for much longer hours at work.

QUALIFICATIONS

One of the questions I asked those at Kodomo Gakuen in a small survey I carried
out was how they would compare the social status (*shakaiteki chii*) of staff in
yōgoshisetsu compared to staff in nurseries, kindergartens, and elementary or
high schools. All but one of those who responded felt, sometimes on reflection,
that it was lower, even if in many cases they had the same qualifications and even
when people recognized what an important and difficult job they were doing.
Some felt that there was an important gender difference here: while the status of
female workers was the same as for women who worked in other caring professions, for male workers it was probably lower than equivalent positions in the
teaching profession. In the main, the (self-perceived) relatively low status of those
working in homes was put down to people in society not knowing about
yōgoshisetsu, the type of people who worked in them, and the type of work they
did.

Some other informants, however, suggested that a further reason for the comparatively low status of child-care staff lay in there being no special qualifications
which allowed residential care workers to see themselves, and be seen by others,

as members of a profession in the same way as teachers. Indeed as one respondent to the question said, people see those who work in *yōgoshisetsu* as closer to admirable volunteers than specialists, an attitude which is perhaps not surprising when, as we have seen, so much of social work delivery in Japan is via the voluntary *minsei.jidōiin* system.

It would be a mistake, however, to give the impression that the majority of residential staff in *yōgoshisetsu* do not have qualifications. Indeed, in a survey carried out in 1998 of almost all the care staff working in *yōgoshisetsu*, 30.1 per cent had four years of tertiary education and a further 53.3 per cent two years (*YnJ*, 2000). It is, rather, that the qualifications they have are not specifically for working in *yōgoshisetsu*. The largest category of staff in *yōgoshisetsu*, the *hobo*, are qualified female nursery nurses who have graduated from tertiary education institutions called *hoboyōseikō* (nursery nurse college). Since 1977, men have also been accepted in these colleges, and graduate as *hofu*, but their numbers have always been very small indeed. Such courses are normally two years in length and involve a combination of practical placements and theoretical training. Ōshima (1990: 102) points out, however, that the training received in *hoboyōseikō*, concentrated as it is on care for children under the age of 6, is increasingly irrelevant as the average age of children in homes increases, with the majority being over the age of 10.

Jidōshidōin rarely have any specialist training in child care at all. The majority have what is known as a *sankamoku shikaku* (three-subject qualification) which means they have earned sufficient credits in three social science subjects considered relevant to child-care work, generally courses such as sociology, psychology, or education at a four-year university. In many ways, the *sankamoku shikaku* is a hangover from the early 1960s when relatively few people continued into tertiary education and even fewer studied social science. It is seen by some as an anachronism now that not only do almost 40 per cent of the peer group attend some form of higher education institution but also social science courses are the most popular—and the easiest to enter—of the courses on offer, especially at academically lower-level institutions.[18] Similarly, many commentators also see it as an anachronism that it is still possible, though increasingly rare, to become qualified as a child-care worker simply by virtue of working in a child welfare institution for two years (what is known as *keiken ni yoru shidōin shikaku*).

It is interesting to note how few of those who do take social welfare courses at university go on to work in social welfare institutions, despite the fact that almost all of them would have undertaken placements in such institutions as part of their degree work. A rapidly increasing number—thirty at the beginning of the 1990s; almost 100 by the end—of universities in Japan offer courses in social work. While these include some good institutions, such as Meiji Gakuin in Tokyo and Dōshisha in Kyoto, it is perhaps symptomatic of the status of such courses that none of Japan's top universities—Tokyo, Kyoto, Keiō, Waseda—offer social work degrees.[19] In the early 1990s Meiji Gakuin undertook a detailed survey of its entrants and graduates. Of an annual intake of around 100 students, about a third each year went on to work in the social welfare field after graduation (roughly the same proportion as those who said they had entered the course because of an interest in a welfare-related profession); a third said they had joined the course because they had failed to get on to the more competitive clinical psychology or education courses; and the final third of students admitted joining the course simply because it was the easiest way for them to get into what is widely regarded as a 'good name' university (Meiji Gakuin, private communication, 1991).[20] The overall result is that the majority of those with qualifications in social welfare do not go on to work in the social welfare field, and the majority of those who work in social welfare institutions have not studied social welfare, although, as we shall see, they may receive considerable in-service training.

RECRUITMENT

One of the biggest differences between public and private *yōgoshisetsu* can be seen in the way in which they recruit their staff. The staff—certainly all the senior staff— of the public homes are recruited in the same way as all people who work in local government in Japan through a mixture of examinations and interviews. Only then are they given relevant (normally two weeks' in-service) training (Tsuzaki, 1997: 89). As a result, according to Matsubara (1992: 5), many of those who end up as child-care workers in public *yōgoshisetsu* do not do so out of choice. They may well have preferred and hoped to work instead in day-care centres such as *hoikuen* where hours are much shorter and the children present fewer problems.

For those who wish to work in private (*minkan*) homes, there is a national organization to which they can submit a curriculum vitae (*rirekisho*) and which acts as a database to which all heads of homes can refer when looking for employees. This doubtless is a system that homes with less good reputations have to rely on for employing staff. A home with an excellent reputation like Kodomo Gakuen, however, can rely and draw on a much more informal network for finding new staff, and indeed will receive more job applications each year than it has staff openings.

Some new staff who come to work in *yōgoshisetsu* have previously worked in jobs completely outside the welfare field. Some of these include members of *dōzoku keiei* families who have transferred from other professions to join the family business. Examples I came across included a qualified vet, a man who had worked in the construction industry, and a man who had spent ten years working as an engineer. Most new members of staff, however, come directly from college, and their relationship to the children when they start is sometimes more like an older brother or sister than a parental figure. This may appear to be reflected in the way they are referred to. Most care staff are called *oniisan* (older brother) and *onēsan* (older sister) regardless of their age and, as one senior social worker commented, it was a little embarrassing to be called *oniisan* when he already had four children of his own. The use of expressions such as *oniisan* and *onēsan*, however, is largely ritualistic. In a survey (Hayashi, 1998: 23) of 448 children in homes aged 10 or more, only 6.7 per cent said that they saw the female staff in homes as big sisters, whereas 9.6 per cent saw them as aunts, 37.9 per cent as mothers, and 37.7 per cent as people doing a job (8.1 per cent either gave some other answer or none at all).[21] Nevertheless, as we shall see in the next chapter, the use of such expressions may be useful in creating bonds of fictive kinship and a 'familial' atmosphere in the homes.

Probably the most common pool of new workers are those who come as *jisshū*, or trainee workers, as part of their social welfare degrees. Most homes have a relationship with a number of nearby universities and nurse-training colleges and will take their students on placement, normally for two periods of between seven and eleven days. For the *jisshū* student this is an intense experience when they have an intermediate status somewhere between the children and the staff of the home. Almost like old-fashioned apprentices, *jisshū* are given the most menial of tasks—such as preparing and clearing the dining hall for meals—and are expected to complete them both efficiently and cheerfully. According to Hagan (1994), who was herself treated as a *jisshū* worker, they are expected to use extremely polite language to the staff of the home; not to chatter among themselves; write detailed evaluations of what they have done each day; and accept advice, however critical, in an obedient manner. Indeed, there are many similarities between the *jisshū* experience in welfare institutions and in Japanese schools and, while both are short in duration, they are exhausting for the individuals concerned, who are continually on edge in case they step out of line. In both cases, the worker or teacher assigned to oversee their practice training is rarely slow to criticize them.

From the point of view of the homes, the *jisshū*, of course, provide a free (in most homes *jisshū* have to pay for their board and lodging) extra pair of hands which must be welcomed even if their presence necessitates a certain amount of time to be spent on induction and training. More importantly, though, the *jisshū* get an opportunity to see if they like the idea of working in *yōgoshisetsu* in general, and in that *yōgoshisetsu* in particular, and the homes get the chance to try out a particular *jisshū* whom they may consider employing in future. Just one measure of how attractive a home Kodomo Gakuen is can be seen in the large proportion of *jisshū* each year who apply to work there, many more than can possibly be accepted.

A further advantage for homes in employing former *jisshū* is that the latter feel a certain obligation to perform well to their former university or college professor, who will continue to visit the home when arranging future *jisshū* placements. This is an important element of Japanese employment practice and can be seen also in the number of workers in homes who have arrived through personal contacts and recommendations: one worker at Kodomo Gakuen, for example, had been involved in the Boy Scout activities at the home and then invited by the head to join the staff as a *jidōshidōin*; another had worked as a volunteer at the home while at university.

While it also involves the use of personal contacts, the employment of former residents as workers is more controversial. As far as I know, there are no figures on how many former residents of *yōgoshisetsu* are now working as staff in *yōgoshisetsu*. There are enough cases, however, for there to be something of a debate over the suitability or otherwise of hiring former residents, although this debate has needed to be carried out in a fairly coded manner to avoid upsetting those to whom it refers. Some people argue that former residents are best placed to empathize with the situation and concerns of current residents in homes, some of whom are only a few years younger than them. Others, though, feel strongly that such former residents have too limited a world-view and are too immature to give current residents the support and guidance they need to succeed in the outside world. The fiercest critique I encountered of the employment of former residents, however, came from a senior member of the residential care workers' union, who felt that the hiring of former residents, as indeed of those known through personal connections, has been a conscious policy of the heads of private homes to militate against the unionization and politicization of the workforce, an issue to which we will return later.

MOTIVATION FOR WORKING IN HOMES

Motivation is difficult to research; when, in a survey of the staff at Kodomo Gakuen, I asked the simple question 'why did you come and work in a child welfare institution?' (*jidō fukushi shisetsu ni tsutometa riyū wo oshiete kudasai*), I received almost universally the simple answer, 'Because I like children' (*kodomo ga suki dakara*). Although sometimes this came with the gloss that a professor had encouraged such a career or that they had worked as a volunteer in a *yōgoshisetsu* and enjoyed it, it seems this may have been the wrong question. When Hagan (1994: appendix A) asked a sample of staff at a home in Osaka, 'Why did you come to work at SJ Home?', she received a rather more interesting range of responses: four members of staff had been to the home as *jisshū* and decided then that they wanted to work there; three thought they could do something for the children; two had found their previous work boring and unchallenging; two had been involved in volunteer work in social welfare; two wanted to work in child welfare; one had been a resident in a home; another remembered the effect of his parents' break-up and the feeling that he wanted to help those who had been through similar experiences; and one responded 'I believe God led me to this work'.

These final two answers are interesting because they are the only examples in two (admittedly small) samples which converge with what some informants ascribed to others as the most common reasons for working in *yōgoshisetsu*—religious belief and personal hardship. Lawrance H. Thompson (1983), himself the son of a missionary and one of the most important intermediaries between the Japanese and Western worlds of social welfare in the post-war period, indeed links the two motivations in his argument that most Christians involved in what he describes as the 'most productive [i.e. successful] of the Christian social welfare projects' in Japan embarked on such projects after some dramatic personal experience.

As we have seen, many *yōgoshisetsu* were set up as charitable foundations by religious organizations, mainly Christian with financial aid from overseas, but also a significant number of Buddhist and new religious (*shinshūkyō*) organizations. As Ninomiya (1998) outlines, however, the number of Christians working in *yōgoshisetsu*, even ones with a Christian foundation, has decreased since the government took over their financing and they began to rely less on funds raised by congregations overseas. He clearly sees this as a negative trend—they have become 'salaried workers whose purpose is gaining income instead of performing a service' (Ninomiya, 1998: 89)—and is particularly upset by the fact that even the heads of so-called Christian institutions do not necessarily need to be Christian. According to a recent report (Nihon Christkyō Shakai Fukushi Gakkai, 1997), however, in a survey of 118 Christian-founded child welfare institutions, some 90 per cent of the heads were Christian, as were some 60 per cent of the staff even though, as we have seen, Christians constitute less than 1 per cent of the total population. The same survey (1997: 12) suggested that around 15 per cent of staff in Christian child welfare institutions were members of other religious groups (and 27 per cent were members of no religious group). There are no similar figures for the staff of non-Christian homes, but the heads of two nominally Buddhist homes both felt that the majority of staff in those homes had no strong religious beliefs. Some indeed, as we shall see, have argued strongly against any religious element in homes at all.

ROLES AND DUTIES OF CARE STAFF

While we have gained some idea of the hours that staff work, and the remuneration they receive, we have little idea of the actual content of their job. As this clearly depends on which part of which day individuals are working, it is perhaps easiest to describe what one individual might have to do if on duty for twenty-four hours, not an impossible scenario in some homes.

In a typical example, two members of staff are in charge of a room of some eight to eleven children. They need to be up in time to wake the children at 6.30 a.m.; get them washed, dressed, and in line for the morning exercises (*radio taisō*) that are performed at virtually all residential institutions in Japan; organized for the morning clean-up (*sōji*); breakfasted and, if it is a school day, off to school with all the correct books, equipment, papers, and anything else especially requested for that particular day.[22]

Once the children are off to school, staff need to air their bedding, clean their rooms, do their laundry and ironing, and keep the records of the individual children in their care up to date. Should one of the children in their care be off sick or if the member of staff needs to visit the school then, just as any parent, they must also look after these matters while fitting in the rest of their jobs around them. Children return from school at a variety of times between 1.30 p.m. and 5 p.m.—depending on the season, the day of the week, what grade they are in, and with what after-school activities they are involved—and their care workers need to be around to greet them, give them something to eat and drink, settle them down to their homework,[23] involve them in the home clean-up, get them to dinner, bathed, and ready for bed.

In between all of these activities, staff would need to attend a variety of meetings: generally at least once a month for the whole staff and weekly in smaller groups; a variety of self-study groups in evenings; meetings with staff from other homes; meetings with parents; meetings with workers from the *jidōsōdanjo*. And of course, around all of this is the need to find time for the most important activity of all, spending quality time with the children in their care. As one new member of staff once confided, it took her at least a year to get into the rhythm of the job, even though she had undertaken placements in *yōgoshisetsu* before starting work.

A care worker in a *yōgoshisetsu*, therefore, fulfils a wide variety of roles as well as working long hours. In some homes, though, these roles are strictly divided by gender.

THE DIVISION OF LABOUR BETWEEN *HOBO* AND *JIDOSHIDŌIN*

Kodomo Gakuen was slightly unusual in that it did not pressurize its female staff who got married or had children to resign as was still the usual practice in many other welfare, including child welfare, institutions in Japan in the early 1990s. It was also unusual in its balance of male and female staff. Of the 7,500 child-care staff in *yōgoshisetsu* in 1990, female staff (*hobo*) outnumbered male staff (*jidōshidōin*) by about 2.5 : 1.[24] At Kodomo Gakuen at that time there were twelve *hobo* and eight *jidōshidōin* (1.5 : 1).

Despite the few exceptions of male *hofu* and female *jidōshidōin*, in most places *hobo* and *jidōshidōin* are positions that are clearly gender-divided.[25] Indeed Hagan (1994) reports the case of one woman who was qualified as a *jidōshidōin* but employed in a home as a *hobo*. In this home, *hobo* and *jidōshidōin* performed clearly separate roles. Female *hobo* worked with the same group of children throughout their time in the home, while the roles of the *jidōshidōin* were changed annually; the *hobo* were responsible for working with the children on an individual basis, while the *jidōshidōin* were responsible for group activities; the *hobo* played the role of 'mother', the *jidōshidōin* the role of 'father'. In terms of lines of command, *hobo* needed the *jidōshidōin* to approve their paperwork. Such gender differentiation in many ways reflects the wider society both in terms of the relationship between public male and domestic female roles and the fact that most *jidōshidōin* have two more years of formal education than most *hobo*.[26]

In some other institutions there was a slightly more equal relationship between the *hobo* and the *jidōshidōin*. At Kodomo Gakuen each room (of around eight to eleven children) had a male and female staff member in charge of it who to a very large degree seemed to share equally the work needed to care for the children. At the smaller *group homes*, which we will discuss later, the domestic workload between the male and female members was also much more equally shared out than in the average Japanese household, though this to a large degree reflected the fact that, for the male staff members, running the *group home* was their full-time job. Indeed, since boys as well as girls were expected to be involved in the cleaning activities within the homes, it could be argued that their socialization experiences were less gender-based than those of most Japanese of their age.

Even at Kodomo Gakuen, however, there was no doubt that the male staff tended to dominate, particularly in management positions. While overall throughout the welfare (and indeed pre-school and elementary education) field, there are many more women than men employed, this is in no way reflected in the number of women in management. Nowhere was this more clearly demonstrated than at the end of the meeting of the heads of all the homes (Yōgoshisetsuchōkai) held at Kyoto in 1991: of the fourteen people sitting on the dais representing the different sections of the meeting, the organizing committee, and Kōseishō, there was not one woman. In the very few cases where women are heads of homes, these are almost all either in homes only for girls (though not all the heads of such homes are women) or else the woman in question is a member of the extended family that set up and ran the home. It is a somewhat curious twist therefore that, whereas more women have qualifications relevant to child care than men, they tend to play subordinate roles in the actual running of *yōgoshisetsu*.

CAREER PATHS

The vast majority of workers who start work in *yōgoshisetsu* are offered contracts of employment in the August to November period of their last year at university or college, and begin work the following April, immediately on graduation. One problem for the heads of homes is that they can only offer to employ someone either on receiving notice of a resignation of a current member of staff or on receipt of extra funding to increase their current staffing level. Moreover, as is the

case with most organizations in Japan, it is extremely unusual for staff to begin
work except in April. While this does have the advantage of enabling the induction and training of all new staff at the same time, it also, as Matsubara (1992: 6)
points out, greatly reduces the flexibility for recruitment in the private homes.
The public homes can always call on the services of others within local government employment, though here too it is unusual for individuals to rotate jobs
except at the beginning of April each year.

In recent years, there has been little problem recruiting sufficient numbers
to work in *yōgoshisetsu*. In part this is because they have been attractive sites
for women, in part because many workers like the opportunity to work with
children, in part because the number of children in *yōgoshisetsu* has been on
the decrease, and in part because in the 1990s, due to the economic recession,
Japanese graduates, especially female graduates, have been faced for the first time
in forty years with the real prospect of unemployment.[27] Indeed in the 1990s there
have been signs of movement into social welfare jobs by those from other fields,
as welfare is perceived to be the one area which can confidently be expected to
expand and offer secure employment for the next twenty years. The real issue for
employment in the homes has been the problem of burn-out.

The immediate reasons for this burn-out are not hard to find. As we have seen,
many residential workers work over 3,000 hours a year with few breaks to
recharge their batteries. Work itself is said by many to be exhausting, not only
because of the hard manual labour of housework involved, but because of the
feeling that any spare time must and should be spent on quality time with the
children in care. Moreover, the problems with which the children come into care,
and with which the care staff have to deal, are perceived to be becoming increasingly complex. Residential staff at a 1990 conference (Jidōyōgo no Kiken wo
Norikoeru tame no Symposium) about working conditions in *yōgoshisetsu*
argued that homes were accepting a higher proportion of older children manifesting a greater proportion of educational problems and delinquent behaviour,
with many dropping out from, or refusing to go to, school.[28] The same conference
received a survey of twenty-one *yōgoshisetsu* in the Tokyo area in which sixteen
reported that staff had been the victims of violence from children in the home
and highlighted the problems in two particular homes, one where only thirteen
out of forty-four staff were fully healthy, and another where five out of sixteen
child-care staff were receiving medical treatment for ulcers while still working.

While some pointed out that rates of pay were insufficient to keep good workers,[29] one *hobo* at the conference fixed on another issue as the main problem in
yōgoshisetsu: low staffing levels and the lack of 'experienced workers' (*veteran
shokuin*) (*Kanagawa Shinbun*, 15 Nov. 1990). This relates to what Matsubara
(1992: 6) describes as 'a chronic shortage of staff at the middle management
level'. We have already discussed staffing levels above, but we need to look at the
complex issue of experienced staff in more detail.

According to Kuraoka (1992: 196), staff in private homes worked on average 62 per cent more hours each year than those in public ones (3,400 against 2,100). This difference is largely explained in terms of the number of staff employed. There are only 1.6 children to each full-time worker in public homes and 2.6 in private homes (figures derived from *KK*, no. 45, 1991: 211).[30] The difference, according to Kuroda (1991: 56–7), is even bigger when it comes to administrative staff, where public homes can have as much as ten times the support staff (*kanrikei*) of private homes, as well as sometimes large numbers of part-time staff (*hijōkin*) who are rarely found in private homes. Similarly, public homes often have one or two nurses (*kangofu*) on their staff, while private homes generally have none (Kuroda, 1991). In terms of size, private homes are generally 70 per cent less spacious per child; while a six-mat room in a private home would have three children, in a public home it would have only two (Kuroda, 1991: 58). Further, the staff in public homes are better paid—except in those few prefectures where the pay is equalized—and receive better benefits for working overtime, as well as being expected to work many fewer hours. According to Kuroda (1991: 58–9), for a qualified *hobo* in her fifth year of employment the difference could be as much as ¥500,000 a year; in her tenth year, as much as ¥1,000,000 (or 20 per cent more than her counterpart in a private home).[31]

There are a number of reasons for these rather stark differences between public and private homes. One relates to the *dōzoku keiei* system that was examined earlier. This system can effectively block off the senior management positions from those who are not of the *dōzoku* family. Further, as Matsubara (1992: 8) explains, there is virtually no exchange or movement of staff between institutions within the same *shakai fukushi hōjin*, so that when employees find themselves stuck at a certain level in a particular institution they have no alternative but to remain in the position for the foreseeable future (which may not be good for either them or those in their care) or to resign altogether. This led to a trend of male workers leaving the profession in their late thirties and early forties. Indeed, one professor of social work estimated that, up to the early 1990s, about 70 per cent of those in *dōzoku keiei* homes left at this stage and found work in companies which could offer better promotion and salary prospects at a time when men of this age were particularly in need of money to pay for their children's high-school and university education. An analysis of *yōgoshisetsu* suggests that the average length of employment for all their staff is less than ten years (derived from *YSI*, 1998).

Even though the trend for workers to leave the world of *dōzoku keiei* institutions in mid-career has been recognized for some time as a potential problem, it has remained something of a sensitive topic within the field as a whole. Even Kōseishō (1991: 24), in a major report on the problems of the shortage in manpower within the welfare field as a whole, mentioned the problem only once and then in a reference buried so deep in the middle of the report that it would make sense only to those already familiar with the issue. According to some commentators, the reason for the ministry's reluctance to face the issue head-on was that the whole residential child welfare sector had become increasingly reliant on the *dōzoku keiei* institutions.

UNIONS

The main reason for the different working conditions in public and private homes relates to the unionization of the respective workforces. There are two unions for those who work in child welfare institutions or offices in Japan. Those who work in public welfare facilities or offices can become members of the large Jichirō (Zen Nihon Jichi Dantai Rōdō Kumiai) union which all local government employees are eligible to join, while those who work in private welfare institutions can join the Hofukurō union (Zenkoku Hoiku Fukushi Rōdō Kumiai).

Jichirō is a very powerful organization, and hence staff in public homes have been able to secure good working conditions. In many public homes, regular care staff do not do night duties, and extra staff have to be drafted in for these. The staff in public homes also seem to include a greater proportion of older and more experienced workers than those at the private homes. One result of these differences, of course, is that public homes are more expensive—one estimate by the head of a private home in Tokyo in 1999 was 2.5 times more expensive—to run than private homes.

On the other hand, according to a senior official, few care staff take up the opportunity to join the Hofukurō union. In the Tokyo area in 1991 only 20,000 out of a possible 400,000 workers (around 5 per cent) were members, and hence its power was extremely muted. In those few homes where the staff were unionized, it could have a major effect on working conditions. The home where the union official worked had always been a strong base for Hofukurō activity, and therefore had some of the best working conditions of private institutions in Japan. This included its own *hoikuen*, which had been set up in the home so that staff could leave their children while working, even overnight. As a result, it was much easier for married staff to continue to work after they had begun a family, and indeed almost all the staff at the home were married and had children. Sixteen of the thirty staff at the home had worked for more than ten years, and the average length of service was around fifteen years, which was probably the longest among all private homes in the Tokyo area.

The Hofukurō union explains its relative lack of members and influence among *yōgoshisetsu* staff in terms of the anti-union antagonism of the heads of homes and their *rijikai*. It argues that, like middle-sized and small companies (*chūshō kigyō*) in Japanese industry, private homes stamp down on attempts to form unions, perceiving them as potential trouble. As one senior union official put it, a strong union, for example, would be able to monitor the way the home operated and spent the money that it received from public funds.[32] According to some commentators, it is not surprising, therefore, that homes prefer to hire docile workers, including former residents, young females, and those with personal connections with the home whom they considered unlikely to become involved in union activities (Tsuzaki, 1997: 97). Moreover, the heads of the private homes have considerable discretion over the promotion of staff which makes it difficult for those who want to work long-term within the homes to cross them.

Kodomo Gakuen did not have a branch (*bunkai*) of the union and there was no union literature visible in the home. According to its head, there was no longer anything on which a union could be active after the Tokyo prefectural authorities had agreed to equalize the pay of staff in private homes with that of workers in public homes; even outside Tokyo, he thought, there was probably only a union branch in one out of every three private homes. Discussion among staff of Kodomo Gakuen seldom turned to matters of wider politics or specific complaints about management, even if they did feel that in general terms they worked too many hours for too little pay. Instead, discussion tended to be focused on the immediate job in hand, and in this staff were encouraged by a well-designed programme of in-service training.

IN-SERVICE STAFF TRAINING

The in-service training that was on offer to staff at Kodomo Gakuen could be divided into two types: external and internal. The former was considerably more optional than the latter and was centred around the local block of six or seven children's homes who formed their own study groups (*kenkyūkai*), the prefectural or city association of *yōgoshisetsu*, and sometimes the national association of all Japan's children's homes.[33] These meetings were largely attended only by the more senior staff who were able to feed in to the discussions the practice in their own institutions. One member of staff at Kodomo Gakuen who was in his third year said that he did not think it would be appropriate to attend—nor indeed was he interested in attending—one such local meeting when I asked him if he would be present. Those who did attend these meetings would be expected to feed back what they had learned to others at either the general Wednesday-morning meetings or as part of the internal training programme.

Kodomo Gakuen was well known locally for its staff training. This was mainly because once a year it hosted a seminar by an American psychotherapist and his Japanese wife about the latest practice in child group-work in the United States, as well as holding lectures by well-known Japanese child welfare specialists.[34] More significant for the staff, however, were the twice-yearly *shokuin gakushū* (staff training sessions), one of which I joined in May 1991. I will describe this event in some detail because it gives some indication of the staff dynamics at Kodomo Gakuen and the skills that senior staff feel need to be developed.

One of the younger female members of staff was the designated *taichō* (team leader), though it became clear this was an organizational rather than a genuine leadership role that had involved visiting all the sites beforehand and making the necessary reservations. A few days before the event we all received a small booklet which she had prepared with a detailed timetable.

The staff were divided into two groups of six members each, and many of the activities throughout the two days were centred on developing group bonding and mutual understanding. The leaders of both groups were male *jidōshidōin*, even though the female workers outnumbered the males on the trip as they did in the home overall, which probably reflected the greater leadership responsibilities that male workers were expected to take in their work.

The trip started with a train ride into the countryside beyond west Tokyo. On arrival at our destination station, everyone stopped for the souvenir photography (*kinen shashin*) that is the prerequisite of all group trips in Japan (Graburn, 1983). This was followed by a visit to a local *udon* restaurant where a generous meal was paid for by the *taichō* out of a special training budget. We then walked the short distance to a joint *yōgoshisetsu* and *nyūjiin* child welfare institution. This proved very interesting for the staff, who were able to compare directly their own working conditions and working practices with those in another institution. This particular home was different from Kodomo Gakuen in a number of important ways: it had children on the same campus from birth to the age of 18 rather than from 2 years of age; it organized few of its own community events but preferred to get its children involved in a much larger range and number of local community events that still existed in what was a comparatively rural area; it had a relatively high proportion of senior high-school children; and it placed a great deal of emphasis on its athletic activities.

Two topics really caught the attention of the Kodomo Gakuen staff. The first was the working arrangements whereby staff could take up to six days off in a block after a few weeks of intensive work. The second was that each room had its own television, radio, and small oven: the children reheated their own food and ate in their rooms in the evening rather than eating together, as part of an effort to make them more like mini-family units than simply dormitories in a large institution.

The pluses and minuses of what we had been told and had seen were debated as we set off to walk to the mountain lodge—the private property of the head's mother (*Gakuen no Okāsan*)—where we would be staying overnight. The evening was spent doing team exercises which had been organized by the senior care worker, the younger brother of the head of the home. The first exercise involved drawing a picture that was being described in detail by someone else. This was then made more difficult as individuals were prevented from asking questions. Although one young member of staff found describing the picture to the rest of her group painfully difficult, and the exercise took much longer than expected, we were not allowed to move on until it had been properly completed.

In the second exercise, each person was given parts of a triangle and asked to complete it. While no one had all the pieces they needed, they were not allowed to request pieces from others, although anyone could give a piece to anyone else whenever they wished. The result was interesting: some people spent the whole time giving pieces to others (in the hope they might receive pieces back); others spent the whole time trying to make as much of a triangle as they could with the pieces that they had in front of them. The result was that few got very near completion.

In the third exercise, we were asked to write down what type of person we thought the others in our group were—their favourite music, colours, places, activities—and then compare them with the lists they had made about themselves. But it was the fourth and final exercise which proved to be the most interesting and controversial. Entitled 'What is most important to you?' (*Anata no ichiban taisetsuna mono wa?*) it asked groups to place in order the eight values of love, health, self-realization (*jiko jitsugen*), service to others (*hōshi*), justice (*seigi*), wealth, fame, and happiness (*tanoshimi*). In the end, the two groups came up with very similar lists, though only one group had been able to reach a consensus among its six members:

Group A	Group B
1 love	health
2 health	love
3 self-development	happiness
4 service to others	self-development
5 justice	justice
6 happiness	service to others
7 not completed	wealth
8 not completed	fame

Within both groups, however, long and serious debate was held as each person tried to explain and convince the others why they had come up with the order they had, and people surprised each other and themselves with the vehemence with which they defended their positions. Where to place the value of 'service to others' was particularly contentious.

The final stage of the evening involved sitting around a long table drinking and eating and listening, mainly to the head and his younger brother, as the senior people present. There was much mutual joking: unmarried staff were teased about their marital status; one member of staff who had turned 40 complained about still being called *onēsan* (big sister) and not *obasan* (auntie); the cook complained that the children never told her if they liked her food (and she was reassured that they did). As is the norm for Japanese parties, the group did not break up into small units (Befu, 1974) and most of the conversation centred on asking the views of the head of the home on a wide variety of topics. But, interestingly, it never included the slightest hint of direct criticism of the management of the home even though being under the influence of alcohol is seen as the one occasion when individuals can legitimately voice such complaints (Moeran, 1998).

One member of staff, however, refused to participate in the party: a senior male *jidōshidōin* with two young children of his own, he worked in one of the small attached *group homes* having previously worked for many years in the main home itself. Throughout he participated only half-heartedly in the group activities and as soon as the final exercise was over he pulled out a mattress and went to sleep. Such passive resistance is a well-known way of objecting to compulsory group activity in Japan, though there is no way of knowing if this was the point he was making since he never mentioned it, and everyone else managed to totally ignore—or pretend to ignore—his actions and his snoring. The rest of us got to bed at around 2 a.m.

We were woken at 6.30 a.m.—the head had left at around 5 a.m. to get back to the home in time for the children who would be getting up there—and immediately set about washing and making a fire and breakfast, again working and eating in our assigned groups. We then walked down to a nearby campsite, did our morning exercises and stretches, sang a few songs, and then set about a project identifying the different plants that we could find about us. A tour of the campsite was followed by an exercise in making a little wooden *omiyage* (souvenir) to take back from the trip. Finally another souvenir photograph was taken at the campsite and we were driven in the home's minibus to a nearby restaurant for lunch. The *taichō* thanked everyone for all their hard work and we all raised our beer glasses in a joint *kanpai*. Most people looked as if they were falling asleep as they made their way to the bus and the cars for the return journey to the home.

It was not difficult to see the effectiveness of the *shokuin gakushū*. It removed staff from their normal working environment and put them through a very tiring regime for two days in a situation where they needed to rely on each other for support and help. Unlike Rohlen's (1996) account of training in a Japanese bank though, the emphasis was more on fun than on physical hardship. Indeed, in many ways the exercises that were carried out were similar to those that are carried out by social workers on away-day training programmes in the UK.[35] Where it perhaps differed was in reinforcing rather than challenging the way that the home was run and, in particular, the paternalistically benevolent role of the head who was seen to supply the funds and provisions that made the event enjoyable. Indeed, the head of each home is, in many ways, the key figure for understanding the way in which it is operated.

HEADS OF HOMES

As with the main staff of *yōgoshisetsu*, heads of homes (universally known, as are the heads of other welfare institutions such as day nurseries, as *enchō sensei*) can be divided into two distinct categories: heads of public homes and heads of private homes.

Heads of public homes (which constitute 10 per cent of all *yōgoshisetsu*) are local government officials who have generally worked in local government throughout their careers. Just as we saw with those who work in the *jidōsōdanjo*, in some areas (such as Yokohama) they will have specialized in welfare work throughout their careers and may even have specialized in working in child welfare. In many other areas, however, they will have had very little or even no experience in these fields. For the latter group, it is suggested that an appointment to head a residential welfare facility is generally either the equivalent of a *madogi-wazoku* (by the window) sideways move which takes them away from the mainstream of local government power at the end of their careers, or a penultimate posting from which they hope to return to something important in the mainstream local government offices. In both cases, as Matsubara (1992: 5) points out, the appointment can be problematic:

Personnel in charge of the management (operation) of [public] children's homes are appointed from the overall personnel rotation within the administrative policy, resulting at times, in appointments of persons with little or no experience in children's home operations. This results occasionally in a negative posture of 'peace-at-any-price' in running the institution 'without serious mishap' until moving on to the next appointment.[36]

The heads of private homes (which constitute the other 90 per cent of *yōgoshisetsu*) come from rather different backgrounds. Thompson (1983) suggests that the original founders of welfare institutions in Japan, particularly Christian foundations, were often extraordinary individuals who had been led to their work by dramatic personal events. Imazeki's account (1991) of the problems and resistance—from the town council, the local population, and even the local education authorities who feared the sudden appearance of 'delinquent' children in their community—that he encountered in setting up a *yōgoshisetsu* in Saitama Prefecture during the 1980s is an indication of the strength of character, purpose, and belief that some of these founders must have possessed. Many of these early pioneers—both during the Meiji boom and the immediate post-war boom in the establishment of *yōgoshisetsu*—were foreigners, and indeed, up to the late 1970s, there were still quite a few heads (both nominal and real) of homes who were not native Japanese.[37]

While very few of today's *enchō sensei* are their original founders, the current generation of heads of private homes still demonstrate some interesting characteristics. First, many homes are religious denominations and their heads remain religious figures though, as Ninomiya (1998) points out, this is no longer as hard-and-fast a rule as it once was. At a meeting of all the heads of *yōgoshisetsu* which I attended in 1991, a significant number of participants wore religious clothing, including nuns in habits and Salvation Army officers in uniform. Though I saw no Buddhist priests in robes, several heads of Buddhist homes were said to be ordained, and the heads of homes associated with new religious movements, such as Seichō no Ie, were assumed to be committed members of those organizations.

Secondly, there appears to be a much wider age range among the heads of the

private homes than among those of the public homes. There are a number of reasons for this. The heads of private homes are appointed by either the *rijikai* of the
home or the *shakai fukushi hōjin* of which the home is a part. There is no stipulation of any retirement age for the heads of private homes (just as in the case of
professors at private universities which are part of *gakkō hōjin*), hence many continue in their positions until they are very old. The head of one *nyūjiin* I visited
was well into his seventies, which was explained by the fact that he was a member
of the family that originally founded the home. On the other hand, the *dōzoku
keiei* system could also lead to a much younger individual being appointed as the
head of an institution through their connection with the founding family. Indeed,
it was widely recognized that the very able and still young head of the old people's
home next to Kodomo Gakuen, who was also, in the early 1990s, the head of the
whole *shakai fukushi hōjin* as well as a part-time professor of social welfare at a
Tokyo university, had partly been able to get so far so quickly because he was the
grandson of the original founder.

Similarly, the *rijikai* of the private homes, unfettered as they are by the senior-
ity promotion system of the local government bureaucracy, are free to make
imaginative appointments outside the normal recruitment system. In Tokyo in
the 1970s, two homes, both facing severe problems which were partly blamed on
their former heads, appointed two new heads in their late twenties—one of
whom had himself been a resident of a *yōgoshisetsu* before going on to university
and study abroad. By all accounts, both of these appointments managed to turn
the *yōgoshisetsu* around, and the heads were popular and supported by the children in their homes. Indeed, when one was transferred by the *rijikai* to another
institution within the same *shakai fukushi hōjin*, former residents protested the
decision.

The *rijikai* of private homes not only have control over appointments, but also
determine the salaries of heads. While the minimum level for salaries are set by
Kōseishō (depending on the size of the home)[38] and paid for by the central and
the prefectural government, the *rijikai* has the power, and sometimes the wherewithal, to top them up as they see fit. As a result, it is thought that while the general staff in private homes are less well paid than those in public homes (except
in those few prefectures where the difference is made up by the local government), the heads of private homes probably receive rather more. The extra provision for the heads of private homes generally comes in the form of free or
subsidized housing, car allowances, expense accounts, and other perks which
mean that the basic salary level bears little relation to the final package. Indeed,
the former head of a private *yōgoshisetsu* who went on to become a university
assistant professor commented that in doing so he had taken a big drop in
income, though not salary, because of losing all these extra payments. James and
Benjamin (1988: 63–4), in their account of *gakkō hōjin*, describe similar practices
as a form of 'disguised profit distribution' which can take place in institutions
which, like *shakai fukushi hōjin*, are technically non-profit-making. Like the heads

of institutions in *gakkō hōjin*, the heads of the private homes generally enjoy a high standard of living that matches their high status in the local community. When the heads of all the homes gather for their annual conferences they generally stay in top-class hotels.

Since the vast majority of heads of homes are male, their qualifications tend to be similar to those of the *jidōshidōin*, and indeed many of the heads of private homes had previously themselves been *jidōshidōin* workers in those homes. Few heads of homes, then, are specifically qualified in child care, and some in *dōzoku keiei* homes may have actually had rather little experience of child care altogether before taking up their positions. In all cases, however, the *enchō sensei* is the most important figure in any *yōgoshisetsu*, especially in dealing with the outside world. He—occasionally she—must persuade local welfare offices to send children to the home, and convince government officials that the home is being run properly. He must persuade employers to take on the home's graduates, and schools to persevere with their more problematic children. He must liaise with the local community, reassure it following problems with children in the home, and encourage it to support the home both financially and through volunteer activity. In many cases heads of the private *yōgoshisetsu* are, or become, quite charismatic figures, and if homes become well known it is often through the name of their *enchō sensei*.

VOLUNTEERS

Yōgoshisetsu make extensive use of volunteers to support the work of their paid employees. In a survey undertaken in 1991, 97.2 per cent of children's homes recorded using volunteers (Sakamoto, 1993a).[39] In most cases volunteers were members of groups which had long had relations with homes, but 81.8 per cent of *yōgoshisetsu* also reported that individual volunteers helped in their home. I was accepted as an individual volunteer at Kodomo Gakuen, and the home had had a number of overseas volunteers at different times, including an American who had spent six months in the home in 1971, an Indonesian student who had been there in 1978, and a Brazilian who had worked in the home in 1980.

There are a number of different types of groups which organize volunteers to work in *yōgoshisetsu*. The most common are those based in nearby universities. According to Sakamoto (1993a), 60 per cent of homes receive volunteers from such groups. Volunteers from local women's groups are received by 55 per cent of *yōgoshisetsu*; a further 38 per cent come from local residents' association groups; 37 per cent come from religious groups; and 17 per cent come from old people's groups. The majority (52.2 per cent) of volunteer groups in homes help the children with their school work (*gakushū shidō*), while a further 20 per cent help them with their recreational activities. Clearly most homes have relations with more than one group, and this is the case at Kodomo Gakuen, which has had a relationship (since 1952) with a volunteer club from a well-known private university in Tokyo, with a local women's group, and with a local old people's group. The university students tutor children in the home once or twice a week. The group of women, mostly in their fifties, make and mend futons and uniforms for the children in the home and, together with the old people's club, help organize the twice-yearly bazaars that raise money towards the children's summer holidays and Christmas presents. Once a month, also, a team of barbers comes to the home and cuts the children's hair for free.[40] Overall, the total number of people who give some kind of voluntary support to the home in terms of their time over the course of a year is very substantial (perhaps as many as 500 individuals), even if in many cases this amounts to no more than half a day helping out at a bazaar.

Many homes also receive financial donations and presents. Sometimes this is through special organizations (*kōenkai*) that homes themselves have set up; sometimes through supporters of the religious organization to which the home is attached; sometimes through local community organizations. This extra funding (often described as *plus-alpha* by the heads of the homes) can, for a few homes, make a significant difference to the overall annual budget. The head of a home in Kyoto, for example, that was linked to, and situated in the grounds of, a large Jōdoshū Buddhist temple, estimated that each year the home received up to 15 per cent of its annual budget from donations from Jōdoshū followers, as well as a large number of direct gifts such as rice, futons, towels, and socks. For capital projects, even larger amounts might be forthcoming: the temple had given the home ¥320 million some twenty years earlier for rebuilding. At Kodomo Gakuen, each of the small *group homes* constructed in the 1980s, which will be discussed later, had been built largely from two single donations, and a large new hall constructed in the 1990s from a number of donations. In many cases, the two types of volunteer support—of money and of time—were linked, such as when volunteers set up and ran the stalls at the two bazaars that Kodomo Gakuen held each year.

From the point of view of the homes, voluntary activity and financial support are crucial aspects of their running. This is especially so in the case of the private *yōgoshisetsu*. While in most cases the total amount of money that a home receives through these means is rarely more than 10 per cent of its total budget (and often far less), it is money which can be spent as the home wishes and hence gives it a measure of, and sense of, independence from the national and prefectural authorities which provided the other 85–90 per cent of its funding (Amenomori, 1997: 198).[41] This sense of independence is extremely important for the homes' self-image. Homes also find themselves in a virtuous circle by raising their own funds since, as we have seen, some of the money which they receive from central and prefectural governments is discretionary and is paid on the basis of new ideas and programmes that they implement.

Much of the volunteer activity in the *yōgoshisetsu* can be traced back to the student movement of the 1960s, when student activists believed that they needed to take a role in improving the quality of life of the least well off in Japanese society.[42] According to some reports, some of these students volunteers did not always see eye to eye with the staff in the homes—a resident of one home in the early 1970s remembers a group of students being asked to leave because they insisted on their right to smoke there—but they were the forerunners of many of the university volunteer clubs that still exist today. The members of these clubs change every year—indeed one of the complaints of children is that individuals suddenly stop visiting them after a period of intensive contact and leave them feeling abandoned—but the club as an entity continues.

Some of those individuals who were involved in the 1960s period of political activity have continued their idealistic commitment to social welfare reform and have remained in volunteer activity. This is particularly the case with women, many of whom are now in their early fifties, and their volunteer activity is still considered radical in some quarters. Imamura (1987: 126), for example, in her account of the lives of Japanese housewives in the 1980s, gives a sense of some of the criticism that women could face if they devoted time to voluntary activities rather than their family:

Social service carries with it an image of the woman participating 'because she enjoys it' and being in a comfortable financial position. This is not necessarily a good image for the woman to create in her neighbourhood, however. It is better to be seen as working hard for one's family rather than having the time and money to put into social service [*boranteia katsudō*]. Social service volunteers all told me that they had been criticized for their activity.

In 1991 I still heard women who participated in social welfare voluntary activity described sarcastically as *yūkan* (members of the leisured class or 'idle rich'). It is perhaps not surprising, therefore, that only 3.9 per cent of the women in Imamura's survey were involved in any form of social service, or that most of these came from the higher income brackets where there was less pressure on them to supplement the family income.

In the early 1990s, there was a general fear that the volunteers who worked in *yōgoshisetsu* were as a group ageing rapidly and were becoming increasingly out of touch with the world of the children in the homes (Yamada, 1992). Volunteer activity in the 1970s had largely been associated with environmental movements and in the 1980s with international relief elements, neither of which brought volunteers in to the *yōgoshisetsu*. Many volunteers were also increasingly frustrated that society still did not understand the nature of volunteer activity: volunteers were still expected to pay their expenses as well as to donate their time, and the idea of actually working full-time for a voluntary organization was considered to be a contradiction in terms (Nakano, 1998: 51–2).

The Hanshin earthquake, however, saw a sudden upsurge in volunteer activity that caught many unawares and led to 1995 being described by some as 'the first year of volunteerism in Japan' (Nakano, 1998: 3). According to the Hyōgo prefectural government, 1.17 million volunteers offered their services in the six weeks after the earthquake. Seventy per cent of them had never been involved in volunteer activity before (Nakata, 1996: 22). Most of them were young, enthusiastic, and not bound to mainstream ideas of volunteer activity. As Nakata (1996: 23) put it: 'The youths flocking the ward office were different from the obedient and respectful "volunteers" that ward officers had known previously . . . for whom volunteer work meant . . . doing whatever they were told to do by the ward officers.'

In the wake of the Hanshin earthquake then, there was a sudden reconsideration of the role of volunteer activity in Japan and a new debate about the development of civil society, based on a model of what many commentators describe as a Western concept of volunteer activity.[43] As we shall see, this has had a major impact on raising awareness about a host of welfare issues, including the care of children in *yōgoshisetsu*.

THERAPISTS AND THERAPEUTIC SUPPORT

In some ways, the most interesting element of the staffing of *yōgoshisetsu* has lain not so much in the categories of those who work in homes as in those who, until recently, have not. Particularly noticeable here has been the almost total absence of specialist psychological and psychiatric support for children who come into care. While many staff may have taken an undergraduate course in basic social psychology, virtually none in any home have been specially trained to deal with cases—ranging from abused children to delinquent behaviour to school refusers—with which they may find themselves confronted.

According to Shinagawa (1999: 26), there was a very brief period at the end of the 1950s when, under the influence of Western 1950s clinical psychologists such as John Bowlby, it was decided to employ clinical psychology graduates in *yōgoshisetsu*, but the idea was abandoned soon after. Since that time there has been very little use of therapists in homes: a survey of almost all *yōgoshisetsu* in 1995 showed that there were only five therapists employed full-time across all the institutions, with a further seven employed part-time (*KK*, no. 50, 1996: 325).

In part, the resistance to the employment of therapists in homes was due to the definition of *yōgoshisetsu* as institutions for children for whom care and protection was necessary, a definition with no mention of therapeutic treatment. When in 1999, therefore, Kōseishō agreed for the first time that it would pay for the employment of part-time psychotherapists (*shinri ryōhōshi*) in roughly 100 *yōgoshisetsu* where more than 10 per cent of children had been shown to be abused, this indicated a major change in policy (*AS*, 16 Jan. 1999). To a large extent this change in policy came from pressure from those in the child welfare world supported by research that showed that a large proportion of children who were coming into care were manifesting serious problems (Ueno, 1999). Indeed, one widely circulated survey (see Table 16) suggested that only just over 40 per

TABLE 16. Major problem behaviours manifested by children on admission to yōgoshisetsu (1 April 1994–31 March 1995)

Problem behaviour	Boys	Girls	Total
Running away from home	114	78	192
Thieving	179	76	255
Truancy	128	76	204
Keeping bad company	85	65	150
Domestic violence	48	15	63
Sexual misconduct	7	34	41
Shoplifting	74	29	103
Smoking	118	42	160
Glue-sniffing	11	9	20
Absconding	63	50	113
Arson	4	1	5
Playing with fire	16	3	19
School refusal	161	129	290
Mute by malice	16	3	19
Maladjustment	8	8	16
Bullying	72	17	89
Victim of bullying	77	37	114
Extortion	21	6	27
Importuning	69	49	118
Bed-wetting/soiling	210	117	327
Neurotic	31	30	61
Borderline school performance	257	142	399
Physical disability	28	22	50
Mental disability	171	85	256
Other	152	99	251
No problem behaviour	1,339	1,300	2,639
TOTAL	3,459	2,522	5,981

Source: KH, 1996: 113.

cent of children admitted to homes were not demonstrating any problematic behaviour at all.

According to some in the child welfare world, the small amount of money that has been put aside for the employment of therapists, as well as the lack of qualified child therapists available for employment, will mean that in practice the new policy will have little effect on the way that children are treated in the vast majority of homes.[44] Instead, homes will have to continue to rely on their previous form of support for children who come into care: helping children adapt and adjust to the group environment of the homes and through that find both confidence and a sense of personal identity. In order to understand how this *group work* or *group dynamics*, as it is often explicitly called (Itō, 1998), operates in practice, we need to look at how children are looked after in *yōgoshisetsu*.

5

The Social Organization of Life in *Yōgoshisetsu*

THE FORMATION OF GROUPS

The organization of children in different *yōgoshisetsu* is normally discussed around two different axes: whether children are placed in small groups (*shōshasei*) or large groups (*taishasei*) and whether they are placed in groups of those who are roughly the same age as themselves (*yokowarisei*) or in groups of children of a range of ages (*tatewarisei*). There is considerable debate about the merits and demerits of all four of these systems, as there is about the proximity in which boys and girls should be placed within a home and the extent to which residents should be required to participate in communal activities. These debates are interesting anthropologically since, although they tend to draw on the work of foreign educationalists (such as Anton Makarenko) and child psychologists (such as John Bowlby), they reflect much wider debates in Japanese society about the relationship between the individual and the group.

Group Homes

The terms *shōshasei* and *taishasei* refer to the size of the individual buildings in any home as well as the overall size of the *yōgoshisetsu* in which children are housed. As we have already seen, *yōgoshisetsu* vary in size from under twenty children to over 200 (the largest category under which Kōseishō can calculate its payments to homes is still 'over 290 children'). In part, difference in size reflects homes' historical foundations. In part, also, it seems to reflect the belief of some prefectural and city governments and the boards of some private homes that economies of scale—in the use of facilities, buying of food, and so on—require homes to be of a reasonably large size. Or, to put this the other way around, as Tsuzaki (1999: 84–5) does, there is no incentive for private homes to spend more money on smaller units for the children in their care. In the course of research, I came across two good examples of this way of thinking. In one case, from the 1970s, the head of a small private home with only thirty children asked the city authorities for money to rebuild it.[1] He was told that the money would only be forthcoming if he increased the capacity of the home to at least eighty children, on the basis that a smaller home was financially less efficient. In the second case, from the 1980s, the attempts by an *enchō sensei* to set up a small *group home* were consistently blocked by the board of governors, on the basis, according to the *enchō sensei*, that the running costs would be too much per head. This was just one of the factors which led him to resign and move to another job altogether.

As this last example suggests, from the late 1970s the debate over *shōshasei* and *taishasei* in terms of the overall size of institutions has mutated into a debate in support of *group homes* versus any institution where all the residents live in a single building. Indeed, the debate about *group homes* has become one of the most important within the Japanese child welfare world in the post-war period.

A study group calling itself the Shōshasei Yōiku Kenkyūkai ('the study group on bringing up children in a small-group living environment') was established in 1979 in order to push for the development of *group homes*. It took most of its examples from the development of such units in Australia and the UK in the 1970s. While the group was small (its early meetings rarely had more than thirty participants), several members were from private homes and, as with most innovations in the world of *yōgoshisetsu*, the first appearance of *group homes* was among the private homes during the 1980s (Miyamoto, 1999). Initially, Kōseishō and most prefectural authorities would only provide the normal maintenance budget per child (calculated in terms of the total number of children in the whole institution) and none of the capital setting-up costs for these *group homes*. Only in 1992—several years after some of the more 'progressive' prefectural authorities—did Kōseishō decide to provide some support towards these costs. In doing so, however, it pressed strongly that these *group homes* should be used in the main for preparing children for the world outside the institution.

While the emergence of *group homes* during the 1980s was an important phenomenon, not least in the light of most of the funding coming from private donations, by 1990 there were still only twenty-six such institutions across the whole of the Tokyo metropolis (Tokyo-to Fukushikyoku Jidōbu, 1990). These could be divided into two types (twelve *family group homes* and fourteen *group homes*)[2] and provided places on average for six children each (around 150 in total or less than 5 per cent of the total number of children in care in the city). Tokyo, however, was far ahead of the rest of the country. By June 1995, the number of *group homes* for the whole country was only just over forty, catering for under 1 per cent of all children in *yōgoshisetsu* (*KK*, no. 50, 1996: 323) and there seems to have been little further development during the rest of the decade.

Kodomo Gakuen was one of the first *yōgoshisetsu* to set up *group homes*. One (H Group Home) was used for preparing older children (four boys and four girls of junior and high-school age) for leaving institutional care, while the other (A Group Home) was used for those in long-term care (*chōkiyōgo*) for whom there was little prospect of a foster placement because of objections from the parents or guardians.[3] This home housed three boys and three girls between the ages of 7 and 16. In 1991 the other children at Kodomo Gakuen lived on the main campus in six large rooms—three had a capacity for eight children; two for ten; and one for twelve—in a manner much more common among *yōgoshisetsu* across Japan than *group home* living.

Organization by Age and Gender

As well as size, the other main consideration for homes is who is placed in each room. The issue is generally discussed in terms of a choice between the principle of putting children of the same age together (*yokowarisei*) versus the idea of putting children of different ages together (*tatewarisei*). In reality, decisions tend to be made in a rather more complex manner than simply along these dimensions, and practice varies greatly not only between homes but also within homes over time.

In a private home in Kyoto, for example, the first organizing principle was to keep siblings together and then try to organize as far as possible on the *yokowarisei* principle of placing together children of the same age. Hence all the children between the ages of 3 and 6 were put together; senior high-school residents had their own rooms; and others were, in theory at least, allowed to choose with whom they wanted to share in groups of four, though it was admitted that this often required some supervision.

A private home in Tokyo, on the other hand, operated totally on the *tatewarisei* principle in the belief that this replicated 'real family life' more closely—what one former *jidōshidōin* called a 'fake family'—than the *yokowarisei* system which they felt was closer to a school dormitory.[4] Indeed, this home was so keen to reconstruct what it felt was a 'real family' atmosphere that it put boys' rooms and girls' rooms on the same floor, something for which, according to one senior member of staff, it had been strongly criticized, especially by staff from homes with a religious foundation.

At Kodomo Gakuen in 1991, girls' rooms tended to be *tatewarisei* and the boy's rooms were *yokowarisei* while the youngest children were all kept together, as in most other homes. The six rooms were organized as in Table 17. Overall, therefore, the home, on its main site and in the two *group homes*, manifested all four major organizing principles—*taishasei* and *shōshasei* on the one hand, and *yokowarisei* and *tatewarisei* on the other hand—as can be seen in Table 18. When the home was rebuilt in the mid-1990s, however, the way that rooms were organized was changed completely so that the main campus came to resemble a series of large *group homes* (with twelve to thirteen children each), where children of

TABLE 17. The organization of rooms at Kodomo Gakuen (1991)

Name of room	Gender	Capacity	Ages
Hibari	boys and girls	8	2–5
Hato	boys	10	10–12, plus one 16–18
Taka	boys	10	5–9
Washi	boys	8	12–18
Komadori	girls	8	5–18
Kanariya	girls	12	5–18

TABLE 18. Organizing principles for accommodating children in care in the Seishin Gakusha (1991)

Organizing principle	*Taishasei* (large groups)	*Shōshasei* (small groups)
Tatewarisei (mixed ages)	Girls in Kodomo Gakuen Main Home	A Group Home
Yokowarisei (same ages)	Boys in Kodomo Gakuen Main Home	H Group Home

both sexes and all ages were housed in either single, double, or, in the case of small children, triple rooms, with their own assigned staff, kitchen, dining-room and bathroom.

Debate Over Group Formation

Debate about organizing principles often developed into intense discussions about the best way to run *yōgoshisetsu* and frequently polarized opinion within the *yōgoshisetsu* community. The Kyoto Conference of the heads of all the homes (Yōgoshisetsuchōkai) in 1991 had a session devoted entirely to discussion of *shōshasei* and *taishasei* systems. At this, critics of the *shōshasei* system, and in particular of the *group homes,* complained that such a system led to the splitting up of sibling groups and the development among those children who were placed in them of a sense of superiority (*yūetsukan*)—one critic used the expression *kizoku-ishiki* (literally, aristocratic feeling)—and that it was better for all children in the home to be treated the same. Supporters of the *shōshasei* system said that it helped children to make friends more quickly, allowed them to play more roles (*yakuwari*), and that the staff—especially if they were a married couple—treated the children more as if they were their own.

These comments reflected much deeper ideological, as well as simply financial, concerns. As mentioned above, the Shōshasei Yōiku Kenkyūkai has for twenty years argued the need for more *group homes* and for children to be cared for in smaller units. On the other hand, those who most strongly object to the idea of smaller homes in Japan have generally been associated with a group which goes under the name of Zenkoku Yōgo Mondai Kenkyūkai (National Study Group on Issues in Child Protection, known as Yōmonken for short). Yōmonken has its origins in the early 1960s as part of a left-wing movement in Japan at the time to introduce practices from the Soviet Union related to the ideology of the 'New Man', in particular the ideas of the Soviet educator, A. S. Makarenko. This movement was especially influential in educational circles, where it became known as the Seito Seikatsu Shidō Kenkyūkai (Student Life Guidance Research Group).[5] There it advocated the idea of getting classes to act as far as possible as collective and cohesive groups in contrast to what it felt at the time was a move towards more individually oriented, and hence potentially elitist, educational philosophies. Indeed, its main focus was on opposing all government interference in

Japanese educational circles, and the group has always been closely associated with Japan's left-wing teachers' unions. For many supporters, however, the big attraction of the Seito Seikatsu Shidō Kenkyūkai—and the reason for its continued existence into the 1990s—has not been so much its political line, but the philosophy it offers for controlling large groups. For this alone, it continues to sell large numbers of books to young and anxious teachers faced by classes of up to forty students.

In many ways, the ideas of Makarenko and his colleagues for organizing groups appeared more suitable to the context of certain social welfare facilities, such as *kyōgoin* and *shōnenin*, than to schools, since their origins lay in Makarenko's experiences of working in reform homes in the pre-war Soviet Union. Here Makarenko forced children to confront their own weaknesses—indeed to manifest faults and weaknesses which they had not yet demonstrated—and then to seek to rebuild themselves and find a sense of worth and identity in the wider group context. When Makarenko's ideas failed to make a major impact in Japanese schools in the 1960s, they were introduced by Yōmonken into the world of *yōgoshisetsu* (see Asakura and Nakamura, 1974: 3, 35; Seki, 1971). In the 1970s, particularly in urban areas such as Tokyo, Yōmonken and its activities enjoyed a period of considerable popularity with residential care workers who, like teachers, had to control large groups of children (Takenaka, 1988). While today its numbers have declined from earlier decades, it still continues to publish actively—in particular targeting those new to residential care work (see Asakura *et al.*, 1996)—and retains an influential core membership, including the head of the Yōgoshisetsu Kyōgikai in 1999.[6]

The argument in support of large groups that Yōmonken has always made—and which has much in common with the argument of its counterparts in the mainstream educational field—is that children flourish and gain confidence when socialized in a group context (*shūdan seikatsu*). Kosaka (1990: 197) explains how such a method, which he calls group dynamics (*shūdan rikigaku*), can be applied in a *yōgoshisetsu*:

A *yōgoshisetsu* is a place where children and staff experience daily life together and a group lifestyle is developed. Hence it can be thought of as a place where the strength of the group can be positively put to use . . . That is to say, through 'group dynamics', which result from the interaction among the children as a group, each child's individualism and abilities can be drawn out and allowed to grow. It is possible too that joy, hardship and sadness, arising within this group lifestyle, can be shared and a feeling of solidarity can be fostered in solving a range of problems. In short, it is a place where the quality of a child's lifestyle can be developed to a high level.

Some commentators (for example, see Aoki in Zadankai, 1991: 21) even suggest that not only Japanese but East Asians in general 'naturally' benefit from living in large groups and hence the smaller *group homes* developed in Europe and Australia and advocated by some within the social welfare world in Japan are not really appropriate to an East Asian context.[7] While few go to this extreme, most accept the appropriateness of group activities in *Yōgoshisetsu*.

Group Activities

Nakane Chie, perhaps the best known of all modern anthropologists of Japan, has characterized Japanese society as one where the group has always been considered more important than the individual and where the individual gains their sense of identity from the group (Nakane, 1970). Many authors have documented how groups are used in areas of Japanese socialization from elementary school (Hendry, 1986; Lewis, 1995) through to company training (Rohlen, 1996). In this context, the difference between those who support *taishasei* and those who support *shōshasei* is to a large extent only a difference of the degree to which the group should be the core of the home's activities. As Hagan (1994: 13) concludes from her survey of the views of the staff in one home about group activities: 'In a certain sense then, some of the staff although they disagree with group living see it as a necessary sacrifice in order to maintain control, an evidently high priority regarding the daily functioning of SJ Home.' Among all homes in Japan, therefore, there is an emphasis on group activities, though the degree to which this is stressed varies considerably.

In many private homes with a religious foundation, for example, all children will be expected to attend religious assemblies at certain times of the week and the year, regardless of their religious background. This indeed has been a matter of considerable debate especially when, as we shall see, Japan signed the UN Convention on the Rights of the Child in 1994, which specifically forbade the enforcement of religious practice. But the homes where religious activity is practised insist that participation in it is integral to being a member of the home's community and sharing in its group identity, and that this is more important than any religious element. Indeed, according to some supporters of the role of private homes in residential child welfare, it is their ability to create a strong institutional tradition and culture—which may often be religious in foundation—with which children can identify which distinguishes them from the always secular and sometimes rather soulless atmosphere of public homes.

The main common group experience of all children in *yōgoshisetsu* across Japan, though, centres on key events during the annual cycle of the home (see Jidō Yōgo Kenkyūkai, 1995: 179, 231–5). Few homes will diverge far from the list of events and activities outlined in Figure III. This basic list, however, can be enormously exceeded in the case of some homes which can invest a great deal of time and effort in group activities. At Kodomo Gakuen, at times, it could feel as if there was a special event happening almost every day, as the outline of events between mid-December and mid-January—a festival period, of course, throughout Japan—shows (see Figure IV).

April	Celebrations for the start of the new school year
May	Children's day
June	Firefly (*hotaru*) hunting
July/August	Fireworks; summer festival; summer camp; *o-bon*
September	*Higan* (autumn equinox)
October	Sports day
November	Cultural festival
December	Christmas party; end-of-year party
January	New Year celebrations
February	*Setsubun* (spring equinox)
March	Girls' festival; Graduation/leaving party

FIG. III Typical annual cycle of events at a *yōgoshisetsu*
Sources: Various homes; Jidō Yōgo Kenkyūkai, 1995: 179.

The list is interesting because while most Japanese children will do many of these traditional events, such as *kakizome* or *hatsumōde,* around New Year, few will participate in all of them every year as would tend to be the case with the children in the *yōgoshisetsu*. While a few events (such as visits to some adventure parks), are limited by age, in general all children of all ages participate in all events. While these events are, of course, supposed to be enjoyable in their own right, the role of the children in organizing as well as participating in them is constantly emphasized, so that they can be seen as strengthening the group bonds between children and between children and staff.

There can be little variation either in the daily routine of children, either within or between homes (Jidō Yōgo Kenkyūkai, 1995: 107). Few homes vary from the daily timetable shown in Figure V, which in many respects is not much different from that of any average school-age child in Japan, where schoolchildren have much less free time, do much more homework, and sleep fewer hours than their counterparts in the United States or western Europe. It does differ, however, in the group cleaning exercises around the *yōgoshisetsu*. Cleaning is something which all Japanese children will experience at school but which very few of those who live with their families, especially boys, will be expected to participate in at home. The biggest differences between the experiences of children in a home and other children, however, is at the pre-school stage and for school-age children at weekends and during school holidays. The majority of pre-school children in Japan spend these formative years with their mothers, most of whom still give up their jobs either on marriage, or, more commonly, on the birth of their first child in order to stay at home to look after them.[8]

The majority of school-age children in Japan, especially boys, are given considerable freedom by parents to do as they wish at weekends and during holidays, provided they have completed their school work. All children in *yōgoshisetsu*, however, are subject to the rules of the home. Homes have a legal responsibility

- Puppet show performance by employees of a Tokyo electric company
- Presentation of a video by the labour union of a department store
- Visit to Sanrio Puroland organized by the Old Boys' Association of the university student volunteers' association
- Visit and presentation from a visitor from Belize as well as several local dignitaries
- Magic show by a university magic group (*kijutsu dōkōkai*)
- Exchange of Christmas presents between pairs (children buy a present and then draw lots to discover with whom they exchange it)
- The end-of-year 'spring clean'
- New Year's evening visit to ring bells at the temple
- Communal *o-sechi ryōri* (the special New Year's meal which children have helped to prepare)
- Presentation of New Year money (*o-toshidama*) to each child by the *enchō-sensei*
- Performance of *kotoshi no ohayashi* (a dance to ward off illness during the coming year)
- *Kakizome* (the first calligraphy of the New Year)
- *Hatsumōde* (the first shrine or temple visit of the year)
- Visit to the home by former residents and their families
- Kite-flying and table tennis tournament
- *Shinnenshiki* (New Year party) and the reading of *Kotoshi no Mokuhyō* (New Year resolutions)
- A party with the current university student volunteers' association members
- Kodomo Gakuen *Ekiden* (marathon) relay race for all staff and residents
- *Seijinshiki* (coming-of-age ceremony) for all graduates and staff who have reached the age of 20 since the previous 15 January
- Party to enjoy the donation of *okashi* (sweets) by a company
- Whole staff meeting to discuss plans for the coming year

FIG. IV Events at Kodomo Gakuen between mid-December and mid-January 1990

to provide a minimum level of care for their children, which means they need to know where they are at all times. At almost all homes, residents of all ages need to get permission whenever they want to go out and to complete a form showing where and when they are going and to sign a book on their return. As a result, many of them are much less confident about going out on their own than are their school peers. As one *hobo* put it, for many of them the world outside the home is a 'foreign country' (Hagan, 1994).

06.30	Wake up, wash
07.15	Morning assembly; cleaning
07.40	Breakfast
08.20	Leave for school in groups
12.00	Lunch for those at home
16.00	Return from school
16.00 – 17.00	Free time
17.00	Cleaning
17.30	Dinner
18.30	Homework
19.30	Free time; bath
21.00 – 23.00	Lights out, depending on room

FIG. V Typical daily timetable in a *yōgoshisetsu*
Source: Various homes; Jidō Yōgo Kenkyūkai, 1995: 179.

THE DEVELOPMENT OF INDIVIDUALITY

Critics of the *taishasei* large-group system say that it requires more rules than the *shōshasei* one and that it creates a 'standardized society' (*kakuitsuna shakai*) where individual residents are relieved of having to make individual decisions because of the array of rules and regulations. Homes which have been moving away from the idea of large groups have been particularly keen to stress the idea of developing the individuality of children within their institutions and, in particular, the ability of individual children to negotiate with staff over how they organize their lives just as other children can discuss issues with their parents. The group, especially a large group, they argue, can not only stifle individuality but can be overly protective in the way in which it offers a place for the child to hide from its problems and avoid the need to develop its personal skills to deal with the world outside. As one teacher with long experience of children from homes commented, such children may be good at co-operative activities but they are weak when they have to act independently. Hence, they find it very hard to manage when they leave the security and protection of the home.

Group homes are perhaps the best example of offering children the space to develop the ability to make decisions for themselves. Kōseishō support for the idea that *group homes* should concentrate on older children suggests that it sees a pattern of early group socialization being followed by more individually oriented experiences. It is significant that the expression *group home* should be English, since in the eyes of some people it is still associated with a Western influence on the Japanese institutional welfare scene, the idea of the needs of individual children being put before those of the group.

There are other practices which have become widespread throughout *yōgoshisetsu* in recent years and which allow children to be given more personal space, even within *taishasei* systems, than previously. For example, most homes have systems of children's councils (*jichikai* or *jidōkai*) where children can discuss ways in which they wish to improve the level of care they receive, though the extent to which these operate successfully seems to vary greatly across institutions.[9] Also, whereas in the 1970s most homes held birthday parties just once a month for those children who had a birthday during that month, today most homes mark individually the birthday of each child.[10] Similarly, homes give children pocket money (around ¥3,000 each month for those in junior high school and ¥5,500 for those in senior high school in 1999) and allow them to spend it as they wish.

While all homes have club activities, both sporting and cultural, children are not obliged to participate, though the merits of doing so will be strongly emphasized and considerable efforts will be made to make them look attractive.[11] A senior worker in one home that placed particular emphasis on trying to develop personal space for its residents explained that a system of keeping very detailed records of the histories of all the children had been instituted which could be read by staff so that they could get to know them individually. But even he, in conclusion, suggested that the main aim in caring for children in *yōgoshisetsu* had to be to find the correct balance between group activity (*shūdan katsudō*) and individual guidance (*kobetsu shidō*).

THE DEVELOPMENT OF HIERARCHY

If the *shōshasei/taishasei* debate is about notions of 'groupism' in Japanese society, then the *yokowarisei/tatewarisei* debate is about another popular theme in the anthropology of Japan, namely that of hierarchy. The classic work on hierarchy in Japan is again Nakane Chie's *Japanese Society* (1970), which was originally published in Japanese under the title *Tateshakai no Ningen Kankei* (literally, Human Relations in a Vertical Society). Nakane suggests that all relationships in Japan, either between groups or between individuals, are essentially hierarchical. These concepts form part of a child's socialization from the time of birth, so that small children learn to distinguish linguistically between older and younger siblings as well as, as Hendry (1986) documents, the correct behaviour to show to them: benevolent care to younger siblings and respect to older ones.

In this context, therefore, the *tatewarisei* system of putting children of different ages together more closely resembles what most regard as a 'traditional' family environment. It also follows what is seen as a 'traditional' local community pattern since, as Hendry (1986) also shows, as children grow up and move out of the immediate family environment into the local community, so older children are given the responsibility of looking after the younger ones who are in turn expected to respect the authority of their elders. According to Nakane (1970), it is essential that these family-based relationships are properly socialized since they are later transposed to the extra-familial context in terms of *senpai–kōhai* (senior–junior) relationships in schools, colleges, and adult life which all carry the same basic role expectations of respect for seniors and benevolence for juniors. For this reason, supporters of the *tatewarisei* system argue that it gives children the necessary training for the outside world, allowing older children to manage responsibility and younger ones to learn to respect authority.

In homes, one often sees older children taking younger ones off to play, teaching them how to do things and consoling them when they have hurt themselves. Older children make sure that younger ones are being looked after before going about their own activities. Indeed, with the low level of staffing available, this kind of system is seen by some as essential for the smooth running of an institution. In many cases, older children are given considerable responsibility and, by extension, power over the younger residents. Some of them are used to this from before they came into the homes since, in many cases, elder siblings have often been substitute parents for younger ones. One former *yōgoshisetsu* resident who went on to train as a nursery nurse felt that her early experience of looking after her siblings and then younger children in the home gave her the experience and insight to take up such a career. One further advantage of the *tatewarisei* system in this context is that, to some extent, it removes children from directly competitive relations with peers, something which may be especially important in the case of shy, disturbed, or slow children who come into the home.

As we shall see later, however, while the relationship between older and younger children within homes can be beneficial to the children involved and often operates effectively and smoothly, it can also be highly problematic. Even in the wider society, *senpai–kōhai* relations can lead to the abuse of juniors by seniors. In the context of a *yōgoshisetsu*—given the fact that children are always together and staff are so few in number—the potential for problems is that much greater. According to some informants, this was a greater problem among boys than girls—indeed one informant suggested that women in general in Japanese society were much less concerned with hierarchical differences than men—and this would seem to be reflected in the organizational system that operated at Kodomo Gakuen in 1991 (Table 18). At one time, apparently, the boys in the home had also been organized in rooms on a *tatewarisei* basis, and at another home where a similar change had taken place in the 1970s, I was told that it was due to the older boys abusing their power and bullying the younger boys. The staff had been unable to stop the bullying in any other way than changing the boys' rooms to the *yokowarisei* principle, as those who had been victimized refused to say exactly what had happened to them.

RELATIONS WITH THE LOCAL COMMUNITY

Unlike Erving Goffman's description of a 'total institution' (Goffman, 1961), *yōgoshisetsu* do not operate in a social vacuum. Indeed, few things are as important to the way that they are run as the nature of the place where they are situated (what is known in Japanese as their *tochigara*) and their relationship with the local community. Not all local communities have welcomed the presence of *yōgoshisetsu* in their midst. Such negative attitudes seem to have been particularly prevalent in the Tokyo region and are used to explain why Tokyo has a large number of its public *yōgoshisetsu* situated outside the area, some as much as two hours or more away in Aichi Prefecture, Shizuoka Prefecture, and Tateyama City at the far end of the Bōsō peninsula in Chiba Prefecture.[12] Kodomo Gakuen, however, has managed to break down such barriers since the founding of the original institution on the same site as today almost ninety years ago, and it provides a good example of the type of community-based *yōgoshisetsu* that Kōseishō would like to see develop.

At the time of its founding, the area in which Kodomo Gakuen was situated was still in the countryside on the outskirts of Tokyo, cut off from the centre by poor communications. As industrialization proceeded, however, and people moved to Tokyo in search of work, so the city began to move west and railway lines were built that enabled those who lived there to travel to the city (see Allinson, 1979). These new suburbs quickly became important manufacturing districts and industrialization brought its normal share of social problems, including problems of juvenile delinquency which led to the establishment of the forerunner of Kodomo Gakuen.

During the war, the area near Kodomo Gakuen was an obvious target for enemy attack since it had military bases as well as industrial plants, though it was not as badly fire-bombed as downtown Tokyo. In the immediate post-war period, the SCAP administration situated one of its biggest bases of American troops in the immediate vicinity, which, though much reduced in size, remains there today. This brought its own set of social problems, perhaps most graphically displayed in Murakami Ryū's (1976) bleak account of life near a base in his best-selling novel, *Kagirinaku Tōmei ni Chikai Blue* (Almost Transparent Blue) which describes a world where the young American soldiers and Japanese locals mixed almost entirely on the basis of drug and sexual experimentation. While *Kagirinaku Tōmei ni Chikai Blue* was a book that, like all Murakami's novels, set out to shock the general Japanese public with a description of a part of their society which most could not even imagine might exist, it contained, according to some of those in the welfare world, more than a grain of truth.

In the early post-war days, many of the children in the newly formed Kodomo Gakuen were of mixed parentage, as indeed were many of the children in homes throughout Japan. More significantly in the long term, however, the immediate vicinity of the home remained a distinctly working-class area throughout the following decades, while Tokyo as a whole became increasingly and homogeneously middle-class. One sign of its working-class nature is the existence of a bicycle-racing track (*keirin*), a spectator sport which is frequented almost completely by men who come to gamble.[13] As we have seen, this means that the local authorities receive extra money for their welfare services. *Yōgoshisetsu* in the area do not benefit directly from this extra money since their financing comes from central and prefectural, not local, government. They benefit indirectly, however, from the fact that the local *jidōsōdanjo* is considerably better staffed than other areas in Tokyo, which is itself considerably better staffed than some other areas of Japan.

Kodomo Gakuen itself is situated directly on one of the main artery roads out of the centre of Tokyo—along which the marathon was run during the 1964 Olympics—which remains as busy as ever today despite the existence of new expressways. The home has a large signboard outside advertising the Seishin Gakusha Shakai Fukushi Hōjin, Kodomo Gakuen, and the old people's home next door. Immediately inside the entrance, one finds an unexpectedly large campus (some 4,788 square metres) which backs on to a small stream across which is a park and baseball ground. It is in the use of this space that Kodomo Gakuen's relationship with the local community is characterized.

The main means by which good relations have been achieved with the local community has been through granting access to its land. Land, as is well known, is at a premium in Japan, especially in large conurbations such as around Tokyo, where almost 25 per cent of the national population of 124 million lives in 5 per cent of the total land space. Park land *per se* is almost non-existent in Tokyo (which has one-tenth of the total parkland space of London), and although new suburbs and residential areas are relatively well provided for in terms of playgrounds (normally a square, sandy space with a climbing-frame and a slide), older residential areas, such as where Kodomo Gakuen is based, are almost completely bereft of such facilities. School playgrounds are often the sole exception, but these are not open to the local community—except normally as emergency evacuation centres in times of earthquake—although schoolchildren themselves will tend to use them at all times of the week and during vacations for their school club activities.[14]

As Table 14 shows, many of those *yōgoshisetsu* which have facilities are willing to share them with the local community. Kodomo Gakuen, however, not only provided a space for the local community, but also a series of activities for local children. It ran an after-school (*gakudō*) club three times a week for up to twenty children of elementary and junior high-school age whose parents were working and could not care for them when school finished.[15] The home also, like many *yōgoshisetsu* in Japan, ran its own *hoikuen* (day-care centre) for its own children of pre-school age. The *hoikuen*, which was set up in 1978, was run along Montessori lines that encouraged children to develop at their own pace. There has, as Hendry (1986) pointed out in the mid-1980s, been a long history of interest in

Montessori methods in Japan as a counterweight to what many parents feel is the excessive homogeneity of the rest of the education system. It was at the urging of members of the local community, therefore, that it was decided to allow local children as well as children from the home to attend the Montessori *hoikuen*, but, as with the *gakudō* club, it was impossible for anyone coming in from outside to tell with any confidence which children were from the home and which from the local community.[16] Each summer, the home ran a five-day programme for children from the local community that included activities that ranged from painting, fishing, canoeing, and barbecues to, in the year I was at the home, English conversation.

Similarly, it was, according to the head of the home, at the urging of the local community that Kodomo Gakuen was one of the first homes to experiment with what it called, using the English words, a *twilight stay* system which provided child care up to 10 p.m. for parents who had to work in the evenings. This programme provided a service in particular for single fathers in the local community who, as we have seen, were caught in the double bind of looking after their children or giving up their jobs unless they could show sufficient commitment to the latter for employers to keep them on. In 1994 the home was commissioned by the government to set up a trial twenty-four-hour, seven-days-a-week telephone counselling service for families or children in the neighbourhood. In 1997 this received over 400 calls a year, almost equally divided between parents, teachers, and children themselves about a variety of issues from child-raising and discipline to child abuse and school refusal.

If accepting local children in the *gakudō* club, the *hoikuen*, and implementing new programmes such as the *twilight stay* system and the telephone counselling service were presented as reactions to the demands of the local community, then other activities were more proactive. Chief among these was probably the part played by the home in a science club for any children in the neighbourhood who wanted to attend, and the local Scout activities. The Boy Scout movement has a long tradition in Japan, and Japanese participants have long been among the keenest at international jamborees. A Boy Scout troop based at Kodomo Gakuen was first established, chiefly for children in the home, in 1967, and in 1997 had some 150 members, representing all levels and age groups of the Scout movement. This was made up of some seventy-eight boys (over the age of 6), of whom twenty were from the home and the rest from the local community, and seventy-one adults, of whom six were staff from the home. The Girl Scout activities started in the home in 1986, and as of 1997 had forty members. These consisted of thirty-four girls over the age of 6, of whom twenty-one were from the home, and six adult leaders, of whom two were members of staff in the home.

Most of the children in the home had tried the Scouts at some time or other during their time there, and even if the children and staff in the home now constituted a minority of the members of the troop (though still a very significant minority considered in relation to the size of the local population), the home itself remained very much the centre of the troop. The troop had had its head-quarters, a beautifully constructed wooden building, in the grounds of the home (though sadly this had to be knocked down when the home was rebuilt in the mid-1990s). It used the back of the home, where it ran down to the stream, to store its equipment and to set up rope runways; it ran stalls at the home's various bazaars, made use of the mountain villa owned by the Gakuen no Okāsan, housed visiting Scouts from overseas, and was led by the home's senior care worker, who was the younger brother of its head and who became head of the home himself in 1992. As with the other activities in the home, it was impossible to tell which children came from the home and which from the local community while they performed their Scout activities, and the home was determined that financially there would be no discrimination between them either.[17]

COMMUNITY EVENTS

Several times a year the home became a focus for the local community in an even bigger way. This was at the various garden parties and bazaars that were run on a regular basis each year. At one level, these were important events for raising funds that both allowed the home to provide extras which could not be supplied through the normal budget and also to retain a measure of independence over its finances and programme. However, it was also stressed by the head that these events were held just as much to generate local community involvement in the activities of the home, and this they certainly did. Indeed, the annual events at the home were among the most important in the local community both in terms of the numbers and the status of those attending.

The first major event of the annual cycle—the Japanese annual cycle generally being seen to start with the cherry blossom in April when schools and universities start their academic years and companies receive their new intake of staff—was the garden party which took place in May. In essence, this was to raise ¥1 million in order to be able to take the children to the beach for four days during the summer, and indeed this amount was reached almost exactly to the yen. The event also brought together in one place and at one time all the major activities of the home and the local community. Stalls and activities were run by the parents of the children at the Montessori nursery, by the Boy and Girl Scout groups, by the science club, by the staff of the home itself, and by a variety of voluntary theatre and performance organizations from local schools and universities. All of these people—and a rough estimate would suggest that they totalled around 250—had given their time and energy voluntarily.

At the same time, the event brought together—quite literally since they were given special tickets and put together in a special fenced-off area—all those the home wished to acknowledge for their help and influence over the preceding year, including local politicians and the city mayor, donors to the home, the maker of a television documentary about the home, and the visiting anthropologist. These special guests were introduced to those present by the *enchō sensei* in a ceremony that opened the bazaar.

The mayor and other local politicians also turned up at the two other major events organized by the home which took place during the year. Their presence was interesting inasmuch as children's homes are prefectural and not city concerns, and receive no money from the local area in which they are based. Hence, local politicians have no direct influence over the home, either in terms of policy or finance. Yet it clearly did no harm to the mayor's political image within the community to be seen at the home, which was one of the best-known and longest-standing welfare institutions in the area. At the same time, it did no harm to the home to have the mayor attend its garden parties, since even if he had no influence over the *yōgoshisetsu*, he might still have considerable influence over the other welfare facilities within the Seishin Gakusha, all of which received money from the city office to support their activities.

Indeed, over the years, Kodomo Gakuen had a good record of attracting important people to its events, and its decennial histories were full of photographs of well-known figures attending such occasions. Most impressively, the home's founder had been able to draw on contacts in the Imperial Household Agency (Kunaichō), where he had previously worked, to arrange for the occasional visit by members of the Imperial Family.

A large crowd also came to the winter bazaar, which again managed to collect almost exactly ¥1 million, this time to buy Christmas presents for the children in the home. But the most impressive event was the meeting of the home's supporters' club (*kōenkai*) to celebrate the fortieth anniversary of Kodomo Gakuen's official foundation. For once this event did not take place in the home itself but in a building hired from the City Hall, and it was an elaborately planned three-and-a-half-hour combination of speeches, reminiscences, performance, and tears which is worth describing in some detail since it provides a good indication of the position of the home within the local community.

The event took place on the Sunday in November nearest the actual date of foundation. The occasion was formal, adults wearing suits, children their best clothes. All the staff were present, even those with a day off. In the lobby, all the guests were asked to sign themselves in a book with a traditional writing-brush dipped in ink. They then presented celebration envelopes (with money inside and their names on the outside) which were discreetly accepted and placed behind the desk, before they were greeted by the *enchō sensei* and the head of the *kōenkai* as they made their way into the Hall. Here everyone found the latest edition of the *Gakuen Diary* (a newsletter put out four times a year about activities in the home), a programme of the concert, and a list of all those who had helped with the arrangements, both individuals and organizations.

The first thirty minutes or so of the meeting was spent on formal introductions and speeches from the stage, on which sat some fifteen individuals in a line. On the right of the dais were three people: the head of the Seishin Gakusha, the head of the *kōenkai*, and the head of Kodomo Gakuen. The head of the Seishin Gakusha spoke first, expressing his hope that the organization would go on for many years and thanking everyone for their support. To symbolize this, a certificate of thanks (*kanshajō*) was given to the representatives of the long-term volunteer organizations within the home, and to a representative of those who had helped organize this special event. The fifteen important guests were introduced in order across the stage, and each proceeded to make a short speech: the local member of the Diet (Shūgiin) said that the area was blessed in having the Seishin Gakusha; the mayor gave thanks to the Seishin Gakusha and Kodomo Gakuen for all its hard work; the head of the Tokyo municipal welfare office thanked Kodomo Gakuen for allowing his office to send so many people who were interested in studying social welfare there over the years; the head of the Tokyo Municipal Social Welfare Association (Tokyo-to Kyōgikaichō), who was also the head of another *yōgoshisetsu* in Tokyo, commented on the excellence of Kodomo Gakuen—'the best home in Tokyo and maybe in Japan'—and sent the congratulations of all the other children's homes in the country. A series of letters of congratulation were read out: from the Yōgoshisetsu Kyōgikai; from the *sotsuenkai* (the association of those who had been residents of the home); from the university student volunteers' association; and from Gakuen no Okāsan (the widow of the founder).

The main entertainment was a lively performance of Latin American music which, after the break, was accompanied by dancing by some of the children from the home together with some of the staff who had clearly been rehearsing together. The climax of the whole event though was a very emotional speech by the *enchō sensei*, who talked to the sound of gentle piano music about his feelings on the home reaching its fortieth anniversary and how much it and the children all meant to him. He told us at the beginning he was going to cry and indeed he was soon on the verge of it; his mother who sat alongside him in a wheelchair was in floods of tears; and it was clear that many of the audience were only just holding back their own emotions too. While this concluded the event on a rather serious note, it was by no means an unusual atmosphere to be created at the end of an important celebration in Japan. Every year, as students graduate from schools and move on to the next stage of their lives, they and their teachers and their parents are reduced to tears by this combination of nostalgic feeling for the past and the sense of the importance of the moment backed up by the accompaniment of piano and other music. The resultant atmosphere, which Victor Turner (1969) has famously called 'communitas', simultaneously highlights the significance of the event and creates a sense of inclusiveness among those who participate in it. In the case of those who live and work in the home, the emotion engendered makes them feel not only that they are part of the home's own strong and unique sense of self-identity but also that the home plays an important role at the centre of the local community.

The meeting of the *kōenkai* was just one example of a conscious policy at Kodomo Gakuen to make the children and staff proud of the *yōgoshisetsu* and not feel that they needed to hide its existence and their presence from the rest of society. As mentioned, the home displayed its presence clearly on its signboard at its gate. The name of the home was emblazoned on the minibus that drove children to major events, where they often wore sweatshirts similarly decorated. The *enchō sensei* often said that he wanted to move away from the old, dark image of orphanages which were isolated from the local society and create an atmosphere where the children—who, he would reiterate, were not in the home through any fault of their own—could feel proud of where they lived. Only if children could develop such a sense of their own worth would they be able to live confidently in the local community, and only if they could live confidently in the local community could they manage in the wider society.[18] The question that needs to be explored, therefore, is how the residents of Kodomo Gakuen fared in the wider community as a result of their experiences in the home.

6

The Effectiveness of *Yōgoshisetsu* as a Form of Child Protection

THE MATERIAL, EMOTIONAL, AND PHYSICAL WELL-BEING OF THE CHILD

There is, of course, more than one way to measure the effectiveness of the care offered in *yōgoshisetsu*. One of the easiest is probably in terms of material needs.

Children in homes tend to be well dressed and well groomed. Even the smallest children have their own clothes which are cleaned and ironed for them. Indeed, care staff often feel that looking after the children's clothes is a full-time job in itself. In most homes there is an abundance of toys for children to play with. Some of these are old toys that have been donated to the home, but many are new, either donated by local companies or bought by visitors or supporters of the home. The fact that children can share toys and have more space to store them probably means that overall they have access to more toys to play with—even if not always the most up-to-date and not always their own—than children who live with their families, where space limitations often means that old toys must be thrown out to make way for new ones. Some care staff at Kodomo Gakuen thought that when outside children came to play at the home they were probably sometimes actually a little jealous of everything that the children in the home had: an abundance of toys; a large space to play in; a wide array of friends always on hand; and a variety of care figures, some of whom were more like big brothers and sisters than parents.

Physical and emotional needs are rather more difficult to measure than material ones. In terms of emotional needs, there is little research on children's own perceptions of their experience of care. Hayashi (1998) asked 448 children (aged 12 or over) living in homes how they felt about their current situation (*genzai no shisetsu seikatsu ni tsuite no omoi*): 4.2 per cent replied they wanted to go to another home; 15.8 per cent that they 'had no choice' (*shikata ga nai*), 33.5 per cent that they wanted to return home, and 40.4 per cent that they were happy to carry on as they were (*ima no mama tanoshiku seikatsu shitai*). These responses, however, are difficult to analyse. There is little contact between children in different *yōgoshisetsu*, so most would have no sense of what it would be like to move to another home. Many children have lost contact with their families and been in homes for such a long time, in many cases as long as they can remember, that it is probably difficult for them to imagine life anywhere else. Other children, as we saw in some of the case studies in Chapter 3, have been waiting for years in the hope of returning to their families at some point.

A more helpful source for the range of perceptions of the experience of children in care may be supplied by the account of the meetings (known as *kōryūkai*) of older children from various homes where they are given free rein to compare and discuss their feelings about being in care. Indeed, the national *kōryūkai* which were started in the early 1990s had been stopped by the end of the decade because of the belief among some homes that they had a bad effect on some of those who attended, who came away with only negative views of their experience. In many areas, however, local *kōryūkai* have continued, and the report that came out of the 1998 meeting in Tokyo (published as *Kodomo ga kataru shisetsu no kurashi* (Children Talk About Life in Residential Care) gives a good indication of the range of feelings (both positive and negative) of older children in homes. Chief among the negative views expressed are complaints about certain members of staff, the lack of choice about the residential institution to which they have been sent,[1] the lack of privacy, the low level of pocket money, and, an issue to which we will shortly turn, stigmatization at school and in the wider community.

Many outside visitors to homes, especially foreign visitors, seem to come away with the sense that, if the material needs of children are being met, the emotional demands are not. 'If you go to Aijien, many [children] just want to sit on your knee and be hugged. That is all they ask for', commented one foreign visitor to a home in Ibaraki prefecture (Ford and Takagi, 1998: 35). Many of those who work in *yōgoshisetsu* also comment on the children's demands for affection. As the head of one home in Tokyo put it: 'The children have everything materially that they need, but the facilities are no substitute for the most important thing: love' (Jordan, *International Herald Tribune*, 29 June 1999). Visitors and staff alike describe the children as extremely *hitonatsukkoi* (amiable even with those they don't know). This they put down to a search for what is called *skinship*, a Japanese coinage of recent invention (Hendry, 1986: 98) that signifies the search for physical contact. They have been denied *skinship* by their own families, and the very low number of staff in homes means that they are also denied it there. As far as I know, there have been no studies of how this lack of attention has affected the lives of those who have passed through the care system.[2]

In terms of physical needs, the situation in *yōgoshisetsu* is also quite complex. On the one hand, the weight and height of all children in *yōgoshisetsu* is constantly monitored and the results of these tests compared with those of the general population. During the first few decades of the post-war period, it would appear that the physical development of children in homes lagged behind the national average. In some ways, this was hardly surprising since children came from less well off families. Some had been born small due to foetal alcohol syndrome; others had been undernourished as infants. Gradually these differences began to disappear, largely through the carefully balanced diets that the nutritionists who worked in homes ensured that the children ate. Indeed, one teacher from the elementary school attended by the children from Kodomo Gakuen commented that they were among the few children she could be confident would come to school each morning with a good breakfast inside them.

For children who have come from problematic, even violent, households, there is little doubt that *yōgoshisetsu* generally provide a measure of stability and safety which they had not previously been able to enjoy. Even the most conscientiously run child welfare institution, however, can never be a completely safe environment, and over the years there have been a number of cases of abuse—by staff on children and by children on children—which demonstrate some of the weaknesses of the management, organization, and monitoring of Japan's system of child protection. Reports of such abuses are fairly few and far between, but the following case studies over a period of some seventeen years (1982–99) have reached the public domain and provide an illustration of some of these problems and the potential for abuse in homes.

1. In 1982 a 6-year-old girl died in a public *yōgoshisetsu* when she hit her head while being bullied by older children at night. At the time, there were only two members of staff on duty, neither with specialist qualifications in welfare work, in charge of some forty children. The girl had only been in the home for five months. Her mother brought a court action against Okayama City Council and the head of the home, citing primarily the latter's failure to act quickly enough when he discovered the girl's injury—he tried first to contact the mother instead of taking the decision himself to get the girl to hospital—and secondly the lack of professionalism among the staff that had prevented them from recognizing what was happening to the child. The judge rejected the application, ruling that the incident was just an accident (*gūhatsuteki jiko*) which the staff could not have stopped and for which, therefore, they should not be held responsible.[3]

2. In Japan's largest, and one of its best known, private *yōgoshisetsu*, based in Osaka, a 7-year-old girl was beaten to death in 1986. It seems that a 15-year-old boy had ordered his juniors to kick and punch her, during which she fell, hit her head against a wardrobe, and died before she got to hospital. According to newspaper reports at the time (*YS*, 18 and 23 Apr. 1986; *AS*, 19 Apr. 1986 and 19 July 1987; *MS*, 19 Apr. 1986), the home fostered the development of strong *senpai–kōhai* relationships and encouraged a culture of control of the younger children by the older ones. Crucially, the whole staff body was in a meeting at the time of the incident. An internal Osaka City Council inquiry, however, concluded that the death was due to the psychiatric illness of the individual boy who had ordered the bullying and that there was no need to re-examine the running of the home or for the matter to be taken further.

3. In 1987 four members of staff beat to death a 13-year-old boy who kept running away from a public *kyōgoin* in Kagoshima in which he had been placed. The boy had come into the institution a few months earlier after stealing money. He constantly ran away, and each time he was caught and brought back he was forced to do *seiza* (sit upright on his knees) and was hit with *shinai* (bamboo staves used

in *kendō*). The boy and the staff appear to have become inured to this system so that each time he was brought back the beating became more severe. On the final occasion, he was tied up before being beaten, and was hit so hard that he died. The administration at first tried to disguise the affair as an accident, but it was reported to the local authorities by a doctor, and when the press broke the story the real events finally emerged. Seven members of staff were tried and found guilty, but the case was dealt with as the moral (ir)responsibility of the individual members of staff involved, and was not seen as symptomatic of wider problems in the child-care system: Kōseishō said that the case was a prefectural issue; the prefecture that it was an institutional issue; the institution that it concerned only those members of staff involved (for a full account see Hanashima, 1994: 231–2). According to Hanashima (1994: 232), 90 per cent of the staff in the home had less than three years' experience of child welfare work, and three of the seven staff members arrested were new recruits aged 23 or 24.

4. According to a report in the *Nara Shinbun* of 19 July 1991, two members of staff at a public *kyōgoin* (one a veteran of twenty years, one with only three years' experience) had been dismissed for having sexual relations with two girls, one of whom (aged 16) was from the home and the other of whom (aged 15) had previously been at the home. An internal inquiry by the prefectural authorities concluded that this issue was purely a problem of the individual morality of the people concerned, and did not concern the running or organization of the institution.

5. In May 1995 a disclosure was made to the police by a group of residents about physical abuse that had been committed by the deputy head (*jichō*) and a *jidōshidōiin* in a private *yōgoshisetsu* in Fukuoka. It included striking one girl in the face and hitting another with the plastic top of a rubbish bin, squeezing a boy around the neck, hitting another with a bat, and pressing a lit cigarette on a third who had been caught shoplifting (*Nishi Nihon Shinbun*, 31 May and 1, 2, 3 June 1995; Hirayū, 1997: 29). Although the Fukuoka City Council authorities criticized the *yōgoshisetsu* for its actions, they decided that the case was best dealt with by the Board of Governors (*rijikai*) of the home itself, which decided that the deputy head of the home should be demoted by one rank, that the other member of staff implicated in the abuse should be required to write a letter of explanation and apology (*shimatsusho*), and that extra training should be carried out in the home. As a result of the publicity around the incident, a note was sent by the association of *yōgoshisetsu* (Yōgoshisetsu Kyōgikai) to the heads of all homes reminding them that physical punishment, 'even if for the sake of the children', was not permitted in *yōgoshisetsu*, and that heads must show leadership in running their homes, an implicit criticism that the head of the home should have been aware of what was happening in his own institution. One further side-effect of the incident was the cancellation of the following year's national *kōryūkai* meeting for children of senior high-school age, in part, it was said, because one of the girls who had made the disclosure of abuse to the police had been negatively affected by the

experience of attending the 1994 meeting. While, through attending the meeting, she had been made aware of the unacceptability of the treatment at the home, she had also subsequently begun to dye her hair red, wear illegal school uniform, and to be persistently late for school, which some took to be an example of her misunderstanding the concept of individual rights that was discussed at the *kōryūkai* meeting.

6. In 1996 children from a private home in Chiba Prefecture wrote to the prefectural governor to say that they had been abused physically and emotionally by the head of the home for several years, and given punishments that included being suspended from a tree, being made to sit in an upright kneeling position (*seiza*) for twenty-four hours without eating or using the toilet (and hence having to urinate in their clothes in front of other children), and being forced to hold a burning tissue (Hirayū, 1997: 30–9; Tsuzaki, 1998: 98–9). When no action was taken, the children ran away to the local *jidōsōdanjo* which had placed them in the home, but they were not allowed to stay there and were advised to return to the *yōgoshisetsu*. According to Tsuzaki (1998: 99) the prefectural authorities expected the head of the home to resign, but he did not since he hoped to pass on his position to his son as his father had done to him. Although they technically had the legal power to intervene, the prefectural authorities decided that they would take no further action, though the case was subsequently taken up by a group of lawyers concerned with children's rights (Hirayū, 1997).

7. In 1996 a female member of staff reported to the head of a private home that a 12-year-old girl in the home had disclosed to her that a *jidōshidōiin* had been sexually abusing her for more than a year. It took several months before the head began an inquiry into the matter, which substantiated the allegation. The member of staff resigned voluntarily with full redundancy pay, but soon afterwards obtained another job in another welfare institution. The head took a voluntary reduction in his salary for two months, which is a common form of apology by senior figures in Japan. No criminal proceedings were enacted. According to Tsuzaki (1998: 99–100), when the allegations were passed on to Kōseishō it left discretion on how to deal with the case to the city authorities, which accepted the above solution in consultation with the home so as to avoid unnecessary publicity.

8. In 1999 the head of a home in Kamakura was dismissed by her *rijikai* following an independent inquiry by an organization called Kanagawa Kodomo Jinken Shinsa Iinkai, headed by a professor from the Japan College of Social Work, into allegations of abuse committed by the home's deputy head, who was her son. He resigned his position in the face of a spate of accusations from former and present staff and residents (*AS*, 30 Aug. 1999; *Kanagawa Shinbun*, 29 Aug. and 3 Sept. 1999; Baba, 1999).

The issues behind the above, distressing, cases, are of course complex and not necessarily in all cases directly comparable. But there are a number of common features which are worth exploring further. Many of these have been picked out by Tsuzaki Tetsuo (1991, 1997, 1998), a former residential social worker and currently head of the Department of Social Welfare at Bukkyō University in Kyoto, who has been an outspoken commentator on the potential for institutional abuse in Japan.

Tsuzaki lists a variety of reasons for abuse by staff in homes. Staff are often under-trained and almost always overworked. At night especially, staffing levels are very low, with up to eighteen children to each member of staff in some homes, and hence it is impossible for staff to keep control of the activities of all the children in their care. It is not surprising therefore, as we have seen earlier, that in many *yōgoshisetsu* older children are mandated to look after younger ones, which, as can be seen in some of the examples above, can occasionally have tragic consequences. Some of those, particularly the senior staff, who work in public homes (especially in *kyōgoin*) did not even choose such work but were posted there as part of the job rotation system of local government administration.

Tsuzaki is critical not only of what he sees as bad leadership but also of what he believes is occasionally a total lack of any leadership at all. This he puts down in part to the fact that many heads of *yōgoshisetsu* are absent from the homes for long periods due to other commitments: sitting on committees, teaching at universities, or setting up other welfare institutions as part of a *shakai fukushi hōjin*.

Another issue which also needs to be addressed in this context relates to the autonomy of the private *yōgoshisetsu*. As we saw earlier, the relation between them and the public authorities is a delicate one: on the one hand they receive public funding and are subject to public scrutiny; on the other, they provide a service for the state by looking after children for whom there is no other appropriate form of care. The *de facto* situation is that the private homes are very much left to regulate and run themselves. The workers in the *jidōsōdanjo* who place children in *yōgoshisetsu* are unlikely to visit them more than once a year, and sometimes not even that often. The homes of course, are subject to inspections (*kansa*), but these are carried out by officials who have no special training in child welfare issues, who have to submit their reports to the Board of Directors of the home which often includes many well-known welfare specialists. At the reporting meeting between officials and the *rijikai* of the Seishin Gakusha which I attended in 1991, the former seemed considerably more nervous than the latter. It is perhaps not surprising, therefore, that while the auditing officials do interview a cross-section of residents, staff, and management in the institutions that they visit, they tend to feel more comfortable focusing on financial rather than care issues.

Even when examples of abuse or possible abuse are reported to the authorities, they are, as we have seen, very loath to act, and in particular to interfere with the authority of the heads of private *yōgoshisetsu*. Since 1995 children in *yōgoshisetsu* in Osaka have been given a leaflet on children's rights (*kenri note*) and the telephone number of a helpline organization (Kodomo no Koe, literally meaning 'children's voice'), but no system has been set up to deal with complaints that come through this process. In one case—indeed by 1998 the only case that most staff knew of—a child rang up to allege physical abuse by a member of staff. The director of Kodomo no Koe contacted a senior official at the local *jidōsōdanjo*, who contacted the head of the home who then spoke to the named member of staff who admitted the allegation. The head then went to the *jidōsōdanjo* to apologize for the actions of his staff member and the case was considered dealt with.

It is very hard to know exactly the extent to which abuse takes place or even is reported in *yōgoshisetsu*, since the first reaction of the authorities in many cases seems to be to stop the news leaking out.[4] The above cases are put together from a variety of sources and are relatively well known among child welfare specialists.[5] Other cases tend only to be reported very locally. It is noticeable, however, that more cases have come to light since the mid-1990s. This has largely been under pressure from local citizens' groups (*shimin dantai*) which have recently become active in many parts of Japan, mainly as a check on abuses of local government funds.[6]

Perhaps most important for future investigations in institutions, however, is the precedent set by the establishment in 1999 of an independent inquiry into allegations of abuse in the homes in Kamakura described in the last example above. No independent inquiries or commissions have ever been set up to report on the implications of—and what lessons could be learnt from—each particular incident for the child-care system as a whole, even though the idea of setting up such commissions is familiar, since British and American reports on children in care are often read as part of university social welfare courses in Japan.[7] Instead, each case has been put down to the problematic behaviour of an individual member or small group of staff.

While there have been no attempts by welfare authorities and homes themselves to examine the extent of the use of physical punishment in homes, the reaction in the newspapers to most of the cases above is that it is a common practice. A report by Hayashi (1998: 23) on a survey responded to by 448 children aged 10 and above (a response rate of 88.5 per cent) from ten *yōgoshisetsu*, one *kyōgoin*, and one short-term facility for the handicapped in Osaka seems to confirm this. Ninety-eight (21.9 per cent) of the respondents said that they had often received physical punishment from a member of staff (*shokuin kara taibatsu wo uketa keiken no umu*); 191 (42.6 per cent) that they had occasionally received physical punishment, and only 153 (34.2 per cent) that they had generally not received it (*hotondo nai*). (Six children did not respond.)

As we will see in Chapter 8, the definition of *taibatsu* (physical punishment) is quite complex. In this context, however, the plea that *taibatsu* should not be used even for the good of the children (see case 5 above) is particularly significant since there has long been a sense among some staff in *yōgoshisetsu* that an element of physical punishment may be needed to help the children prepare for the outside world. One former care worker who had worked in *yōgoshisetsu* in the 1970s remembered being told by the head of the home that staff occasionally needed to show children in care, by force if necessary, the correct way to behave since when they went out into the world they would be on their own and would need to behave better and make fewer mistakes than others in society in order to survive.

THE EDUCATIONAL NEEDS OF THE CHILD

Education is perceived to be the main means by which social status is acquired in modern Japanese society. Success is not seen as being related to social, ethnic, or class background, but purely as the result of effort and perseverance. The best-known exemplar of this ethic is the figure of Ninomiya Sontoku, whose statue is still found outside some elementary schools in Japan and in the pre-war period was found outside all of them. Ninomiya's statue portrays a man walking along carrying firewood on his back and reading a book, and symbolizes the rise to political and social eminence in the Tokugawa period of a man born into such dire poverty that he had to study by the light of the moon while collecting fire-wood in order to earn money to pay his uncle who looked after him. There could be few better role models for children in *yōgoshisetsu*, the vast majority of whom come from the poorest families within society.

Yet this educational meritocratic ideology is seriously belied by the lack of 'success' of children in *yōgoshisetsu*. There are many ways in which one can measure educational 'success' in Japan, but the two key ones are the length of time children stay in the education system and the particular institution, within the strict hierarchy that exists at each level after compulsory education, that they finish in. On both measures, the situation of children from *yōgoshisetsu* stands in very stark contrast to that of the general population of children in Japan.

School Achievement and Continuation Rates

Since the early 1970s, the vast majority of children in Japan have continued in the education system for a further three years beyond the compulsory age of 15. Indeed, this figure has come to be so close to universal that many consider 'compulsory education' to be, in effect, up to the age of 18.[8] As Table 19 shows, the education of children in *yōgoshisetsu* has lagged a long way behind the national average. In 1961, proportionally ten times as many children in the general population stayed on for senior high school as did those in *yōgoshisetsu*; by the late 1960s, the ratio was still 3.5:1. Since the early 1970s, by which time almost all children in Japan were attending senior high school, the proportion of those in children's homes has incrementally increased year by year and the gap has narrowed. Even in the mid-1990s, however, only around 60 per cent of all eligible children in *yōgoshisetsu* entered senior high school.[9] Further, a far higher proportion of children from *yōgoshisetsu* dropped out of senior high school before completion than the national average of around 2 per cent. According to a 1989 survey of the 1,337 children in Tokyo who entered public high schools during the five-year period between 1984 and 1989, 198 (14.8 per cent) dropped out for a variety of reasons, including 'behavioural problems' (60), poor academic records (32), and inability to adjust to school (29) (Takahashi, 1998*b*: 46). The significance accorded these figures in the eyes of most commentators is summed up well by Okano and Tsuchiya (1999: 90) when they write:

Many studies on poverty and schooling conclude that one of the most effective solutions for inhibiting the reproduction of *seikatsuhogo* families [families on welfare] and poverty from one generation to the next is the completion of high schooling . . . high schools with 'appropriate' orientations are considered as means of preventing these young people from taking up insecure jobs and unemployment, early marriage and birth. In short, high schools are expected to keep these young people occupied until they become more mature.

According to Okano and Tsuchiya (1999: 85), continuation rates to high school for children from *yōgoshisetsu* are lower even than those for single-parent families (85.5 per cent) and for families on welfare support (78.5 per cent).

Equally significant for those children from *yōgoshisetsu* who do continue to senior high school is the type of school they attend. Until the late 1970s, more continued on to training schools than to academic high schools, and in 1990 six times as many went to such institutions than in the general population. These

TABLE 19. Comparative proportions of children from *yōgoshisetsu* and in the general population continuing into the non-compulsory education system or to employment (1961–93) (%)

Year		Regular school	Non-regular (training) school	Total	Work (part-time school)
1961	Children in homes	5.8	4.5	10.3	89.7
	National average	59.3	3.0	62.3	37.7
1969	Children in homes	9.4	13.9	23.3	76.7
	National average	75.9	3.5	79.4	20.6
1974	Children in homes	19.5	21.8	41.3	58.7
	National average	88.3	2.5	90.8	9.2
1980	Children in homes	31.5	16.6	48.1	51.9
	National average	92.1	2.1	94.2	5.8
1984	Children in homes	35.4	16.6	52.0	48.0
	National average	92.9	1.0	93.9	6.1
1990	Children in homes	49.5	13.0	62.5	37.5
	National average	95.0	1.0	96.0	4.0
1993	Children in homes	54.0	6.6	60.6	39.4
	National average	95.0	1.0	96.0	4.0

Sources: Fukushima, 1986: 182; *KH*, 1992, 154–7; *KK*, no. 50, 1996: 198; Nichibenren, 1995: 299; Zenshakyō, 1991: 416.
Note: about 2,500 children in *yōgoshisetsu* complete compulsory education each year and must decide whether to continue in education or seek work.

schools are the lowest rung of the education system at this level and, effectively, might be considered work-related apprenticeships. Further, a 1991 survey (*KK*, no. 45, 1991: 365) showed that very nearly half of all those attending regular senior high schools were in fact attending vocational senior high schools compared to less than 30 per cent in the general population. While at least one-third of the curriculum in vocational schools is given over to general education, they have much lower status than the academic senior high schools (Dore and Sako, 1989).

The educational situation of children from *yōgoshisetsu* has been clear for a very long time. The problem first really impinged on the public consciousness, however, with the publication in 1983 of Ogawa *et al.*, *Bokutachi no jūgosai* (Us at Fifteen), which pointed out that only a third of children in *yōgoshisetsu* were continuing on to regular senior high school, against a national figure that was already approaching 95 per cent. The manner in which this educational failure has been explained since provides interesting insights into Japanese ideas about education and socialization.

It is interesting, for example, that the comparatively low proportion of children in *yōgoshisetsu* who continue into the non-compulsory education system should be perceived as a problem at all. Research on children in institutions in Europe, for example, has until recently hardly touched on the issue of educational success (or failure).[10] In Japan, though, the education of all children has been considered since the Meiji period to be of public and not just personal significance. Moreover, as we have seen, educational success in Japan is premised on the public ideology that the system is essentially meritocratic and that everyone has the same potential to succeed if they invest enough personal effort. In such an educational ideology—which many have suggested has been responsible for bringing about the extremely high average levels of education in Japan in the post-war period—there is enormous resistance to explaining educational differences in terms of genetic inheritance, even though most teachers in Japan to a large extent base their practice on implicit assumptions of 'natural ability'.[11]

Those who work with children from *yōgoshisetsu*—both in the homes and in the schools—share the general reluctance to relate educational success to genetic factors despite what might appear to be contrary evidence. A recent survey suggests that 5 per cent of children from *yōgoshisetsu* attend schools for those with a handicap (*yōgogakkō*) and 2 per cent of those who attend mainstream schools are placed in classes for slow students (*tokushu gakkyū*), a combined total that is roughly seven times higher than in the general population (*YnJ*, 2000). Instead, the relative lack of educational success among children in the homes is ascribed to a variety of social or environmental factors (see e.g. Okano and Tsuchiya, 1999: 88–90; Sakamoto, 1993b) of which the most common is probably that the parents—especially the mothers—of children in *yōgoshisetsu* have not given them the stimulus to do well in the educational system.[12] As the head of one home put it, such parents are very *laissez-faire* (*hōnin*) about their children's education.[13]

Others explain the comparative lack of educational success among children in *yōgoshisetsu* in terms of the poor health (physical and mental) of their parents. Poor school records are blamed, in several cases, on foetal alcohol syndrome and, as we have seen, there is some evidence to suggest that a high proportion of the parents of children in care are suffering from various forms of mental illness and/or retardation.

Most agree, however, that the environmental issues involved in the education of children in *yōgoshisetsu* extend beyond just their parenting. Many point out that the children have long been discriminated against by the formal educational system in Japan. For many years in the post-war period it was simply economically impossible for children from homes to go to senior high school, since there was no public money available to fund them to attend what was technically a non-compulsory institution. Only in 1973 was a special budget (*tokubetsu ikuseihi*) made available to pay for the school expenses of children at *yōgoshisetsu* at public senior high schools which explains the sudden doubling shown in Table 19 of the number of children from homes at such institutions between 1969 and 1974.[14]

There were still no public funds available, however, for children from *yōgoshisetsu* to attend private senior high schools. Private senior high schools have played an important role in the expansion of non-compulsory education in post-war Japan and, from the early 1970s, have been attended by over 30 per cent of senior high-school students. Apart from a few exceptions, mainly in major metropolises such as Tokyo and Kyoto, private senior high schools have generally had lower status (and entry requirements) than public ones. They have largely been a means to enable those who would otherwise have had to drop out of the education system to remain within it, even if at a price (see James and Benjamin, 1988). It was not until 1988 that the government agreed to provide money for children from *yōgoshisetsu* to attend private senior high schools, and since then roughly the same proportion of children from homes attend private schools as from the general population.

Even then, serious inequalities remained in the education provided for children from *yōgoshisetsu*. In Japan, as is well known, there runs alongside the formal education system a widespread informal system built around cram schools known as *juku*. From the age of around 10 onwards, almost all boys in urban areas and a very high proportion of girls will attend a *juku* at least once a week, and the proportion and duration of attendance increase the longer children stay in the education system. The education received in *juku* provides an important complement to that given in the mainstream schooling system. It is not designed (as cram schools often are in Western countries) specifically for slower students, but to ensure that all students can keep up with, and if possible get a little ahead of, a mainstream syllabus that has become fuller and fuller as the mainstream education system has become more and more competitive. Attendance at *juku* has become virtually mandatory for children who want to do well in the Japanese school examination system and thereby get into one of the better (generally public and hence cheaper) high schools and universities. It has until recently, however, been impossible for Kōseishō financially to support children from *yōgoshisetsu* at *juku* for the simple reason that the government as a whole, and in particular the Ministry of Education, has refused officially to recognize the existence of this informal sector.

Few *yōgoshisetsu* have been able to support from their own funds the often very high cost of sending children to *juku*. Instead, children from homes have had to rely on help from the staff and on volunteer teachers from outside. Unlike many of the teachers in *juku*, these helpers are not qualified, though they have sometimes been successful in the support they have been able to offer and, as we have seen, the volunteer teachers also provide one of the important links between children in the home and the outside world. Indeed, when in 1997 Kōseishō introduced a minimal scheme which paid up to ¥8,300 a month for children in homes in their third (and final) year at junior high school to attend *juku*, according to the head of one *yōgoshisetsu* only two of the children in his home took up the offer. The others, particularly the boys, preferred to continue to receive the individual tuition (*kobetsu shidō*) provided by the female students of a nearby university.

The final institutional educational barrier relates to tertiary education. In Japan, over one-third of the age cohort has gone on to some form of tertiary education since the middle of the 1970s, and nearly 40 per cent by the mid-1990s. The desire to go to university among children in *yōgoshisetsu* would not appear to be far out of line with that of children in the general population. A 1989 survey of 6,401 children from homes between the ages of 15 and 18 suggested that only 52 per cent definitely did not want to go to university (*KH*, 1991: 108). In reality, however, very few indeed are able to attend tertiary education, and those that do have to rely on special funding arrangements made either by their prefectural welfare offices or the homes in which they live.[15] The main reason, though, why so few are able to attend university is that their school records are rarely good enough.

It seems that children in *yōgoshisetsu* fall behind academically almost as soon as they come into care, if they are not already behind. In part, this is because the majority of children when they are placed in homes simultaneously become what are known in Japanese as *tenkōsei* (school movers). In 1996, for example, only 30 per cent of the children at Kodomo Gakuen had been placed in the home by the local *jidōsōdanjo*. The other 70 per cent had had to move there from other parts of Tokyo and, since it is very unusual for children of compulsory school age to be allowed to attend a school which is not the one nearest to where they live, this meant changing school.[16]

There has been very little research into the effect of changing school on children in Japan. To some extent at least, any negative effect is mitigated by the fact that the curriculum and style of teaching is almost exactly the same in every school throughout Japan. If children do not miss any school, therefore, they should have no trouble adjusting to the new environment. In the case of children from *yōgoshisetsu*, however, they have often moved several times before being placed in a home, and many have missed a considerable amount of their schooling. Further, according to Yokoshima (1977), *tenkōsei* who do not join their new schools at the start of the academic year can find it difficult to break into the tight-knit groups which have already formed in the classes they join, and may face ostracism and possible bullying.

Even after they settle into the school environment, many children in *yōgoshisetsu* cannot catch up with their peers. As Sakamoto (1993b) points out, the environment inside *yōgoshisetsu* does not always allow students to study in peace. In some homes, senior high-school students have their own rooms, though in most they are still required to share. Very few children of below senior high-school age have private study space in a country which, despite the cramped conditions in which many families live, has, as Merry White (1987: 145) has memorably described, fetishized the child's study space and furniture, adding bells to desks so that mothers can be summoned to supply food and drink to enable the child to continue working uninterrupted.

Relations with Schools and Teachers

Much of the educational experience of children from *yōgoshisetsu* depends on the relationship between the home and the school and between the children and their teachers. Since children must attend the elementary and junior school that is nearest, the relationship with these schools is normally of a long-standing nature. The fact that teachers are rotated between state schools every five to seven years, however, means that many of them may have had little experience of children from *yōgoshisetsu*. The head of Kodomo Gakuen was rung up by a teacher at one Tokyo senior high school, for example, to ask what kind of handicap (*shōgai*) the child they were about to accept from the home had despite the fact that the school had previously taught another child from the home.

The nearest elementary school for the children at Kodomo Gakuen was some twenty minutes' walk away[17] and once a year all the teachers from the school who had children from the *yōgoshisetsu* in their classes visited the home as a group along with the school's principal and deputy principal for an hour and a half as part of their official home visit (*katei hōmon*) system.

The local school worked hard to integrate the children from the *yōgoshisetsu* as quickly as possible. They were divided up between classes—even twins were separated—to avoid them forming exclusive groups and, in discussion, the teachers and staff at the school expressed the view that there were few differences between the children from the home (as a group) and the other children in the school. Those differences that were pointed out were in the main of a positive nature such as that children from the home were good at doing things collectively because of their experience of group activities. One teacher pointed out that the children sometimes demonstrated a need for physical contact (*skinship*), but added that this was not exclusive to children from the home. The teachers collectively insisted on the fact that school records were simply a result of individual differences (*seiseki kojinsa*) and not related to whether children came from a *yōgoshisetsu* or not.

Not all homes or children in care have such a positive response from teachers. Children at the Tokyo *kōryūkai* in 1998 cited a long list of bad experiences at school and complained of discrimination by teachers, parents, and fellow students (Kodomo ga Kataru Shisetsu no Kurashi Henshūiinkai, 1999: esp. pp. 67−8, 117−19). One physical education teacher regularly singled out children from the *yōgoshisetsu* with the order *shisetsu no kodomo atsumare* ('children from the home get together'). Children from *yōgoshisetsu* complained that they were always blamed when things went missing at school. Parents would tell their children that children in *yōgoshisetsu* were supported by their (taxpayers') money, which would lead to teasing and bullying. Indeed, some children said that they did everything that they could to hide from friends at school the fact that they lived in a *yōgoshisetsu*.[18]

On the other hand, teachers who had children from *yōgoshisetsu* in their class were not always positive in their views of them. Several complained that they were badly behaved and disruptive and that their extra demands for attention were difficult to deal with when teachers had up to thirty-nine children in their classes.[19] In this, teachers also receive pressure from the parents of other children in the class, who fear that any extra time the teacher needs to spend on 'children with problems' (*mondaiji*) detracts from the time they can give to their own child and to the class as a whole. In an educational meritocracy where one's own social and economic status is so closely tied to the success of one's children in the educational system, such concerns are real ones, even if they may be exaggerated.[20]

School Refusers (Futōkō)

A curious irony about the educational problems of children in *yōgoshisetsu* is that since 1992 the homes have been the site of a programme to help children in the community who have refused to attend school (a syndrome normally termed *tōkōkyohi*) to return to the education system. This is a complex topic that needs some background explanation.

While the phenomenon of *tōkōkyohi* has been recognized in Japan since the 1960s, it only began to engage public attention in the early 1980s with the reported sudden doubling (to over 20,000) of the number of children at junior high school (ages 12−15) who missed more than fifty days of school a year. By 1990 the number had doubled again to over 40,000, and in 1997, when the definition of *tōkōkyohi* was widened to include all those who missed school for more than thirty days in an academic year, it surpassed 84,000 (1 in 53) junior high-school students and 20,000 (1 in 378) elementary school children (*DY*, 8 Aug. 1998).

These statistics, however, do not fully demonstrate the significance given in Japan to the phenomenon of *tōkōkyohi*. The term covers a very wide range of reasons why children do not attend school which might otherwise not be connected. These range from truancy, to fears of being bullied or ostracized in school, to feelings of inadequacy in dealing with the school curriculum, to anxieties about leaving a difficult family environment in case it has changed irreparably on return from school.[21] According to Lock (1986) in the early 1980s, the term served to homogenize the individual experiences of children, and they and their families were made to feel responsible for their failure to attend school, while counsellors and teachers were charged with getting them to return. The late 1980s saw some revision of this view and a new term—*futōkō* (school non-attendance)—was coined, which was both more neutral in its meaning and recognized that there was a wide range of reasons why such large numbers of children were increasingly missing so much of their schooling (Yoneyama, 1999: ch. 8).

Throughout the 1980s and 1990s the growing phenomenon of *tōkōkyohi* and *futōkō* fuelled a national debate about the problems of the Japanese educational and family systems. It raised questions about the competitiveness of the school curriculum; about the homogenization of schoolchildren and schools' intolerance of diversity; about the use of physical punishment by teachers in schools; about the pampering of children by parents, especially mothers; about the absence of father-figures in the family (as more company employees were posted to new jobs in different cities and left their wives and families behind for longer); and about the breakdown of communication between family members. More significant than the debate, however, for those families with a child who refused to go to school, was the emergence of a large, and largely unregulated, industry that offered to help.

The programmes and approaches that have been set up for tackling the problem, as it is seen, of *tōkōkyohi* are extremely diverse both in practice and in price. These extend, in practical terms, from withdrawing children completely from the Japanese education system and sending them overseas alone, to engaging in extensive family therapy in Japan, and, in terms of approach, from shock therapy to excessive concern for the well-being of the child (Yoneyama, 1999). In 1992, however, the government officially adopted a new policy towards children who refused to go to school and became more active in setting up programmes to tackle the problem. One of the earliest government initiatives (in April 1992) was to allow *yōgoshisetsu* to accept those who refused to go to school, and to receive state money from Kōseishō for doing so.

At first glance, the idea of sending children who refuse to go to school to a *yōgoshisetsu* is hard to understand. It has long been posited by some experts, however, that one type of *tōkōkyohi* (known as *hikikomori tōkōkyohi*, literally 'confining oneself indoors school refusal syndrome') is as much a problem of the child not wanting to leave home as of it not wanting to go to school. For this type of child, an argument was made that *yōgoshisetsu* might provide an alternative base from which the child could try again to return to the education system. Several homes accepted school non-attenders from the start-date in 1992. By 1995, twenty institutions were offering a programme, including Kodomo Gakuen, which set up a *group home* for such children very near its main campus. No staff in *yōgoshisetsu* were trained, however, in how to work with *tōkōkyohi* nor, as we have seen, did they have trained therapists, though a few could call on a clinical psychologist for occasional advice.

In several cases, children placed in *yōgoshisetsu* have been successfully reintegrated into the school system, in part because they and their families have been given the space to sort out their problems, in part because the move to a home also meant a change of school. Despite this success, however, some critics still feel that placing children who are having problems with their academic careers in an environment where children statistically have educational records far behind the national average is far from satisfactory. For the government, on the one hand, and the homes, on the other hand, however, there has been a certain logic to the system. In the case of the former, it demonstrates that it is serious about addressing what is felt by many to be an issue of national importance; moreover, it is able to do so at minimal cost because the number of children in *yōgoshisetsu* has been decreasing and many homes have spare capacity. For the latter, filling this spare capacity has become essential if they are to remain open, and accepting children who do not attend school is a good demonstration of their changing role in society. These are both topics to which we will return later.

PREPARATION FOR LIFE AFTER *YŌGOSHISETSU*

Perhaps the most important measure of the success of *yōgoshisetsu* is what happens to children when they leave the homes. Technically speaking, when a child leaves the formal education system, it also leaves the *sochi seido* system through which the state provides funding to the home for it and, unless the home is prepared to care for the child at its own expense, it is expected to leave the *yōgoshisetsu* within one year and live independently in the wider society. This can be as early as 15 years of age.

In many countries, of course, it is not at all unusual for adolescents to live independently from the age of 15. In Japan, however, very few leave home before the age of 18 and the vast majority continue to live with their parents—perhaps with interludes to live in university and then company dormitories—until they get married in their late twenties.[22] There is some irony in the fact, therefore, that those who are least prepared to succeed in a society which places such a premium on educational background find themselves forced to make their own way in the world many years earlier than those who are better qualified.

Wherever possible, *yōgoshisetsu* try to find a way to allow residents, especially those who are not educationally able, to be able to stay on in the institutions after the age of 15. One common system is to enrol those residents who work during the day in night senior high schools or on a correspondence course. In 1991 four students at Kodomo Gakuen were in this situation. During the day they worked in a bookshop, a tyre shop, a video factory, and an aluminium-producing factory; three were registered for night school, one on a correspondence course. Not all of them, it was clear, were fully committed to their academic work but, as the staff saw it, it at least kept them in their care for a little longer.

Some residents, however, are determined to leave the home environment at the age of 15. As one former resident put it, it was not necessarily that they hated being in a home, but that they hated studying. Until the revision of the Child Welfare Law in 1998, there was no state provision for helping such former residents once they were living in the community, and there was no statutory requirement on the local child and social welfare agencies to provide support. Instead, the burden fell on individual *yōgoshisetsu*, and here it is clear that provision varied enormously.

Until only about twenty years ago, the ideal scenario for those leaving a *yōgoshisetsu* was that they should be apprenticed to a traditional Japanese craftsman such as a carpenter or house builder. While they may not have received a salary, they would have been provided with board and lodging and a secure environment and would have ended up with a trade. Over the past twenty years, however, such apprenticeships have all but disappeared in Japan. Today, *yōgoshisetsu* seek out jobs where the individual can as far as possible live in company housing or else live in accommodation near the home in which they previously resided, so that they can receive some level of unofficial support.[23] Many homes are able to draw on long-term contacts to find jobs for their graduates. At a home in Nagoya, for example, many graduates found work through the network of members of the Mukyōkai (Japanese non-Church Christian movement) or other Church movements with which the home was associated, or through an association set up for all children in homes in Nagoya City known as the Yotsubakai (Four-Leafed Association) (Shield, 1991: 27). Where homes do not draw on personal contacts, it can be rather more difficult for children from *yōgoshisetsu* to secure jobs. The head of one home in Kyoto detailed a number of cases from the recession-hit 1990s when residents or former residents had had job offers suddenly removed when it was discovered that they were, or had been, in *yōgoshisetsu*.

Kodomo Gakuen invested a lot of time in acquainting its residents with the world of work before they left the home. Many residents were able to do part-time work in a coffee-shop that had long had connections with the home, and the home had good relations with a number of local companies where residents could gain work experience. A *jidōshidōin* at the home was responsible for what was called, using the English expression, the *aftercare* of residents, which meant their preparation for independent living in the wider society. This involved not only teaching them practical skills such as how to budget and pay bills, but more difficult skills such as interpersonal communication, for which there simply is no time in the tightly packed school curriculum. Kodomo Gakuen had a reputation for being good at preparing its residents for independent living, but everything that it did was on its own initiative and without support—financial or otherwise—from the local or central government authorities. Many of those who had left the home came back regularly to talk to their former carers, particularly the *enchō sensei*, and to ask advice. The head had acted as the symbolic go-between (*nakōdo*) at the weddings of several former residents. Many former residents also kept in touch with each other through an association that had been running for many years. Others, though, set off on their own and if they did not want to keep in touch with the home, then they quickly lost all contact.[24]

Very little research appears to have been undertaken on what happens to former residents of *yōgoshisetsu* once they leave care.[25] Hayashi (1992) undertook a survey of those who had left homes in Osaka between 1985 and 1989 which gives an indication of the work experiences of residents during the first few years after leaving care. The vast majority in this survey of 259 leavers went into manufacturing and construction jobs (47 per cent) or the retail and service sectors (42 per cent), but their careers seem to have been marked by instability. Only 29 per cent had never changed jobs, and 25 per cent had changed jobs within a year of starting their first employment.

In 1991 I carried out a survey of the former residents of a home in west Tokyo.[26] The survey, though small, provided some interesting data. First of all, the average length of time the respondents had spent in the home varied from five to sixteen years, but averaged over ten years, which is double the national average for that age cohort. Working on the assumption that mainly those who had relatively successful transitions to independent life would have stayed in touch with the home and its former residents, and that respondents to an unsolicited questionnaire—even when supported by a letter from a former colleague and allowing anonymous responses—would again tend to be those who were more rather than less successful in society (a major limitation of such a survey), this suggests that long periods in residence are not necessarily a bad thing for some children who go into care, especially when, as was the case with all respondents here, that period in care is in a single institution and can thereby offer a certain measure of stability. None of the respondents in the survey had any experience of fostering.

A related feature of the responses was the very limited contact with parents or other guardians that the survey appears to show. Once, or sometimes twice, a year would appear to have been typical. Indeed, a significant proportion seemed not to know exactly why they had been placed in care in the first instance.

On leaving the home, however, former residents had a wide variety of experiences. Almost all moved either into a company dormitory of some kind or into the house of the head of the company for which they had gone to work. The exceptions were two who moved into their own apartments and one who returned to live in the family home. As with Hayashi's survey, one of the most noticeable features of the respondents is the number and variety of jobs they had done in a relatively short space of time. Of sixteen respondents, two were still studying and three others had stayed in the same job since leaving the home, one pointing out that he had been with the same firm for nine years since joining it at the age of 15. The other eleven had all changed jobs, most of them several times, including two who had had five different jobs within ten years: one man had worked as a cook, a salesman, and an engineer.

These changes of job need to be placed in some kind of economic and social context. On the one hand, both Hayashi's and my surveys cover a period, the 1980s, when the job market in Japan was particularly buoyant. Rather than unemployment, many companies faced severe financial problems through being unable to complete orders due to a lack of workers. Throughout the decade, there were more job openings than applicants, and towards the end of the 1980s Japanese businesses had to use foreign workers to fill positions. On the other hand, Japanese employers have rewarded the loyalty of workers, and a wage structure (known as *nenkō joretsu*) has been developed to benefit those who remain with a company for long periods of time. While this pattern has never applied to the same extent to those in small companies as it has to large firms, or to those who enter the workforce from junior or senior high school as much as to those who have completed tertiary education, it does appear that the number of times these particular samples of former *yōgoshisetsu* residents changed jobs is out of line with the national pattern.[27]

One of those in the small survey of former residents that I undertook described in a follow-up interview the problems that men, in particular, but also many women had in holding down a regular job when they left the home. Almost all those she knew ended up doing some form of manual labour (*nikutai rōdō*). Very few became white-collar workers, in part because they were better at working with their hands, in part because they did not have the educational qualifications for white-collar work. The women, in particular, were vulnerable to falling into bad company, and some she knew had ended up in *boshiryō* or with their own children in *yōgoshisetsu*. In many cases, she believed, former residents were able to do better the 'second time around', but in general it still took a long time for those who had spent time in care to settle down completely in society. This was largely, she felt, because of the lack of support systems.[28]

Jiritsu Enjo Homes (*After-Care Facilities*)

One of the revisions in the 1998 child welfare law was the official government recognition of *jiritsu enjo homes* (after-care facilities) as public welfare institutions. The battle to set up such homes is best exemplified in the life of Hirooka Tomohiko, who resigned his post as an assistant lecturer in chemistry at the University of Tokyo to devote himself full-time to work in a *jiritsu enjo home*, a prototype of which he had been involved in establishing in 1965.[29]

Hirooka's original idea (Seishōnen to tomo ni Ayumukai, 1997: 47) was that *jiritsu enjo homes* should be available to any child—either on leaving junior high school or on dropping out of senior high school—who had previously been in a *yōgoshisetsu, kyōgoin,* juvenile prison (*shōnenin*), foster care, or even from a normal family. They simply needed to be recommended or introduced to the home by any one of a number of official organizations—*jidōsōdanjo,* welfare offices (*fukushi jimusho*), family courts (*katei saibansho*), probation offices (*hogokansatsusho*), hospitals, or schools. He argued passionately that those who were in the care of the state (including those placed in institutions because of their delinquent behaviour) must be offered support by the state until at least the age of 18.

Hirooka's writings vividly depicted the problems faced by those who were forced to make their own way in society from as young as the age of 15, yet, for many years, few followed his lead. Largely this was because of the financial implications of setting up homes which were not recognized as official care institutions and which, if they followed Hirooka's model based on small *group homes,* required much greater levels of staffing and funding per resident than was common elsewhere in the child welfare world in Japan. In 1984, however, such institutions in Tokyo became eligible for the first time for prefectural funding (*KH,* 1994: 138) and in 1989 for money from Kōseishō, though in both cases only for capital costs. This led to the real birth period of *jiritsu enjo homes,* and by 1996 there were eighteen such homes in the whole country, though in total they could only offer residential places to less than 160 children (Murata, *KH,* 1996: 114).[30] From the late 1980s, an increasing number of *yōgoshisetsu* also developed facilities and dormitories where residents who otherwise would have had to leave the home were able to stay. One home in Nagoya had a block where former residents of the home could stay when they came to visit, a system half-way between offering full-time residence and none at all (Shield, 1991: 27).

When in 1998 the revised Child Welfare Law officially recognized *jiritsu enjo homes,* it seemed that that Hirooka's dream had finally been realized, though he died too early (in 1995) to see it for himself. The institutions were officially recognized and renamed *jidō jiritsu seikatsu enjo jigyō* (institutions for supporting an independent life for children), but they had to be self-supporting institutions and still were not eligible for funds, other than capital costs, from local or central government. At one such home in Kyoto, therefore, every resident is on a private contract and pays rent for his food and accommodation (on average around ¥30,000 a month) depending on his earnings. The home, which was set up by a former worker from, and under the auspices of, the next-door *yōgoshisetsu,* is in a new purpose-built institution for which 80 per cent of the funding came from the city government and 20 per cent from Kōseishō. It opened in 1994 in the grounds of a Buddhist temple in the centre of Kyoto, and has space for ten boys who can stay for between three and twelve months. It has three full-time staff, one of whom lives in. Apart from the rent it receives from its residents, the home also receives support from a network of over 600 supporters as well as an Internet sales project, and during the daytime, while the full-time residents are out at work, it runs an intensive private programme for school non-attenders whom it tries to prepare for a return to the education system.

The boys at the Kyoto *jiritsu enjo home* were put in contact with it through a variety of channels including police and courts worried about young men possibly getting involved in a life of crime, and the local *fukushi jimusho* (welfare offices) worried whether they could manage to live independently in society. In 1998, though, there were no children who had come from *yōgoshisetsu*. The head described the relationship with *yōgoshisetsu* in the area as poor and put this down to their sense of inadequacy in not being able to provide properly for their own former residents. Despite the development of such institutions, therefore, it is clear that the vast majority of residents from *yōgoshisetsu* still go into the outside world under-educated, ill prepared, and with little support for what they are about to face. The main question, of course, is what alternatives there are. We will explore some of these in the next chapter.

7

Alternatives to *Yōgoshisetsu*: Fostering and Adoption

FOSTERING

There is one service provided by Kodomo Gakuen which has not been discussed. Since 1973 it has also housed what is called a *yōiku katei centre* staffed by two full-time workers to recruit and register foster-parents within the locality, introduce them to appropriate children, help them through the procedures with the local *jidōsōdanjo*, which has exclusive authority over foster placements, and then provide support for them while fostering. The centre, one of ten in Tokyo, had twenty foster-families registered in 1997, of which sixteen had foster-children placed with them.

The existence of a *yōiku katei centre* at Kodomo Gakuen might suggest that a significant number of children who come into the care of the state are fostered rather than placed in residential institutions. This, however, is not the case. As Table 20 shows, both the absolute and the relative number of children fostered in Japan has declined markedly over the past forty years. In 1955, 20.3 per cent of all

TABLE 20. Changes in the number of children in child protection institutions and foster placements in Japan (1955–95)

	Yōgoshisetsu (A)	*Nyūjiin* (B)	Fostered (C)	% Fostered C/A+B+C
1955	32,944 (—) [100]	2,755 (—) [100]	9,111 (56.2%) [100]	20.3
1965	32,346 (88.0%) [98.2]	3,188 (82.6%) [115.7]	6,909 (33.4%) [75.8]	16.3
1970	30,933 (90.3%) [93.9]	3,331 (81.5%) [120.9]	4,729 (29.9%) [51.9]	12.1
1975	30,084 (86.6%) [91.3]	3,292 (78.5%) [119.5]	3,851 (31.5%) [42.3]	10.3
1980	30,787 (88.2%) [93.5]	2,945 (69.6%) [106.9]	3,188 (29.6%) [35.0]	8.6
1990	27,423 (80.5%) [83.2]	2,599 (67.6%) [94.3]	2,876 (28.7%) [31.6]	8.7
1995	25,960 (78.3%) [78.8]	2,566 (68.5%) [93.1]	2,377 (24.0%) [26.1]	7.7

Sources: Sakamoto, 1994: 175; *KH*, 1998: 113.

( ) = % of available places being taken up.
[ ] = relative % compared to 1955.

children in care were in foster homes; in 1965, in 1975, and in 1990, the proportion dropped successively to 16.3 per cent, 10.3 per cent, and 8.7 per cent. By 1995 it was just 7.7 per cent.

As Table 21 demonstrates, while the number of registered foster-carers has declined over the past forty years, the proportion who have actually fostered children has declined much faster. In 1995 less than 25 per cent of registered foster-parents were actually fostering, while almost 70 per cent of available places in *nyūjiin* and almost 80 per cent of places in *yōgoshisetsu* were being used (see Table 20). To give just one example of what these figures mean in practice: in the whole of Osaka in 1996 there were forty-eight children (less than 3 per cent) in foster placements out of a total of 1,675 children in care (Osaka-fu Kodomo Katei Centre, 1997: 46). This is strikingly similar to the situation in 1951 when fifty-two (4.5 per cent) out of 1,146 children were fostered (Kikiwada, 1968: 189).

The only three (very short) accounts by foreign observers of Japan's child protection system—two from the UK (Davis, 1983; Neilson and Meekings, 1997) one from the US (Jordan, *International Herald Tribune*, 29 June 1999)—published outside Japan that I have come across all concentrate on the lack of fostering and adoption. For these authors, this is what distinguishes the Japanese system most clearly from the north European and North American, as Table 22, produced by the Sato Oya Kai (Foster-Parent Association) in Japan, seems to show. Table 22 is, however, rather misleading. This is perhaps not surprising since it aims to show just how much Japan is out of line, in terms of fostering, from these other OECD countries. A table produced by a study group in Tokyo in 1996 (Tokyo-to Shakai Fukushi Kyōgikai, 1996b: 84), which tries to show how *little* Japan is out of line,

TABLE 21. Number of registered foster-families, families fostering children, and children in foster care (1949–96)

	Registered foster-families (A)	Active foster-families (B)	Children in foster placements	% of registered families fostering (B)/(A)
1949	4,153	2,909	3,278	70.0
1953	13,288	7,271	8,041	54.7
1955	16,200	8,283	9,111	51.1
1960	19,022	7,751	8,737	40.7
1965	18,230	6,090	6,909	33.4
1970	13,621	4,075	4,729	29.9
1975	10,230	3,225	3,851	31.5
1980	8,933	2,646	3,188	29.6
1985	8,659	2,627	3,322	30.3
1991	8,163	2,183	2,671	26.7
1993	8,090	2,083	2,561	25.7
1995	8,059	1,940	2,377	24.1
1996	7,975	1,841	2,242	23.1

Sources: Kōseishō Jidōkateikyoku, 1998: 256; Kōseitōkeikyōkai, 1992: 116; Nihon Sōgō Aiku Kenkyūjo 1988: 236.

TABLE 22. Proportion of children in care in residential institutions and in foster-home placements in seven selected countries (1981) (%)

	Foster placements	Residential institutions
England	60	40
Holland	54	46
Sweden	85	15
Finland	67	33
New Zealand	60	40
America	79	14
Japan	9	90

Source: Sato Oya Kai, 1990: 55.

is based on an almost completely different set of OECD nations (only Holland is in common). Madge (1994) also gives a rather different picture for the overall position of fostering versus residential care in Europe as a whole (see Figure VI) which appears to demonstrate a split between a southern (Catholic) Europe and a northern (Protestant) Europe. Portugal, Spain, Greece, and Italy are all relatively dependent on residential placements, while Sweden and England are much more dependent on a system of foster care.[1]

Japan may not be totally out of line with OECD countries in terms of the proportion of children in care who are in residential institutions—although it is at one extreme end of the spectrum—but it does differ in that the proportion of those in residential institutions in relation to those being fostered or on care orders at home has increased over the past forty years. As Madge says (1994: 137), the major trend within Europe over the past four decades has been the decline in residential care in favour of other forms of care and a movement from 'care and containment' to providing and maintaining family and community support mechanisms. As she graphically puts it (1994: 68), the conventional wisdom has become that a 'bad' family is usually better than a 'good' children's home. In England, for example, the proportion of children in care being fostered rose from around 50 per cent to 65 per cent just in the decade between 1985 and 1995 (Berridge and Brodie, 1998: 12). The questions that need to be explored is why so few children are fostered in Japan, and why the number has been decreasing. These questions seem particularly pertinent given some of the problems around residential care we discussed in the previous chapter. One survey indeed suggests that the small number of children who are fostered in Japan do significantly better in the education system than those who live in *yōgoshisetsu*: between 15 and 20 per cent more a year of children in foster placements continue to senior high school than those in homes, which brings them almost in line with the national average (*KK*, no. 50, 1996: 198).

The relative absence of fostering in contemporary Japan is all the more surprising in the light of there being a long tradition of it in Japanese society. Interestingly, this 'tradition' is never referred to in accounts of the contemporary foster

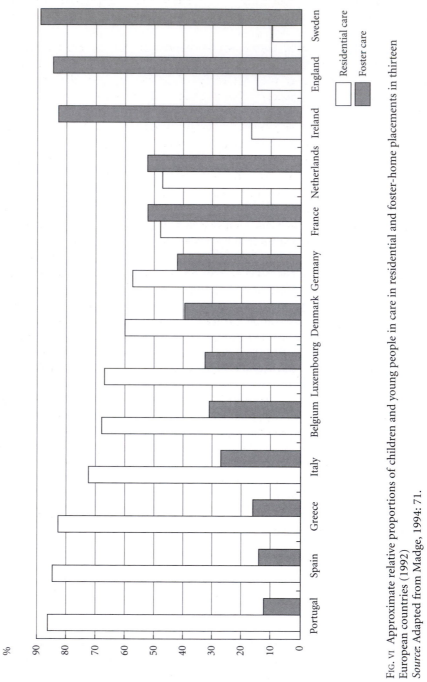

Fig. vi Approximate relative proportions of children and young people in care in residential and foster-home placements in thirteen European countries (1992)

Source: Adapted from Madge, 1994: 71.

system and, conversely, those who write about fostering practices from an anthropological or historical perspective rarely, if ever, refer to the contemporary situation.

Foster-children in Japan are known as *satogo* (*sato* means 'natal place'; *go* means child). The origins of the word seem to lie in the practice in the medieval period of many children of the aristocracy being brought up by their mother's family (matrilateral cognates) (Nihon Shakai Minzokugaku Kyōkai, 1954: 503–5).[2] Noguchi (1988: 26) suggests that some urban families thought that the experience of living in the countryside would enable the children to grow up strong and healthy; others, however, have argued that the practice related more to keeping children, particularly those born in 'unlucky' years, out of harm's way—both for their own good and the good of the family.

Fostering was certainly still widespread in pre-war Japan, especially among the elite. In describing how the status culture of the aristocracy was acquired and passed on, Lebra writes about how not only fathers but also mothers were generally uninvolved in child-rearing. Children were largely brought up by servants (what she calls 'surrogate parenthood') or by foster-parents (*sato oya*), as happened for example with the late Emperor Shōwa and his brother. Some interviewees in her study recalled the abuse they received at the hands of these care-givers, and many children, it would appear, were left permanently with peasant foster-parents (who needed their labour) by their birth families (who wanted fewer mouths to feed), a practice known as *sato nagare*.[3] The peasant families would also receive money (*satobuchi*) for fostering children, sometimes on the understanding that they would be returned if the designated successor died out or proved unsuitable.

Prior to 1945, foster-children lacked civil or social rights, especially in regard to their foster-parents. There were advocates of a state fostering system, such as Ishi'i Jūji (Yoneyama, 1993: 33), the founder of the orphanage in Okayama discussed earlier, but fostering was essentially undertaken privately. Foster-parents received no state support, and the experience of foster-children varied enormously from treatment as full kin to being used as just an extra pair of hands (Komatsu, 1992: 143–7).

In the immediate post-war period—a time of great social, political, and economic upheaval in the country—there is evidence of an especially large number of private foster arrangements being made (Vogel, 1963: 240–1). There was still very little state support for these arrangements (Komatsu, 1992) and there was no system to check on the well-being of the children involved (Kikuchi, 1991). In almost all cases, however, the natal family and the fostering family knew each other, and the fostering family knew something of the background of the child it was fostering.

This last point is significant because probably the most common explanation for the relatively small number of children in care who are fostered in Japan today is the reluctance among Japanese to look after children when their background is not known. Many people simply quote the expression (which is also sometimes used when discussing a prospective spouse) *Doko no uma no hone ka wakaranai* (You don't know from which horse the bone comes) to make this point. As one parent who fostered a child in Kyoto explained, there is a strong tendency in Japan to explain any problem that a child of unknown background who is fostered has on the fact that he or she is fostered. Indeed, she knew of one woman who had fostered and then adopted a child from a *yōgoshisetsu* who decided that it was best to pretend that the child was that of a relative so as to avoid comments of just this type.

According to some informants, there is a rather ambivalent view about foster-parents in general in Japan. As a worker in a centre for recruiting foster-parents put it, most Japanese think it is very difficult to bring up one's own children, and that it must be much more difficult to bring up someone else's. Foster-parents are seen as exceptional, 'self-sacrificing' people (*tokushika*), definitely unusual and perhaps even a little strange.

It was largely to try and create a more positive image that a new law covering fostering was introduced in 1987. Administratively, the new law transferred authority in this area, which had previously been exercised by prefectural governors, to local public bodies. More practically, it attempted to increase the number and improve the image of foster-parents and parenting by reducing the amount of investigation potential foster-parents had to go through before registration; by providing better training for foster-carers; by utilizing non-government organizations to publicize[4] the activities of and train foster-carers; and by simplifying the standards expected of foster-parents—previously they had had to own their own homes—to simply having an understanding of child care and offering a stable family life (Yamamoto, 1988).[5]

As Table 23 shows, following the new law there are three official categories of foster-parent in Japan. *Tanki sato oya* (short-term foster-parents) provide short-term fostering or relief care when parents are ill for periods of between one month and a year. *Yōshi sato oya* are those who foster with a view to adoption under the new adoption law (discussed below). *Yōiku sato oya* are those who foster so as to provide care for children who need it but without necessarily a view to adopting. There are also other unofficial forms of fostering. Many *yōgoshisetsu*, for example, have a system that they themselves have arranged whereby children stay with a 'foster-family' during New Year and O-bon (the midsummer festival when the souls of the dead are welcomed back) celebrations.[6] As Table 23 shows, however, only about 3,000 children were being fostered in the mid-1990s despite the fact that the new law had been in force for almost a decade. There are a number of factors which help explain why the new fostering system has not been as effective as either hoped or expected.

First, despite being on average slightly longer than placements in homes (Takahashi, 1987: 9), foster placements have all too often proved unsuccessful. The following case was recounted by a child psychotherapist who had been

TABLE 23. Numbers per year in the different categories of foster placements in Japan in mid-1990s

Yōiku sato oya (1995)	Yōshi sato oya (1995)	Tanki sato oya (1996)
1,940	521*	571

Sources: KH, 1998: 113; Takami, 1996: 97.
* Figure based on the assumption that foster parents foster for one year on average before adoption is finalized.

invited to advise staff on how to work with 'problem' children (*mondaiji*) in a *yōgoshisetsu*. He did not think it atypical.

X was abandoned when he was less than 1 and placed in an infant's home (*nyūjiin*) from where he transferred to a *yōgoshisetsu*. Unusually, a foster-family was found for him but, at the age of 4, he was rejected and returned to the children's home. His foster-mother said he insisted on spying on her while she was having a bath and that it was beyond her ability to deal with his unhealthy behaviour. (The therapist related the behaviour of the boy to having been in a Catholic *nyūjiin* where nuns showed him no affection; he desperately wanted *skinship* from his foster-mother, but she found his attentions perverted.) He was found another foster-family with whom he stayed until he was 10 or 11, when he started stealing money from the family and again was returned to the *yōgoshisetsu*. Now (aged 17) he was having a lot of problems in the home and was persistently stealing from other children and staff. (The therapist believed that his motivation, in part at least, was that he wanted 'to be loved even if bad' since the one thing he had always been denied was unconditional love.)

Komatsu (1992: 146) explains the high rate of breakdown of foster placements in terms of the lack of state support for foster-carers who, he says, 'More than anywhere else . . . are squeezed between low practical support on the one hand and high expectations on the other'. Foster-parents said that they received at most two or three visits a year from the local *jidōsōdanjo* while they were fostering, despite the fact that many foster-parents are childless with little or no experience of child care,[7] and many of them are relatively old in Japanese terms to be looking after young children. In 1990 almost 10 per cent of foster-fathers and 6.5 per cent of foster-mothers were over 60 years old; 40 per cent and 30 per cent respectively over 50; and only 0.4 per cent and 1.1 per cent under 30 (Sato Oya Kai, 1990: 9).

Ozawa (1991: 13) and Takami (1996: 100) alternatively argue that the recent decline in fostering in recent years in Japan is related mainly to economic and social changes: the increase in housing costs (which was particularly significant during the bubble economy of the 1980s), the decrease in extended families, and the expanded participation rates of women in the labour force. To this some have added the fear of unemployment during the 1990s as Japan has been in extended recession. The idea that fostering could itself be seen as an occupation for those properly qualified, so minded, and accredited has not been accepted in Japan.[8]

One of the main concerns of the 1947 Child Welfare Law was that there should not be abuse of child-support expenses which explained, in part, the reluctance of those without substantial means to volunteer to foster. Even today, anyone who considers fostering with any apparent financial motives is viewed very suspiciously by the workers who approve foster-families.

Another reason frequently given for why fostering in Japan remains so limited is the fact that fostering and adoption are often confused in people's minds. *Jidōsōdanjo* workers, for example, frequently point out that it is the natural parents and guardians of the children—with, in Japan, the weight of the law on their side—who, confusing adoption and fostering, prevent their children from being fostered in case they lose control over them and cannot get them back. As a result, in the case of about 60 to 70 per cent of the children who are fostered, both their parents have either died or are uninterested in contesting the placement (Kikuchi, 1991).[9]

In the case of those who apply to be foster-parents, there is also a tendency to conflate or confuse the categories of fostering and adoption.[10] Since a high proportion of those who foster do so with a view to adopting, many registered foster-parents are very fussy about which children they will foster. Only 7 per cent of registered foster-parents, according to one survey, are not fussy at all about the child they take, and 50 per cent of children fostered are under 3 years of age and 80 per cent are under 6 (Tokyo-to Yōiku Katei Centre, 1991: 10).

One further reason for the failure of the new fostering policies, according to some commentators, has been the vested interests of the *yōgoshisetsu* which currently look after over 90 per cent of children in care. It is interesting that in Tokyo in the early 1990s just six of the thirty-seven homes provided half of all the children who were fostered from *yōgoshisetsu* (Tokyo-to Yōiku Katei Centre, 1991: 9). These were mainly the homes which had attached to them a *yōiku katei centre*, a publicly funded unit established with the express purpose of improving the system of foster care in Tokyo. Such centres had been established to get those who worked in fostering and children's homes to work more closely together, in the interests of the children, rather than, as had hitherto sometimes seemed the case, in opposition (see Takahashi, 1987).[11]

Many other homes, however, have been much less keen to pursue foster placements. They have argued that they provide 'professional care' whereas the care provided by foster-parents is 'amateur care', particularly when the children have emotional problems or have been abused (see Yamamoto, 1988: 6; Zadankai, 1991: 21).

ADOPTION

If few children in care are fostered, then it is perhaps not surprising that even fewer are adopted even though, like fostering, adoption has a long history in

Japan. According to Bachnik (1988: 14), 'adoption has been widely practised in Japan for at least 1300 years'. To some extent, indeed, it might be thought of as the defining feature of the Japanese kinship system. Patterns of adoption are certainly more widespread and flexible in Japan than in neighbouring countries such as China and Korea with which it shares so many other cultural practices.[12] Adoption has been particularly prevalent among the upper classes. Samurai records suggest that by the nineteenth century up to 40 per cent of samurai families adopted sons or daughters. The practice was so widespread that, in the Tokugawa period, one scholar, according to Lebra (1993: 107 ff.) picked it out as a major cause of social chaos, describing it as both 'barbaric' and 'evil'. Most commentators, though, were not so critical of adoption as a social practice and some saw it as a useful system for the elderly without children to ensure that they were cared for in their old age in return for passing on their inheritance (Kurosu and Ochiai, 1995).

The type of adoption that was practised in pre-modern Japan, and which indeed remains the most prevalent type today, was essentially adoption of kin relatives (including younger brothers, uncles, and grandchildren) for purposes of succession, and can only be understood in relation to the structure of the Japanese household, known as the *ie*. Figure VII shows the *ie* in diagrammatic form. The *ie* had become fixed, in theory if not necessarily in practice, as the basic social unit by the Tokugawa period (1603–1868) and was disseminated throughout society as an ideal kinship model during the period of Meiji modernization. In the context of discussion about adoption, a number of important features about it need to be kept in mind.

(*a*) Certain roles and positions—for example head, successor—are only defined in the context of the *ie*. Hence, an *ie* is distinct from a 'family' where genealogy rather than position is paramount.

(*b*) It is a corporate body which has its own status, assets, career, and goals.

(*c*) It has an existence over and above its immediate membership. Current members of the *ie* are only temporarily looking after it and their main purpose is to pass it on to the next generation in the best possible condition and with the best possible leadership. Ideal succession within the *ie* is male primogeniture, but if the eldest son is not considered competent, then a younger son or even daughter may replace him. If there is no appropriate successor within the family, then an 'outsider' should be recruited through adoption. Whatever happens, continuity must be ensured.

Adoption to ensure the continuity of an *ie*, unlike fostering, creates a fictive parent–child relationship by law. The adopted child—or sometimes adopted couple—has the same legal rights as a natural child or children, unlike an illegitimate child, whose inheritance is only half that of legitimate siblings. In some senses, this type of adoption might be considered akin to marriage in the way in which the adoptee is chosen and incorporated into the household, and indeed a

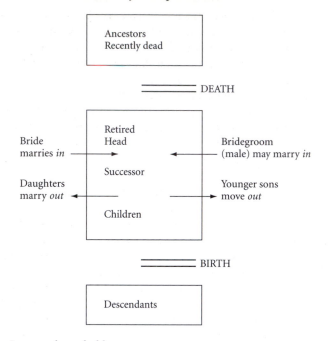

FIG. VII *Ie*: The Japanese household
Source: Adapted from Hendry, 1981: 17.

large number of such adoptions have always taken place at the time of marriage. Kitaōji (1971: 1047) even suggests that marriage in Japan might be better thought of as a type of adoption. Adoption is generally known in Japanese as *yōshi engumi* (generally shortened to *yōshi*). *Yōshi* means both adoption and the adopted person; *engumi* consists of two characters meaning 'relation' and 'matching', and can be translated as 'alliance'. Like marriage, too, adoption ties of this type can be broken in a type of 'divorce' (*rien*).[13]

In Japan, therefore, adoption has historically been distinguished by the following characteristics (see Bachnik, 1988: 14–15):

(*a*) the primary focus is the 'house' (*ie*) not the adoptee;
(*b*) the adoptees are not foundlings, but usually close relatives whose natal home is known;
(*c*) the adoptee is relatively old (the vast majority are adults);
(*d*) no legal distinction is made between adoptive and natural child.

The system is remarkably flexible. A brother can be adopted as a son; a son-in-law can be adopted, as can a married couple. If the ranks or reputations of two households involved in marriage are considered incompatible, then a daughter can gain 'suitability' by being adopted by another household, although there is no need for her ever to actually live with her adoptive parents.[14] This indeed was the case with the bride of Prince Chichibu, brother of the Shōwa emperor and uncle of the current emperor. In the Meiji Civil Code the only limitations on adoption were, in the case of kin, the prohibition on adopting someone of a higher generation, such as an uncle or aunt, and, in the case of non-kin, adopting someone who was older.

How were these pre-war practices, which can be traced so far back in Japanese history, modified in the modern period? In theory, the post-war civil code banned any adoption that was enacted purely in the interests of the *ie*. Emphasis was laid on the rights of the potential adoptee and, for the first time, the courts were given a role in the adoption of children. In practice, however, the new civil code ran alongside the previous code rather than replacing it, and the adoption of adults and children for the purpose of continuing the *ie* remained very popular. In separate post-war village studies, Beardsley (1959: 238) and Befu (1963: 37) found that around 25 per cent of all households were succeeded by adoption; Nakane (1967: 67) and, at a slightly later period, Bachnik (1983: 163) came up with figures of nearly one-third of households in some villages. Among elite families, where the political and economic considerations of adoption were even more important, the figures may have been even higher. Among post-war prime ministers, Yoshida Shigeru was adopted, and two prime ministers, Kishi Nobusuke and Satō Eisaku, were actually brothers—the younger brother, Nobusuke, being adopted to succeed to his father's natal household (the Kishi family), his father having been adopted to his mother's natal household (the Satō family) (Hara, 1995: 3). Perhaps not surprisingly, the adoption of a competent heir has historically been particularly stressed among merchant families and indeed, to some extent, this still remains the case today (Fruin, 1983: 240–1).

While it is still easy and not uncommon to adopt someone to continue an *ie*, the general perception of this practice is increasingly confused. Katō (1989: 164–6) suggests, however, that the main reason for the continuation of adult adoptions has gradually come to be to create a kind of contract that exchanges inheritance rights for offering care in old age in a period where more and more people have no children to look after them in later life. Other informants and researchers (see, e.g. Yonekura, 1984: 6) suggest a rather more negative view of the practice, which is that there must be something wrong, sad, or suspicious about a person who decides to adopt. Adoption can be used as a means to avoid inheritance tax (*sōzoku-zei*)—which explains why 80-year-olds sometimes adopt 70-year-olds—or as a system for homosexual couples to ensure inheritance between them if one partner dies. Children are sometimes adopted by relatives so that they can live in the catchment area of a particularly good state school. Employers, in the period of a shortage of manual workers in the late 1980s, were reported to be adopting illegal workers from overseas so as to keep them in the country.[15] Adoption may even be used as a means of avoiding debt-collectors since it is one of the few ways one can legally change one's family name in Japan. A common response in discussions about adoption, therefore, is *kawaisō* (how sad) for all concerned, though particularly for a marrying-in man who, so the well-known saying goes, should refuse to be adopted if he still has at least three pints of rice to his name. Nevertheless, as the 1998 Kōseishō White Paper (*KSH*, 1998: 102) points out, the number of such adoptions has remained steady at 80,000 to 90,000 over the past thirty years.

Another popular post-war category of adoption has been the adoption of one's illegitimate children, step children, or grandchildren. This relates to the Household Register Law (Kosekihō), the complex system of family registration which was originally imported from China in the sixth century and, according to Kashiwazaki (1998: 284), 'provided successive Japanese rulers with a model of defining and controlling their subjects'. Since the Meiji period, every Japanese person has been placed in one, and only one, household register (*koseki*) which provides legal proof of his or her identity. A *koseki* can consist of a married couple, or of a married couple and their unmarried children (natural or adopted) of the same surname, or of an individual with unmarried children (natural or adopted) of the same surname, or of just an individual over the age of 20. Many step-parents adopt their stepchildren in order to set up a new *koseki* as a way of ensuring legal guardianship. While Article 798 of the 1947 version of the Civil Code made it mandatory for anyone proposing to adopt a minor to obtain the permission of the Family Court, an exception was made for those adopting lineal descendants of their own or their spouse, including grandchildren, on the basis that the well-being of such children was unlikely to need monitoring (Katō, 1989: 161–2).

In all the above categories of adoption, the adoptive parents know the background of the individual who is being adopted. In the vast majority of cases the two families are related. As Table 24 shows, the great majority (66.8 per cent) of such adoptions are of adults (those over 20), some of whom are quite elderly. While adoptions of those under 20 are evenly split between males and females, the great majority of adult adoptions (around 80 per cent) are of males (Yuzawa, 1983: 24).

There are two other much less common forms of adoption of children in Japan, however, where the background of the child is not always known. The first of these generally involves children being adopted by non-Japanese couples, often outside Japan. The adoption by foreigners of Japanese children largely started in the immediate post-war occupation period (Asahi Shinbun Osaka Shakaibu, 1995). In all, just one agency, International Social Service (ISS), arranged 2,028 adoptions between 1952 and 1975, of which 75 per cent were with foreigners living in Japan and 25 per cent were overseas (including Japanese living overseas) (Itō, 1977: 114). The practice still continues and during the 1990s there were annually around 300 Japanese children adopted overseas (*KK*, no. 50, 1996: 267). Of these, according to Moriki (1998) about 20 per cent went to the US. A high proportion of such adoptions has been of mixed-blood children or of children with some physical or mental handicap for whom it has proved particularly difficult to find adoptive placements in Japan.[16] Kikuchi (1998: 110) suggests, how-

TABLE 24. Estimated number of adoptions by age in Japan (1983)

Age	No. per year	Average no. per age year
0	874	874
1–5	8,588	1,718
6–11	12,768	2,128
12–14	2,850	950
15–19	3,268	654
20–29	33,364	3,336
30–39	14,706	1,471
40–49	4,978	498
50–59	3,116	312
60–69	760	76
70–79	114	11
TOTAL	85,386	

Adoption of minors (under 20): 28,348 (33.2%)
Adoption of adults (over 20): 57,038 (66.8%)

Source: Yuzawa, 1983: 24. (Yuzawa has extrapolated these figures from a 1982 Justice Ministry survey of some 2,247 cases.)

ever, that one further reason for the continuation of overseas adoptions may be that the birth of such children does not need to be recorded on the mother's *koseki*, the significance of which will become clear later.

The second form comes the nearest in Japan to what Goody (1969) has described as the 'modern European understanding' of the term 'adoption'. This form of adoption has only comparatively recently been introduced into Japan and is known as *tokubetsu yōshiengumi* or, more simply, *tokubetsu yōshi* (special adoption).

The impetus behind the introduction of the *tokubetsu yōshi* system in Japan can largely be traced back to a famous controversy in the 1970s (see Kikuchi, 1998: 85–91). Kikuta Noboru was a doctor who specialized in both abortions and infertility treatment and recognized an inherent contradiction in his work. Abortion rates in Japan not only historically but also today are, by international standards, high, and it is still one of the main forms of 'family planning' (Hodge and Ogawa, 1991).[17] Kikuta believed that one reason for the high abortion rate was that anonymous adoptions were impossible because of the *koseki* (family registration) system. The Household Register Law (Kosekihō) of 1871 made it compulsory to record that a woman had given birth—under any circumstances. Since the *koseki* has in the past been needed for such basic acts as obtaining a driving licence or a passport, applying to schools or companies, and may still today be requested by such people as prospective parents-in-law (although they have no legal right to do so), the potential stigma involved in recording an illegitimate birth can cause major problems later in life not only for the mother but for her whole family.[18]

According to Kikuta, it was easy to find potential adoptive parents from among those he assessed as infertile; his only difficulty was to persuade women having abortions to give up their child for adoption instead. He claimed to have relayed some 220 babies to adoptive parents from the early 1970s and to have recorded them (illegally) as their natural children (*jisshi*) and ensured that there was no trace on the natural mother's family register.[19]

Kikuta's radical approach won him few friends at the time in the child welfare and medical establishment. He bypassed the *jidōsōdanjo* on the basis that they took an unsympathetic attitude to women who gave up their children for adoption and would place the children in infant homes (*nyūjiin*). He was attacked by other doctors, many of whom made large sums of money from abortions, kicked out of the national association of obstetricians in 1973, and suspended by Kōseishō for six months in 1979. Indeed, despite his attempts to explain his actions through the media at the time, he was widely vilified as a 'child seller' when his activities first came to light as the result of a newspaper advertisement offering babies to childless couples.

However, partly as a result of Kikuta's lobbying, a new law was introduced in 1988 whereby children could be registered by adoptive parents as their natural children. Rather confusingly, the expression *tokubetsu yōshi* (special adoption) was used for this new form of adoption.[20] The law contained a number of strict regulations which were designed to protect the welfare interests of the child (Yamamoto, 1988):

(*a*) the adoption must be concluded by a Family Court (*katei saibansho*);[21]
(*b*) it ends all legal relationship between the adopted child and its biological parents;[22]
(*c*) parents must be married and over 25; the child must be under 6 when the process of adoption officially starts;[23]
(*d*) adoption is possible only in cases where the biological parents are really unsuitable and adoption is in the interests of the child;
(*e*) it may not be nullified by the adoptive parents;
(*f*) there will be a minimum six-month trial period during which adoptive parents remain under investigation by the *jidōsōdanjo*;[24]
(*g*) normally parents will be encouraged to become foster-parents first.

In addition, under the *tokubetsu yōshi* system, adopted children are no longer expected to support their birth parents in old age, and lose any rights to inherit from them. This, it was hoped, would reduce the potential for conflict between adopted children and their blood siblings.

The new law however has not had the impact that Kikuta's personal experience had suggested it would, although his memory would appear to have been almost totally rehabilitated by the late 1990s judging from the tone of the hour-long documentary on his life aired by Asahi TV on 23 October 1998. While there were 1,814 adoptions in 1988 through the *tokubestu yōshi* system, numbers declined successively over the following years to around 400 a year in 1996 (Aoki, 1994: 24). As Table 25 shows, indeed, the total number of child adoptions has declined dramatically since the *tokubetsu yōshi* system was introduced.

TABLE 25. Figures for *futsū* (normal), *tokubetsu* (special), and *kokusai* (international) adoptions of children (1985–96)

Year	Futsū yōshi * = under 20 ** = under 18	Tokubestu yōshi (all under 6)	Total futsū and tokubetsu adoptions	Kokusai (international) yōshi
1985	3,245*	—	3,245	—
1986	3,296*	—	3,296	—
1987	2,876*	—	2,876	—
1988	2,421*	1,814	4,235	—
1989	2,151*	1,933	4,084	—
1990	2,037*	1,178	3,215	—
1991	1,529**	619	2,148	381
1992	1,310**	509	1,819	359
1993	1,258**	520	1,778	337
1994	1,205**	491	1,696	339
1995	1,111**	521	1,632	299
1996	971**	426	1,397	—

Sources: Iwasaki, 1992: 56; Kikuchi, 1998: 81; *KH*, 1998, 102; *KK*, No. 50, 1996: 267.

Note: The *tokubetsu yōshi* system came into effect in 1988; 1985–90 figures for *kokusai yōshi* are not available.

The number of child adoptions needing to be sanctioned by the courts (*futsū yōshi*) has declined from about 40,000 a year during the early 1950s, to around 2,000 at the end of the 1980s to under 1,000 by the mid-1990s. Katō (1989: 163) explains the first part of this trend in terms of the decrease in the average size of families (from over four children in the 1950s to less than two at the end of the 1980s) which meant that fewer families had 'spare' children that they were willing to allow relatives to adopt. Yuzawa (1994: 43) explains it in terms of: there being less demand for adoptive children because the costs of bringing up children are considered so high; improvements in the social welfare system having made the elderly more independent; and the number of small businesses and of self-employed people having declined greatly, which has made people less worried about keeping family names and occupations going. The continued decline in the 1990s may be related to the introduction of the *tokubetsu yōshi* system, which created considerable confusion in many people's minds about the whole adoption process. The reasons for the declining number of *tokubetsu yōshi* adoptions needs to be explored in more detail.

One of the main reasons for the failure of the *tokubetsu yōshi* system must relate to the fact that the birth of the baby given up for adoption continues to be marked on the mother's *koseki*. This is to prevent the possibility, however remote, of adopted children marrying someone to whom they are related by blood. For many women, therefore, a termination must still be seen as preferable to giving up a baby for adoption. Most of the other reasons, however, are almost exactly the same as those that explain the low numbers of children being fostered. Indeed, since 84 per cent of parents who adopt children through the *tokubetsu yōshi* have been *yōiku sato oya* foster-parents (*KSH*, 1998: 102), there is a close relation between the two. As for the children, 90 per cent of those adopted through the *tokubetsu yōshi* system are the children of single, unmarried mothers, often where an abortion has not been effected in time. However, as the American journalist Mary Jordan (*International Herald Tribune*, 23 June 1999) found when she went to Japan to investigate adoption practices, in most cases where the mother is unable to look after a child, her relatives still often prevent it from being adopted even if they are unwilling to take it in themselves.[25] As a result such children must be placed in *nyūjiin* and *yōgoshisetsu*.

There has been a debate in Japan from the beginning of the post-war period about the relative advantages and disadvantages of the fostering and adoption of children who come into care, on the one hand, and placement in residential institutions, on the other (see Kikiwada, 1958, 1968). Those in favour of fostering and adoption have often drawn on the work of Western psychologists and psychiatrists—Goldfarb in the 1940s, Bowlby in the 1950s, Tizard and Hodges in the 1970s and 1980s—about the dangers of 'maternal deprivation', the deleterious effects of long-term institutionalization, and in particular the need for the 'normalization' of the experience of children who are placed in care. More recently, fostering and adoption have been supported on financial grounds, in part drawing on the example of the reforms in the 1980s under Mrs Thatcher's Conservative government which saw the closure of most children's homes in the UK (Cliffe and Berridge, 1991). Fostering, as currently carried out in Japan with very little support for foster-parents, is much cheaper than caring for children in institutions. In Tokyo, in the mid-1990s, the foster allowance was ¥100,000 per child, while it cost around ¥240,000 a month to care for a child in a *yōgoshisetsu*; in Aichi Prefecture the figures were ¥78,100 and ¥220,500 respectively (Yamanta, 1995: 73). These arguments, however, have had little effect on national rates of fostering or adoption.

Those in favour of residential care have, as we saw in Chapter 5, argued that there are many advantages for children in Japan who grow up in institutions, including the chance to learn how to co-operate and get on with others. Equally significantly, they point out the potentially damaging effects when a fostering arrangement breaks down, sometimes referring to research from the UK (see Berridge and Cleaver, 1987).

Whatever the arguments, the fact is that, despite the introduction of both new fostering and adoption systems in the late 1980s, the actual number of children who come into the care of the state who are fostered and/or adopted has continued to fall in the 1990s. This trend explains in part why the number of children in *yōgoshisetsu* has remained relatively stable despite the fall in the overall number of children coming into care. It has been this stable base that has allowed *yōgoshisetsu* to develop a new role in the Japanese child-protection system, as we shall see in the next chapter.

8

Towards a New Role for *Yōgoshisetsu*

THE LACK OF CHANGE IN *YŌGOSHISETSU* IN THE POST-WAR PERIOD

On 8 January 1996 the Kōseishō vice-minister Tada Hiroshi held a press confer-ence on the Ministry's plan to reform Japan's post-war child welfare system. In what appears to have been an unusually frank speech, he picked out *yōgoshisetsu* as an institution particularly in need of change: '*Yōgoshisetsu* were built to take in orphans in the post-war period', he is quoted as saying in one newspaper (*Kumamoto Nichinichi Shinbun*, 9 Jan. 1996), 'but times have changed.'

It is hard in many ways to disagree with Tada's view that *yōgoshisetsu* have not kept up with the times, especially when one reads some of the concerns about *yōgoshisetsu* voiced by the head of a home in the late 1950s: '[I]t is generally accepted that privileged children belong in their own home, that less privileged ones are sent to foster homes and the institution is the only place for the most underprivileged children' (Kikiwada, 1958: 87). According to Kikiwada (1958: 88):

- Many children are placed in institutions rather than under foster care because it is cheaper and because Japan does not yet understand the importance of the foster home.
- Many institutions are still congregate and of dormitory type.
- Professional services, such as psychiatric, psychological, remedial reading, casework, and group-work services are not well developed.
- Adequate financial support is lacking.
- The administrative structure in institutions is weak, with boards of directors having very few administrative responsibilities.

A visit to many *yōgoshisetsu* today conveys the feeling that not much has changed. As we have seen, institutional care still predominates over foster care; in many homes, children still live in large dormitories in hospital-like buildings, run by a small, non-specialist, and overworked staff; there is virtually no therapeutic, psychiatric, or remedial casework; many homes still rely significantly on charita-ble funds; and the responsibilities of boards of directors remain ill defined and are not always closely monitored. What has changed, of course, is that while Japan in the 1950s was a developing country still recovering from the ravages of fourteen years of war between 1931 and 1945, today it is an economic superpower second only to the United States.

It is not hard to explain why the system for children in care should have changed so little over the past fifty years. Put simply, there has been no pressure for change. The children in the homes themselves have had no voice, no economic and political leverage, to try and bring about change. Indeed, until the early 1990s, when the first *kōryūkai* (meeting) was arranged for senior high-school children in *yōgoshisetsu*, there was not even a forum in which they could compare their experiences. Even after the annual meetings were begun, some homes did not allow their children to participate, citing high costs, and, as we saw in Chapter 6, when a child involved in one of the meetings subsequently started behaving 'badly', there was criticism of some of the 'messages' that children were picking up at them. It was decided, therefore, that the meetings should no longer be used for educating children about their rights but simply enjoyable holiday camps. But since most homes already ran such camps for their residents, they could see little point in sending children elsewhere and in 1999 the national meetings were cancelled altogether, though some local areas ran their own versions.

If children in care do not have political or economic power, nor do their parents. In many cases, the parents are simply not around; in others, they are not in good enough mental and physical shape to organize on behalf of their children. Even when they are in reasonable mental and physical health, they generally have neither the money nor the access to political power to act as a pressure group. Indeed, according to some of the staff in *yōgoshisetsu*, many parents who place children in care feel looked down upon by society for not being able to look after them themselves. It is not surprising, therefore, that there has never been any attempt by parents to organize on behalf of their children and pressurize the government to provide better services for them.

The Japanese government, in its turn, has been content to allow the status quo in child protection to continue. As we have seen, welfare provision in Japan has generally been focused on supporting the most productive elements of society and has concentrated on health and education. In the 1990s, government spending on personal social services as a proportion of GDP did rise overall, but in the case of child welfare was largely focused on dealing with the issues raised by the declining birth rate (*shōshika shakai*). Hence, government expenditure has increased considerably in response to powerful middle-class demands for an increased supply of day-care (*hoikuen*) places and an increased number of after-school (*gakudō*) clubs to care for children while their parents were still at work.[1] The interests of these middle classes have rarely overlapped with those of children in *yōgoshisetsu*. While most middle-class mothers can appreciate the need for day care and after-school clubs, there has been little idea in Japan that anyone's child might end up in the child protection system. Indeed, there may even have been the sense that only the fecklessness of parents can explain a child coming into care, and such fecklessness should not be encouraged by the state providing too generous a system of alternative care. As a result, the government has faced little pressure from voters to spend more money on welfare facilities like *yōgoshisetsu* and expenditure has, in some areas, even been cut. For example, throughout the

1990s, public *yōgoshisetsu* have continued to be closed down, mainly because the prefectural authorities, which had been forced to take on a larger share of the funding for these public institutions from the central government, were looking for ways to make cuts in their overall child welfare budgets in order to meet rising costs elsewhere, particularly in services for the elderly.

In the 1960s, Nagata (1968: 192) pointed out that most change in the child welfare system came about as a result of the initiatives of private institutions and was often despite and not because of the leadership of public officials: 'Some public officials have no initiative and do only what they are told . . . On the other hand, private welfare workers have spirit, zeal, and courage but they lack the necessary funds.' As a result, some private homes have changed over the past fifty years and some of these changes are an impressive testament to individual vision, effort, and the ability to raise private funds, since the public authorities have very rarely led the way and even less often provided the money for such changes.

In general, though, most private homes have changed very little. In some cases, this was because they were not able to raise the necessary funds. In some cases, their attention was on setting up other welfare institutions as part of a *shakai fukushi hōjin*. In many cases, where the original home was the project of a particular individual, his or her descendants simply saw the maintenance of the status quo as their primary duty; they had neither the interest nor the energy to make changes, or they felt that there was no need to change. In general, therefore, *yōgoshisetsu* were under no pressure, from children, parents, government, or each other, to change. Nor was any pressure applied by unions or other organizations working on behalf of children in care.

Of course, all homes relied on the *jidōsōdanjo* to place children in them. Yet while the workers in the *jidōsōdanjo* mostly had their own (mental) hierarchy of homes, and knew where they would prefer to place children, in general they tended to share the children around between the homes in their area. Many workers in the *jidōsōdanjo* felt obliged to keep up the long-term relationship with local homes, especially, as is so often the case in Japan, if they had personal contacts with the individuals or families that ran them.[2]

In the early 1990s, however, the situation for *yōgoshisetsu* began to change dramatically. For the first time, they (and the government) had an interest in changing the system of child protection.[3] This pressure came from three quite separate directions: the rapid decline in the birth rate in Japan; the ratification by Japan of the UN Convention on the Rights of the Child; and the 'discovery' of child abuse in Japanese society.

YŌGOSHISETSU AND THE DECLINE IN THE BIRTH RATE

The so-called '1.57 shock', discussed briefly in Chapter 2, was a cause for much discussion at the 1991 meeting of the heads of all the *yōgoshisetsu* (Yōgoshisetsuchōkai) in Kyoto. The proportion of children in the population, the absolute number of children, and the birth rate were all set to decline throughout the 1990s. In 1998, indeed, there would be fewer children (aged 15 or younger) than at the time of the first census in 1920, and in 1997 the number of elderly (those aged 65 and over) would exceed the number of children for the first time in Japanese history. There might be considerable regional variations in the fig-ures—21 per cent of the population in Okinawa was 15 or younger; in Tokyo this figure was 12.7 per cent, the lowest in the country (*DY*, 7 May 1998)—and the birth rate was predicted to rise slightly between 1998 and 2005 as members of the second post-war baby boom began to have children of their own, but there was no doubt that the overall number of children in the population would continue to decline. Many *yōgoshisetsu* feared that they would be forced to close.

Looking from the outside, the closure of a *yōgoshisetsu* might be taken as a pos-itive sign that there were fewer children in need of residential care in Japanese society. In 1991 many homes were already a long way under capacity even though, as we have seen, children were on average staying longer in homes and fewer of them were going to foster placements. Some homes took advantage of this under-capacity to ensure, for example, that all of their residents of senior high-school age had their own rooms. There was no doubt, however, that if the trend contin-ued some private homes as well as the public homes would need to close, and that closure would mean the end of long and often distinguished histories of residen-tial child welfare work. In some cases, closure would also mean the removal of a cornerstone of a *dōzoku keiei* family business. This in turn might raise questions about the suitability of the *shakai fukushi hōjin* to operate other welfare institu-tions, such as old people's homes and nurseries. At the 1991 conference, the heads of all homes were made aware, if they were not aware before, that *yōgoshisetsu* would need to find a new role in society if they were to survive far into the next century (see *YSno40nen*, 1987: 103–53).

To some extent, the immediate problem of declining numbers was dealt with by the development of new categories of children who were eligible for placement in a *yōgoshisetsu*. Three such schemes were introduced in 1991 and 1992: a *twi-light stay* system for single parents working in the evening; a *tankinyūsho* (short-stay) scheme, for a parent or parents with no alternative arrangement for caring for their children while they were in hospital for a few days; and, most controver-sially of all, as we saw in Chapter 6, a programme to place school non-attendees in *yōgoshisetsu*. These programmes actually only became available in a minority of *yōgoshisetsu*—by 1996, 186 offered short-stay programmes, seventy-nine had *twilight stay* programmes, and twenty had programmes for *tōkōkyohi* (*KK*, no. 50: 1996)—but they not only helped to bring more children into the homes, but also, at least in the immediate vicinity of the homes concerned, helped to foster the perception of *yōgoshisetsu* as not so dissimilar to *hoikuen* and other day-care institutions.

At the same time, according to some informants, children who might previ-ously have been placed in *kyōgoin* because they were considered liable to commit acts of delinquency were increasingly being placed in *yōgoshisetsu*. Certainly, the numbers of children being placed in *kyōgoin* continued to fall during the 1980s and early 1990s (see Table 5) and while in 1977, 1982, and 1987 only 7.8 per cent, 10.5 per cent, and 9.4 per cent of children in *yōgoshisetsu* were thought to have been involved in anti-social behaviour (*han-shakaiteki mondai kōdō*) (Kita, 1996: 59; Tokyo-to Shakai Fukushi Kyōgikai, 1986/7: 209), in 1995 the figure appeared to be much higher (see Table 16). It was certainly the subjective experience of those working in *yōgoshisetsu* in some areas of Japan, particularly Tokyo, that more of what they called *mondaiji* (problem children), or sometimes a '*wild child*', were being admitted to the homes than had been the case twenty years earlier.

YŌGOSHISETSU AND THE UN CONVENTION ON THE RIGHTS OF THE CHILD

If the falling birth rate provided one impetus for *yōgoshisetsu* to begin to reconsider their role in society, a second impetus was provided by the discussions surrounding Japan's ratification of the UN Convention on the Rights of the Child. Japan became a signatory to the Convention on 21 September 1990, and the proposal for its ratification was submitted to the Diet in March 1992. After a further two years' discussion, Japan became the 158th country to ratify the Convention (on 29 March 1994) and it took effect on 22 May of the same year (Matsushima 1996: 125). Ratification, however, did not put an end to debate, which was resumed with renewed vigour in 1998 when the United Nations Committee on the Rights of the Child (Japan) considered a report from the Japanese government on how it had gone about implementing the Convention.

At one level, the debate throughout the 1990s was focused on the appropriateness of introducing a convention at all that referred to children as independent individuals endowed with human rights—and which obligated governments to protect the 'best interests' of the child—into a society where children had historically been viewed as dependent subjects in need of protection. Japan, of course, was far from alone in having such debates. As the authors of the UNICEF publication *The Best Interests of the Child* (Alston 1994) asked, can a universal declaration be of practical use when applied to a specific cultural context?[4] Or in the case of this particular convention is there a danger of imposing what might generally be conceived as largely Western-derived[5] concepts of 'the child' and 'rights' on to a society with very different ideas about what these concepts mean?

One of the most significant consequences in Japan of the debates about the UN Convention was the emergence of a number of domestic non-governmental human rights organizations which were established to pressurize the government to ratify the Convention and then to conform to its obligations by enacting new legislation and to make adults and children themselves generally more aware of

issues of children's rights (Kita, 1998: 34–8). These groups included the Jidō
Kenri Kyōkai (Children's Rights Council), ARC (Action for the Rights of Children), and Kodomo no Jinkenren (Federation for the Protection of Children's
Human Rights), as well as a number of more locally based groups. The most vocal
and powerful voice in these debates, however, belonged to Nichibenren (the Japan
Federation of Bar Associations). Nichibenren, of which all lawyers are automati-
cally members, is an interesting organization. Its power emanates from the very
high status of lawyers in Japanese society. Each year, a quota of fewer than 1,000
(out of 30,000) applicants pass the law exams which allow them to go on to practice. As a result, Japan has a much lower proportion (1 : 9,199) of lawyers per
head of the population than other OECD countries such as France (1 : 3,468), the
UK (1 : 879), or the USA (1 : 358) (Oda, 1992: appendix 2), and an even greater
sense that those who do become lawyers are part of an elite. Despite such elitism,
however, and quite unlike, for example, the conservative Japanese Medical Association, Nichibenren has always retained a radical image, probably best exemplified by the fact that it has frequently been headed by a lawyer specializing in
human rights law, despite the fact that such lawyers constitute only a small proportion of the membership. It has vigorously pursued issues of human rights, and
from the beginning of the 1990s was an energetic and vocal champion of the UN
Convention on the Rights of the Child.

Nichibenren and other organizations set out largely to oppose the insistence of
the Japanese government—in particular the Ministries of Education, Health and
Welfare, and Justice—that even when Japan ratified the Convention, it would not
be necessary to modify any existing laws concerning children since the necessary
protection of their rights was already enshrined in the post-war Constitution
(Matsushima, 1996: 126). Any apparent conflict between Japanese legislation and
the Convention, according to the government, was simply a question of how the
Convention was interpreted (Kita, 1992: 4). Since Japanese is not an official UN
language, there was indeed room for interpretation and it was not surprising,
therefore, that there soon existed in Japan three competing Japanese translations
of the Convention—by the government, by the Japanese branch of UNICEF, and
by the Kokusai Kyōikuhō Kenkyūkai (Study Group on International Education
Law)—supporting the interpretations of three different interest groups (see
Nichibenren, 1993: 554–637).

Some government officials in Japan argued that the idea of 'interests' which
underlies the concept of the 'best interests of the child' in the Convention was one
that had become a central plank of Anglo-Saxon thinking over a long history of
bloody struggle, but was not one with which the Japanese were familiar (Tokyo-
to Shakai Fukushi Kyōgikai, 1996a: 16).[6] Others argued that the emphasis on
rights among children would only encourage selfishness and social confusion (see
Kita, 1992: 6). Perhaps most powerful of all, however, was the argument than an
emphasis on rights would conflict with what Matsushima (1996: 142) has called
Japan's 'ancient "national harmony" or "family harmony" philosophy'. In Japan,

the rights of the family have generally even in the modern period prevailed over those of individual members of the family, including children. Many in Japan felt that this explained the continued stability of the Japanese family—lower divorce rates, greater care for parents—compared to most Western societies, where the rights of the individual prevailed over those of the family (see Ozawa, 1996 for an overview of these discussions).

It was no surprise, therefore, that when, in its report to the UN committee in May 1998, the Japanese government announced that it had fulfilled, or was in the process of fulfilling, all the requirements of the Convention, Nichibenren responded by submitting a counter-report accusing the government of having failed to understand and implement many of its main tenets. Some of Nichibenren's (1997: 95) strongest criticisms were reserved for the continuing role of *yōgoshisetsu* in Japanese society: 'In Japan, it has long been taken for granted that children in institutions should receive a level of care inferior to that extended to children living in normal surroundings since welfare, especially the welfare of children, has been seen as a favour rather than as a right.' Among the features of *yōgoshisetsu* that the Nichibenren report (1997: 95–102) highlighted for particular criticism were the continued use of physical punishment (*taibatsu*); the lack of specialist treatment for children who had been abused; the inadequate levels of funding, staffing, and privacy (including an unreasonable emphasis on rules regulating children's daily lives); the children's poor school advancement rates; inadequate after-care facilities; and the inability to take into account individual children's desires both about where they were placed and how they were treated there. It criticized the government for scarcely altering the minimum standards of care in homes over the previous fifty years, despite Japan's astonishing rates of economic development, and for not monitoring homes closely enough.

The Nichibenren report specifically mentioned incidents of physical abuse by staff in homes and expressed concern that physical punishment was still widely tolerated. It called for a body to be set up that could independently monitor the daily life of children in *yōgoshisetsu*, since children themselves were unable to insist on their rights, and for local authorities only to assign those with specialized qualifications to work in *jidōsōdanjo*.[7] Finally, it recommended that all children in care should at least be given the option of staying on in a *yōgoshisetsu* up to the age of 18, even if they left school at 15.

In June 1998 the UN Committee on the Rights of the Child (Japan) considered the Japanese government's report alongside that of Nichibenren and also heard from three Japanese children who had been brought to the meeting in Geneva by a Japanese non-governmental organization. One of these was a 17-year-old girl who had spent thirteen years in a *yōgoshisetsu* in Tokyo, who expressed the view that staff in homes would never be able to ensure the 'best interests' of the children in their care when so much of their time and effort had to be invested in *kanri* (control) due to the size, structure, and staffing levels of homes. Her sentiments were echoed in the final report of the UN Committee (United Nations,

1998), which was critical of the continuing reliance on residential institutions and the level of care that they provided. It urged the Japanese government to work more closely with the various children's rights organizations to change the child welfare system in Japan.

The UN Committee was clearly disappointed at the way in which the Convention had been implemented in Japan by 1998. It may well have underestimated, however, the wider ramifications of the debates that had surrounded Japan's ratification of the Convention. The groups which emerged during the 1990s determined to monitor the government's performance in regard to the Convention—which could be seen as part of the wider development of citizens' groups (*shimin dantai*) following the Kobe earthquake and the inability of the bureaucracy to deal with the subsequent crisis—brought about important changes in the child welfare system. These included the establishment in a number of areas (such as Tokyo) of children's rights ombudsmen, and the issue to children in *yōgoshisetsu* in many areas (such as Tokyo and Osaka) of booklets which set out their rights and explained what to do and whom to contact if they felt that these had been violated. Perhaps most importantly, the debate about children's rights which had largely been generated by the Convention was responsible, at least in part, for the 'discovery' in the 1990s of the existence of child abuse in Japan.

CHILD ABUSE

As we saw in Chapter 3, the official view has always been that children come into care because of their parents' problems rather than because they have problems of their own. It is particularly noticeable how few children appear to have been admitted because they have been abused. In 1987 this category accounted for just 2.9 per cent of children, of whom, according to Tsuzura (1990: 38), around 4.5 per cent were the victims of sexual abuse. This looked very different from the situation in the UK where sexual abuse alone was reported to be the main cause for the admission of around one-third of all children in homes (Warner, 1992).

In the late 1980s, as Ikeda (1987:204) pointed out, the majority of Japanese, including many professionals in child welfare, believed that there was no, or virtually no, child abuse in Japan. In this regard, some argued, Japan was quite different from most Western nations. The apparent absence of abuse was generally explained in terms of the stability of the Japanese family, community, and wider society (see Wagatsuma, 1981 for a good example of this argument).

For example, the structure of the Japanese family, it was maintained, made the likelihood of child abuse much lower than in Western societies. 'Traditional' family ties remained strong (60 per cent of the elderly still lived with someone of a younger generation, as opposed to 8 per cent in the UK and 14 per cent in the US). This meant not only extra hands to help but extra eyes to detect abuse.

Crude divorce rates (the number of divorces per total population) were less than half those of the UK and almost one-quarter those of the USA (*JIC*, 1987: 92). Annual illegitimacy rates were still below 1 per cent (compared to around 30 per cent in US and UK and over 50 per cent in some European countries).[8] Teenage mothers were almost non-existent.[9] Japan not only had one of the highest proportions of the population getting married (less than 5 per cent of men and women aged 50 or less had never married) but also one of the highest average ages at first marriage for both men (28) and women (almost 26) (Ochiai, 1996: 55). Few women had followed the path of an increasing number of women in western Europe and North America of bringing children up by themselves. Single-parent families constituted less than 1.5 per cent of all households (Peng, 1995).

Both the status and style of motherhood were also seen as playing a major role in preventing child abuse in Japan. Japan had a well-documented and sharply drawn division of labour around gender (male: public sphere; female: domestic sphere)[10] where the two roles were ideologically supposed to complement each other. For women, the dual role of mother and wife was seen as a professional one, and fulfilling it well conferred high status. Non-working women described themselves as *sengyō shufu* (professional housewives) on official forms (Imamura, 1987).[11] With 96 per cent of mothers in Japan finishing senior high school and over 40 per cent completing some form of tertiary education, Japanese mothers were almost certainly the most highly educated in the world as well as, on average, among the most mature in years at the time they became mothers.

Other factors that were also seen to make child abuse unlikely included the continuing stability of the community, the high status of community institutions, and the acceptance of the authority of the state. The system of local police boxes (*kōban*) meant a much closer relationship between members of the police force and the local community than in most Western societies. The *minsei.jidōiin* system meant that any abuse of children within the local community should be picked up very early by voluntary welfare workers who were members of the same community. Teachers enjoyed high status in society and parents listened to and accepted their advice. Schools gave regular physical check-ups to all children and insisted that parents follow up any concerns by visiting their doctors.

Finally, the stability of post-war society more generally was seen as important in explaining the absence of abuse of children. As sociologists who often argued a link between the two might have put it, the lack of deprivation precluded an increase in depravation. The fruits of Japan's impressive post-war economic growth had been relatively equally shared throughout society. Over 90 per cent of the population annually declared themselves to be members of a mass middle class, and there was a widespread belief in both the cultural homogeneity of the Japanese population and the lack of significant minority groups. Recorded rates for all forms of serious crime were very low compared with all other OECD countries; murder rates were one-fifth, rates of reported rape one-tenth, rates of robbery one-sixtieth of those in the UK. Arrest rates were remarkably high—98 per cent for murder and rape; almost 80 per cent for robbery (*JIC*, 1987: 92)— and those arrested were almost always convicted. People in Japan had the sense that they and their children lived in a very safe country. Overall, therefore, it seemed that for a wide variety of reasons Japan diverged from the view of many experts at the time (see Korbin, 1987) that child abuse was a concomitant feature of all developed societies.

'Hidden' Child Abuse

It should be said that even before the 1990s not everyone in Japan accepted that there was no child abuse in the country.[12] Ikeda (1987), for example, suggested that those few cases of abuse which were reported were probably only those instances where it was impossible for the abuse to be ignored any further; others explained the low rates of reported abuse on factors such as a lack of a well-articulated sys-tem of reporting and recording child abuse and a strong reluctance to get involved in the personal business of others in part, according to Kitamura *et al.* (1999: 24), because of fears of being sued by victims' parents for defamation.

Technically, under Article 25 of the 1947 Child Welfare Law, anyone who saw a child who was not being properly cared for was obliged to report it to the *jidōsōdanjo* or the local welfare office. The law, however, was not backed up by any sanction. Very few people reported their concerns about children with whom they had no direct link; in 1990 of the 12,000 child welfare cases referred to the twelve Tokyo *jidōsōdanjo*, only 0.9 per cent were referrals by neighbours. Even doctors and teachers often appeared unwilling to report suspicions of abuse (Hashimoto, 1996: 146). A 1991 survey undertaken by Nichibenren in the Kinki district of Japan suggested that less than half of the doctors in the area would uncondition-ally report to *jidōsōdanjo* child abuse cases which they came across in the course of their work (*JTW*, 12 Dec. 1994). Similarly, while teachers at the compulsory school level (up to the age of 15) were obliged to visit students at home at least once a year, it would appear that they very rarely took suspicions of possible child abuse any further than talking directly to the parents and/or guardians involved.

Even when cases were taken further, some critics suggested that the local gov-ernment workers in the *jidōsōdanjo* were reluctant to seek recourse to the law for fear that a case they brought would be unsuccessful and that this might harm their future careers in local government. As a result, the trend appeared to be to redefine cases of suspected child abuse as *yōiku kanren* (general concerns to do with bringing up children) and attempt to advise the parents on correct and acceptable practice, rather than seek to remove the child, even temporarily, to a safer environment (see Table 1).[13]

Similarly, there was considerable evidence that the police were reluctant—and of course Japan was far from alone in this—to get involved in domestic 'disputes'. The section of the police that dealt with such cases, recently renamed the *seikatsu anzenka* (life safety section), had little or no specialist training in dealing with issues of abuse and tended to be looked down on by other sections of the force. According to various voluntary civil rights groups, girls who were picked up by the police for teenage prostitution sometimes claimed that they had been abused at home, but were often taken back there without their allegations being examined (*JTW*, 13 June 1994).

Even if the police did wish to pursue a case, it was widely recognized that the courts were reluctant to become involved in issues of child abuse because of the rights afforded to parents in Japan. According to Kamiide (1990: 8), although there was a provision for removing parental powers under Article 33–6 of the Child Welfare Law, there were only ten instances where this was in force in 1990. In any case, even when courts placed children in *yōgoshisetsu*, parents retained the right to remove them when they wanted. The following case described by Ikeda (1982: 489 and 1984: 11), was not, she claimed, uncommon:

We know of one case of a twin girl[14] who was abused by her mother. She was starved and burned with cigarettes among other things. The police discovered the girl and put her in a child welfare institution through a [*jidsōdanjo*]. However, one year later the parents came along promising not to abuse the girl any more. The father signed a statement and swore to divorce his wife if she mistreated the girl any more. The girl was returned to her family who then moved to another town. As was expected, she was abused again by her mother.

As Ikeda notes, once a child was removed from an institution by its parents, the case was considered closed and there was no follow-up work undertaken with the family or monitoring of the child. Some homes were sensitive to this and, as a result, there were examples of children being hidden in homes or moved around between homes as the only means of protecting them from parents or guardians who wanted to claim them back (see Sargeant, 1994).

Defining Child Abuse

During the 1980s a handful of groups dealing with child welfare issues began to question whether the apparently low level of child abuse in Japan compared to Western societies was actually due to a different definition of abuse. Two surveys, for example, suggested that a large proportion of those who were abusers were not aware, or would not accept, that what they had done constituted abuse (Fujimoto, 1994: 35–70). In a 1983 survey (N = 416), only 10 per cent of perpetrators admitted to being conscious that they were committing abuse; 60 per cent admitted performing the actions involved but did not perceive them to be abusive; and 20 per cent blamed others for their actions. In a 1988 survey (N = 1,039), the proportion who admitted performing the actions but not perceiving them as abusive had dropped slightly, but was still around 50 per cent. A high proportion of those abused (at least 50 per cent) had themselves been abused when young.

One of the most interesting features about the first surveys of child abuse in

Japan were the definitions they used of what constituted abuse (see Fujimoto, 1994). A 1973 survey, the first to be carried out by Kōseishō, used the five categories of abandonment, murder, *oyako shinjū* (discussed below), murder by abandonment, and abuse, which was defined as causing physical injuries by violence, not providing food over a long period, and endangering life (see Table 26).

The survey was undertaken in the light of reports of an increase in the number of infants being abandoned by mothers in coin lockers which had recently been installed in Japanese railway stations. Indeed over a quarter of all murdered babies who had been abandoned were, according the survey, found in coin lockers, and while counter-measures were taken in 1981 which dramatically reduced the number, the practice continued, as did other forms of murder by abandonment (see Kouno and Johnson, 1995).[15] According to some commentators, however, there was a considerable degree of sympathy towards the mother in such cases. If the mother of the abandoned baby was found she was rarely given a prison sentence because, as Kouno and Johnson (1995: 28) explain, she was 'considered to have been in a mentally unusual situation during and after the pregnancy'.[16]

The category of *oyako shinjū* perhaps gives the most interesting insight into how ideas about abuse are linked to the relationship between parent and child in Japan. *Oyako shinjū* is also known variously in Japanese as *boshi shinjū*, *fushi shinjū*, and *ikka shinjū*, where the first word in each expression refers respectively to parent–child, mother–child, father–child, and whole family and the word *shinjū* connotes a double suicide committed out of love. (It is indeed the word used for a suicide pact made by lovers.) Neither in Japanese—nor in English translation—is the word murder ever used in what is, in practical terms, the murder of the child by the parent followed by the parent's suicide.

TABLE 26. Survey of the abuse, abandonment, and murder of children under the age of 3 (1973) N = 423

	Natural father		Natural mother		Step-parents		Others		Unknown		Total	
	No.	%	No.	%	No.	%	No.	%	No.	%	No.	%
Abuse	6	23.1	16	61.5	2	7.7	2	7.7	0	—	26	6.1
Abandonment*	26	18.7	74	53.2	0	—	2	1.4	37	26.7	139	32.9
Murder by abandonment*	7	5.1	51	37.2	0	—	0	—	79	57.7	137	32.4
Murder	9	16.7	40	74.1	1	1.9	4	7.4	0	—	54	12.7
Oyako shinjū	12	17.9	53	79.1	0	—	2	3.0	0	—	67	15.8
TOTAL	60	14.2	234	55.3	3	0.7	10	2.4	116	27.4		

Source: Fujimoto, 1994: 38 (based on an original survey by the Children and Families Bureau, Kōseishō).

* The distinction in the survey between 'abandonment' and 'murder by abandonment' refers largely to where the child was found abandoned. In the former case, children were generally left in open public areas such as parks, hospitals, or post offices with the intention that they should be found and taken into care; in the latter case, they were found locked in their own homes or coin lockers and had been left to die.

The practice of *oyako shinjū* has a long history in Japan,[17] but high rates have particularly been recorded in times of economic depression. Indeed, in the 1930s it became so widespread that it was in response to it that the government enacted the first child welfare legislation in 1933 (Jidō Gyakutai Bōshihō, the Prevention of Cruelty to Children Law) and 1937 (Boshi Hogohō, the Mothers' Aid Law). The practice continued, however, into the post-war period. In 1983 alone according to one source (Garrison, 1984), there were 400 reported incidents involving over 1,000 deaths.[18]

Describing what is in effect child murder as family suicide is revealing of social attitudes. Even more revealing, though, are accounts of the criticism of parents who have committed—or who have attempted to commit—suicide without first killing their children. Takahashi (1977) and Garrison (1984) both describe the case of a mother who unsuccessfully attempted suicide and was severely criticized for not having murdered her children first; she successfully performed *boshi shinjū* at her next attempt. The specifically cultural nature of *oyako shinjū*, however, is best demonstrated when the practice has taken place overseas, a well-documented example of which is the so-called 'Santa Monica *Oyako Shinjū* Case' (see Woo, 1989).

In 1985 a Japanese mother in her mid-thirties, on discovering her husband's infidelity and with one failed marriage behind her already, decided to commit suicide and took her two children (aged 4 years and 6 months) to the beach with her. She managed to drown the children in the Pacific ocean, but was herself rescued by others who were on the beach at the time, and she subsequently found herself facing prosecution for the double murder of her children. The Japanese-American community, with support from Japan, managed to collect a 25,000-name petition on her behalf appealing that the case should be viewed as an example not of child murder but of *oyako shinjū*. Her supporters argued that there had been no malice towards the children in what she had done; indeed she had done it out of her love for them and hence she should be given a lenient, probationary sentence. According to Woo (1989), her American lawyer was unwilling to pursue this cultural defence, not least because in arguing that she knew what she was doing in killing the children she would be seriously prejudicing her own position in terms of American law. Instead, he found a number of American psychologists who were able to diagnose her mental state at the time of the incident as one of 'introjection'—the inability to distinguish her own life from those of her children which in American cultural terms could be termed a form of temporary insanity—and therefore neatly turned a cultural practice (*oyako shinjū*) into a psychological pathology.

The practice of *oyako shinjū* goes a long way in demonstrating the different perceptions of the parent–child relationship in Japan and the United States. In Japan the child is often described as a *mono* (object) which is an extension of, rather than separate from, the parent (Yamamura, 1986: 34). The rights of the family come before those of the child, and where the child has clearly suffered this can be explained in terms of the over-zealous actions of an adult who was acting only in the best interests of the family. According to Wagatsuma (1981: 120), writing in the early 1980s, the fact that Japanese parents were more likely to kill or abandon their children than keep and abuse them explained the apparently low rate of the forms of child abuse that were practised in other societies. Similarly, Ikeda (1987: 206) made a distinction between what she called Japanese-style (*Nihongata*) forms of abuse (such as abandonment and *oyako shinjū*) and 'Western' (*ōbeigata*) forms of abuse (such as sexual and physical maltreatment).[19]

In 1988, however, a large survey of child abuse in Japan was undertaken which did not include the category of *oyako shinjū* at all (see Table 27). Instead, the definition of abuse used was 'physical violence, abandonment and desertion, neglect or refusal to protect, sexual assault, emotional abuse and prevention from attending school' (Tsuzaki Tetsurō, 1996: 112–16). These categories were much closer to definitions of abuse in North America and northern Europe at the time. The figure for sexual abuse in the survey (less than 5 per cent of all abuse cases), however, reflected a situation in Japan which was quite different from that in the US and UK where, as Hacking (1991) pointed out, sexual abuse had by itself in the late 1980s become virtually synonymous with the category of child abuse.[20]

La Fontaine (1988, 1990) has argued that it was the redefinition of child sexual abuse in terms of an abuse of power that led to a major change in the perception of abuse in general in the UK in the mid-1980s. The redefinition of incest as child abuse was a particularly important step. In Japan the view of incestuous relationships according to some commentators has been, as La Fontaine (1988: 6) said the view was in the UK in the mid-1980s, 'oddly muted'. Allison (1996: 7), for example, examines in detail articles which explored the issue of mother–son incestuous

TABLE 27. Survey of abuse of children under the age of 17 (1 April–30 September 1988) N = 1,039

Main abuser	Type of abuse						
	Physical violence	Abandonment/ desertion	Refusal to protect	Sexual assault	Emotional abuse	Forbidden to go to school	Total
Natural father	106	39	111	20	28	13	317
Stepfather	29	3	17	10	1	—	60
Live-in father	15	—	3	9	2	2	31
Foster-father	—	—	—	1	—	—	1
Natural mother	79	162	235	—	20	10	506
Stepmother	15	—	7	—	12	—	34
Live-in mother	4	1	5	—	3	—	13
Foster-mother	1	—	—	—	—	—	1
Other people	26	—	13	8	2	3	52
Unknown	—	24	—	—	—	—	24
% affected	26.5	22.0	37.7	4.6	6.5	2.7	

Source: Fujimoto, 1994: 59 (based on a survey by the Association of Heads of Jidōsōdanjo (Jidōsōdanjochōkai)).

relations in the 1970s and 1980s in Japan, the tone of which she describes as ranging 'from condemnatory to sympathetic and almost celebratory'.[21]

Japanese law still does not recognize incest (*kinshin sōkan*) as a crime—though morally it may be abhorred—unless rape or indecent assault has taken place (which may be difficult to prove) and the victim is prepared to press charges (which is very hard for them to do). Child sexual abuse reporting, therefore, has almost always been limited to the sexual abuse of girls over the age of 10 (almost always by adult men) or the forcing of children to perform obscene acts with a third party (Ikeda, 1987: 70). In Table 27, all but one of the 48 cases of sexual abuse were of girls over the age of 10. In all but one case, the perpetrator was a man.

The definition of physical abuse in the late 1980s and early 1990s was also unclear in Japan. Indeed, when the first child-abuse hotlines were set up in Osaka and Tokyo respectively, they immediately received twenty calls a day, mainly from mothers wanting to know whether what they were doing to their children constituted abuse and, if so, what they could do to stop it (Nashima, *JTW*, 13 June 1994). By the end of the first year of both hotlines, some 90 per cent of all calls were on the same theme (Katō and Tatsuno, 1998: 108–9). Much of the uncertainty reflected by these callers related to the fact that the use of physical force against children was described using a number of different expressions: *taibatsu* (corporal punishment), *chōkai* (disciplinary punishment), *gyakutai* (abuse), and the more general term *shitsuke* (training).[22] Only the third of these terms carries a totally negative connotation, while the others could all be used in a positive sense depending on the context. The right of parents to use *chōkai* 'in so far as it is necessary' is indeed enshrined in article 822 (*chōkaiken*) of the revised Civil Code (Oda, 1997: 168).

Confusion about the appropriateness of physical punishment was not restricted to domestic situations. Legally, the position on using force against children in education is very clear. Physical punishment is banned in all Japanese schools (Gakkō Kyōikuhō, Article 11). In reality, the use of physical discipline has often been accepted as an integral part of turning Japanese children into adult members of Japanese society (Field, 1995: 59). A 1984 survey, for example, suggested that physical punishment was practised in almost all (97 per cent) of Japanese schools (*AS*, 30 May 1984). Perhaps more significant, however, were surveys which suggested that the majority of parents (regularly about 70 per cent) supported the use of discipline as being good for their children (*kodomo no tame*).[23] The use of physical punishment by staff in *yōgoshisetsu* was banned by law with the revision of the Child Welfare Law in 1998, but a survey carried out almost two years later suggested that only 30 per cent of homes had actually instituted rules prohibiting it and only 15 per cent instructed their staff about children's rights (*AS*, 12 Apr. 2000).

The 'Discovery' of Child Abuse in Japan0

The 1988 survey seemed to show a sudden 450 per cent increase in cases of child abuse dealt with by the *jidōsōdanjo* since a previous survey only five years earlier.

Certain groups immediately declared that the statistics were the 'tip of the ice-berg' (*hyōzan no ikkaku*) (see Ueno, 1994: 9) and that child abuse was a serious issue that needed to be confronted in Japan. Partly in response to these concerns, in 1990 Kōseishō established a common definition of child abuse—limited to the four categories of physical abuse, neglect or the refusal to protect, sexual abuse, and psychological abuse (see *KH*, 1997: 91 for a fuller definition);[24] established the category of 'abuse' (*gyakutai*) among the reasons for a consultation at *jidōsōdanjo*; and began to collect statistics annually.

As so often in the history of child welfare in Japan, however, the first major initiatives in dealing with the perceived new and growing problems of child-abuse were private. These were the establishment of two child-abuse telephone counselling services (*jidō gyakutai sōdan denwa*) in 1990 and 1991 in Osaka and Tokyo respectively. The Osaka line was set up by a voluntary group which called itself Jidō Gyakutai Bōshi Kyōkai (Association for the Prevention of Child Abuse, APCA). It received 90 per cent of its funding from the Kansai Television Company—which screened three one-hour documentaries on child abuse in 1989—and it was a non-profit-making, non-governmental organization staffed by part-time workers.[25]

A year later a voluntary organization called Kodomo no Gyakutai Bōshi Cen-tre (Centre for Child Abuse Prevention, CCAP) set up a line in Tokyo. In both the Kansai and the Kantō regions, the main actors in constructing the debate about child abuse were lawyers, paediatricians (such as Kobayashi Noboru), nurses at the local health centres (*hokenfu*), academics such as Ikeda Yoshiko, and a few well-known and outspoken individuals who worked in family courts, *jidōsōdanjo*, and *yōgoshisetsu*.

The opening of the Tokyo line in May 1991 was preceded by a large conference which brought together a number of different groups to discuss child abuse from a variety of perspectives. This conference, together with the opening of the telephone lines, precipitated a sudden growth in awareness of child abuse in Japan and a new vocabulary—specifically the expression *jidō gyakutai*—quickly entered the public arena.[26] During the second half of 1991, articles appeared not only in medical and legal journals but also in popular women's magazines and newspapers. NHK, the national broadcasting company, aired 'specials' on child abuse on three consecutive nights in September. New special-interest groups were also formed: the 'WE' group in Yokohama for professionals and victims; the Stop Child Sexual Abuse (STOPCSA) group for victims only. A number of mothers who had abused or were abusing their children set up their own self-help group to tackle the problem called the Kodomo wo Gyakutai Shite Shimau Haha Oya Tachi (Mothers who Cannot Stop Abusing their Children).

By the mid-1990s, discussion of child abuse had begun to become a regular part of the world of child welfare specialists. Official figures on child abuse, while still very low by North American and north European standards, had begun to show the kind of exponential growth that many of those societies had seen in the

1970s and 1980s (see Figure VIII).[27] Newspaper headlines such as *Kodomo gyakutai sōdan, nananen de gobai* (Consultations on child abuse increase fivefold in seven years, *AS*, 26 Oct. 1998) reflected not so much an increase in child abuse as an increased awareness among professionals of its existence and a greater sophistication in identifying and recording possible cases.

The increase in professional awareness of child abuse was made most noticeable by the increasing number of prefectures and major cities (Hokkaidō, Fukushima, Tochigi, Saitama, Gunma, Yokohama, Shizuoka, and Wakayama) which followed the example of Osaka and Tokyo and set up their own organizations to monitor and advise on cases of abuse. These organizations included institutions such as health centres, schools, hospitals, and clinics. An association called Nihon Kodomo no Gyakutai Bōshi Kenkyūkai.JaSPCAN (Japan Society for the Prevention of Child Abuse and Neglect) was established as an umbrella organization to bring together the many regional and local groups. Its third and fourth meetings in 1997 and 1998 in Yokohama and Wakayama were attended by over 1,500 professionals from almost all areas of child welfare.[28]

In late 1999 the issue of child abuse was forced into the public consciousness even more strongly. In part this was due to a new child sex law introduced in November 1999 in the light of what was perceived to be a growing problem of young girls offering under-age sex in exchange for money (a phenomenon known as *enjo kōsai*) and of international criticism of Japan as the source of 80 per cent of the commercial child pornography available on the Internet (*DY*, 10 Dec. 1998). In part, it was due to a growing awareness of how far Japan was out of line with some Western societies in dealing with the issue of domestic violence, following the arrest of the Japanese consul in Canada for abusing his wife: he is alleged to have said that what he had done was acceptable practice in Japan. In part it was due to the continuing efforts of a number of groups, including doctors, lawyers, and those in the child welfare world to continue to raise awareness of the issue. Newspapers mounted a number of investigations into the subject, and a survey by the *Mainichi Shinbun* reported that between January 1997 and April 1999 eighty-three children had been killed as a result of abuse inflicted on them by their parents or other adults (Yamashina, *MS*, 26 Aug. 1999).

In July 1999 Kōseishō published the results of its own survey which revealed that 328 children had died as a result of abuse over the five-year period between 1992 and 1997. One-quarter of these cases were in lone-mother families; 80 per cent of deaths were through assault; 20 per cent were through neglect or abandonment (*AS*, 28 July 1999). This followed hard on an earlier announcement that fifteen children had died in 1997 from abuse which had already been brought to the attention of *jidōsōdanjo* (*AS*, 31 Mar. 1999).[29] As a result of this, it sent a circular to all *jidōsōdanjo* which greatly broadened the type of case that they should deal with under the category of abuse. These included cases of neglect where parents left babies alone in prams on the ground floor while they shopped on the second floor, cases of physical abuse even where an 'assault does not leave an external

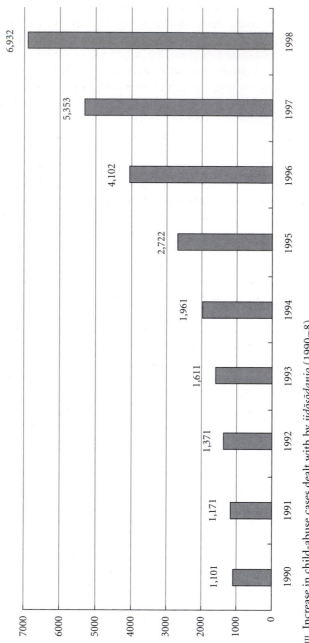

Fig. VIII Increase in child-abuse cases dealt with by *jidōsōdanjo* (1990–8)
Sources: *KH*, 1998: 111; *AS*, 2 Nov. 1999.

wound' (*gaishō ga nokoranai bōkō*), and cases of psychological abuse where parents discriminated against one child in favour of another (*AS*, 5 July 1999).

By the late 1990s, therefore, there had been a major reappraisal of the notion at the beginning of the decade that Japan was immune from the problem of child abuse that afflicted industrial societies in the West. In some reports, the issue of child abuse in Japan took on the aura of a moral panic so that, rather than simply discovering the possibility of child abuse in society, some sections of society were beginning to suggest that it was endemic. One widely disseminated survey (*YS*, 10 Aug. 1999), carried out by the Centre for Child Abuse Prevention in Tokyo, suggested that as many as 40 per cent of mothers actually either abused or mistreated their children.[30]

Under pressure of reports of the dramatic increase in cases of child abuse, the government announced that to tackle the problem it would increase its budget by an unprecedented 90 per cent to ¥900 million from April 2000 (*YS*, 29 Aug. 1999). This new money was to be spent on a number of new programmes including the establishment of 100 committees across the country with members from schools, day-care centres, local government welfare offices, and the newly established urban child and family support centres which were mostly based at *yōgoshisetsu*. These committees were charged with raising awareness in the community about child abuse, especially among the police, doctors, and teachers. In particular, they were to take some of the burden away from the *jidōsōdanjo*, whose workers, who often already had an average caseload of over 50 active cases, were in danger of being swamped by the increase in the number of child-abuse referrals. It was reported that even family courts in some areas—again notably Osaka and largely under pressure from a small number of human rights lawyers—were becoming aware of child-abuse issues and becoming more willing to consider the removal of parental rights so that children could be forcibly taken into care by staff from *jidōsōdanjo*. At the same time, Kōseishō announced that *minsei.jidōiin* and *shūnin jidōiin* should be seen as another social agency alongside the *jidōsōdanjo* to whom child abuse allegations could be referred (*AS*, 22 Sept. 1999). This was a further sign of the expanding role in social work provision being given to a system that few had expected to survive the immediate post-war period.

The 'discovery' of child abuse was largely as a result of the campaigns of a variety of different groups in Japanese society. The role that the media played was particularly important. The media in Japan have often played the main role in focusing government attention on specific social problems, and indeed in some ways child abuse can be seen as simply the latest in a long series of social problems which the media have discovered in Japanese society over the past two decades and given easily recognized labels such as: *gakkyū hōkai* (collapse of the classroom); *tōkōkyohi* (school refusal syndrome); *ijime* (bullying—of children by other children); *kōnai bōryoku* (school violence—by pupils against teachers); *kateinai bōryoku* (domestic violence—by children against their parents). Japan's mass media are marked by their homogeneity—it is sometimes argued that editors of major newspapers believe that readers do not want to feel that their paper is too far out of touch with the mainstream of public opinion—and hence once the issue of child abuse had been picked up by one part of the media (led mainly by the Mainichi media group based in Osaka, which has seen itself as being in the vanguard of child-abuse debates over the past decade) it was predictable that others would jump on the bandwagon. All the above social problems have gone through remarkably similar stages—'discovery': definition; the collection of statistics that seem to show a sharp increase in incidence; the implementation of measures to tackle it; and its gradual control and disappearance—and, to some extent, it might be argued that *jidō gyakutai* (child abuse) is just the latest passing fad of the media.

Such an account, however, ignores the significance of the explanations that are given to each social problem as it emerges and does not explain why some problems but not others quickly gain currency as issues which need state intervention. The explanations that were given for the emergence of child abuse in Japan, for example, tied in with broad-ranging debates that were going on in Japan at the end of the twentieth century, including discussions of individual rights and the changing family structure. Fujimoto (1994: 35) provided a good example of some of these arguments when he wrote: 'Child abuse has never been a big social problem on a national level in Japan . . . However with an infiltration of European and American life style[s] [on] social, economic and cultural levels . . . social problem[s] such as child abuse which occurred in Europe and America affected Japan seriously.'

Explanations for the increase in child abuse in the late 1990s have focused on the nuclearization of the Japanese family. New mothers have had virtually no experience of child care (as their mothers had had with, for example, nephews and nieces), nor have grandparents been around to advise or prevent them from abusing their own children. Further, the nuclear family that has developed has never been formed, as in Western societies, around the husband–wife relationship, but instead centres, some have said to an unhealthy degree, on the mother–child one. In post-war sociological works on the Japanese family, the father has often been described as being more firmly 'married' to the company than to his wife.

This 'Japanese' form of the nuclear family has been seen as being unhealthy for the socialization of the child. The father-figure has often been absent and often under excessive stress at work, where he has been forced to spend long hours with colleagues after normal working hours. He has hardly been involved in the rearing of his children at all, and they have often became excessively dependent on their mothers.[31] As a result, the nuclear family has been seen as being particularly stressful for mothers. This stress has been exacerbated, according to Ohinata (1995a, 1995b), by what she has called the 'myth of motherhood', the idea that women are naturally (*sententeki ni*) programmed to be good and caring mothers. This myth, according to Ohinata, has meant that women are unprepared for motherhood when they first face it and often feel inadequate and unable to seek help when they experience problems. To add to their problems, mothers in Japan have been put under intense pressure to perform as perfect parents. Much of this pressure has come from cultural expectations: mothers have been expected to suffer for the sake of their children (Azuma, 1986: 7) and expected to consistently work on improving their parenting skills (what Befu (1986: 24–5), calls 'role perfectionism'). Should they fail in any mothering skills, then their inadequacy has been constantly reinforced by images of parenthood presented in the enormous quantity of child-training literature which emphasizes that there is a way to do everything properly (see Dingwall, Tanaka, and Minamikata, 1991).[32]

The combined effects of lack of support from a husband, extended family, or the wider community, plus the myth of motherhood and the idea that women are directly responsible for the success of their children has been recognized in the notion that many women suffer from what is known as *ikuji neurosis* (child-rearing neurosis).[33] In a 1994 survey of mothers with children under the age of 15, only 23 per cent of Japanese respondents replied that they found bringing up children rewarding (*tanoshii*) compared to 54 per cent in South Korea and 72 per cent in the USA (*AS*, 20 Nov. 1996). In the early 1990s books on the problems of bringing up children became increasingly popular in Japan (see Shiina, 1993; Tachibana, 1992). Perhaps most revealing of the pressures on mothers have been surveys which have suggested that mothers are the main abusers of children (see Table 28).

Figures which suggest that women have been mainly responsible for abuse to an extent merely reflect the idea that they are primarily responsible for the care of their children. Some feminist historians, indeed, have suggested that the 'discovery' of child abuse can be correlated with a greater proportion of women entering the workforce. Gordon (1988), for example, has documented how rising concerns about child abuse in the United States have closely mirrored increases in female participation in the labour force implying, she suggests, that the continual 'rediscovery' of child abuse is in fact a male discourse to keep women in the domestic sphere.[34] It is possible that a similar argument can be made for the 'discovery' of child abuse in Japan at the end of the late 1980s when, as a result of the bubble economy, there were major changes not only in female participation rates in the workplace but also in the levels to which women were able to advance. The Japanese government, in its 1998 *Kōsei Hakusho* (Annual Report on Health and Welfare), however, took a rather different view: 'In cases of abuse, excluding sexual abuse, natural mothers were the perpetrators twice as often as natural fathers, *reflecting the much greater burden of parenting that is placed on mothers*' (KSH, 1998: 110; italics added).

The 'discovery' of child abuse made it easier for the government to put in place more state-funded systems in the community to support women with families and thereby help both to ease their situation and to encourage other women in the belief that having a family could, in future, be rewarding. At the same time,

TABLE 28. Gender of main abusers in cases of child abuse (1996) N = 1,559

	Non-sexual abuse	Sexual abuse
MEN		
Natural father	416	47
Stepfather	63	15
Adoptive father	58	12
Common-law husband	34	4
Grandfather	11	1
Uncle	3	4
Total	585 (37.5%)	83 (87.4%)
WOMEN		
Natural mother	823	3
Stepmother	50	
Adoptive mother	18	
Foster-mother	2	
Common-law wife	1	
Grandmother	16	
Aunt	5	
Total	915 (58.7%)	3 (3.1%)
GENDER NOT GIVEN		
Siblings	12	5
Others	19	4
Unknown	28	
Total	59 (3.8%)	9 (9.5%)
TOTAL NO. OF CASES	1,559	95

Source: KSH, 1998: 111.

the government tried to link growing awareness of child abuse with the issue of children's rights (*KSH*, 1998: 110):

Domestic child abuse is not always easy to distinguish from discipline [*shitsuke*]. However, as stressed in the Convention on the Rights of the Child, it is essential to set up a system whereby people within the community [*chiiki jūmin*] unfailingly report their concerns about child abuse both as a means of reviewing the relationship between parents and child within the concept of the child as an 'individual endowed with their own rights' [*kenri no shutai*] and within the context of ensuring 'the best interests of the child' [*kodomo no saizen no rieki*].[35]

A year later, at the end of 1999, it was announced that there was already a great increase in the number of reports to *jidōsōdanjo* about suspicions of child abuse from members of the public (*MS*, 16 Nov. 1999). The government also announced plans to bring in mandatory reporting procedures of suspicions of abuse which would increase the figures still further (*YS*, 19 Apr. 2000). The rising rate of reported child abuse led some experts to suggest that the real rates in Japan were no lower than those in Western societies (Kitamura *et al.*, 1999: 21).[36]

TOWARDS A NEW ROLE FOR CHILD PROTECTION
INSTITUTIONS IN JAPAN

The 'discovery' of child abuse in Japanese society has had an effect on the role of *yōgoshisetsu* in two ways. On the one hand, it has changed the perception of the care that homes need to provide for many of the children who are placed in them. Until the late 1990s, the view of *yōgoshisetsu* was that they were to provide an alternative form of care for those children whose parents could not look after them. In many ways, they were simply a continuation of old-fashioned orphanages, despite the fact that, as we have seen, only a small minority of the children in them were technically orphans. Increasingly, however, during the 1990s, it came to be recognized that many children had suffered considerably before coming into care. While officially at the start of the decade only around 3 per cent of children were in care because of 'abuse' (*gyakutai*), to a large extent this figure reflected the fact that the vast majority of children in homes were still placed there 'voluntarily' by parents or guardians who for obvious reasons did not wish 'abuse' to be put down as the main cause for admission. A large-scale survey carried out by academics from Nihon Shakai Jigyō Daigaku (Japan College of Social Work)[37] in Tokyo (Tsutsumi *et al.*, 1996) suggested that a substantial proportion (around 40 per cent) of children who came into care were from very abusive backgrounds and in need of special care. The head of Kodomo Gakuen in 1999 estimated that about half of the children in the home had suffered some form of abuse and, even when they had not been directly abused, in many cases they had been indirectly damaged by the break-up of their families. Equally importantly, he felt, many had been abused by individuals who had themselves been abused, and something had to be done to stop them going on to be abusers themselves.

In some respects, Tsutsumi *et al.* (1996: 213–14) advocate turning *yōgoshisetsu* into institutions which resemble today's children's homes in the UK (see Sinclair and Gibbs, 1998) with highly specialist forms of care on offer to finely distinguished groups of children. To some extent, it would appear that their work was responsible for Kōseishō agreeing to pay from April 1999 for part-time therapists to work in homes where more than ten children had been abused before they came into care. The small scale of this initiative must call its effectiveness into question. It is very unclear, also, how the relationship between part-time therapists and full-time residential staff will develop. Nevertheless, there is no doubt that the increase in the number of cases of abused children that are uncovered will, if only marginally, improve the staffing ratio in homes. It will also mean an increase in the number of children placed in *yōgoshisetsu*; throughout the 1990s around one-fifth of abuse cases dealt with by the *jidōsōdanjo* have resulted in children being placed in *yōgoshisetsu*, which has meant an increase from 366 such children in 1993 to 1,391 in 1998 (*Tokyo Shinbun*, 29 Nov. 1999). Between 1990 and 1998 the number of children officially placed in homes because of abuse increased dramatically from 3.5 per cent to 21.1 per cent (*YnJ*, 2000). While *yōgoshisetsu* may be better able to help children who have been abused, the emergence of an increasingly large number of abused children may at the same time help *yōgoshisetsu* to survive. Ueno (1999), indeed, suggests that *yōgoshisetsu* have been centrally involved in raising awareness of the problem of child abuse in Japan as a means of survival in a period of dramatically declining numbers of children in the population.

The second way in which the 'discovery' of child abuse has affected the role of *yōgoshisetsu* is in the increased role that the homes have been given in the wider community as the site of the new urban child and family support centres. A plan drawn up by the association of the heads of all the homes (Yōgoshisetsuchōkai) in 1995 saw the 'future role of *yōgoshisetsu*' as comprising three main interconnected areas (see *KH*, 1996: 103): (*a*) an alternative to family care; (*b*) a family support service; and (*c*) a medico-educational, independent living service to aid the proper development of all children. Under this plan, *yōgoshisetsu* would retain their residential function (though offering increasingly specialist support) but also look out for those who have been in the care system and are trying to make their way in the wider society. They would also become the site to which families in the community would turn when they need support. Underlying their new direction was the message that in future anyone might want or need to call on the services of *yōgoshisetsu*, not just society's most feckless parents.

The survival of individual *yōgoshisetsu* will largely depend on how quickly they can adapt to their new role in society. Over a five-year period from April 1999, the government, despite vigorous opposition from the national association of *yōgoshisetsu*, is gradually introducing as part of its basic social welfare structural reform (*shakai fukushi kiso kōzō kaikaku*) the beginnings of a market principle into the funding of *yōgoshisetsu*. They will no longer be paid on the basis of their capacity but according to the number of children for which they actually care. *Jidōsōdanjo* have been instructed to send children only to homes that offer the most appropriate care for their needs, unlike the earlier system where it seemed in many areas that children were simply shared equally across the available homes. The effectiveness of the changes will of course largely depend on how vigorously different *jidōsōdanjo* implement the new policy and how much they feel bound by old ties of loyalty to those homes they have always used, often over several decades.

In 2000, as a result of the redesignation of homes for physically weak children, there are more *yōgoshisetsu* (556) than ever before and, against all the expectations of less than a decade earlier, this number appears set to rise even further. Kōseishō announced in late 1999 that it would authorize the establishment in urban areas of independent, family-style *yōgoshisetsu* designed to care for six or fewer children (instead of the previous minimum capacity of twenty) and that ten model homes would be set up in the next year. These homes would be based in a normal house in a normal housing area and children would live a normal family life within the local community (*AS*, 4 December 1999). Individual *yōgoshisetsu*, therefore, will doubtless start to become more specialized as their role begins to diversify as has happened in the UK. While some homes will continue with residential care in much the same fashion as before, others may decide to take in only children presenting severe behaviour problems (generally now known by the term *shogū konnanji*—children needing complex treatment), or only older children. Others may concentrate on community services such as telephone helplines for families seeking advice. Others may provide a half-way house for children who have left school but need a base from which to operate in the community.

Kodomo Gakuen has in many ways been a model for the new-style *yōgoshisetsu*. By the late 1990s it represented a multi-purpose child welfare agency all based on one site, as can be seen in its own new organization chart (Figure IX). It offered residential care (but with an increased prospect, if it could find the qualified staff, of therapeutic treatment in its three purpose-built counselling blocks); short-term stay (while parents were ill) and *twilight stay* (while lone parents were working during the evenings); services for those who refused to go to school; a non-residential workshop for individuals in the community over the age of 20 who still needed support; a foster-parent recruitment and support centre; a twenty-four-hour telephone counselling and advice line; an after-school club; and a day nursery, as well as a host of activities for members of the local community and from the old people's home next door. While Kodomo Gakuen was exceptional (though not unique; see Date, 1998) in the way it changed during the 1990s, most other homes find themselves subject to exactly the same external and internal pressures at the start of the twenty-first century. Those homes which do not adapt to the new situation will doubtless find it difficult to survive in the new market situation.

Market forces mean that the public *yōgoshisetsu* will continue to close and may not exist at all in ten years' time. These homes have become too expensive to run: staff stay longer, their salaries are linked to length of service, and, as members of the powerful Jichirō union, they can refuse to work the long hours of those in private homes and hence other staff have to be hired to cover for them. While, as we have seen, public homes have generally had better staffing ratios and better facilities per child, there are few individuals and organizations which will have an interest in fighting their closure.

The closure of the public homes is a good example of the efforts by central and local government to try and control and cap an escalating welfare bill as the society ages. The government has clearly recognized the significance of trying to raise the fertility rate through programmes such as the *Angel Plan*, but implementation of this has been hit in some degree by the enormous expenditure that was needed to implement the two *Gold Plans* of 1990 and 1994 to provide welfare for the aged. One way that the government has been able to reduce some welfare costs has been to pass public institutions over to private organizations. For example, in the late 1990s the Seishin Gakusha was given a *hoikuen* to run by the local city

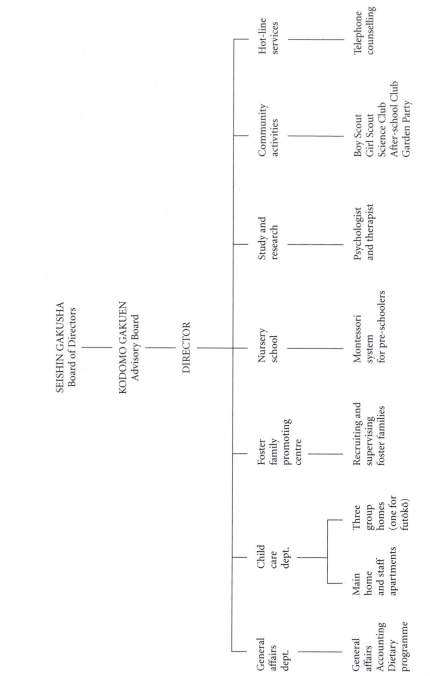

SEISHIN GAKUSHA
Board of Directors

KODOMO GAKUEN
Advisory Board

DIRECTOR

General affairs dept.
- General affairs
- Accounting
- Dietary programme

Child care dept.
- Main home and staff apartments
- Three group homes (one for futōkō)

Foster family promoting centre
- Recruiting and supervising foster families

Nursery school
- Montessori system for pre-schoolers

Study and research
- Psychologist and therapist

Community activities
- Boy Scout
- Girl Scout
- Science Club
- After-school Club
- Garden Party

Hot-line services
- Telephone counselling

FIG. IX Organization chart of Kodomo Gakuen (1999)

government which it had itself received from the prefectural government. The new role provided for private *yōgoshisetsu* is a relatively cheap way of meeting the new demands of child protection and combating child abuse. It avoids the need to set up a professional child social work system—for which there are no plans— and relies on those who are already in the child welfare field and have experience of dealing with children with problems. The fact that *yōgoshisetsu* and their heads are often well known in the local communities where they have been situated for many years may, indeed, make it easier for local families to approach them than the officials who sit in the *jidōsōdanjo* at the town or city hall. It may indeed be the case that the new *toshi jidō katei shien centres* based at *yōgoshisetsu* will grad- ually begin to replace the role of the *jidōsōdanjo* in child protection work in Japan.[38] If so, then the new role of *yōgoshisetsu* in Japanese society will provide a good example of the type of mixed economy of welfare—the combination of public and private working together—that has characterized much post-war wel- fare in Japan.

After forty years of virtually no change, *yōgoshisetsu* changed very rapidly dur- ing the late 1990s and look as if they will change even more rapidly at the start of the next decade. The speed of this change is interesting and has come about as a result of the convergence of a number of factors and interests: the desire of the private *yōgoshisetsu* to survive; the desire of the government to introduce policies to support families in the community and encourage women to have children without adding excessively to the rapidly rising welfare bill; the demands for the implementation of the UN Convention on the Rights of the Child both inside and outside Japan; the growing awareness of 'child abuse'. While in 1991 many *yōgoshisetsu* feared that they would have to close in the near future, by 2000 their role in the child welfare system had broadened and their numbers appeared set to increase. Similarly the *dōzoku keiei* system of a group of family-run institutions, the quasi-voluntary *minsei.jidōiin* system, and the system of *jidōsōdanjo* staffed by local government bureaucrats will continue to operate. If anything, these three pillars of the child welfare system in Japan are likely to be forced to work more closely together than has been the case in the past to deal with the rising aware- ness of child abuse and the need for children to be protected. As a result, while the Japanese system of child protection has been placed under many of the same political, economic, and demographic pressures as those of other advanced, industrial societies over the past fifty years, it will remain distinctively different in the way it operates as the new millennium starts.

NOTES TO CHAPTER 1

1. Although I can find no independent verification of either fact, several informants told me that Nakasone Yasuhiro, prime minister throughout much of the 1980s in Japan, had a granddaughter with Down's syndrome and that the state's support for Down's syndrome children increased substantially during his prime ministership.

2. Sinclair and Gibbs (1998: 13) point out that children who are voluntarily placed by their parents in homes in the UK should technically be referred to as 'looked after', while only those on court orders are actually 'in care' of the state. Like them, however, I have decided to avoid the clumsy expression 'looked after' and describe all children in residential or foster homes in Japan or the UK as 'in care' whether their placements have been voluntary or involuntary.

3. I am fully aware of course that it would be naive of me not to expect others to use my work either to criticize or endorse the system. Indeed, a paper I delivered in Japan in 1991 about children's rights and *yōgoshisetsu* (published in English: see Goodman, 1996) was cited in a Diet committee meeting about the use and abuse of physical punishment in *yōgoshisetsu*, a topic to which we will return later.

4. There have, however, in recent years appeared in English a few books on the problems of Japan's ageing society (Formanek and Linhart, 1997; Long, forthcoming; Palmore and Maeda, 1985) and some interesting ethnographies of old people's homes (Bethel, 1992; Kinoshita, 1992). There is also a small literature on Japanese welfare policy in a comparative and very broad sense (Boling, 1998; Campbell, 1992; Gould, 1993; Rose and Shiratori, 1986) and some work on the development of ideas about social welfare in Japanese society (Anderson, 1993; Garon, 1997; Takahashi, 1997a), but, as we shall see, virtually nothing about the *minsei.jidōiin* system, which forms the backbone of the delivery of personal social services, virtually nothing about the welfare offices which make the decisions on placements in institutions, and very little about the contemporary systems of adoption and fostering or about the current debates on children's rights and child abuse. On *yōgoshisetsu*, I have managed to find precisely three articles of two pages each (Davis, 1983; Ford and Takagi, 1998; Neilson and Meekings, 1997) written by non-Japanese since the end of the Second World War. There is of course some material put out in English by various Japanese government agencies, and the journal *Child Welfare: Quarterly News From Japan* publishes useful but very short (500–1,000 words) articles on various aspects of the system. I have cited these English-language references where possible so as to make them accessible to other readers, but this material on its own tends to be difficult to follow unless placed in the much broader historical and social context that it is hoped this account will provide.

5. At first gloss, a comparison between *yōgoshisetsu* and child protection institutions in other Asian countries, in particular Taiwan and South Korea, might seem more appropriate from a cultural and historical perspective than a comparison with institutions in the UK. In the Japanese literature, however, the child welfare system is virtually only ever compared with the systems of other OECD countries, and in such accounts the British system seems to be the most common comparative point of reference in discussions of *yōgoshisetsu* in Japan (see e.g. Kosaka, 1996; Tsuzaki, 1991).

6. I am fully aware of the dangers of reducing complex issues of child protection to such simple either/or formulas. Those in the child protection fields in both Japan and the

UK need to take into account a host of issues when they make decisions about what to do when a child is referred to them, many of which relate to that particular child, place, and time. Nevertheless, some of the stark contrasts that emerge when comparing the British and Japanese child protection systems—and the list that follows concentrates on contrasts rather than similarities—do suggest that it is useful, even if only heuristically, to compare some of the basic ideas underlying contemporary child protection decisions in both countries. For similar reasons, Hayden *et al.* (1999: 29) reduce debates about child welfare in the UK to just three main dimensions: the tension between family-based and institutional care; the tension between intervening too early and too late in child protection cases; and the perception of the link between childhood deprivation, depravation, and later criminality. They are also keen, however, to stress the autonomy of individual workers within any child protection system and the fact that no system is ever static.

7. Figures from Colton and Hellinckx (1993) suggest that the proportion in Germany is roughly similar to that of the UK and in France is about double.

8. See Akiyama, 1997 for a detailed account of how this particular dichotomy is discussed in Japan.

9. In the UK, the number of children in residential care declined from 29,700 in 1981 to 10,600 in 1991 to 6,500 in 1998, while the number of children fostered remained relatively stable during the same period at between 33,000 and 35,000 (Hayden *et al.*, 1999: 36). In the US, the number of children in orphanages declined from 144,000 in 1933 to 95,000 in 1951 to 77,000 in 1963 to 43,000 in 1977, and by 1980 'the orphanage for all practical purposes ceased to exist' while the number of children fostered had increased from 165,000 in 1961 to 394,000 in 1977 (Shughart and Chappell, 1999: 142, 154).

10. As Pringle (1998: 40) points out, in the UK since the 1970s and subsequently also in Sweden, Denmark, and Germany, 'increasingly, family placement and residential care are being provided by not-for-profit charities, having largely in the past been the preserve of the public sector'.

11. In 1992 I took a group of Japanese residential social workers to visit a children's home in south London. They were astonished that we could walk past the home two or three times without being able to identify it, before eventually a neighbour was able to point us to the right building. As Sinclair and Gibbs (1998: 82) point out, 'a home catering for four residents is starting to resemble a large foster home'.

12. The Children's Act (1989) does not actually specify fixed ratios of staffing, but states that these depend on the role and purpose of the individual unit concerned. Berridge and Brodie (1998: 121) actually found a ratio in the twelve homes they researched of close to two members of staff to each child.

13. In both Japan and the UK, direct costs for fostering per child per year are much lower than for residential care—in Japan about ¥1.2 million (£6,000), in the UK about ¥1.6 million (£8,000) depending on the individual circumstances of the child being fostered—although, as McKenzie (1999) points out in his argument supporting residential care over fostering in the US, such direct cost figures do not take into account the costs of social workers and others who support fostering services.

14. The 1969 Act reflected an increasing blurring of the boundary between 'deprived' and 'depraved' children. 'Delinquent children', as they came to be called in the 1960s, were

seen to be a product of their social environment and hence more the responsibility of the child-care system than the juvenile justice system. As Hayden *et al.* (1999: 24) point out, this change dramatically altered the public perception of children in care. In a survey carried out in the late 1990s in UK children's homes, Sinclair and Gibbs (1998: 178–9) found that half the male and a quarter of female residents had previous convictions, and nearly 40 per cent of those with no previous convictions acquired one if they stayed in the home longer than six months. None of the children at Kodomo Gakuen had a criminal record.

NOTES TO CHAPTER 2

1. *Kokeshi* dolls are still bought today throughout Japan as souvenirs (*omiyage*) or as presents, though their original meaning appears to have been totally forgotten (Kouno and Johnson, 1995: 27).
2. According to Jolivet (1997: 119), little girls and babies displaying abnormalities were most at risk, and there was a general belief that a woman should not have more than three children. Wagatsuma (1981: 132) notes that historically babies were sometimes abandoned if both parents were in their unlucky year (*yakudoshi*), usually 42 for fathers and 33 for mothers.
3. The idea that social policy should be seen essentially as a device for mitigating social tension has been important throughout modern Japanese history, espoused most rigorously in the Meiji period by the Association for the Study of Social Policy (*Shakai Seisaku Gakkai*) (Mouer and Sugimoto, 1986: 71–4). For more detail on the influence of German social theory in Japan during the Meiji period, see Pyle, 1974.
4. It should be pointed out that a better candidate for originator of the welfare commissioner system in Japan is Okayama Prefecture where the Governor, Kasai Shinichi, instituted a 'social reform advisory system' (*saisei komonsei*) in 1917 (see Tatara, 1975: 153; Zenkoku Minsei.jidōiin Kyōgikai, 1986: 8). Historical accounts, however, have tended to concentrate on the significance of the *hōmeniin* system that developed a year later, possibly because it gave its name to the system as a whole.
5. It was also in response to the rice riots that the government introduced the Health Insurance Act (Kenkō Hokenhō) in 1922, which came into force in 1925 and which Gould (1993: 36) calls 'the first genuine social security measure'.
6. According to two left-wing commentators, Chūbachi and Taira (1976: 425), the strength of the system lay in combining two distinctive elements, surveillance and welfare aid, in 'an ignominious marriage of authoritarian government and the charitable spirit of local leaders'. This dual role was perhaps most clearly demonstrated in the surveillance of those in the local community released from prison or thought to be delinquent (Hastings, 1995: 86).
7. This was an attitude which the early occupation forces were particularly keen to change—since it was felt to lead to a potentially dangerous degree of subservience to the state—and replace with concepts of 'citizenship' and 'rights'.
8. For more on the significance of repaying debts at this period in Japanese history, see Benedict's classic wartime account, *The Chrysanthemum and the Sword* (1946: chs. 4–6).
9. As Itō (1995: 260–1) points out, although all those who study social welfare know the

English word 'social worker', many identify themselves more closely with the Japanese term which literally means 'social welfare secretary'. The use of the term 'social worker', therefore, is clearly problematic.

10. Exactly how generous government expenditure has been in comparison with that of other OECD countries remains very difficult to measure, as many commentators (Gould, 1993; Jacobs, 1998; Kwon, 1998) have pointed out, both because the way in which welfare is provided and calculated is so different and also because Japan's welfare system developed so much later. For example, while most of those who retire today in Japan receive pensions that are commensurate with those received in other OECD countries, many of the very old in Japan are still receiving tiny pensions, and the pension system as a whole in Japan has still to fully mature—which in part explains Japan's apparent overall lower welfare expenditure compared to some other countries (Ferries, 1996: 225–6).

11. See Baba Keinosuke (1980) for the most-cited account of what constitute the main features of the Japanese-style welfare system.

12. Kirsten Refsing, personal communication, describing a conference she attended in Hokkaidō in the late 1970s.

13. For an extreme version in English of the argument that Japanese welfare is a direct result of Japanese cultural and historical practices, see Nakagawa Yatsuhiro's (1979) oft-cited article on 'Japan, the Welfare Super-Power' (originally published in the highly respectable *Chūō Kōron* in 1978).

14. As Lee (1987: 250), says, 'The slogan of 1973, "Welfare First, Growth Second" was replaced gradually by "Reconsider Welfare", "Welfare State Disease", "Japanese Style Welfare State", and others.'

15. This needs to be placed in the wider context of a society where in the early 1990s only 0.75 per cent of the population received welfare payments, while tax evasion, especially by the self-employed, was believed by many to be endemic.

16. An even more extreme imbalance exists in the case of probation officers where, in 1992, 48,836 *hogoshi* (volunteer probation officers) worked under a mere 970 professional workers (*hogokansatsukan*) who were all employed as civil servants (Yokochi, 1994: 14). As of 1994, the age profile of *hogoshi* was also more extreme than that of *minsei.jidōiin*: 91 per cent were over 50, 67 per cent were over 60, and 20 per cent were over 70, and the average age was over 62. Women accounted for just over 20 per cent of those appointed (Rehabilitation Bureau, 1995: 12–13). For accounts in English of the *hogoshi* system, see Hamai *et al.*, 1995: 88–92, 180–4, and Johnson, 1996: ch. 9.

17. There are interesting parallels here, increasingly being made in the UK, between the different positions of an ever-present Church and a visiting social welfare profession in inner-city communities.

18. Ben-Ari contrasts this with the generally low status (not unconnected with the fact that many of its members are women) of the social work profession in most industrialized societies.

19. The problem, of course, is exacerbated by the very small number of single mothers in Japanese society. Another example of this rather negative view of *minsei.jidōiin* can be seen in the decision by the Kyoto municipal government in 1998 to mail questionnaires to single-parent families rather than have *minsei.jidōiin* deliver them personally, as previously, following complaints from many of the parents that they regarded the

visits as intrusive. This plan backfired somewhat, however, when the authorities accidentally mailed the questionnaire to many households where one parent was Japanese and the other foreign, since in such cases both parents are listed as single in their residence and foreign registration documents, a mistake which the locally based *minsei.jidōiin* would have been much less likely to make (*DY*, 6 Nov. 1998). The strongest criticism of the *minsei.jidōiin* system, however, that I have heard has been from some of the workers in child guidence centres (*jidōsōdanjo*) who are very reluctant to call on the services of people whom they feel are not only unqualified but often behave inappropriately in their dealings with members of the local community.

20. Though it could also be argued that it is a very effective means of avoiding benefit fraud.

21. It should be pointed out that in 1950, which is generally used as the baseline in Japanese illustrations of the ageing society, Japan had its youngest population during the twentieth century as a result of the post-war baby boom. A higher proportion (more than 5 per cent) of the population was over the age of 64 at the start of the twentieth century.

22. Japan's declining birth rate is an immensely complicated topic and it is far from easy to predict future trends. The average number of children that married women are having has remained at around 2.2 over the last three decades; the decrease is almost totally due to a sudden increase in women of reproductive age deciding not to get married and not to have children. This is largely because of a conscious choice to stay in employment: the fertility rate for working women in the late 1990s is 0.60, against 2.96 for those not working (Harada, 1998: 223). Whether such women will decide to have children at a later stage still remains to be seen, and will determine the overall fertility rate over a much longer period than simply a single decade. Nevertheless, the subtleties of this debate, while recognized by the experts in Japan, have seldom been translated into the popular media where there remains the belief that Japan currently faces a 'population crisis'.

23. To be fair to the Japanese administrations of the 1980s, it needs to be noted that they were fully aware of the implications of the ageing society (see e.g. the 1985 White Paper on the Japanese economy), and the introduction of the consumption tax in 1989 was in part to generate funds to tackle the issue. The fact, however, that the tax was so unpopular suggests that the government had failed to convince the Japanese public at large of the gravity of the situation.

24. While Japan's personal tax burden is relatively low in comparison with north European and North American competitors (see Ka, 1999: 120), raising taxes to generate further welfare revenue became impossible in the recession of the 1990s. Indeed, the government cut taxes in the hope of stimulating the economy into recovery.

25. One sometimes hears of progressive caseworkers suggesting to people that they live separately from their families in order to qualify for welfare support which they will not be able to get while remaining together. The criteria for received *seikatsu hogo* (livelihood protection) remain very strict in Japan and preclude ownership of a range of material objects including cars and air conditioners.

NOTES TO CHAPTER 3

1. The level at which individuals are appointed as *jidōfukushishi* varies greatly between different areas. In Tokyo, they are never lower than *kakarichō* (the first level of management) and hence would be at least 35 years of age. These positions sometimes are referred to as *muninsho kakarichō* (managers with no one to manage). In a survey in 1999 of all workers in *jidōsōdanjo* (with a response rate of just under 60 per cent), only 20 per cent had more than ten years' experience in the field, over 60 per cent had less than five, and 10 per cent had less than one (*AS*, 26 Nov. 1999).

2. Using simple mathematics, if the 1,200 *jidōfukushishi* have to deal between them with some 310,000 cases a year, each has more than 250 cases to work through. In a survey of all workers in *jidōsōdanjo* (with a 58.5 per cent response rate), around 60 per cent said they were holding more than fifty cases as of 1 November 1999 (*AS*, 26 Nov. 1999). Even if some of these are relatively simple, they still involve a great deal of bureaucratic paperwork and recording and there have been many accounts of 'burn-out' among child welfare officers in recent years (Jidōsōdanjo wo Kangaerukai, 1998).

3. The main reason for this appears to lie in a discrepancy between the Civil Court Law (Minpō) and the Child Welfare Law (Jidōfukushihō). As Kashiwame (1997: 7), a former official at the Child Welfare Section of Kōseishō, explains, while it was possible for children to be placed in homes compulsorily under Article 28 of the Jidōfukushihō, parental rights remained in the hands of the guardians under the Minpō. Kamiide (1990: 8), writing in 1990 as head of the national association of *jidōsōdanjo*, said that in nearly half of the cases where it was considered essential to separate a child from its parent it was difficult to obtain parental consent, and in nearly 30 per cent of cases where children were placed in care parental consent was still being withheld and the placement disputed. Kōseishō issued a circular in 1997 which recommended that the unreasonable demands of parents in such a situation should not be upheld, but the complete removal of parental rights remains very rare indeed and staff in the *jidōsōdanjo* still prefer to find other ways around the problem.

4. There are a number of other welfare institutions which also slightly overlap with the services of *yōgoshisetsu*. Among these are sixteen centres for emotionally disturbed children (*jōcho shōgai tanki chiryō shisetsu*, generally known as *jōtan*), first set up in 1961, with 770 places which catered in 1996 for around 580 children. Many of the children in these institutions, as with those in *kyōgoin* and *yōgoshisetsu*, are considered to have come from severely deprived family environments which are largely to blame for their anti-social or often asocial behaviour. In operation, however, they are very different from *yōgoshisetsu*. They provide short-term care and aim to reintegrate the children into society through programmes of group therapy and vocational activity. Hence they are highly therapeutic in nature and their programmes are based on individual psychiatric and psychological treatment; indeed, admission to the facilities is described as 'hospitalization'. (For an interesting description in English of some of the activities of such an institution, see Ishikawa and Sakaguchi, 1989.)

5. On average, in the case of lone-mother families almost 80 per cent of income comes from employment and about 15 per cent from various forms of state support (Sakuraya, *KH*, 1995: 161). As Peng (1997: 122) points out, this means a much greater proportion of income packages comes from work than in comparable families in the UK and Canada.

6. The proportion of lone-father families created due to the death of the mother has always been around 5 per cent higher than the case for lone-mother families caused by the death of the father (Sakuraya, *KH*, 1995: 161).

7. In the immediate post-war period, custody of the children was still normally granted to the father in the case of divorce. It was granted more often to mothers than fathers for the first time only in 1965, since when the gap has grown continuously in favour of maternal custody (Matsubara, 1988: 4). There is no provision for shared custody in Japanese divorce which explains why, according to Matsushima (1996: 137), only 26 per cent of fathers stay in touch with their children after the mother has been awarded custody.

8. Peng points out other ways in which the welfare system in Japan has increasingly made life difficult for lone mothers to look after their children themselves, such as the 1985 Child-Rearing Allowance Law under which lone mothers cannot receive child-rearing allowance if their husband's income exceeds ¥6 million, regardless of whether he provides any support for the family or not. Peng (1997: 132, 137) concludes, however, that while there has been a steady decline in lone mothers' relative income in comparison with those of all other families, ironically their personal financial situation may have actually improved following divorce or separation from their husbands because with it came greater control over the family budget. For a recent celebration of lone parenthood in Japan, see Single Mothers' Forum, 1994.

9. As Peng (1997: 127) points out, there was considerable discussion in the early 1980s about the position of lone-father families in contemporary Japanese society following the screening of the popular film *Kramer vs Kramer*. There were some positive effects from this for lone fathers, known as the *Kramer taisaku* (the Kramer measures), such as the extension in 1982 of the home-help system to cover them during times of sickness. All other support for lone-father families, however, still depends on local government practices (Matsubara, 1988: 8). Indeed, men can find themselves financially penalized if their wife dies, since they lose the wife-support tax break enjoyed by married men. The reason for the lack of legislation to support single fathers, according to Ikeda (1984: 9), seems to lie in the expectation that they would have a high rate of remarriage, as was indeed the case until the mid-1960s.

10. Sometimes the number of those in the *boshiryō* is measured in terms of household units, sometimes in terms of individuals.

11. The illegitimacy rate in Japan, which was around 9 per cent at the beginning of the twentieth century, has remained consistently under 1 per cent since the 1950s, even after the time limit on abortions was reduced to twenty-two weeks in 1976.

12. In 1995 there were 1,962 staff (85 per cent full-time) for 1,755 residents, a ratio better than 1 : 1, although this included office and other support staff as well as direct carers (*NTN*, 1998: 44–5).

13. The two other major figures in the development of child welfare in the early Meiji period were Tomeoka Kōsuke (1864–1934), who set up the first juvenile correctional facilities (today's *kyōgoin*), and Ishi'i Ryōichi (1867–1937), who established the first facility for children with a handicap, both of whom, like Ishi'i Jūji, were Christian and spent time studying social welfare in North America (Nagashima, 1996: 55).

14. The histories of a number of the child welfare institutions I examined included photographs of visits by members of the Imperial Family. This would even appear to be

the case for Japanese children's homes set up among overseas Japanese communities (see Kuramoto, 1976: 83).

15. This movement was part of the promotion of state Shintoism as the state religion with the emperor as its leading figure.

16. Constitution of 1946, Article 89: 'No public funds or other property shall be expended or appropriated for . . . any charitable . . . enterprises not under the control of public authority'. There was of course some irony implicit in this regulation—which was essentially promulgated to prevent the use of state funds to support Shintō activities—in that the majority of extant welfare institutions in Japan at the time were Christian-founded establishments, many of which had been set up by American missionaries in the pre-war period, as well as in the fact that support for proposed new homes was mainly coming from overseas Christian groups. In many areas of Japan, the child welfare system in the immediate post-war period was designed by American child welfare specialists, some of whom, such as Alice Carroll, who designed the systems in Osaka, Miyagi, and Fukuoka, are still held in great esteem in child welfare circles today (see Osaka-fu Shakai Fukushi Kyōgikai, 1996: 193), even if on their departure it is clear that a variety of circumstances, largely financial, made it impossible to implement many of their plans.

17. The law also for the first time set down minimum standards of care for children in homes: there should be no less than one nursery nurse (*hobo*) for every eight children, as well as medical and management staff; 80 per cent of the costs of keeping children in homes were to be met by the state, with the remaining 20 per cent to be paid either by the family or by local government; and grants given to homes should be standardized across the nation.

18. The Elizabeth Saunders Home was founded in 1948 by Sawada Miki, granddaughter of Iwasaki Yatarō, founder of the Mitsubishi industrial empire. It was named after an impoverished British woman and long-term resident of Japan, who donated her life savings of $170 to the establishment, and is currently run by Sawada Shinichi, the 76-year-old son of its founder (*JTW*, 31 Oct. 1999). For an analysis of the marginal situation of those of mixed blood in the immediate post-war period, see Burkhardt (1983).

19. There are few statistics kept on the religious background of *yōgoshisetsu* and it is very hard to get a clear picture of what is not, in any case, a static situation: some homes which were set up by religious foundations seem to have lost their religious flavour, while occasionally a new head of a home or a board of trustees will introduce a religious element into a home that had not previously had it. According to Morinaga (1975: 412), there were fifty-five Buddhist *yōgoshisetsu* in the early 1970s, thirty-five of which had been founded in the post-war period. Probably the most accurate information available, however, concerns homes set up by new religious movements: in 1989, for example, there were thirteen *yōgoshisetsu* affiliated to Tenrikyō (Tenrikyō Shakai Fukushishisetsu Renmei, 1989: 4–16). The significance of the religious background of homes lies, as we shall see, in two main areas: the extra funding that this can sometimes produce, and the extent to which children in the homes are required to participate in religious activities.

20. Not all figures for the numbers of public and private homes are consistent. This is because some figures are based on their foundation and some on their current

organization, and there are fifteen homes which were founded with public funds but which by 1991 were being run by private (*minkan*) organizations (*KK*, no. 45, 1991: 211). The figures used in Table 7 are based on who currently runs the homes since, as we shall see, this is what has the greatest effect on the care of children within them.

21. In introducing an article about *yōgoshisetsu* in the popular magazine *Bessatsu Takarajima*, Baba (1999) has to spend no less than seven paragraphs (and almost 800 characters) explaining exactly what they are and distinguishing them from *kyōgoin*, *yōgogakkō*, and *kojiin*.

22. See a pamphlet put out by Osaka Jimusho Katei Yōiku Sokushin Kyōkai, *Kai-in ni natte kudasai* (Please Become a Member of Our Association), n.d.: page 2.

23. The *Nakumonoka* (Yōgoshisetsu Kyōgikai, 1977; 1990) volumes and others like them are the source of some controversy in the child welfare world, and the genre is sometimes referred to by critics as *o-namida chōdai* (please cry for me). The volumes consist mainly of stories told by children in homes that have been collected by the heads of homes and submitted to the editors. The volumes still sell well, continue to be updated and republished (the first volume went through twenty-two editions in thirteen years after first appearing in 1977), and generate funds for the Yōgoshisetsu Kyōgikai. The criticism of the volumes is that they play on old-fashioned sentiments of charity in order to raise awareness and funds. Similar serious criticism of the Yōgoshisetsu Kyōgikai from among its own membership was voiced when, at its 1991 conference, it announced that it had accepted a donation of ¥50 million (at the time almost £300,000) from Promise Sarakin, one of Japan's largest money-lending companies, to which at least some of the parents of children in *yōgoshisetsu* had over the years become indebted. A representative of Promise Sarakin was presented with a certificate of thanks at the formal ceremony that marked the opening of the annual conference, but there was considerable discomfort among some members of the association about the appropriateness of accepting such money.

24. Throughout my fieldwork one of my biggest concerns was about the ethical issue of collecting personal information on individual children which they themselves were not in a position freely to deny me. I decided early in the research therefore not to seek such information from staff, though obviously it sometimes came up in the course of conversations, and I rarely knew why a particular child was in the home although I was aware of the overall patterns of admission. The following cases, therefore, come from another (unpublished) source altogether—about a *yōgoshisetsu* I never visited— and hence their provenance should not be identifiable. They tally closely with the cases that I came across at Kodomo Gakuen and other homes (see also Kita, 1996: 56–8), and I am grateful to the researcher who has given me permission to use them here.

25. Part of the reason for implementing this reform at this particular time was that while in earlier generations there had been an excess of demand over supply for day-care places, by the mid-1990s the placement ratio (the number of children in the facilities to the total number of places available) was down to 80 per cent (Suzuki, 1998: 30). As the 1998 White Paper on Health and Welfare (*KSH*, 1998: 156) pointed out, however, in many, especially urban, areas in Japan there still remains a great unmet demand for places for children under the age of 3 (see also Funabashi, 1999: 34).

26. When these committees were set up in early 1998 most members were doctors, mainly psychiatrists and paediatricians, lawyers, and professors of welfare, and were already

members of the Shakai Fukushi Shingikai. To avoid conflicts of interest, those who worked in child welfare institutions were not supposed to sit on the committees. Most committees met once a month to consider just a couple of particularly complex placements.

27. These centres had been trialled over the previous four years in some areas of Japan, sometimes under the name of *advocate centres*, and numbered around twenty-five in 1998 when their status was officially recognized in the revised Child Welfare Law (Takahashi, 1998*a*: 141).

28. For a good overview of, and commentary on, the details of the revisions of the Child Welfare Law, see Takenaka (1998), where the old and new versions are laid out alongside each other.

NOTES TO CHAPTER 4

1. Ben-Ari (1997) and Hendry (1986) have described this process in detail at the level of pre-school socialization; Satō (1991) and Lewis (1995) at the level of elementary schools; Singleton (1967) and Cummings (1980) at the level of junior high school. For an overview of much of this literature, see McVeigh, 1998.

2. Uniformity is particularly noticeable at the city level where it can be more easily monitored, but it remains the fact that one can tell a Japanese elementary or junior high-school child almost immediately anywhere in the country from their dress and the buildings they study in; and one can predict when they will hold certain events, and what they will eat in the course of a week and study in the course of a year, with a considerable degree of confidence. The strength of this observation is perhaps most obviously supported by the reporting as news cases of institutions that break from these patterns.

3. The budget is allocated on a remarkably complicated formula but, in 1995, a home with around fifty children could receive about ¥115 million a year (or around ¥2.3 million per child) topped up with discretionary grants from local authorities (Jidō Yōgo Kenkyūkai, 1995: 209–11). From 1999 budgets will increasingly be allocated on the basis of the number of residents rather than on the home's capacity as hitherto.

4. Homes can take children from the age of 2 onwards, though there is occasionally flexibility on this in order to keep siblings together. The state will continue to financially support the care of a child in a home until one year after they have left the education system, although in some cases arrangements can be made for children to stay until the age of 20 even if they have left school.

5. Allinson (1979) describes in detail how funds from the Tokyo Keibajō (Tokyo racecourse) in Fuchū Honmachi are used to support welfare services in Fuchū City in west Tokyo.

6. Although it is not clear from Table 14, and I can find no figures to support the contention, my impression from visiting a variety of homes is that they are divided between those which have all or many of the facilities listed in the table and those which have few or none, rather than some having some on the list and others having others.

7. The Shōshasei Yōiku Kenkyūkai, which campaigns for children to be housed in smaller buildings, defines *shōshasei* as a building which can accommodate up to a maximum

of fifteen children, which would considerably reduce this number (Iwasaki, 1999: 57–8).

8. I have seen no research on why fewer girls than boys go into *yōgoshisetsu* and can only surmise that members of the extended family are more willing to take in girls. This is certainly the case, as we shall see, with foster-families in Japan. Interestingly, though, once children are in care, there is no significant difference between the average length of time boys and girls spend there (*YnJ*, 1990: 105)

9. Since such a high proportion of children who are in care in Japan are in institutions, and since movement between institutions is relatively rare (less than 5 per cent of children in homes had come there from other homes; only 1 per cent from foster-family breakdowns—*YnJ*, 1990: 54), the figures in Japan provide a reasonably accurate picture of the population of children in homes and avoid many of the snapshot problems provided in countries like the UK (see Rowe, 1989) where the movement of children in and out of homes is much more rapid.

10. It is very common in Japan to place institutions in hierarchical order like this. For example, all institutions of higher education are unofficially ranked every year in terms of the entrance scores of their entrants. While the system in the case of *yōgoshisetsu* was not, for obvious reasons, as clear as that for educational institutions, most people in the field had a strong sense of where individual homes ranked.

11. There has long been confusion and overlap between *hoikuen* (day-care centres) and *yōchien* (kindergartens) in Japan, and indeed, in some areas of Japan, the differences are minimal. In general, *hoikuen* provide child care for working mothers while *yōchien* provide pre-school classes and education. All *hoikuen* are open until 5 p.m. and an increasingly large number until 7 p.m., though few beyond that time, which makes it difficult for parents with long journeys or anti-social working hours. *Yōchien* have tended to be open only a few (three or four) hours a day and take children from the age of 3, but increasingly, in order to keep running, have been extending their opening hours and taking younger children. Most important for this account, *hoikuen* are regulated by Kōseishō (and hence are welfare institutions) and *yōchien* by Monbushō (and are educational ones).

12. The system of homes for the elderly in Japan has undergone a number of reforms in the post-war period, and today there is a variety of different types. *Yōgorōjin homes* provide care for those over 65 with limited financial resources who are basically in good health but unable to live on their own; a *keihi rōjin home* (literally 'low-fee old people's home') is the official term for any of several kinds of residential care facility for individuals with a low income over the age of 60, where the amount paid by the individual for the care they receive is limited by government regulation; *tokubetsu yōgo rōjin home* is an accredited nursing home for the elderly which provides nursing care for bed-bound individuals over the age of 65. While the above three types of homes for the elderly are the only such institutions recognized and controlled by the government, there is also a large number of non-accredited privately run institutions and facilities for the elderly.

13. The Seishin Gakusha grew so rapidly during the 1990s with the demand for old people's homes and other services for the elderly that in 1997 it split into two separate parts.

14. The largest *shakai fukushi hōjin* which I came across in 1991 was one in west Tokyo that had twenty-seven institutions under its umbrella with around 700 employees.

15. Residential child-care staff at Kodomo Gakuen did technically have a day in lieu of a *saijitsu kyūka* (national holiday) owing to them once a month as well as five days of summer holiday, which they could take in a block as personal vacation, but very few of them (as indeed is reported to be the case with most Japanese workers with their personal holiday allowance) took all of these. One member of staff reckoned he had taken about eight days' holiday the previous year, of which several were used up on the staff trip (*shokuin ryokō*). Over the whole year, he calculated that he had about seventy to eighty complete days off, or six days a month, which is considered the norm in the profession. Whereas, in most other professions, the main reason given for not taking holiday entitlement is to avoid inconveniencing one's fellow-workers, in *yōgoshisetsu* it is so as not to reduce time with the children in the home. Other homes worked on different timetables. One home in the same area as Kodomo Gakuen gave workers much heavier timetables for three weeks of the month, but then gave them a complete week of rest. Some Kodomo Gakuen staff thought this was a good idea since it would allow workers to get a complete break from the home once a month (at the moment they rarely have long enough even to visit parents in other prefectures), and come back to work refreshed each time. From 1993 Kōseishō, worried about the high rate of burn-out (*moetsuki*), especially after three to four years in the job, among child welfare staff, officially reduced working hours to forty a week in both *yōgoshisetsu* and *kyōgoin*, though it is not clear that this had a major effect on the actual working practices in such institutions, since no extra budget was provided to increase man-power. In a survey in 1998, only 8.6 per cent of staff were working forty or less hours a week (*YnJ*, 2000). (See Yōgoshisetsu Kyōgikai, 1996: 30, for an outline of how offi-cial hours at work in *yōgoshisetsu* have been reduced from forty-eight to forty between 1973 and 1997.)

16. These were all homes with members of the residential care workers' union, Hofukurō, who collected the figures for Kuraoka.

17. The basic salaries of staff who work in the public *yōgoshisetsu* is higher than those of staff in the private homes, since they are employed as public servants. In 1991, how-ever, some six prefectures, including Tokyo, made up the difference through a system known as *kōshi kakusa zeisei jigyō* (tax programme for dealing with differentials between the public and private sectors), which also operates in other welfare areas where there are both public and private institutions.

18. For an interesting analysis of courses offered at tertiary level, see James and Benjamin (1988).

19. To put this another way, academics and practitioners in Japan were generally very sur-prised to hear that in the early 1990s it was possible to get a Certificate of Qualifica-tion in Social Work (CQSW) from Oxford University. One result of the small number of top universities in Japan offering courses in social welfare is that few of those employed in the local government offices (who normally come from such universities) have taken such courses. As Itō (1995: 261) points out, the system seems to be contra-dictory: 'For the people who study social work in a university, the opportunity to become a field social worker is closed, whereas for any bureaucrat in local govern-ment, the option is open.'

20. It is widely believed that the name of the university from which one graduates is more important for future employment prospects in Japan than the course one has

followed. Since very few universities undertake entrance interviews and rely almost totally on examination scores, it is virtually impossible for lecturers to screen potential applicants for their motivations in joining a course.

21. A similar range of views of their care staff can be seen in the very direct observations of children in care collected in Kodomo ga Kataru Shisetsu no Kurashi Henshūiinkai, 1999.

22. Until my own children began to attend Japanese elementary school and nursery in 1998, I had not fully appreciated the extraordinary demands that such institutions place on parents in terms of getting their children ready each day. The *renrakuchō* (communication book) that institutions send back with children each day after school frequently contained a page or more of instructions for things that needed to be prepared, bought, repaired, or decided by the next day.

23. Even children in the first grade of elementary school (age 6) will have daily homework assigned to them, the amount of which increases the longer they have been in school.

24. The proportion of male staff has been on a steady increase since the early 1980s, when it stood at around 25 per cent, to over 35 per cent in 1995 (Yōgoshisetsu Kyōgikai, 1996: 28), perhaps reflecting the generally higher status of social welfare work in the past two decades.

25. It was in part to get over the gender division of workers in child welfare institutions that in 1998 the official titles of *hobo* and *hofu* were changed to the gender-neutral term *hoikushi* (care worker). In practice, though, there was no discernible increase in the very small number of men choosing to take the qualification.

26. The starting salary of a *hobo* is about 7 per cent lower than that of a *jidōshidōin* (Kuroda, 1997: 151).

27. Even in the 1980s bubble economy, however, when there were up to 10 per cent more job openings than applicants, there was no suggestion—as was the case for example with welfare institutions for the aged—that Japan might need to call on foreign workers, mainly from neighbouring countries, to work in children's homes (see Matsubara, 1996: 94).

28. This symposium was sponsored by the Tokyo Associations of Yōgoshisetsu, Shakai Fukushi Kyōgikai Jidōbukai, Jidōsōdanjo Mondai Kenkyūkai, and the Tokyo Kyōshokuin Kumiai—representing a cross-section of public and private employer and union organizations who had co-operated in the collection of the data—and was attended by around eighty people. For a full report of the symposium, see *Kanagawa Shinbun* (Kanagawa newspaper; 15 Nov. 1990).

29. In a 1991 survey which asked students of social welfare to select which one from a list of ten possible improvements would increase the number of people desiring to work in welfare institutions, pay and benefits (30.6 per cent) and working hours and holidays (23.8 per cent) accounted for more than half the answers (*Fukushi Tenbō* (Welfare Outlook), July 1991).

30. The difference is mainly due to the fact that public homes have special budgets to hire people to do night duties while this duty is undertaken by the general staff in private homes (Kuroda, 1991: 58).

31. For an overview of some of these findings and the rather problematic methodology which produced them, see Mutō and Takahashi, 1990.

32. Eiwa (1998), in his analysis of the finances of a number of old people's homes in Shikoku, demonstrates in great detail how it is possible to double-account the money

that large welfare organizations receive from government. During the 1990s there were a number of financial scandals (normally involving deals between welfare institutions and construction companies) in the rapidly expanding market of institutions for the aged. I have only ever heard of two cases, however, where *yōgoshisetsu* were implicated in financial irregularities, both of which were private, *dōzoku keiei* institutions without unions.

33. Many senior staff in *yōgoshisetsu* are extremely active in various research projects, and publish extensively as part of their study groups. Asakura *et al.* (1996: 195–200) list some of the most popular outlets for the writings of *yōgoshisetsu* staff, many of which have been drawn upon to construct the account provided here.

34. In 1991 a lecture was given by Yoshizawa Eiko, the doyenne of child welfare studies in Japan, who had herself worked in a *yōgoshisetsu* before becoming a university professor, and had largely been responsible for putting child welfare on the university curriculum through her writings in the 1960s and 1970s.

35. In fact I suspect that some of the exercises, which were taken from a volume published by the YMCA in Japan, may have originally come from Western manuals on group work.

36. The former Kōseishō official Miyamoto Masao describes in great detail the system whereby bureaucrats in Japan are promoted, not so much on what they achieve as on how few mistakes they make, in his best-selling book *O-yakusho no okite* (published in English as *Straitjacket Society*, 1995).

37. In a list of all the homes in 1977 (*Ysno30nen*: 152–75), some thirty out of 530 (or over 5 per cent) had foreign heads. Thirty years later, there were no foreign heads of homes, though the foreign origins of some homes can still be seen in the names of around 5 per cent written in the *katakana* script reserved for foreign words, e.g. St Joseph, Sion, St Francisco (*YSI*, 1998).

38. In 1995 the basic starting salary for a new head in a 'small' (fifty children or fewer) home was set at ¥254,300 a month. For the purposes of comparison, the salary of a *jidōshidōin* in the same position was ¥193,900 and of a *hobo* was ¥180,500, which constituted 73 per cent and 71 per cent respectively of that of an *enchō sensei* (Kuroda, 1997: 151).

39. While I assume that those few homes which did not have any volunteers were public homes, it is clear that the majority of public homes do also accept volunteers.

40. This seems a common practice at *yōgoshisetsu*, though whether it has some historical basis I have been unable to ascertain.

41. A relatively small amount of funding comes in the form of fees paid by wealthier parents (normally single fathers) who have placed children voluntarily in homes. The amount that these parents pay is determined on the same scales as when parents are assessed for paying *hoikuen* fees, and the vast majority of parents are assessed as being too poor to pay anything, or else are not around to be assessed. For those who are asked to make a contribution towards the costs of maintenance of their children, at the top of the scale (for someone with a monthly income of over ¥600,000), this would amount to around ¥120,000 a month, which would cover about 50 per cent of the actual cost of care in the home. I only heard of one case, a single-father company director, who was paying this level of maintenance fee.

42. According to one informant who was himself a volunteer in a *yōgoshisetsu* in the early 1970s, many of these groups were allied to left-wing political groups such as the youth sections of labour *unions* (*rōdōkumiai no seinenbu*) and the young communists

(*minsei*). As far as I know, however, this explicit political affiliation is no longer seen in the current university volunteer groups which indeed appear, like most Japanese student groups of the 1990s, essentially apolitical.

43. For an example of this new thinking see Tanaka, 1996. For overviews of the whole non-profit sector and for descriptions of organizations in the educational, religious, medical, and other areas of Japanese society which share many of the characteristics of the *shakai fukushi hōjin*, see Amenomori (1997: 195–206) and Yamamoto (1998). One of the major debates in the wake of the surge of volunteer activity was the idea that voluntary organizations should be given legal rights and tax incentives along the lines of those offered to similar organizations in other OECD countries (see NIRA, 1996). Adachi (forthcoming) suggests that the new, Western-style model of volunteer is now actively in competition with the previous 'tradition' of community volunteers such as *minsei.jidōiin*, which we saw in Chapter 2.

44. Kodomo Gakuen has three rooms purpose-built and fully equipped for therapy in the mid-1990s, but none of these was in use in early 1999 because of the lack of qualified therapists.

NOTES TO CHAPTER 5

1. *Yōgoshisetsu*, as with normal domestic homes in Japan, would appear to be knocked down and rebuilt on the same land more often than similar institutions in western Europe and the United States. This can be explained by the fact that the ratio of the cost of the building to the value of the land is roughly 1 : 4 in Japan compared to roughly 4 : 1 in the UK.

2. *Family group homes* are institutions set up independent from *yōgoshisetsu* and run by a married couple who are registered as foster parents. A *group home* is an extension of, and run by staff from, the main home, who may be also be a married couple though normally are not. *Group homes* can be on the same campus as their 'parent' *yōgoshisetsu*, but more normally are established elsewhere as branch (*bunen*) homes. During the 1990s the minimum size for a *yōgoshisetsu*, however, remained twenty children and hence it was still impossible to establish a *group home* as an independent institution.

3. These are the two most common usages of the *group home* system, together with a third, which is to place all the youngest children straight from *nyūjiin* in a *group home* together in the belief that these are the children who will benefit most from close physical contact with staff and will find it hardest to adjust to a large institution with children up to the age of 18.

4. Though it was admitted that these days, with an average family size of only 3.2, a large number of children in Japan do not have even one sibling.

5. For a fairly rare example of Makarenko's writings in English, see Makarenko, 1965. Far more, perhaps most, of Makarenko's writings have been translated into Japanese. By pure coincidence, perhaps the biggest name at that time in the Seito Seikatsu Shidō Kenkyūkai, Ōnishi Chūji, was a Japanese language teacher at the school where I carried out research on *kikokushijo* in 1984–5 and hence I was already familiar with the thinking and approach of this group (see Goodman, 1990: 120–3)

6. For an overview and examples of the thinking and influence of Yōmonken in contemporary child welfare in Japan, see Asai, 1991, Nozawa, 1991, and Takenaka, 1995.

7. The idea that East Asians are somehow 'naturally' inclined towards forming groups is a common theme in Japanese folk psychology and is generally explained in deterministic terms, such as that people who live in rice-growing cultures, like those in East Asia, need to co-operate in groups, as opposed to those who live in hunting cultures, which demand individual initiative (see e.g. Ishida, 1971).

8. There remains a strong belief in Japan that mothers should look after their children full-time at least until the age of 3, a belief vigorously attacked in the 1998 Kōseishō White Paper as responsible for over-anxious parenting and discouraging women from having children (*KSH*, 1998: 84).

9. At Kodomo Gakuen, as well as an elected executive board of five members, the *jichikai*, which met on the first Sunday of each month, had three further committees (educational, management, and health), so that almost all children from grades 3 to 9 seemed to have an official position. It was a little hard to tell, therefore, whether the *jichikai* was an example of group activity or of developing individual decision-making skills. The senior high-school students (grades 10–12) had their own autonomous committee.

10. Birthdays, the ultimate ego-centred festival of the ritual calendar, have historically rarely been individually recognized in Japan and even today most nurseries continue the practice of holding only monthly birthday parties. The fashion more generally in society today though is for families to celebrate each child's birthday.

11. As well as its Boy Scout group, which we will look at later, Kodomo Gakuen had a *sadō* (tea ceremony) club for two hours every Friday afternoon—run by a volunteer teacher from the local community which was attended by about ten children, mainly girls— as well as a smaller *shodō* (calligraphy) club and music, dancing and painting lessons for children who wanted them. It had a softball team for boys aged 7 to 10, a baseball team for boys between 10 and 15, and a volleyball team for girls of the same age, which all participated in the local inter-*yōgoshisetsu* tournaments which were held about three times a year, and a dodgeball club for the younger children.

12. These institutions (known as *tōgai shisetsu*) have been used mainly to place children who have no family or relatives thought likely to visit them. Apart from being a response to the opposition expressed by Tokyo residents, the city authorities built homes in such areas because the land was much cheaper to buy and develop.

13. One of the very few things I have been warned off attending in Japan was the *keirin*, since I was told that spectators tended to get drunk and could get aggressive. There was a similar view of horse-racing (*keiba*) until the early 1980s when, largely due to the popularity of one jockey with young female fans, it underwent a complete renaissance and became a fashionable venue for young people of both sexes and all classes (see Nagashima, 1998b).

14. Club activities in Japan tend to be much more focused on the school than based within the local community, as is often the case in the UK or the US. In part this may be explained by the lack of space in the local community. A 1988 government-commissioned report on educational reform urged schools to open their space more to the local community (see Roesgaard, 1998: 192), though there is little sign ten years later that this has been acted upon.

15. In the early 1990s, there was something of a national outcry in Japan about latch-key children who were having, from the age of 6, to look after themselves until their parents returned from work. Following the *Angel Plan* of 1994, there has been an

enormous investment and increase in the number of after-school clubs throughout the country, most of which are actually based in the schools themselves.

16. The *hoikuen* developed a policy of always having more children from the local community than from the home to prevent the former feeling excluded by the latter, who already spent all their time together.

17. In 1991 three children from the home applied to go to the international jamboree. Two failed to be accepted, and it was thought fairest that the third one should not go either. The head of the troop expressed some relief at this result since it would have been very expensive to send the children. It was clear, however, that had two or all of the children been accepted, then the money would have been found somehow for them to attend.

18. The concept of identity being formed as if through a series of ever-widening concentric circles—self, family/institution, local community, wider society—is a very common theme in much of the sociology and anthropology of Japanese society (see e.g. Hamaguchi, 1977; Kuwayama, 1992; Lebra, 1976).

NOTES TO CHAPTER 6

1. In a survey by Sinclair and Gibbs (1998: 45), about 40 per cent of children in UK children's homes indicate that they had been given some choice, not only about which home but indeed whether they should go into a residential institution at all or stay with their families or go to a foster placement. Very few children in *yōgoshisetsu* would have been involved in similar issues, which are resolved by discussion between parents or guardians and staff in the *jidōsōdanjo*.

2. In 1985 Yokogawa, a journalist specializing in educational issues, published a book entitled *Kōhai no Karute* (A Desolate Card) which very briefly focused public attention on the potentially disastrous effects of the lack of personal attention given to those who come into the care of the state. The book tells the true story of a man who was born in prison and spent all his childhood in a *nyūjiin* and *yōgoshisetsu* during the 1960s and 1970s—where his emotional needs were totally ignored and he was badly bullied by both fellow residents and staff—and who, in 1983, was found guilty of raping and murdering a female student in a case which received wide publicity at the time.

3. See Kuraoka, 1992, an academic specializing in welfare law, for a full, and passionate, account of this case.

4. It is important not to over-exaggerate national differences here. In many of the institutional abuse scandals in the UK local authorities also appear to have been very reluctant to respond to initial claims of abuse by either residents (past or present) or staff. (See, for example, the report on abuse in homes in North Wales by Waterhouse, Clough, and le Fleming, 2000.)

5. Kodomo no Koe Kenkyūkai (Children's Voice Study Group) documents in great detail (1993: 11–47) a total of twenty-three cases which it feels raise important questions about the rights of children and parents in child-care cases, though these are generally not as serious as the cases cited above.

6. For example, physical and emotional abuse in a *yōgoshisetsu* in Shimane Prefecture in 1998 was reported in the local pages of the *Yomiuri Shinbun* (26 July and 1 Aug. 1998) after a citizen's group calling itself 'Kodomo no Jinken Ombudsperson' compiled a

report and submitted it to the newspaper following an approach by a child in the home. This group was founded by a local housewife who had recently moved to Shimane, and whose daughter was suffering from school refusal syndrome (*tōkōkyohi*), and is run on a totally voluntary basis.

7. The case of Dennis O'Neill, murdered by his foster father in 1945, is mentioned in many Japanese introductory social work textbooks. The case greatly bolstered the significance of the just-established Curtis Committee, which was responsible for setting up children's departments in the UK, and led to the Monckton Report (available in Japanese). The report on the death of Maria Colwell in 1974 is available in Japanese; the cases of Jasmin Beckford, Tyra Henry, and Kimberley Carlisle are often cited; and the report that looked into the ramifications of several of these cases, the Barclay Committee (1982), is widely available and still read in Japan today. I found a Japanese translation of at least one other recent report—the Pindown Report on Staffordshire Children's Home Policy by Levy and Kahan—produced within six months of the British report being published in 1991.

8. The best demonstration of this is that children of senior high-school age who, once they have entered senior high school then refuse to attend, are classified as having *futōkō* (school non-attendance), even though senior high-school education is not compulsory.

9. There are interesting regional variations in the proportion of children from *yōgoshisetsu* going to senior high school, according to a 1987 survey (*KH*, 1991: 108). At the top were Tottori (73.3 per cent), Toyama (69.2 per cent), Kumamoto (67.7 per cent), Nagano (66.1 per cent); at the bottom, Fukushima (17.3 per cent), Aichi (25.9 per cent), Tochigi (26.6 per cent), Fukui (27.8 per cent). Since these are all rural prefectures, however, the difference is probably accounted for by very small numbers of children. Indeed, the senior residential worker in one home made the point that since the number of children in *yōgoshisetsu* of senior high-school age is such a tiny population in the context of the whole of the Japanese education system, very small numbers of children deciding to go, or not to go, to senior high school in a particular year could make a big difference in the overall statistics. While there is clearly validity in this point, it does not reflect the general concern among those who work in the sector about what remains a large gap between the number of children in *yōgoshisetsu* and the number of children in the general population who are continuing on to senior high school. This concern is supported by the results of a Kōseishō survey in 1989 of 3,190 children in their final year of junior high school of whom only 10 per cent said they definitely did not want to go to senior high school and 6.1 per cent were still undecided (*KH*, 1991: 108).

10. According to Madge (1994: 83), there were in the early 1990s no figures in any European country on the educational advancement rates of children in residential care. In the UK in the late 1990s, however, there has been growing concern about the educational experience of children in care. In general, as Sinclair and Gibbs (1998: 128) conclude, 'the educational performances of children who are looked after is extremely low relative to almost any comparison group, and the consequence is that the young people leave care seriously disadvantaged'. According to Hayden *et al.* (1999: 44, 112, 115, 117), 25 per cent of those in care in the UK who are of compulsory school age are not attending school (either because of absenteeism or exclusion),

less than 20 per cent stay in education post-16, and 75 per cent leave school with no GSCE examination passes; the last two figures compare with around 70 per cent and 6 per cent respectively in the general population.

11. The best example of this practice can be seen in the widely used *hensachi* labelling system on which teachers, parents, and students base their judgement as to which university students should apply to (see Hurst, 1984), and the common, informal distinction that teachers make between *dekiru ko* and *dekinai ko* (able and less able children).

12. The relationship between mothers and schools in Japan is a complex and important one in understanding the educational 'success' of individual children. Even those mothers who would prefer to avoid being seen as the stereotypical *kyōiku mama* (educational mothers) are compelled by demands from schools to invest an enormous amount of time and energy as soon as their children start compulsory education in helping them keep up with their school work. For a good ethnographic comparison of the role of the mother in Japanese and American elementary education, see Benjamin, 1997.

13. Another related explanation that I heard was that the influences that the children received while still in the womb had rarely been positive and frequently negative (such as hearing parents fighting) and that this would have affected their later performance. The significance in Japan of 'influences while still in the womb' (*taikyō*) is discussed in Hendry (1986).

14. Previously all those at senior high school had been funded by individual *yōgoshisetsu* from their own charitable funds. Since it was largely chance which decided to which home a particular child was sent, this system was manifestly unfair, particularly in the context of an education system which was based on equality of opportunity.

15. At Kodomo Gakuen, in 1991, there was one girl who attended a night university. The Seishin Gakusha found the money for the entrance fee (¥460,000) and allowed her to continue to live in the home although it no longer received state money for her. The home also arranged a job for her at a coffee-shop, where she worked during the day and which paid her ¥120,000 per month plus her travel expenses and meals.

16. A very small number of *yōgoshisetsu* have their own elementary and junior high schools staffed by qualified teachers who come in from outside. These are in very rural areas (such as Wakayama Prefecture) where there are not enough children in the local community to keep a school running.

17. Almost all children in Japan walk to school, often in groups from the same neighbourhood, a practice known as *shūdan tōkō*, which is designed to encourage ideas of neighbourhood co-operation.

18. In a survey of all children in *yōgoshisetsu* in 1985, around 3.4 per cent (just under 1,000) of those who responded complained of discrimination and bullying at school, which was seen as the result of the fact that they were from *yōgoshisetsu* (Tsuzaki, Tetsurō 1996: 106–8).

19. Something on which, as far as I know, there has been no research is the effect of the school curriculum on children from *yōgoshisetsu*. As many commentators have pointed out (see Horio, 1988), Monbushō enforces a conservative line on the images of Japanese society that are presented in the school textbooks. According to Nakanishi (*DY*, 20 July 1998), for example, the Ministry insisted on the insertion in a textbook

of the following sentence: 'A family—and the home in which it lives—is the entity within which we are born and raised. It plays an important role as a place where we can find peace of mind.' There is a virtual absence in the textbooks of alternative family styles, despite the fact that these are increasing in Japanese society (see Lunsing, 1995: ch. 3), which must make it difficult for children from *yōgoshisetsu* to know how to deal with the messages being presented to them.

20. Imazeki (1991) actually ascribes these anxieties more to the local education authorities than to individual parents. Schools still consider it their responsibility to educate all children of compulsory school age within their catchment area. Very few children from homes, therefore, are excluded from elementary or junior high schools, however problematic their behaviour. This contrasts strongly with the UK, where children in care are ten times as likely to be excluded as those not in care (Hayden *et al.*, 1999: 115).

21. It is interesting that in Japan no significant distinction has generally been drawn between school refusal and truancy, since the expectation is that all children will understand the importance of schooling for their life chances and will not wish to miss any of it. In one survey in the mid-1990s, however, 10 per cent of children gave as their main reason for not attending school that they wished to play truant, while 10 per cent cited problems of bullying and other problems at school; the other 80 per cent of responses fell into very vague categories such as 'confused or mixed emotions', 'general feeling of lack of energy', and 'no particular reason' (*DY*, 28 July 1997). Only very recently have experts in the field acknowledged that there may be two main categories of children: those who want to go to school but cannot and those who do not feel it necessary to go to school at all (*DY*, 17 Aug. 1998).

22. Indeed, the comfort of living with (and off) one's parents is given as one of the main reasons among women for the increasing average age of marriage and delay of parenthood in Japan which has led to the drop in fertility. The proportion of working, unmarried women living with their parents in Japan rose from 70 per cent in 1975 to 80 per cent in 1996 for those in their twenties, and from 50 per cent to 70 per cent for those aged 30–34 (*KSH*, 1998: 104).

23. A few children return to live with their families when they start work. As one resident in a *yōgoshisetsu* who was considering this option pointed out, however, this can be problematic if the family is receiving welfare benefits, since any income they receive will be included in the household income which may make the family ineligible for state support (Kodomo ga Kataru Shisetsu no Kurashi Henshūiinkai, 1999: 65).

24. In March 1999, the TBS network broadcast a documentary entitled *Setsunai Ai* (Painful Love) which followed the attempts by the former head of a home in Shikoku to stay in touch with a boy, who had been in his care since he was a toddler, after he went to Tokyo to start his first job. In the course of the programme, the former head gradually lost his ability to influence the boy, who continually changed jobs and appeared to be drifting into delinquency, and by the end he had lost contact altogether.

25. I was unable to discover exactly why there was this serious and glaring gap in the literature. The most common explanations that I received were that *yōgoshisetsu* did not want to participate in such research since they feared it would be an indictment of the care that they provided, and that university social welfare departments felt inhibited from undertaking such research since it would jeopardize their relationship with the

homes, on which they relied for placements for their students. It should also be pointed out that in any case such surveys are not easy to conduct. Shōji Yōko (1984: 9) describes the problems that were involved in a survey carried out by the Japan College of Social Work (Nihon Shakai Jigyō Daigaku) of one particular home which was able to locate fewer than half of the total number of former residents.

26. My questionnaire was distributed through the OB Kai (association of former residents) of the home. After lengthy discussions, I agreed the text of the questionnaire with one of the members of the association and her husband, and then mailed them fifty copies of it together with stamped, self-addressed envelopes. They incorporated a covering letter of support and sent the questionnaires to the members of the society who were able to return them to me anonymously, though in fact five individuals did include their own names and addresses on the envelopes. In total, I received sixteen responses as well as the news that one member of the society had recently died of tuberculosis for which he had been unable to afford treatment. (His daughter, I was also told, was now in a *yōgoshisetsu* since his divorced wife was not able to look after her.) I was also able to interview one other member. The average age of respondents was just under 25, which meant that most had left the home within the previous ten years, and they were divided evenly by gender.

27. Okano and Tsuchiya (1999: 90) cite another survey from 1988 in which almost 28 per cent of those from *yōgoshisetsu* who went to work after middle school quit their job within the first eight months.

28. Just as I was completing this book I received out of the blue an e-mail from a woman, married to a former resident of a *yōgoshisetsu*, asking if anyone had ever followed up what happened to children after they left the care system. She thought that homes should be made to see what had happened to many of their former residents, and graphically described her own knowledge of some of those who had been in the home with her husband. 'The ones we know range (guys) from someone my husband's age in prison for murder [actually as the *migawari* (scapegoat) for a *yakuza* gang he got involved with] to someone a bit younger in a mental hospital to several twenty somethings . . . who are kind of drifting on the edges of the underworld and resurface at our place once every couple of months for a good meal, and (girls) from someone who married a 40-year-old straight out of the home and had his baby and a nervous breakdown within a year, and has now separated from him and lives with someone else, to an 18-year-old . . . who is pregnant by a guy who won't marry her, but wants to keep her baby, and so may be either living with us come the New Year or (hopefully not) in a *boshiryō*. Oh and there is also at least one guy I knew who (at 23) committed suicide.'

This account is the nearest that I have come across to suggest that the experiences of those who have been in *yōgoshisetsu* may not be so far out of line with the experiences of those who have been in the care system in the UK where, according to Hayden *et al.* (1999: 44, 133), 40 per cent of children leave care at the age of 16; 16 per cent of young women leaving care are either pregnant or already mothers; and 38 per cent of young prisoners have been in care at some time in their lives, as have 30 per cent of young single homeless people. Frost, Mills, and Stein (1999: 109) suggest that perhaps as many as 50 per cent of beggars and 66 per cent of prostitutes in the UK have also had experience of being in care.

29. For a collection of Hirooka's writings and an overview of his work, see, Seishōnen to tomo ni Ayumukai, 1997. For a brief piece in English, see Hirooka, 1989.

30. A 1994 survey of the then seventeen *jiritsu enjo homes* shows the following capacities: twenty residents—two homes; ten residents—six homes; nine residents—one home; six residents—eight homes. Six of the homes were mixed; four for boys only, and five for girls only. Almost 45 per cent of the places were available in Tokyo, which had taken the lead in this field (*KH*, 1994: 139). To put these figures in context, every year about 300 residents of *yōgoshisetsu* who finish junior high school do not stay on in the education system and hence, technically, have to leave the homes within a year (see *KH*, 1992: 154, 156–7).

NOTES TO CHAPTER 7

1. The major exception here is Catholic Ireland, which has a long history of fostering (Madge, 1994: 62). Madge (1994: 138) suggests that residential child care has an unusually low status in England compared to most of the rest of Europe. Curiously though, as many authors have commented (Bullock, Little, and Millham, 1993: 21; Kahan, 1994: 8, 23–4) private fee-paying boarding schools in England, long attended by children from the upper and upper-middle classes, are not tainted with the same negative images of institutionalization and stigmatization as residential children's homes. This implies that the status of residential institutions is more closely associated with those who use them than with the form of care they offer.

2. The expression *sato no oya* (*oya* means 'parent' or 'parents') is still used in Japan to talk about the parents of one's wife, or by wives to talk about their own parents.

3. This practice is similar to what Kopytoff and Miers (1977: 55 ff.) call 'adoptive slavery' or 'acquired persons' in some African societies.

4. Many in Japan still think, for example, that foster-parents receive no payment for taking in children. In fact they receive between ¥75,000 and ¥115,000 a month depending on individual circumstances and the prefecture in which they live.

5. In theory, the new law opened the way for single or divorced parents to be registered as foster-parents for the first time (Takami, 1996: 100). In practice, it appears the criteria for registration as a foster-parent remain quite strict (Takei, 1999). According to a leaflet put out in 1997 by the Katei Yōgo Sokushin Kyōkai, a private organization which recruits foster-parents in the Kansai area, they must be married for more than three years, be no more than forty years older than the child they will foster, have an annual salary of at least ¥3 million, and live in a house with more than two rooms.

6. At Kodomo Gakuen, this system was known as a *short-stay home* (using the English words) and was set up in 1986. In Tokyo more generally it was known as the *friend home programme* (again using the English words) and catered for around 600 infants and children from homes a year (Tokyo Metropolitan Government, 1995: 44). Some in the welfare world are very critical of these placements and one foster specialist expressed privately the view that the families involved treated the children a bit like 'pets', which could be returned when they grew tired of them, and questioned why they did not take a more active fostering role.

7. According to the Katei Yōgo Sokushin Kyōkai, in a 1988 survey conducted in Kobe of 158 foster-parents on their main motivation for fostering (only one answer being

allowed), 42 per cent of men and 34 per cent of women gave as their reason the fact they were childless.

8. It is significant, for example, that, in Tokyo, foster-parents cannot place their children in the state-subsidized *hoikuen* (day-care centres), but only in the non-subsidised *yōchien* (kindergartens), since a placement in the former would be considered to be receiving a double welfare benefit. Under the employment law, also, no child-care leave is available for those who foster, and indeed at least one fostering agency encourages foster-mothers to give up their jobs (see Katei Yōgo Sokushin Kyōkai, 1997).

9. The foster placements of the other 30–40 per cent can be very problematic. In a government-commissioned report that was released in late 1999, 80 per cent of the children in the sixty-five foster homes surveyed had suffered some form of abuse—ranging from sexual abuse to neglect—before coming into care. Thirty-nine of the sixty-five foster-families stated that children placed in their care had been removed, without permission, by parents or guardians, and many were subsequently discovered to have been re-abused (*AS*, 3 Nov. 1999). A separate survey from 1992 of all children in foster placements found that the main reason given for coming into care was abuse (*gyakutai*) or 'refusal to care' (*yōiku kyohi*), categories which overall accounted for less than 8 per cent of all children in care (Kita, 1996: 54).

10. The expression *sato oya* (foster-parent) is frequently misused in Japan. Those who adopt children whose background they do not know are often described as *sato oya* rather than adoptive parents (see e.g. Murakami Ryū's influential novel *Coin Locker Babies* (Murakami, 1980: 15–16). To compound the confusion, the English term 'foster-parent' has been increasingly used since the 1980s by non-governmental organizations in Japan to refer to those who sponsor the education and health of children in developing countries and, following the Hanshin earthquake in 1995, look after pets whose owners can no longer care for them. In the late 1990s, some people most readily associated the term *sato oya* with those who temporarily look after someone else's *tamagotchi* (computer animal).

11. In part the model used for these centres was the Barnardo's organization in the UK, which moved from concentrating on residential to foster care in the 1970s.

12. According to Bachnik (1988: 15), Japanese adoption in the Nara period (710–94) had already developed its own particular flavour and diverted from Chinese practice. For a brief comparison of Japanese, Chinese, and Korean historical ideas about adoption, see Kurosu and Ochiai (1995: 262).

13. In the mid-1980s, there were almost 19,000 cases of adoptions being revoked a year, a figure that was remarkably constant over at least the previous decade. This constituted around 20 per cent of all adoptions, a figure far higher than the divorce rate in Japan (see Saikō Saibansho Jimu Sōkyoku, 1988: 5–6).

14. Hence it is important to note that adoption does not necessarily imply co-residence, while fostering does.

15. These examples come from a meeting of the Jidō Fukushihō Kenkyūkai (Child Welfare Law Study Group) held in Tokyo on 22 October 1991.

16. A girl from Kodomo Gakuen who was adopted in the 1990s by a French couple who had lived for six years in Japan—and already had an adopted Vietnamese daughter—was very small for her age. It was thought unlikely, therefore, that she would find adoptive parents in Japan and that it would be in her best interests to be adopted overseas.

17. The contraceptive pill was only made legal in Japan for the first time in 1999. The delay in introducing it was largely put down to the opposition of doctors, many of whom were involved in the massive business—some estimates put the figure as high as 1.5 million cases a year—of performing abortions (Norgren, 1998: 172).

18. Kikuta frequently contrasted the situation of such mothers with that of criminals who do not have their crimes recorded on their *koseki*. Ihaya (*JTW*, 25–31 Mar. 1991) cites the extreme case of a girl who was raped, but was too frightened to have an abortion and decided to keep the baby. As a result, she was ejected from home by her mother who agreed to accept her back only when she agreed to a termination which meant that the family register would be kept 'clean'.

19. Different sources variously put the number of adoptions Kikuta arranged as between 100 and 220. His sudden death in August 1991, aged 65, left many questions unanswered.

20. As can be seen, there are already enormous problems with the translation of *yōshiengumi* (or *yōshi*) as 'adoption'. As Bachnik (1983: 171) points out, 'the "adoption" of a younger brother is incomprehensible to an English speaker'. The same, of course, applies to the translation of 'adoption' as *yōshiengumi*, and some of those involved in setting up the new *tokubetsu yōshi* system wanted it to be given a 'Westernized' name, written in *katakana* (the syllabary used to write foreign words in Japanese) to distinguish it from old ideas about adoption. They were prevented from doing so, however, by the drafting committee of the Ministry of Justice (Hōmushō), which insisted that *katakana* words could not be used in framing Japanese laws (Noda Aiko, personal communication). For a good outline written for the lay public of the basic differences between *tokubetsu yōshi* and *futsū yōshi*, see Yoshioka *et al.* (1995: 43).

21. The court needs to be convinced by the applicant and the Family Court social worker that the potential adoptee is in need of the care being offered (*yōhogoyōken*). If it is not convinced of this, then the application for adoption will be rejected, thereby ensuring that the child's, and not the applicant's, rights and needs are placed first (see Ishizaka, 1990: 34).

22. While it would appear that in most cases the adopting parents are given only minimal information about the birth parents, the names and addresses of all parties who can be traced—sometimes one of the birth parents has disappeared—appear on the *hanketsugaki* (court judgement paper) so it is actually possible for them to contact each other.

23. It would also appear that in practice, if not in law, those who adopt through the *tokubetsu yōshi* system should not have children of their own, since 90 per cent of parents adopting through the system are childless (*KSH*, 1998: 102).

24. In practice, though, it would appear that adoption takes considerably longer than six months to complete due to lack of manpower in the relevant court offices; in some cases it can take up to two years. During this interim period, however, the adopting parents receive money as foster-parents.

25. Jordan suggests that there might be a significant underground system where couples who want to adopt are instructed to turn to obstetricians who operate by the 'shadow rules'. She quotes one source who suggests that doctors broker 'hundreds of children' each year, but another informant dismisses this as anecdotal. She concedes, however, that the total number of adoptions of unrelated children in Japan can still be only a minute fraction of the 60,000 or so adoptions in the United States each year. It is also

proportionally much less than in the UK, even though adoption in the UK has declined rapidly in recent years, from around 25,000 cases in 1968 to 6,000 in 1998, in line with changes in child welfare policy (Hayden *et al.*, 1999; 199).

NOTES TO CHAPTER 8

1. Some areas of Japan now guarantee working mothers a full-time, subsidized place at a local *hoikuen*. Between 1990 and 1998, the state budget for *gakudō* clubs increased sevenfold (*KH*, 1998: 122). A further increase by 60 per cent is planned by 2004 (*MS*, 11 Dec. 1999).
2. One former head of a *yōgoshisetsu* once suggested that the head of a home which was not having children placed in it might occasionally visit the local *jidōsōdanjo*, with a bottle of sake, to enquire if children would be placed there in the near future.
3. Boudreaux and Boudreaux (1999) also explain the change in orphanages in the US from the 1960s onwards in terms of interest-group politics. In that case, however, according to the Boudreaux, the most powerful interests were those of professional fieldworkers who argued for fostering over institutional care, since they would take over responsibility for such a system. This, they claim, was one of the main reasons for the demise of the orphanage in the US.
4. For discussions about how the UN Convention was introduced, always problematically, into the United States, Australia, Britain, and Russia see Cohen (1995), Rayner (1995), Freeman (1995), and Harwin (1995) respectively.
5. Judith Ennew (1995), discussing the relevance of the Convention to street children in Brazil, argues that the 'child' in the Convention is a 'Northern' as opposed to a 'Southern' child. In the context of Japan, however, the distinction is always made between a 'Western' (basically northern European/North American) versus 'Eastern' (generally meaning East Asian) concept of the child.
6. Boyden (1990) is among a handful of Western commentators who also feel that the UN Convention on the Rights of the Child imposes a European and American capitalist view of the child and childhood on other societies. Ishida (1986) points out that when the concept of rights was first discussed in Japan at the end of the nineteenth century, it was always introduced in a negative manner as something born of selfishness and not of filial piety. It would be a mistake, however, to assume that the concept of individual rights was still so radical a hundred years later in the 1990s. Japan has, for example, since the 1940s had a system of *jinken yōgoiin* (civil liberties commissioners) who are charged with investigating human rights violations and promoting human rights ideas although, according to Neary (1997), the commissioners have generally avoided criticism of government policies and their method of acting as a conciliation service may actually sometimes prevent individuals from pursuing their rights.
7. The enormous increase (of about 300 per cent) in the number of universities offering courses in social welfare during the 1990s will almost certainly mean that more of those who get jobs in *jidōsōdanjo* will have some relevant social welfare education even if there is not a change in policy, as demanded by Nichibenren, to make this mandatory.
8. While these figures were widely circulated in this form in Japan, they needed some contextualization. In the UK, for example, while 35 per cent of children were born to unmarried mothers, in 70 per cent of these cases both parents were registered as living

at the same address. On the other hand, in recognition of the importance to a Japanese child of having a socially recognized father (*pater*), a husband was sometimes registered as a child's father even if it was known that he was not the biological father (*genitor*) (Shimazu, 1994: 83).

9. Kojima (1986: 136) cites a 1980 study which suggested that almost 90 per cent of teenagers who became pregnant had abortions. Further in the 1980s, only about 5 per cent of abortions were performed on teenagers, compared to 25 per cent in the UK (Hayashi, 1989: 20). According to Norgren (1998: 62), however, the pattern of abortions began to change quite rapidly in the 1990s, with an increased proportion being performed on unmarried and younger women.

10. For analyses of the construction of gender in Japan, see Brinton, 1993; Iwao, 1993; Lebra, 1984; and Smith, 1987.

11. The then prime minister Kaifu made a speech, much criticized by feminists, at the UN at the start of the UN Year of the Child (1991) in which he declared that the reason that Japan had few social problems and a well-educated population was that women stayed at home and looked after their children.

12. Some commentators in the US during the 1980s also described some Japanese cultural practices such as co-sleeping and co-bathing as potentially or even actually abusive, though their writings tell us as much about American social values as they do about Japanese society. For reference, these articles can be found mainly in the journal edited by the psycho-historian Lloyd DeMause entitled *The Journal of Psychohistory* (see DeMause, 1987, 1991, 1998; Kitahara, 1989a, 1989b). The source of the evidence cited in most of these articles is often very unclear; they are conspicuously circular in their referencing; and some of their reasoning borders on the bizarre. Kitahara (1989a: 50–2), for example, connects Japanese views of incest with Japan's foundation myth based on the incestuous relationship between the sibling deities Izanami and Izanagi. It should be added that in the same journal the practices of many other countries are described in similarly negative terms in support of DeMause's central contention that 'the history of humanity is founded upon the abuse of children'.

13. All *jidōsōdanjo* have attached to them a unit in which children can be placed for temporary care (*ichiji hogo*) without, it would appear, any time limit. It is unclear whether parents can remove their children from such facilities without permission, and it is partly because of this uncertainty, and the problems to which it might lead, that some workers in *jidōsōdanjo* are reluctant to make use of these facilities.

14. Twins have been felt to be particularly susceptible to abuse (Tanimura, Matsui, and Kobayashi, 1990). This mainly reflects the greater pressure on mothers in bringing up the children, though some also relate it to the birth of twins in Japan being stigmatized as 'animal behaviour' (Kitahara, 1989a: 64).

15. Comparing rates of homicide, especially of children, is notoriously difficult, but the evidence suggests that the rate of child homicide in Japan is at least as high as in other OECD countries (see Costin, Karger, and Stoesz, 1996: 172).

16. The case in 1996 of a British woman who was arrested at New York airport attempting to board a flight back to the UK with the dead body of her newborn baby under her coat highlights how views of such cases are far from straightforward even in the US. The US authorities felt compelled to prosecute on behalf of the dead child; the defence team argued strongly that the mother was a victim herself since she was

suffering from severe depression and in need of psychiatric treatment. While the latter (defence) argument is common in Japan, I have never come across the former (prosecution) one. The only direct comparative study of mental health and abuse which I have seen—looking at Japanese-American and Samoan-American families in Hawaii—suggests that in that context the Japanese community was more likely to blame abuse on mental illness (Dubanoski and Snyder, 1980: 223).

17. The expression itself probably dates from the mid-1920s when abortion was made illegal—in a state-driven attempt to increase the fertility rate—and many unwanted babies were born.

18. Figures for *oyako shinjū* are clearly difficult to collect and there is wide variation in the numbers given for different years. The crux of the problem is that no official figures are kept and hence researchers have to rely on newspaper reports, and many cases either do not reach the newspapers or else are reported only in local editions. From the top end of the scale, Pinguet (1993: 49) cites an unidentified source giving a figure of 494 cases in 1975; Takahashi (1977: 66) says that there were fifty-nine cases during April, May, and June 1974; Tsuji (1982: 2) gives a figure of eighty cases reported in the Tokyo edition of the *Asahi Shinbun* for 1978; CAPNA (1998: 63–4), again working from media reports, suggests that there were fifty-four incidents leading to the deaths of seventy-six children in 1996 and 1997 combined. In surveys of *oyako shinjū*, it would appear that 70–80 per cent are in fact cases of *boshi shinjū* (mother and child suicide); almost all involve married parents, generally in their thirties; and it would seem to be a largely urban phenomenon, although this may reflect the rate of reporting as much as the actual practice. The vast majority (over 80 per cent) of the children who died were aged 7 or less.

19. If *oyako shinjū* and abandonment in coin lockers are practices which seem very alien to Western readers, it should be pointed out there are practices which are common in many northern European and North American societies which are equally hard for many Japanese to understand. These extend from male circumcision—of which there is no tradition in Japan (Wagatsuma, 1981: 121)—to putting children to sleep in separate beds and even separate rooms from an early age, to leaving them to cry on their own, to the practice of taking out toddlers on reins to stop them running into traffic (Gough, 1995: 5). Similarly, as many anthropologists have recorded (see Hendry, 1986: 110–11), Japanese parents tend to punish their children by shutting them out of the house, while in Europe and America it is more likely that they would shut them in.

20. According to Pringle (1998: 33), however, within Europe the focus on sexual abuse is peculiar to the UK.

21. While it is difficult to measure such things, it would seem that if there is a slightly higher preponderance of mother–son incest cases in Japan than elsewhere (for which the evidence in any case is very weak), it is still the case (despite media and other reports to the contrary—see Kitahara, 1989b) that they represent only a small fraction of all incest cases. Allison (1996) ascribes the attention focused in the 1970s and 1980s on such cases to a conservative, probably mainly male, backlash against the increased number of women in the workplace and a perception that women were becoming increasingly selfish in fulfilling their desires to have both children and a career.

22. As Hendry (1986: 11) points out, the Chinese character for *shitsuke* is made up of two

parts meaning 'body' and 'beauty', and is a crucial concept in child-rearing in Japan, in which the body is used as a site for socialization.

23. In a 1996 survey undertaken by the All Japan Parents and Teachers Association, only 25.6 per cent of respondents said that corporal punishment should never be administered by a teacher (see http://www.indis.co.jp/sugita). The most extreme example, however, of the apparent social acceptance of physical punishment in the socialization of children is probably the case of Totsuka Hiroshi. During the 1980s, at the Totsuka Yacht School in Aichi Prefecture, Totsuka, a former Olympic yachtsman, reigned over a regime of extreme discipline that was intended to 'improve' the anti-social behaviour of children with emotional problems who had been placed by their families in his care. Three children died and two went missing presumed dead as a result of treatment received at the home, and Totsuka was arrested and tried for murder. In 1992 the Nagoya District Court acknowledged that the two deaths were the result of injuries inflicted on them, but handed down suspended sentences to Totsuka and three instructors in the school on the grounds that they had acted not for profit but in what they believed was the best interests of the children. Soon afterwards, Totsuka reopened the school and had no problem finding parents willing to entrust children to his care in the belief that his extreme regime of socialization, which included beating and confining children, was in the best interests of their children. The institution was only closed in 1997 when the Nagoya High Court, on appeal by the prosecution in the original case, overturned the lower court decision and sentenced Totsuka to six years in prison (*Mainichi Daily News*, 13 Mar. 1997; Yoneyama, 1999: 94–5).

24. Some subsequent statistics also include the category of *tōkō kinshi* (prevention of children from attending school), but the numbers are so negligible that they are normally excluded. In Tokyo, for example, they amount to between one and three cases per year (Tokyo-to Fukushikyoku, 1998: 23). For a good account of the debates over the definition of child abuse in Japan in the early 1990s, see Jidō Gyakutai Bōshi Seido Kenkyūkai, 1993.

25. When the line was set up, concerns were expressed over the role of a major television company and the potential for 'commercial exploitation'. As a result, the line has been run by a board of twenty members, of whom ten or more must be employees of the local government.

26. An analysis by Ueno (1994: 5) of the keyword expression *kodomo no gyakutai* (child abuse) in the *Asahi Shinbun* (Tokyo edition) showed two uses in the last six months of 1988, nine instances in 1989, twenty in 1990, twenty-two in 1991, twenty-one in 1992, and twenty-two in 1993.

27. As Gilbert (1997: 3) writes in his introduction to a study of child abuse in comparative perspective, 'child abuse reports to confidential doctors climbed from 3,179 to 13,220 in the Netherlands between 1983 and 1993 . . . in Belgium the number of reports increased by 70 per cent between 1986 and 1992 . . . and in Quebec, Canada, the number of reports jumped by 100 per cent from 1989 to 1992'. In the United States (with double the population of Japan) the number of reported cases of child abuse rose from 7,000 in 1967, to 60,000 in 1972, to 1.1 million in 1980, to 2.3 million in 1993 (Gilbert, 1997: 3; Hacking, 1991: 259). The number of children on the child protection register in England almost quadrupled from 12,388 in 1984 to 45,300 in 1991, and the rate of sexual abuse registrations (the largest category of registrations) increased sevenfold between 1983 and 1986 (Berridge, 1997: 86–7).

28. One group conspicuous by its absence in meetings of child abuse specialists during the 1990s was the police. In the late 1990s, Miyamoto and Ishibashi (1998) undertook a survey of police involvement in child abuse cases. This survey covered 315 members of JaSPCAN, including sixty doctors, forty-three workers from *jidōsōdanjo*, forty health workers, and thirty-six teachers. Of the respondents, 263 (83.5 per cent) had dealt with abuse cases of whom only ninety-three (35 per cent) had even communicated with the police, including twenty-eight of those working in *jidōsōdanjo* and nineteen doctors. Thirty of the ninety-three reported that nothing further happened as a result of their communication and that in one case the abuse had actually got worse. Only thirteen cases led to arrest.

29. Two television documentaries on NHK and Yomiuri TV in April 1999 covered the same story of a 6-year-old boy, Masato-kun, who was killed despite the fact that no fewer than three *jidōsōdanjo* in two different areas of Japan had been aware that he was being abused. The NHK documentary (*Close-Up Gendai*, 29 June 1999) was highly critical of the *jidōsōdanjo* in question and, for probably the first time, workers at *jidōsōdanjo* found themselves under pressure for not having intervened earlier, as happened in the UK following the growth in awareness of child abuse in the 1980s particularly following the Jasmine Beckford case (see Franklin and Parton, 1991; Hayden *et al.*, 1999: 26–7).

30. The survey was in part in response to a number of reported deaths of children left in cars while their parents were playing *pachinko* (a Japanese form of pinball). It defined abuse very broadly and asked mothers if they had ever done any of sixteen different things to their children, including shouting at them, slapping their hands, leaving them while they were crying or leaving them alone in a car. Respondents were scored two points for those things which they said that they did often and one for those they did occasionally. Those with eleven or more points were defined as abusing their children; those with between seven and ten points as bordering on abuse. Nine per cent of mothers were found to be 'abusive' and a further 30 per cent as 'bordering on abuse'.

31. A survey of six countries carried out by Kōseishō suggested that Japanese fathers had the least contact with their children (*KSH*, 1998: 88). A survey from the early 1990s suggested that 30 per cent of fathers spent under fifteen minutes a day on weekdays playing or talking to their children, and only 50 per cent spent more than thirty minutes. Even on Sundays, over 40 per cent of fathers spent less than an hour interacting with their children (Yuzawa, 1994: 66).

32. These images of the perfect family are, of course, particularly difficult for those bringing up children with any form of handicap. According to Kamiide (1990: 6–7), cases of child abuse in Japan are most likely to involve children who have been born prematurely, have developmental problems, and are emotionally or behaviourally disturbed.

33. See Kojima (1986) for the history of the development of this phenomenon in postwar Japan. This idea is of course not unique to Japan. It has long been recognized that there are high rates of depression among mothers with children under 5 in the UK: see Brown and Harris (1978). Such examples from other societies, however, are rarely, if indeed ever, mentioned in the Japanese literature.

34. For a comparable argument from the UK, see Reder, Duncan, and Gray (1993: 8–13), who document the relationship between the concept of 'child abuse' and changing social and historical views of children and families over the past 200 years.

35. A further, more overtly political, reason for Kōseishō to highlight the 'discovery' of child abuse—and thereby be able to demand an increase in its budget from the Ministry of Finance to put in place measures to tackle it—may be related to the fact that, under administrative reforms, Kōseishō will be merged with the Ministry of Labour (Rōdōshō) in January 2001. It is hence keen to enlarge its area of influence (and budget) as much as possible before that happens. Kōseishō actually grew considerably in status throughout the 1990s. This was in part due to the demands of the ageing society which dramatically increased its budget and influence; in part because it was run by two charismatic politicians, Kan Naoto and Koizumi Junichirō, during much of the decade. Kan in particular raised the profile of the ministry by apologizing for its maladministration of blood transfusions in the 1980s, which had led to several people contracting AIDS.

36. One interesting feature of the rising rates of reported child abuse during the 1990s was that the relative proportions of different categories of abuse generally remained the same. In almost all years, just over half of all cases involved physical abuse; around 30 per cent related to cases of neglect; 10 per cent involved psychological abuse; and around 6 per cent involved sexual abuse. Kitamura *et al.* (1999: 24) suggest that the comparatively low rate of reported sexual abuse may be related to embarrassment at investigating suspicions, and fears of stigmatizing victims.

37. Though technically a *gakkō hōjin*, and hence a private institution, in practice Nihon Shakai Jigyō Daigaku has had the same status as a national university (*kokuristsu daigaku*) since it was set up in 1946, except that it receives most of its funding from Kōseishō rather than Monbushō. In the 1970s and 1980s, the radical line of some of its academics often led to tension between it and Kōseishō, but since the 1990s it appears to have worked much more closely with the Ministry and its research projects are often drawn upon by policy-makers.

38. This is certainly one way of interpreting a survey that found that 60 per cent of prefectures and major cities would be cutting the budgets of their *jidōsōdanjo* from April 2000, some of them by as much as 10 per cent (*MS*, 6 June 1999).

GLOSSARY (INCLUDING DATES OF MAJOR PERIODS IN JAPANESE HISTORY)

This glossary has relied heavily on Nakamura, Kojima, and Thompson's excellent *English–Japanese/Japanese–English Social Welfare and Related Services Glossary* (Tokyo: Seishin Shobō, 1981).

The pronunciation of Japanese vowels is similar to that of Italian vowels. Vowels are given double length when modified by a macron (e.g. ō, ū). Consonants are pronounced in a fashion similar to English. Each element of a double consonant (e.g. kk) should be treated separately. G is hard. Words are pronounced in an even fashion with little variance in pitch.

Ainu: early inhabitants of the Japanese islands, gradually pushed back to the northernmost island of Hokkaidō, where their current numbers are estimated at around 25,000. Very few are of pure Ainu blood

Angel Plan: government initiative in 1994 to implement policies that would increase Japan's birth rate

boshiryō: accommodation for lone-mother families

boshi seikatsu shien shisetsu: institutions to support the lives of single mothers and children; new name for *boshiryō* from April 1998

burakumin: hamlet people; euphemistic term used in most Western-language material to describe members of Japan's outcaste class who were officially distinguished by their low-caste occupations until 1870

chōnaikai: neighbourhood associations

chōriin: kitchen staff

daimyō: feudal lord

dekasegi: literally 'to go out and earn money'; migrant work

dōzoku: group of related households

dōzoku keiei: management by a group of related households

Eikoku-byō: British disease; derogatory term used in Japan to describe the social and economic problems in the UK of the 1970s

eiyōshi: nutritionist

enchō sensei: head of a welfare facility

fukushi: welfare (often with a negative connotation)

fukushi gannen: first year of welfare; designation given to 1973 as the start of a new welfare era in Japan

fukushi jimusho: welfare office; front-line publicly administered service delivery agency, charged with fulfilling the provisions of the six basic welfare laws and required to be established in any political jurisdiction with more than 100,000 inhabitants

fukushi minaoshi: reconsideration of welfare; movement in the 1970s to restrict expansion of the provision of welfare largely as a result of the 'oil shock' of 1973

fushiryō: accommodation for lone-father families

futōkō: school non-attendance

gakkō hōjin: school corporation

gakudō (hoiku): after-school care for children in elementary school (ages 6–12) whose parents are at work

Gold Plan: government plan in 1990 to increase public spending on facilities for the aged in Japan; supplemented by a *New Gold Plan* in 1994

gonin gumi seido: the organization of peasants into units of five families which were held mutually responsible for the actions of all their individual members; used as a form of political control during the Tokugawa period

group home: small-scale child residential institution

gyakutai: abuse, ill-treatment

Heian period: AD 794–1185

hobo: female child-care worker, in either residential or day-care institutions

hoboyōseikō: nursery nurse training college

Hofukurō: Zenkoku Hoiku Fukushi Rōdō Kumiai; union for workers in private welfare and care institutions

hofu: male child-care worker, in either residential or day-care institutions

hoikuen: day-care centres (generally open at least ten hours a day, offering child care for working parents)

hoikushi: male or female child-care worker; gender-neutral term introduced in the 1990s

hōmeniin: district volunteers; pre-war predecessor of the *minseiiin* system, originated in Okayama Prefecture in 1917 and officially recognized in 1936

Hōmushō: Japanese Ministry of Justice

ichiji hogo: temporary care; mechanism available to *jidōfukushishi* to place children about whom they have concerns in temporary care units attached to *jidōsōdanjo*

ie: house or household

ikuji neurosis: child-rearing neurosis

Jichirō: Zen Nihon Jichi Dantai Rōdō Kumiai. The largest labour organization in Japan with a membership in the early 1990s of around 1.25 million. It was founded in 1954 to represent public sector workers.

jidō: child or children

jidōfukushishi: child welfare officer; caseworker specializing in children's problems attached to a prefecturally administered *jidōsōdanjo*

jidō fukushi shingikai: child welfare advisory council; established at national and local levels to survey, debate, and make recommendations regarding child welfare issues

jidō gyakutai: child abuse

jidō gyakutai sōdan denwa: child abuse telephone hotlines; first set up in 1990 and 1991 in Osaka and Tokyo respectively

jidōiin: child welfare volunteer; system instituted in 1947 whereby those appointed as *minseiiin* serve concurrently as child welfare volunteers to promote the health and welfare of mothers and children in their communities

jidō jiritsu shien centre: institutions to help children develop their own self-supporting capability; new name for *kyōgoin* from April 1998

jidōkai: student or children's council

Jidō Kenshō: Children's Charter, document published on 5 May (Children's Day) 1951 as an official guideline for the nation's work with children

jidōshidōin: child guidance worker; worker in residential care institutions, generally with an undergraduate degree with some emphasis on sociology, psychology, and education

jidōsōdanjo: child guidance centres; primary public agency charged with supervising and carrying out the provisions of the Child Welfare Law

jidō yōgoshisetsu: child protective institutions; new official name for *yōgoshisetsu* from April 1998

jihi: mercy; Buddhist concept still important in debates about social welfare provision in Japan

jimushokuin: office staff

jinken yōgoiin: civil liberties commissioners

jisshū: trainee workers; trainee practice

jōcho shōgai tanki chiryō shisetsu: institutions for emotionally disturbed children, generally known as *jōtan*

juku: private schools where children study outside normal school hours

kaihō: nursing, care; generally without any negative connotation

Kamakura period: AD 1185–1333

kankain: obsolete term referring to a system of residential care and education for delinquents provided for under the Kankain Law of 1900

kansa: audit and inspection; carried out by public officials of both public and private institutions that receive public money

Kansai: 'West of the Barrier'; the Kyoto–Kōbe–Osaka area

Kantō: 'East of the Barrier'; the Tokyo area

kataoya: step-parent

katei hōmon: visit by home-room teacher in state elementary and junior high schools to the home of each pupil in their class

katei saibansho: Family Court; established in 1948, each court has two sections, one dealing with mediation and arbitration of family problems, the other with problems of juvenile delinquency or adult offences that relate to the welfare of juveniles. General philosophy of the court is that of problem-solving rather than harsh application of law

Katei Yōgo Sokushin Kyōkai: private fostering and adoption agency based in the Kansai region

kikokushijo: Japanese returnee schoolchildren

kōban: local police box

Kodomo no Hi: Children's Day; annual public holiday on 5 May to promote the welfare of children, established in 1948

kōenkai: supporters' association attached to an individual or institution

kōhai: one's juniors in an organization

kojiin: obsolete term meaning orphanage

kome sōdō: rice riots of 1918 resulting from the rising cost of living, especially of rice, after the First World War, and influenced by the ideology of the Russian Revolution

kōmuin: public official, civil servant

konketsuji: children with one Japanese and one non-Japanese parent

kōreika shakai: society that is ageing

kōryūkai: meeting to exchange experiences

Kōseishō: Japanese Ministry of Health and Welfare

koseki: household register

Kunaichō: Japanese Imperial Household Agency

kyōgoin: educational protective facilities

kyojakuji shisetsu: homes for physically weak children

mabiki: literally 'thinning out' as in thinning out rice seedlings to ensure that healthy plants have room to grow; refers to murder of infants in feudal Japan when families faced severe shortages

Meiji period: period between 1868 and 1912 when Japan was formally ruled by the Emperor Meiji

minkan shisetsu: private institutions; voluntary agencies

minseiiin: quasi-voluntary, semi-official community volunteers who act as a liaison between the community in which they live and local welfare offices and other community resources. Most *minseiiin* are also appointed as *jidōiin*, with a special brief to look after children in their neighbourhood

minsei.jidōiin: full title of those appointed as *minseiiin* with the added brief of looking after children in their neighbourhood

Monbushō: Japanese Ministry of Education, Science, Sports, and Culture

mondaiji: literally 'problem child or children'; term used for children in *yōgoshisetsu* manifesting behavioural problems

Muromachi period: AD 1392–1568

Nara period: AD 646–794

Nichibenren: Japan Federation of Bar Associations

Nihongata shakai fukushi shakai: Japanese-style social welfare society

nisei: second generation; term used to refer to those in *yōgoshisetsu* of whom one or both parents have themselves been in care

nyūjiin: residential infant care facilities

OB kai: Old Boys association; association of those (male or female) who have graduated from an institution

Okinawans: inhabitants of the chain of Ryūkyū Islands to the south-west of the Japanese mainland, the largest of which is Okinawa, originally an independent kingdom

oyako shinjū: 'parent–child suicide'; more accurately, child murder–parent suicide

pachinko: Japanese form of pinball used for gambling

rijikai: Board of Directors

rōjin home: old people's home

sankamoku shikaku: three-discipline qualification; qualification to become a *jidōshidōin* based on having taken courses in sociology, psychology, and education at university

sarakin: loan companies (often offering easy money at very high interest)

satogo: foster-child

sato oya: foster-parent(s)

seikatsu hogo: livelihood protection; broad programme of public assistance under the 1950 Daily Life Security Law, which aims to catch any cases which are not covered by other forms of assistance

seiza: sitting on one's haunches or knees

senpai: one's seniors in an organization

sensei: one who goes before; general term of respect towards seniors

shakai fukushi hōjin: social welfare juridical person; corporate status provided for under Article 22 of the 1951 Social Welfare Services Law, whereby a private welfare administrative organization can be accredited to provide specified publicly recognized welfare services and receive public funding for these programmes

shakai fukushi shingikai: social welfare advisory council; established at national and local levels to survey, debate, and make recommendations regarding all welfare issues apart from those dealt with by the *jidō fukushi shingikai*

shakaifukushishuji: public assistance caseworkers charged with the administration at the local level of services provided for under the six basic welfare service laws (*shakai fukushi roppō*)

shimin dantai: citizens' groups

shinri ryōshi: psychotherapist

shitsuke: training

shōgai: any kind of mental or physical handicap

shogū konnanji: children needing complex treatment

shokuin gakushū: in-service staff training

shōshasei: system of small-scale residential living

Shōshasei Yōiku Kenkyūkai: Study Group on Bringing Up Children in a Small-Group-Living Environment

shōshika shakai: society with a declining birth rate

Shōwa period: period between 1926 and 1989 when Japan was formally ruled by the son of the Taishō emperor

shūdan katsudō: group activities

shukuchoku: night duty

shūnin jidōiin: quasi-voluntary community welfare volunteers created in the mid-1990s to support the work of *minsei.jidōiin* in the area of child welfare

shūnin shidōin: senior care worker position in a residential institution

skinship: physical (non-sexual) contact

sochi seido: placement system, whereby public funds are used to pay for welfare services provided by public or private institutions based on a standard fee per month per person

sotsuenkai: association of those who have been residents of an institution

taibatsu: physical/corporal punishment

taishasei: system of large-scale residential living

Taishō period: period between 1912 and 1926 when Japan was formally ruled by the third son of the Meiji emperor

tankinyūsho: short-stay system of accommodation provided in *yōgoshisetsu* for children while guardian(s) are hospitalized or otherwise temporarily unavailable

tanki sato oya: short-term foster-parent(s)

tatewarisei: system of dividing up a group so as to place together those of different ages

teiin: official maximum quota for number of residents that an institution can take, on the basis of which budgets have largely been decided

tenkōsei: students who change school within Japan

tōkōkyohi(shō): school refusal syndrome; psychological problem ascribed to children who refuse to attend school

tokubetsu yōshi(engumi): special adoption; new adoption system introduced in 1988

Tokugawa period: period between 1603 (when Tokugawa Ieyasu was awarded the title of *shōgun*) and 1868. Also known as the Edo period because the military government headed by the *shōgun*, known as the Tokugawa *bakufu*, was based in Edo (present-day Tokyo) while the Imperial Family in Kyoto was virtually powerless

tonarigumi: term for neighbourhood associations during the pre-war and wartime periods

toshi jidō katei shien centre: urban child and family support centre; system set up in the mid-1990s to provide advice and support to families in urban neighbourhoods, generally based at *yōgoshisetsu*

twilight stay: system of accommodation provided in *yōgoshisetsu* for children while guardian(s) work during the evening after day-care centres have closed

yakuza: member of Japanese organized crime syndicate

yōchien: kindergarten (generally open only part of the day and offering pre-school education)

yōgogakkō: school for children with mental or physical handicap

yōgoshisetsu: residential child protection institution

Yōgoshisetsuchōkai: Association of Heads of Yōgoshisetsu

yōgoshisetsuji: children who live in *yōgoshisetsu*

Yōgoshisetsu Kyōgikai: Association of Yōgoshisetsu

yōikuin: obsolete term for home for orphans which was run like a workhouse

yōiku katei centre: family care centre; system of centres set up in Tokyo in the 1970s to encourage the fostering of children who come into care; many based at *yōgoshisetsu*

yōiku sato oya: foster parents who do not necessarily intend to adopt

yokowarisei: system of dividing up a group so as to place together those of the same ages

Yōmonken: short for Zenkoku Yōgo Mondai Kenkyūkai (see below)

yōshi: adopted person; adoption
yōshi engumi: adoption
yōshi sato oya: foster-parents who intend to adopt
zainichi-Kankokujin: Korean residents in Japan, generally with Korean nationality
Zenkoku Yōgo Mondai Kenkyūkai: National Study Group on Issues in Child Protection

REFERENCES

AARRE, KAREN, 1998. 'The Child Welfare Debate in Portugal: A Case Study of a Children's Home', in Iain R. Edgar and Andrew Russell (eds.), *The Anthropology of Welfare* (London: Routledge).

—— 2000. 'Changing Attitudes Towards Children in Care in Portugal in the 1990s: A Case Study of a Children's Home', D.Phil. thesis (University of Oxford).

ADACHI, KIYOSHI, forthcoming. 'The Japanization of Social Welfare and the Future of Welfare Reform in Japan', in Susan O. Long (ed.), *Caring for the Elderly in Japan and the US: Practices and Policies* (London and New York: Routledge).

AKAISHI, CHIEKO, and YOSHIOKA, MUTUSKO, 1998. 'Kongaishi (Children Born out of Wedlock)', in Sakakibara Fujiko (ed.), *Koseki Seido to Kodomotachi* (Children and the Household Register System) (Tokyo: Akashi Shoten).

AKIYAMA, TOMOHISA, 1997. 'Basic Issues of the Social Work Profession in Japan', *Japanese Journal of Social Services*, 1, 35–40.

ALLEN, MATTHEW, 1994. *Undermining the Japanese Miracle: Work and Conflict in a Coal-Mining Community* (Cambridge: Cambridge University Press).

ALLINSON, GARY D., 1979. *Suburban Tokyo: A Comparative Study in Politics and Social Change* (Berkeley and Los Angeles: University of California Press).

ALLISON, ANNE, 1996. *Permitted and Prohibited Desires: Mothers, Comics and Censorship in Japan* (Boulder, Colo.: Westview Press).

ALSTON, PHILIP (ed.), 1994. *The Best Interests of the Child: Reconciling Culture and Human Rights* (Oxford: Clarendon Press).

AMENOMORI, TAKAYOSHI, 1997. 'Japan' in Lester M. Salamon and Helmut K. Anheier (eds.), *Defining the Nonprofit Sector: A Cross-National Analysis* (Manchester and New York: Manchester University Press).

AMES, W. L., 1981. *Police and Community in Japan* (Berkeley and Los Angeles: University of California Press).

ANDERSON, STEPHEN J., 1993. *Welfare Policy and Politics in Japan: Beyond the Developmental State* (New York: Paragon House).

AOKI, SUSUMU, 1994. 'Tokubetsu Yōshi Engumi no Saibansho no Mondaiten' (Problems in the Special Adoption System Court Judgement System), *Hōritsu no Hiroba* (Feb.), 24–30.

Asahi Shinbun Japan Access, 1992. 'Welfare Rolls Shrink, but for Wrong Reasons' (31 Aug.).

ASAHI SHINBUN OSAKA SHAKAIBU (ed.), 1995. *Umi wo Wataru Akachan* (Babies Who Cross the Seas) (Osaka: Asahi Shinbun).

ASAI, HARUO, 1991. *Jidōyōgoron Ronsō (Controversies in Child Protection Theories)* (Tokyo: Aiwa Shuppan).

ASAKURA, KEIICHI, KANDA, FUMIO, KITA, KAZUNORI, and TAKENAKA, TETSUO (eds.), 1996. *Jidō Yōgo e no Shōtai: Wakai Jissensha e no Tebiki* (An Invitation to Child Protection: A Handbook for Young Practitioners) (Kyoto: Minerva Shobō).

—— and NAKAMURA, KUNIYUKI, 1974. *Shisetsu no Kodomotachi: Shūdan Yōgo no Riron to Jissai* (Children in Institutions: The Theory and Practice of Group Protection Work) (Tokyo: Minerva Shobō).

AZUMA, HIROSHI, 1986. 'Why Study Child Development in Japan?', in Harold Stevenson, Hiroshi Azuma, and Kenji Hakuta (eds.), *Child Development and Education in Japan* (New York: W. H. Freeman).

BABA, CHIE, 1999. ' "Ienaki Kodomotachi" ga Tomo ni Kurasu Ie' (The House Where "Children Without Homes" Live Together), *Bessatsu Takarajima*, 462 (Sept.), 10–33.

BABA, KEINOSUKE, 1980. *Fukushi Shakai no Nihonteki Keitai* (The Japanese-Style Welfare Society) (Tokyo: Tōyō Keizai Shinpōsha).

BACHNIK, JANE M., 1983. 'Recruitment Strategies for Household Succession: Rethinking Japanese Household Organisation', *Man*, NS 18/1, 160–82.

—— 1988. 'Adoption', in *Kōdansha Encyclopedia of Japan*, vol. i (Tokyo: Kōdansha).

Barclay Committee, 1982. *Social Workers: Their Role and Tasks* (London: Bedford Square Press).

BAYLEY, DAVID H., 1976. *Forces of Order: Police Behavior in Japan and the United States* (Berkeley and Los Angeles: University of California Press).

BEARDSLEY, RICHARD K., 1959. *Village Japan* (Chicago: Chicago University Press).

BEFU, HARUMI, 1963. 'Corporate Emphasis and Patterns of Descent in the Japanese Family', in Richard K. Beardsley and Robert J. Smith (eds.), *Japanese Culture: Its Development and Characteristics* (London: Methuen).

—— 1974. 'An Ethnography of Dinner Entertainment in Japan', *Arctic Anthropology*, 11 (supplement), 196–203.

—— 1986. 'The Social and Cultural Background of Child Development in Japan and the United States', in Harold Stevenson, Hiroshi Azuma, and Kenji Hakuta (eds.), *Child Development and Education in Japan* (New York: W. H. Freeman).

BEN-ARI, EYAL, 1991. *Changing Japanese Suburbia: A Study of Two Present-Day Localities* (London and New York: Kegan Paul International).

—— 1997. *Japanese Childcare: An Interpretative Study of Culture and Organization* (London: Kegan Paul International).

BENEDICT, RUTH, 1946, repr. 1977. *The Chrysanthemum and the Sword: Patterns of Japanese Culture* (London: Routledge & Kegan Paul).

BENJAMIN, GAIL, 1997. *Japanese Lessons: A Year in a Japanese School through the Eyes of an American Anthropologist and her Children* (New York and London: New York University Press).

BERRIDGE, DAVID, 1997. 'England: Child Abuse Reports, Responses and Reforms', in Neil Gilbert (ed.), *Combatting Child Abuse: International Perspectives and Trends* (New York: Oxford University Press).

—— and BRODIE, ISABELLE, 1998. *Children's Homes Revisited* (London: Jessica Kingsley).

—— and CLEAVER, HEDY, 1987. *Foster Home Breakdown* (Oxford: Basil Blackwell).

BESTOR, THEODORE C., 1989. *Tokyo Neighborhood* (Stanford: Stanford University Press).

BETHEL, DIANA LYNN, 1992. 'Life on Obasuteyama, or, Inside a Japanese Institute for the Elderly', in Takie Sugiyama Lebra (ed.), *Japanese Social Organisation* (Honolulu: University of Hawaii Press).

BOLING, PATRICIA, 1998. 'Family Policy in Japan', *Journal of Social Policy*, 27/2, 173–90.

BOUDREAUX, KAROL C., and BOUDREAUX, DONALD J., 1999. 'Social Security, Social Workers and the Care of Dependent Children', in Richard B. McKenzie (ed.), *Rethinking Orphanages for the Twenty-First Century* (Thousand Oaks, London, and New Delhi: Sage Publications).

BOYDEN, JO, 1990. 'Childhood and the Policy Makers: A Comparative Perspective on the Globalization of Childhood', in Allison James and Alan Prout (eds.), *Constructing and*

Reconstructing Childhood: Contemporary Issues in the Sociological Study of Childhood (London, New York, and Philadelphia: Falmer Press).

BRINTON, MARY C., 1993. *Women and the Economic Miracle: Gender and Work in Postwar Japan* (Berkeley and Oxford: University of California Press).

BRONFENBRENNER, MARTIN, and YASUBA, YASUKICHI, 1987. 'Economic Welfare' in Kōzō Yamamura and Yasukichi Yasuba (eds.), *The Political Economy of Japan*, vol. i: The Domestic Transformation (Stanford: Stanford University Press).

BROWN, GEORGE W., and HARRIS, TIRRIL, 1978. *Social Origins of Depression: A Study of Psychiatric Disorders in Women* (London: Tavistock Publications).

BULLOCK, ROGER, LITTLE, MICHAEL, and MILLHAM, SPENCER, 1993. *Residential Care for Children: A Review of the Research* (London: HMSO).

BURKHARDT, WILLIAM R., 1983. 'Institutional Barriers, Marginality and Adaptation among the American-Japanese Mixed Bloods in Japan', *Journal of Asian Studies*, 42/3, 519–44.

BURKS, ARDATH W., 1985. 'Japan: The Bellwether of East Asian Human Rights?', in James C. Hsiung (ed.), *Human Rights in East Asia: A Cultural Perspective* (New York: Paragon House).

CAMPBELL, JOHN CREIGHTON, 1983. 'Social Welfare', in *Kōdansha Encyclopedia of Japan*, vol. vii (Tokyo: Kōdansha).

—— 1992. *How Policies Change: The Japanese Government and the Aging Society* (Princeton: Princeton University Press).

CAPNA (Child Abuse Prevention Network Aichi), 1998. *Mienakatta Shi: Kodomo Gyakutai Databook* (Unseen Deaths: Child Abuse Data Book) (Nagoya: CAPNA Shuppan).

CHECKLAND, OLIVE, 1994. *Humanitarianism and the Emperor's Japan, 1877–1977* (London: St Martin's Press).

CHILDREN AND FAMILIES BUREAU, 1979. *A Brief Report on Child Welfare Services in Japan* (Tokyo: Ministry of Health and Welfare).

CHŪBACHI, MASAYOSHI, and TAIRA, KŌJI, 1976. 'Poverty in Modern Japan: Perceptions and Realities', in Hugh Patrick (ed.), *Japanese Industrialization and its Social Consequences* (Berkeley and Los Angeles: University of California Press).

CLARK, RODNEY, 1979. *The Japanese Company* (New Haven and London: Yale University Press).

CLIFFE, DAVID, with BERRIDGE, DAVID, 1991. *Closing Children's Homes: An End to Residential Care?* (London: National Children's Bureau).

COHEN, CYNTHIA PRICE, 1995. 'Children's Rights: An American Perspective', in Bob Franklin (ed.), *The Handbook of Children's Rights: Comparative Policy and Practice* (London: Routledge).

COLLICK, MARTIN, 1988. 'Social Policy: Pressures and Responses', in J. A. A. Stockwin, Alan Rix, Aurelia George, James Horne, Daiichi Itō, and Martin Collick, *Dynamic and Immobilist Politics in Japan* (Basingstoke: Macmillan).

COLTON, M. J., and HELLINCKX, W. (eds.), 1993. *Child Care in the EC: A Country-Specific Guide to Foster and Residential Care* (Aldershot: Arena).

COSTIN, LELA B., KARGER, HOWARD JACOB, and STOESZ, DAVID, 1996. *The Politics of Child Abuse in America* (New York and Oxford: Oxford University Press).

CUMMINGS, WILLIAM K., 1980. *Education and Equality in Japan* (Princeton: Princeton University Press).

DATE, NAOTOSHI, 1998. ' "Yōhogojidō" Care no Ōro to Fukuro' (The Road There and Back of the Care of 'Children in Need'), *Atarashii Kazoku*, 33, 52–74.

DAVIS, LEONARD, 1983. 'Legacy of the Past', *Social Work Today*, 15/13 (29 Nov.); repr. in *Social Care: Rivers of Pain, Bridges of Hope* (London: Whiting & Birch, 1992).

DEMAUSE, LLOYD, 1987. 'The History of Childhood in Japan', *The Journal of Psychohistory*, 15/2, 147–52.

—— 1991. 'The Universality of Incest', *The Journal of Psychohistory*, 19/2, 123–64.

—— 1998. 'The History of Child Abuse', *The Journal of Psychohistory*, 25/3, 16–36.

DINGWALL, ROBERT, TANAKA, HIROKO, and MINAMIKATA, SATOSHI, 1991. 'Images of Parenthood in the United Kingdom and Japan', *Sociology*, 25/3, 423–46.

DORE, RONALD P., 1958. *City Life in Japan* (Berkeley: University of California Press).

—— and SAKO, MARI, 1998. *How the Japanese Learn to Work*, 2nd edn. (London: Nissan Institute/Routledge Japanese Studies Series).

DOWER, JOHN, 1999. *Embracing Defeat: Japan in the Wake of World War II* (New York: W. W. Norton).

DUBANOSKI, RICHARD A., and SNYDER, KAREN, 1980. 'Patterns of Child Abuse and Neglect in Japanese- and Samoan-Americans', *Child Abuse and Neglect*, 4, 217–25.

EIWA, RYŪNOSUKE, 1998. *Naze Kōreisha Fukushi wa Fushoku suru no ka?* (Why is Welfare for the Elderly Going Rotten?) (Matsuyama: Sōfūsha Shuppan).

ENNEW, JUDITH, 1995. 'Outside Childhood: Street Children's Rights', in Bob Franklin (ed.), *The Handbook of Children's Rights: Comparative Policy and Practice* (London: Routledge).

FERRIES, JONATHAN, 1996. 'Obasuteyama in Modern Japan: Ageing, Ageism and Government Policy', in Roger Goodman and Ian Neary (eds.), *Case Studies on Human Rights in Japan* (Kent: Curzon Press, Japan Library).

FIELD, NORMA, 1995. 'The Child as Laborer and Consumer: The Disappearance of Child-hood in Contemporary Japan', in Sharon Stephens (ed.), *Children and the Politics of Culture* (Princeton: Princeton University Press).

FORD, MARK L., and TAKAGI, YŌKO, 1998. ' "Oliver" with a Japanese "Twist" ', *Look Japan* (Sept.), 34–5.

FORMANEK, SUSANNE, and LINHART, SEPP (eds.), 1997. *Aging: Asian Concepts and Experiences, Past and Present* (Wien: Österreichischen Akademie der Wissenschaften).

FOWLER, EDWARD, 1996. *Sanya Blues: Laboring Life in Contemporary Tokyo* (Ithaca and London: Cornell University Press).

FOX HARDING, LORRAINE, 1991. *Perspectives in Child Care Policy* (London and New York: Longman).

FRANKLIN, BOB, and PARTON, NIGEL (eds.), 1991. *Social Work, the Media and Public Relations* (London and New York: Routledge).

FREEMAN, MICHAEL, 1995. 'Children's Rights in a Land of Rites', in Bob Franklin (ed.), *The Handbook of Children's Rights: Comparative Policy and Practice* (London: Routledge).

FROST, NICK, MILLS, SUE, and STEIN, MIKE, 1999. *Understanding Residential Child Care* (Aldershot, Brookfield, USA, Singapore, and Sydney: Ashgate Arena).

FRUIN, MARK W., 1983. *Kikkōman: Company, Clan and Community* (Cambridge, Mass.: Harvard University Press).

FUJIMOTO, TETSUYA, 1994. *Crime Problems in Japan* (Tokyo: Chūō University Press).

FUKUSHIMA, KAZUO, 1986. 'Yōgoshisetsu to Kodomo no Jinken' (Children's Homes and Children's Rights), *Jurist*, 43, 181–5.

FUNABASHI, KEIKO, 1999. 'Reassessing the Value of Children', *Japan Echo*, 26/1, 32–9.

GARON, SHELDON, 1997. *Molding Japanese Minds: The State in Everyday Life* (Princeton: Princeton University Press).

GARRISON, LLOYD, 1984. 'The Puzzle of Oyako-Shinjū', *Time* (11 June), 41.

GIFUKEN JIDŌFUKUSHI KYŌGIKAI, 1992. *Heisei 4 Nendo Gifu-ken Kōkōsei Kōryūkai Happyōsho* (Report on the Senior High School Meeting in Gifu Prefecture in 1992) (Gifu: Kōkōsei Kōryūkai).

GILBERT, NEIL (ed.), 1997. *Combatting Child Abuse: International Perspectives and Trends* (Oxford: Oxford University Press).

GILL, TOM, forthcoming. *Men of Uncertainty: The Social Organisation of Day Laborers in Contemporary Japan* (New York: SUNY Press).

GOFFMAN, ERVING, 1961. *Asylums: Essays on the Social Situation of Mental Patients and other Inmates* (Garden City, NY: Anchor Books).

GOODMAN, ROGER, 1990. *Japan's 'International Youth': The Emergence of a New Class of Schoolchildren* (Oxford: Clarendon Press).

—— 1996. 'On Introducing the UN Convention of the Rights of the Child into Japan', in Roger Goodman and Ian Neary (eds.), *Case Studies on Human Rights in Japan* (Kent: Curzon Press, Japan Library).

—— forthcoming. 'Images of the Japanese Welfare State', in Harumi Befu and Sylvie Guichard-Anguis (eds.), *Japan Outside Japan* (London: Routledge).

GOODY, JACK, 1969. 'Adoption in Cross-Cultural Perspective', *Comparative Studies in Society and History*, 11, 55–78.

GORDON, ANDREW, 1985. *The Evolution of Labor Relations in Japan* (Harvard University: Harvard East Asian Monographs).

GORDON, LINDA, 1988. *Heroes of Their Own Lives: The Politics and History of Family Violence* (Harmondsworth: Penguin).

GOUGH, DAVID, 1995. 'Child Abuse in Japan', unpublished paper (Oct.).

GOULD, ARTHUR, 1993. *Capitalist Welfare States: A Comparison of Japan, Britain and Sweden* (Harlow: Longman).

GRABURN, NELSON, 1983. *To Pray, Pay and Play: The Cultural Structure of Japanese Domestic Tourism* (Aix-en-Provence: Centre des Hautes Études Touristiques).

HACKING, IAN, 1991. 'The Making and Molding of Child Abuse', *Critical Inquiry*, 17 (Winter), 243–88.

HAGAN, KELLY, 1994. 'Socialising Children in *Yōgoshisetsu* (Children's Homes) in Japan', BA diss. (Oriental Studies, University of Oxford).

HAMABATA, MATTHEWS MASAYUKI, 1990. *Crested Kimono: Power and Love in the Japanese Business Family* (Ithaca and London: Cornell University Press).

HAMAGUCHI, ESHUN, 1977. *Nihonrashisa no Saihakken* (The Rediscovery of Japaneseness) (Tokyo: Nihon Keizai Shinbunsha).

HAMAI, KŌICHI, VILLÉ, RENAUD, HARRIS, ROBERT, HOUGH, MIKE, and ZVEKIC, UGLIJESA (eds.), 1995. *Probation Around the World: A Comparative Study* (London and New York: Routledge).

HANASHIMA, MASASABURŌ, 1994. *Kyōgoin no Kodomotachi* (Children in Educational Protective Facilities) (Kyoto: Minerva Shobō).

HARA, YOSHIHISA, 1995. *Kishi Nobusuke: Kensei no Seijika* (Kishi Nobusuke: A Politician of Influence) (Tokyo: Iwanami Shoten).

HARADA, SUMITAKA, 1998. 'The Ageing Society, the Family, and Social Policy', in Junji Banno (ed.), *The Political Economy of Japanese Society*, vol. ii: *Internationalization and Domestic Issues* (Oxford: Oxford University Press).

HARWIN, JUDITH, 1995. 'Russian Children's Rights', in Bob Franklin (ed.), *The Handbook of Children's Rights: Comparative Policy and Practice* (London: Routledge).

HASEGAWA, SHIGEO, 1980. 'Yōgoshisetsujidō no Jinken Shingai no Jittai to sono Haikei' (The Conditions and Background to the Infringement of the Rights of Children in Homes), in Zenkoku Shakai Fukushi Kyōgikai (ed.), *Oyaken to Kodomo no Jinken* (Parental Rights and the Human Rights of Children) (Tokyo: Zenshakyō Yōgoshisetsu Kyōgikai).

HASHIMOTO, MEIKO, 1996. 'Becoming Aware of Child Abuse', *Japan Quarterly*, 43/2, 145–52.

HASTINGS, SALLY ANN, 1995. *Neighbourhood and Nation in Tokyo, 1905–1937* (Pittsburgh and London: University of Pittsburgh Press).

HAYASHI, HIROYASU, 1992. 'Yōgonenreiji no Jittai to Jiritsu Enjō no Arikata' (The Situation of Older Children Who Have Been Through Care and How their Independence Should Be Supported), *Osaka-shi Shakai Fukushi Kenkyū*, 15, 25–35.

—— 1998. ' "Ima, Shisetsu de Seikatsu suru Kodomotachi" ' Chōsa kara (From the Survey 'Children Who Live in Institutions Today'), *Harappa*, 180, 18–23.

HAYASHI, KENJI, 1989. 'Adolescent Sexual Activities and Fertility in Japan', in *Proceedings of the Seminar on Child Welfare Services in Thailand and Japan, February 14–15, 1989* (Bangkok: Japan Research Institute on Child Welfare, Tokyo).

HAYDEN, CAROL, GODDARD, JIM, GORIN, SARAH, and VAN DER SPEK, NIKI, 1999. *State Child Care: Looking After Children?* (London: Jessica Kingsley).

HEMPHILL, ELIZABETH ANNE, 1980. *The Least of These: Miki Sawada and her Children* (New York and Tokyo: Weatherhill).

HENDRY, JOY, 1981. *Marriage in Changing Japan* (London: Croom Helm).

—— 1986. *Becoming Japanese: The World of the Pre-School Child* (Manchester: Manchester University Press).

HIRANO, TAKAYUKI, OKA, TOMOFUMI, MACHINO, HIROSHI, and AKASAKA, YUKIO, 1987. *Fushi Katei* (Lone-Father Families) (Kyoto: Minerva Shobō).

HIRAYŪ, MASATO, 1997. 'Jinken Kaifuku no Ba toshite no Shisetsu' (Children's Homes as the Site for Recovering Human Rights), in Masato Hirayū (ed.), *Shisetsu de Kurasu Kodomotachi* (Children Who Live in Institutions) (Tokyo: Akashi Shoten).

HIROOKA, TOMOHIKO, 1989. 'The "Ikoi-no-Ie" (Rest Home) Movement', in *Proceedings of the Seminar on Child Welfare Services in Thailand and Japan, February 14–15, 1989* (Bangkok: Japan Research Institute on Child Welfare, Tokyo).

HIWATARI, NOBUHIRO, 1993. 'Sustaining the Welfare State and International Competitiveness in Japan: The Welfare Reforms of the 1980s and the Political Economy', Institute of Social Science, Tokyo, discussion paper.

HODGE, ROBERT WILLIAM, and OGAWA, NAOHIRO, 1991. *Fertility Change in Contemporary Japan* (Chicago and London: University of Chicago Press).

HORIO, TERUHISA, 1988. *Educational Thought and Ideology in Modern Japan: State Authority and Intellectual Freedom*, ed. and trans. Steven Platzer (Tokyo: University of Tokyo Press).

House of Commons (Health Committee), 1998. *Children Looked After by Local Authorities* (London: HMSO).

HURST, G. CAMERON III, 1984. *Japanese Education: Trouble in Paradise?* (University Field Staff International Reports, no. 40: Asia).

ICHIKAWA, RYŪICHIRŌ, 1985. 'Factors Responsible for Delinquency on the Part of Children

Admitted to Homes for the Training and Education of Juvenile Delinquents', *Child Welfare: Quarterly News from Japan*, 5/3, 2–13.

IIJIMA, YOSHIHARU, 1987. 'Folk Culture and the Liminality of Children', *Current Anthropology*, 28/4, 41–8.

IKEDA, YOSHIKO, 1982. 'A Short Introduction to Child Abuse in Japan', *Child Abuse and Neglect*, 6, 487–90.

—— 1984. 'Child Abuse in Japan', *Child Welfare: Quarterly News from Japan*, 5/2, 2–12.

—— 1987. *Jidō Gyakutai* (Child Abuse) (Tokyo: Chūō Kōronsha).

ILLICH, IVAN, 1977. *Disabling Professions* (London and Salem, NH: M. Boyars).

IMAMURA, ANNE E., 1987. *Urban Japanese Housewives: At Home and in the Community* (Honolulu: University of Hawaii Press).

IMAZEKI, KIMIO, 1991. 'Aru Yōgoshisetsu no Negai: Fukuin no Shakaika wo Mezashite' (The Aspirations of One Children's Home: Towards Spreading Glad Tidings Through Society), *Christkyō Shakai Fukushigaku Kenkyū*, 24, 4–10.

ISHIDA, TAKESHI, 1971. *Japanese Society* (New York: Random House).

—— 1986. *The Introduction of Western Political Concepts into Japan*, Nissan Occasional Paper Series, no. 2 (Oxford: Nissan Institute of Japanese Studies).

ISHIKAWA, KEIJIRŌ and SAKAGUCHI, SHIGEHARU, 1989. 'Trial Measures Undertaken by Kotorisawa Gakuen Institute: Activities of a Short-Term Treatment Facility for Emotionally Disturbed Children', *Child Welfare: Quarterly News from Japan*, 10/1, 2–10.

ISHIZAKA, FUMIKO, 1990. 'Tokubetsu Yōshi Jishō Oboegaki' (Notes on the Beginning of the Tokubetsu Yōshi Phenomenon), *Atarashii Kazoku*, 17, 33–7.

ITŌ, SAYAKO, 1998. 'Jidō Yōgo no Kihon Genri' (Basic Principles of Child Protection), in Shigetake Yoshida (ed.), *Jidō Yōgo no Genri to Naiyō* (The Contents and Principles of Child Protection) (Gifu: Mirai), revised version.

ITŌ, YONE, 1977. 'Sengo Nihon no Konketsuji Mondai to Gaikokujin Katei e no Yōshiengumi ni tsuite' (On Adoption by Foreign Couples and Japan's Mixed-Blood Children Issue in the Post-War Period), in Yōgoshisetsu Kyōgikai (ed.), *Yōgoshisetsu Sanjūnen* (Thirty Years of Child Protection Institutions) (Tokyo: Yōgoshisetsu Kyōgikai).

ITŌ, YOSHIKO, 1995. 'Social Work Development in Japan', *Social Policy and Administration*, 29/5, 258–68.

IWAO, SUMIKO, 1993. *The Japanese Woman: Traditional Image and Changing Reality* (New York: Free Press).

IWASAKI, MIEKO, 1992. 'Zadankai' (General Discussion), *Atarashii Kazoku*, 21.

—— 1999. 'Shōshasei wo Dō Teigi suru ka' (How to Define Small-Group Living), in Shōshasei Yōiku Kenkyūkai (ed.), *Naze Shōshasei Yōgo ka* (Why Small-Group Living Should Be Supported) (Fukushima: Shōshasei Yōiku Kenkyūkai).

JACOBS, DIDIER, 1998. *Social Welfare Systems in East Asia: A Comparative Analysis Including Private Welfare*, CASE paper 10 (London: LSE Centre for Analysis of Social Exclusion).

JAMES, ESTELLE, and BENJAMIN, GAIL, 1988. *Public Policy and Private Education in Japan* (Basingstoke: Macmillan).

JIDŌ GYAKUTAI BŌSHI SEIDO KENKYŪKAI (ed.), 1993. *Kodomo no Gyakutai Bōshi: Saizensen kara no Hōkoku* (The Prevention of Child Abuse: A Report from the Front Line) (Osaka: Toki Shobō).

JIDŌSŌDANJO WO KANGAERUKAI (ed.), 1998. *Jidōsōdanjo de Deatta Kodomotachi* (Children Encountered at the *Jidōsōdanjo*) (Tokyo: Minerva Shobō).

JIDŌ YŌGO KENKYŪKAI (ed.), 1995. *Yōgoshisetsu no Kodomotachi* (Children in *Yōgoshisetsu*) (Osaka: Osaka Shoseki).

JNC–ICSW (Japan National Committee–International Council of Social Welfare), 1986. *Social Welfare Services in Japan* (Tokyo: JNC–ICSW).

—— 1988. *Law, Social Welfare, Social Development* (Tokyo: JNC–ICSW).

—— 1990. *Social Welfare Services in Japan* (Tokyo: JNC–ICSW).

JOHNSON, ELMER, 1996. *Japanese Corrections: Managing Convicted Offenders in an Orderly Society* (Carbondale, Ill.: Southern Illinois University Press).

JOLIVET, MURIEL, 1997. *Japan: The Childless Society? The Crisis of Motherhood*, trans. Anne-Marie Glasheen (London and New York: Routledge).

KA, LIN, 1999. *Confucian Welfare Cluster: A Cultural Interpretation of Social Welfare* (Tampere, Finland: Acta Universitatis Temperensis 645).

KAHAN, BARBARA, 1994. *Growing Up In Groups* (London: HMSO).

KAMIIDE, HIROYUKI, 1990. 'Child Abuse in Japan: From a Survey by the National Association of Child Guidance Center Directors', *Child Welfare: Quarterly News from Japan*, 11/1, 2–9.

KAMIZONO, SHŌJIRŌ, 1999. 'Igirisu no Jidō Fukushi: Hōteki Haiki kara' (Child Welfare in England: From a Legalistic Perspective), in Shōshasei Yōiku Kenkyūkai (ed.), *Naze Shōshasei Yōgo ka* (Why Small-Group Living Should Be Supported) (Fukushima: Shōshasei Yōiku Kenkyūkai).

KAPLAN, MATTHEW, KUSANO, ATSUKO, TSUJI, ICHIRO, and HISAMICHI, SHIGERU, 1998. *Intergenerational Programs: Support for Children, Youth and the Elderly in Japan* (New York: SUNY Press).

KASHIWAME, REIHŌ, 1992. 'The Current Situation, Trends and Issues in Child Guidance Centers', *Child Welfare: Quarterly News from Japan*, 13/1, 2–13.

—— 1997. 'The System for Dealing with Child Abuse in Japan: Issues and Counter-Measures', *Child Welfare: Quarterly News from Japan*, 17/4, 2–13.

KASHIWAZAKI, CHIKAKO, 1998. 'Jus Sanguinis in Japan: The Origin of Citizenship in a Comparative Perspective', *International Journal of Comparative Sociology*, 39/3, 278–300.

KASUGA, KISUYO, 1989. *Fushikatei wo Ikiru* (Living in Lone-Father Families) (Tokyo: Iwanami Shoten).

KATEI YŌGO SOKUSHIN KYŌKAI, 1997. *Oyako e no Dōhyō* (Milestones on the Path to Becoming a Parent-Child Unit) (Osaka: Katei Yōgo Sokushin Kyōkai).

KATŌ, ICHIRŌ, 1989. 'The Adoption of Majors in Japan', in John M. Eekelaar and David Pearl (eds.), *An Aging World: Dilemmas and Challenges for Law and Social Policy* (Oxford: Clarendon Press).

KATŌ, YŌKO, and TATSUNO, YŌKO, 1998. 'Denwa Sōdan ni okeru Gyakutai Yobō no Tatewari' (The Role of Telephone Consultation in Child Abuse Prevention), in Nihon Kodomo no Gyakutai Bōshi Kenkyūkai (ed.), *Dai Yonkai Gakujutsu Shūkai Programme* (Programme of the Fourth Academic Meeting [of the Japan Study Group for the Prevention of Child Abuse]) (Wakayama: Nihon Kodomo no Gyakutai Bōshi Kenkyūkai).

KIKAWADA, JOHN S., 1958. 'Present Status of Child Welfare Work in Japan', in Dorothy Dessau (ed.), *Glimpses of Social Work in Japan* (Kyoto: Social Workers' International Club of Japan).

—— 1968. 'The Function of Children's Institutions', in Dorothy Dessau (ed.), *Glimpses of Social Work in Japan* (Kyoto: Social Workers' International Club of Japan).

KIKUCHI, MIDORI, 1991. 'Nihon no Satooya Seido, Yōshi Seido o Kangaeru' (Reflections on Japan's Adoption and Fostering Systems), unpublished paper presented to the Jidō Fukushihō Kenkyūkai (Child Welfare Law Study Group) (Tokyo: 22 Oct.).

—— 1998. 'Tokubetsu Yōshi Seido to Koseki' (Household Registers and the Special Adoption System), in Fujiko Sakakibara (ed.), *Koseki Seido to Kodomotachi* (Children and the Household Register System) (Tokyo: Akashi Shoten).

KINOSHITA, YASUHITO, 1992. *Refuge of the Honored: Social Organization in a Japanese Retirement Community* (Berkeley, Los Angeles, and Oxford: University of California Press).

KISALA, ROBERT, 1992. *Gendai Shūkyō to Shakai Ronri: Tenrikyō to Risshō Kōseikai no Fukushi Katsudō wo chūshin ni* (Contemporary Religion and Social Ethics: On the Social Welfare Activities of Tenrikyō and Risshō Kōseikai) (Tokyo: Seikyūsha).

KITA, AKITO, 1992. 'Towards Ratification of the Convention on the Rights of the Child', *Child Welfare: Quarterly News from Japan*, 12/3, 2–11.

KITA, KAZUNORI, 1996. 'Shisetsu Yōgo no Taishō' (The Object of Child Protection Institutions), in Keiichi Asakura and Atsushi Mineshima (eds.), *Kodomo no Seikatsu to Shisetsu* (Children's Lives and Institutions) (Kyoto: Minerva Shobō).

—— 1998. 'Kodomo no Kenri' (Children's Rights), in Shigetake Yoshida (ed.), *Jidō Yōgo no Genri to Naiyō* (The Contents and Principles of Child Protection) (Gifu: Mirai), revised version.

KITAHARA, MICHIO, 1989a. 'Childhood in Japanese Culture', *The Journal of Psychohistory*, 17/1, 43–72.

—— 1989b. 'Incest—Japanese Style', *The Journal of Psychohistory*, 16/4, 445–50.

KITAMURA TOSHINORI, KIJIMA NOBUHIKO, IWATA NOBORU, SENDA YUKIKO, TAKAHASHI KŌJI, and HAYASHI IKUE, 1999. 'Frequencies of Child Abuse in Japan: Hidden but Prevalent Crime', *International Journal of Offender Therapy and Comparative Criminology*, 43/1, 21–33.

KITAŌJI, HIRANOBU, 1971. 'The Structure of the Japanese Family', *American Anthropologist*, 73/3, 1036–57.

KODOMO NO KOE KENKYŪKAI (ed.), 1993. *Jidō Fukushi Shisetsu ni okeru Jidō no Kenri Hoshō no Jittai ni kansuru Chōsa Kenkyū* (Survey Report on the Situation of the Protection of Children's Rights in Child Welfare Institutions) (Tokyo: Kodomo no Koe).

KODOMOGA KATARU SHISETSU NO KURASHI HENSHŪIINKAI (ed.), 1999. *Kodomo ga Kataru Shisetsu no Kurashi* (Children Talk about Life in Residential Care) (Tokyo: Akashi Shoten).

KOJIMA, HIDEO, 1986. 'Becoming Nurturant in Japan: Past and Present', in Alan Fogel and Gail F. Melson (eds.), *Origins of Nurturance: Developmental, Biological and Cultural Perspectives on Caregiving* (Hillsdale, NJ and London: Lawrence Erlbaum Associates).

KOMATSU, RYŪJI, 1992. 'The State and Social Welfare in Japan: Patterns and Developments', in Paul Close (ed.), *The State and Caring* (Basingstoke and London: Macmillan).

KONOMI, YŪ, 1996. *Kodomo no Kenri to Jidō Fukushihō* (Children's Rights and the Child Welfare Law) (Tokyo: Shinzansha Shuppan).

KOPYTOFF, IGOR, and MIERS, SUZANNE, 1977. 'African "Slavery" as an Institution of Marginality', in Igor Kopytoff and Suzanne Miers (eds.), *Slavery in Africa: Historical and Anthropological Perspectives* (Madison, Wis.: The University of Wisconsin Press).

KORBIN, JILL E., 1987. 'Child Sexual Abuse: Implications for the Cross-Cultural Record', in Nancy Scheper-Hughes (ed.), *Child Survival* (Dordrecht and Lancaster: D. Reidel).

Kosaka, Kazuo, 1990. 'Shisetsu Yōgo no Jissai' (Practice in Protective Institutions), in Susumu Iida, Kyōji Ōshima, Kazumu Miyamoto, Yoshihito Toyofuku, and Kazuo Kosaka, *Yōgoshisetsu Naiyō Sōron* (An Outline of Practice in Children's Homes) (Kyoto: Minerva Shobō).

—— 1996. 'EC Shokoku, Igirisu no Shisetsu Yōgo Kaikaku no Dōkō' (Reform Trends in English and Some EC Welfare Institutions), in Keiichi Asakura and Atsushi Mineshima (eds.), *Kodomo no Seikatsu to Shisetsu* (Children's Lives and Institutions) (Kyoto: Minerva Shobō).

Kōseishō, 1991. *Hoken Iryō, Fukushi Manpower Taisaku Honbu Chūkan Hōkoku* (Intermediate Report from the Policy Unit on Staffing in Welfare and Health Related Institutions) (Mar.) (Tokyo: Kōseishō).

Kōseishō Jidōkateikyoku (ed.), 1998. *Jidō Fukushi: Gojūnen no Ayumi* (Fifty Years of Child Welfare) (Tokyo: Kōseishō Jidōkateikyoku).

Kōseitōkeikyōkai (ed.), 1992. *Kokumin no Fukushi no Dōkō* (Trends in Public Welfare), 39/12 (Special number of the monthly *Kōsei no Shihyō*—Welfare Index).

Kouno, A., and Johnson, J. F., 1995. 'Child Abuse and Neglect in Japan: Coin-Operated Locker Babies', *Child Abuse and Neglect*, 19/1, 25–31.

Kuramoto, Ford H., 1976. *A History of the Shonien, 1914–1972: An Account of a Program of Institutional Care of Japanese Children in Los Angeles* (San Francisco: R & E Research Associates).

Kuraoka, Sayo, 1992. *Kazuko Rokusai Ijime de Shinda: Yōgoshisetsu to Kodomo no Jinken* (Kazuko Died Aged 6 from Bullying: Children's Homes and Children's Rights) (Tokyo: Hitonaru Shobō).

Kuroda, Kunio, 1991. 'Koko made Aita Shisetsu no Kōmin Kakusa' (The Great Gap Between Public and Private Institutions) *Fukushi Tenbō*, 12, 55–61.

—— 1997. 'Shisetsu Seikatsu Suijun to Seido Mondai' (The Standard of Life in Institutions and Problems with the System), in Shigeyuki Kinoshita and Haruo Asai (eds.), *Jidō Yōgo no Kaikaku: Jidō Fukushi Kaikaku no Shiten* (Reforming Child Protection: From the Perspective of Child Welfare Reform) (Osaka: Toki Shobō).

Kurosu, Satomi, and Ochiai, Emiko, 1995. 'Adoption as an Heirship Strategy under Demographic Constraints: A Case from Nineteenth-Century Japan', *Journal of Family History*, 20/3, 261–88.

Kuwayama, Takami, 1992. 'The Reference Other Orientation', in Nancy Rosenberger (ed.), *Japanese Sense of Self* (Cambridge: Cambridge University Press).

Kwon, Huck-ju, 1998. 'Democracy and the Politics of Social Welfare: A Comparative Analysis of Welfare Systems in East Asia', in Roger Goodman, Gordon White, and Huck-ju Kwon (eds.), *The East Asian Welfare Model: Welfare Orientalism and the State* (London and New York: Routledge).

—— 1999. *Income Transfers to the Elderly in East Asia: Testing Asian Values*, CASE paper 27 (London: LSE STICERD).

LaFleur, William R., 1992. *Liquid Life: Abortion and Buddhism in Japan* (Princeton: Princeton University Press).

La Fontaine, J. S., 1988. 'Child Sexual Abuse and the Incest Taboo: Practical Problems and Theoretical Issues', *Man*, ns 23/1, 1–18.

—— 1990. *Child Sexual Abuse* (London: Polity Press).

Large, Stephen S., 1992. *Emperor Hirohito and Shōwa Japan: A Political Biography* (London: Routledge).

LEBRA, TAKIE SUGIYAMA, 1976. *Japanese Patterns of Behavior* (Honolulu: University of Hawaii Press).

—— 1984. *Japanese Women: Constraint and Fulfillment* (Honolulu: University of Hawaii Press).

—— 1993. *Above the Clouds: Status Culture of the Modern Japanese Nobility* (Berkeley: University of California Press).

LEE, HYE KYUNG, 1987. 'The Japanese Welfare State in Transition', in Robert Friedman, Neil Gilbert, and Moshe Sherer (eds.), *Modern Welfare States: A Comparative View of Trends and Prospects* (Brighton: Wheatsheaf Books).

LEWIS, CATHERINE C., 1995. *Educating Hearts and Minds: Reflections on Japanese Pre-Schools and Elementary Education* (Cambridge: Cambridge University Press).

LOCK, MARGARET, 1986. 'Plea for Acceptance: School Refusal Syndrome in Japan', *Social Science and Medicine*, 23/2, 99–112.

LONG, SUSAN O. (ed.), forthcoming. *Caring: People, Practices and Policies for Late Life in Japan and the United States* (London and New York: Routledge).

LUNSING, WIM, 1995. 'Beyond Common Sense: Negotiating Constructions of Sexuality and Gender in Japan', Ph.D. thesis (Oxford Brookes University).

LYNN, RICHARD, 1988. *Educational Achievement in Japan: Lessons for the West* (London: Macmillan Press in association with the Social Affairs Unit).

MACFARLANE, ALAN, 1998. *The Savage Wars of Peace: England, Japan and the Malthusian Trap* (Oxford: Blackwell).

MCKENZIE, RICHARD B. (ed.), 1999. *Rethinking Orphanages for the Twenty-First Century* (Thousand Oaks, London, and New Delhi: Sage Publications).

MCVEIGH, BRIAN, 1998. *The Nature of the Japanese State: Rationality and Rituality* (London: Routledge).

MADGE, NICOLA, 1994. *Children and Residential Care in Europe* (London: European Children's Centre and National Children's Bureau).

MAKARENKO, ANTON S., 1965. *Problems of Soviet School Education* (Moscow: Progress Publishers).

MARUO, NAOMI, 1986. 'The Development of the Welfare Mix', in Richard Rose and Rei Shiratori (eds.), *The Welfare State: East and West* (New York and Oxford: Oxford University Press).

MASAMURA, KIMIHIRO, and HIGUCHI, KEIKO, 1996. 'Care for the Elderly: Who Will Bear the Burden?', *Japan Echo*, 23/4, 38–47.

MATSUBARA, YASUO, 1988. 'Single-Parent Families, Mother and Child Homes', *Child Welfare: Quarterly News from Japan*, 9/1, 2–10.

—— 1992. 'Current Situation and Issues Faced by Children's Homes in Japan: Emphasis on Manpower Problems', *Child Welfare: Quarterly News from Japan*, 12/4, 2–9.

—— 1996. 'Social Work in Japan: Responding to Demographic Dilemmas', in M. C. Hokenstad, S. K. Khinduka, and James Midgley (eds.), *Profiles in International Social Work* (Washington, DC: National Association of Social Workers Press).

—— 1997. 'Jidōiin Katsudō no Ishiki to Kadai: Shūnin Jidōiin no Yakuwari ni yosete' (Themes and Awareness of Jidōiin Activities: The Role of the Shūnin Jidōiin), *Gekkan Fukushi* (Dec.), 60–7.

MATSUSHIMA, YUKIKO, 1996. 'Controversies and Dilemmas: Japan Confronts the Convention', in Michael Freeman (ed.), *Children's Rights: A Comparative Perspective* (Aldershot: Dartmouth).

MAXWELL, JOSEPH L. III, 1999. 'Funding our Children's Future: The Interplay of Funding and Regulatory Philosophies on Private Children's Homes', in Richard B. McKenzie (ed.), *Rethinking Orphanages for the Twenty-First Century* (Thousand Oaks, London, and New Delhi: Sage Publications).

MIYAMOTO, KAZUMU, 1999. 'Shōshasei Yōiku Kenkyūkai no Ayumi to sono Hyōka' (An Account and Evaluation of the Small-Group Living Research Group), in Shōshasei Yōiku Kenkyūkai (ed.), *Naze Shōshasei Yōgo ka* (Why Small-Group Living Should Be Supported) (Fukushima: Shōshasei Yōiku Kenkyūkai).

MIYAMOTO, MASAO, 1995. *Straitjacket Society: An Insider's Irreverent View of Bureaucratic Japan* (Tokyo: Kōdansha International).

MIYAMOTO, SHINYA, and ISHIBASHI, NAOKO, 1998. 'Kodomo e no Gyakutai e no Taiō ni kansuru Kenkyū: Keisatsu to no Renkei no arikata ni kansuru kentō' (Research on How to Deal with the Abuse of Children: An Examination of Co-operation with the Police), in Nihon Kodomo no Gyakutai Bōshi Kenkyūkai (ed.), *Dai Yonkai Gakujutsu Shūkai Programme* (Programme of the Fourth Academic Meeting of the Japan Study Group for the Prevention of Child Abuse) (Wakayama: Nihon Kodomo no Gyakutai Bōshi Kenkyūkai).

MOERAN, BRIAN, 1998. 'One Over the Seven: Sake Drinking in a Japanese Pottery Community', in Joy Hendry (ed.), *Interpreting Japanese Society: Anthropological Approaches*, 2nd edn. (London: Routledge).

MORIKI, KAZUMI, 1998. 'Koseki Seido to Gaikokujin, "Kokusai Kekkon" no Kodomotachi' (The Household Register System and Foreigners: Children of 'International Marriages'), in Fujiko Sakakibara (ed.), *Koseki Seido to Kodomotachi* (Children and the Household Registration System) (Tokyo: Akashi Shoten).

MORINAGA, MATSUNOBU, 1975. *Shakai Fukushi to Bukkyō* (Social Welfare and Buddhism) (Tokyo: Seishin Shobō).

MOUER, ROSS, and SUGIMOTO, YOSHIO, 1986. *Images of Japanese Society: A Study in the Structure of Social Reality* (London: Kegan Paul International).

MURAKAMI, RYŪ, 1976. *Kagirinaku Tōmei ni Chikai Blue* (Almost Transparent Blue) (Tokyo: Kōdansha).

—— 1980. *Coin Locker Babies* (Tokyo: Kōdansha).

MUTŌ, MOTOAKI, and TAKAHASHI, MASAHIKO, 1990. 'Yōgoshisetsu no Konnichi Kadai to sono Jittai: Rōdōjikan no Tanshuku to Kōshikakusa wo Megutte' (The Conditions and Current Topics of Children's Homes: The Issues of the Public/Private Divide and the Shortening of Working Hours), *Jidō Fukushi Kenkyū*, 19, 99–107.

NAGASHIMA, NOBUHIRO, 1998a. 'Gambling and Changing Japanese Attitudes Towards It', in Sepp Linhart and Sabine Frühstück (eds.) *The Culture of Japan As Seen Through its Leisure* (New York: SUNY Press).

—— 1998b. 'The Cult of Oguricap: Or, How Women Changed the Social Value of Horse-Racing', in D. P. Martinez (ed.), *The Worlds of Japanese Popular Culture: Gender, Shifting Boundaries and Global Cultures* (Melbourne: Cambridge University Press).

NAGASHIMA, YUTAKA, 1996. 'Jidō Fukushi no Rekishi' (The History of Child Welfare), in Katsuaki Hanawa, Katsumi Tokuda, and Kazuko Takatama (eds), *Wakariyasui Jidōfukushigaku* (An Introduction to the Study of Child Welfare) (Tokyo: Bunka Shobō Hakubunsha).

NAGATA, ELIZABETH, 1968. 'The Plight of the Private Institution', in Dorothy Dessau (ed.), *Glimpses of Social Work in Japan* (Kyoto: Social Workers' International Club of Japan).

NAKAGAWA, YATSUHIRO, 1979. 'Japan, the Welfare Super-Power?', *Journal of Japanese Studies*, 5/1, 5–51.

NAKAMURA, YŪICHI, KOJIMA, YŌKO, and THOMPSON, LAWRANCE H. (eds.), 1991. *Social Welfare and Related Services Glossary* (Tokyo: Seishin Shobō).

NAKANE, CHIE, 1967. *Kinship and Social Organisation in Rural Japan* (London: Athlone).

—— 1970. *Japanese Society* (Harmondsworth: Penguin Books).

NAKANO, LYNNE YUKIE, 1998. 'Civic Volunteers in a Japanese Neighborhood: Negotiating Status in a Marginal Place', Ph.D. thesis (Yale University).

NAKATA, TOYOKAZU, 1996. 'Budding volunteerism', *Japan Quarterly*, 43/1 (Jan.–Mar.), 22–6.

NAKURA, M., 1995. 'Iryō to Shūkyō to no Kakawari' (The Relationship Between Medicine and Religion), in Bukkyō to Iryō wo Kangaeru Zenkoku Renraku Kyōgikai (ed.), *Inochi to Nihonjin* (Life and the Japanese) (Tokyo: Hakubasha).

NEARY, IAN, 1997. 'The Civil Liberties Commissioners System and the Protection of Human Rights in Japan', *Japan Forum*, 9/2, 217–32.

NEILSON, WENDY, and MEEKINGS, ROGER, 1997. 'Old Problems Passed On to No Rising Sons', *Local Government Chronicle*, (28 Nov.), 16–17.

NICHIBENREN (NIHON BENGOSHI RENGŌKAI) (ed.), 1993. *Kodomo no Kenri Jōyaku to Kazoku, Fukushi, Kyōiku, Shōnenhō* (Convention on the Rights of the Child and the Family, Welfare, Education, and the Juvenile Justice Law) (Tokyo: Kouchi Shobō).

—— 1995. *Kodomo no Kenri Manual* (Manual on Children's Rights) (Tokyo: Kiri Shobō).

—— 1997. *Towareru Kodomo no Jinken: Kodomo no Kenri Jōyaku Nichibenren Report* (On the Charge of Children's Rights: Nichibenren's Report on the Implementation of the Convention on the Rights of the Child) (Tokyo: Kouchi Shobō).

NIHON CHRISTKYŌ SHAKAI FUKUSHI GAKKAI (ed.), 1997. *Gendai no Christkyō Shakai Fukushi: Ishiki, Genjō, Kadai* (Current Christian Social Welfare: Awareness, Conditions, and Topics) (Nagoya: Nihon Christkyō Shakai Fukushi Gakkai).

NIHON SHAKAI MINZOKUGAKU KYŌKAI (ed.), 1954. *Nihon Shakai Minzoku Jiten* (Dictionary of Japanese Folklore) (Tokyo: Seibundō Shinkōsha).

NIHON SŌGŌ AIKU KENKYŪJO (ed.), 1988. *Nihon Kodomo Shiryō Nenkan* (Annual Statistical Review of Children in Japan) (Nagoya: Chūō Shuppan).

NINOMIYA, AKIIE, 1998. 'Christianity and the Postwar Changes in the Welfare System', *Japan Christian Review*, 64, 84–92.

NIRA (National Institute for Research Advancement), 1996. *Volunteer nado no Shien Hōsaku ni kansuru Sōgōteki Kenkyū: Volunteer Katsudō no Shien to Volunteer Dantai no Hōjinka* (Comprehensive Study on Volunteer Activities and Other Measures of Support: The Support of Volunteer Activities and the Incorporation of Volunteer Organizations) (Tokyo: Sōgō Kenkyū Kaihatsu Kikō).

NOGUCHI, TAKENORI, 1988. 'Satogo' (Foster-Child), *Kōdansha Encyclopedia of Japan*, vol. xx.

NOMOTO, SANKICHI, 1998. *Shakai Fukushi Jigyō no Rekishi* (The History of Social Welfare Work) (Tokyo: Akashi Shoten).

NORGREN, TIANA, 1998. 'Abortion Before Birth Control: The Interest Group Politics Behind Postwar Japanese Reproduction Policy', *Journal of Japanese Studies*, 24/1, 59–94.

NOZAWA, MASAKO, 1991. *Jidō Yōgoron* (The Theory of Child Care) (Kyoto: Minerva Shobō).

OCHIAI, EMIKO, 1996. *The Japanese Family in Transition: A Sociological Analysis of Family Change in Postwar Japan* (Tokyo: LTCB International Library Foundation).

ODA, HIROSHI, 1992. *Japanese Law* (London, Dublin, and Edinburgh: Butterworth).

—— 1997. *Basic Japanese Laws* (Oxford: Clarendon Press).

OGAWA, TOSHIO, HASEGAWA, MASATO, MURAOKA, SUEHIRO, TAKAHASHI, MASANORI (eds.), 1983. *Bokutachi no Jū-go sai: Yōgoshisetsu no Kōkōshingaku Mondai* (Us at Fifteen: The Advancement to Senior High School of Children in *Yōgoshisetsu*) (Kyoto: Minerva Shobō).

OHINATA, MASAMI, 1995a. 'Kindai no Kodomo no Aisenai Hahaoya no Kenkyū kara Miete Kuru Mono: Omotoshite Shinrigaku ni okeru Hahasei Kenkyū no Tachiba kara' (Research on the New Mothers who Cannot Love their Children: From a Psychological Perspective), *Kazoku Kenkyū Nenpō*, 20, 20–31.

—— 1995b. 'The Mystique of Motherhood: A Key to Understanding Social Change and Family Problems in Japan', in Kumiko Fujimura Fanselow and Atsuko Kameda (eds.), *Japanese Women: New Feminist Perspectives on the Past, Present and Future* (New York: City University of New York, The Feminist Press).

OKANO, KAORI, and TSUCHIYA, MOTONORI, 1999. *Education in Contemporary Japan: Inequality and Diversity* (Cambridge: Cambridge University Press).

OSAKA-FU KODOMO KATEI CENTRE (ed.), 1997. *Kodomo to Katei no Takumashii Jiritsu ni Mukete: Osaka Kodomo Katei Hakusho* (Towards the Strong Independence of Children and Families: White Paper on Osaka Children and Families) (Osaka: Osaka-fu Kodomo Katei Centre).

OSAKA-FU SHAKAI FUKUSHI KYŌGIKAI (ed.), 1996. *21 Seki no Kodomo to Katei e no Message* (A Message to Children and Families for the Twenty-First Century) (Osaka: Osaka-fu Shakai Fukushi Kyōgikai).

ŌSHIMA, KYŌJI, 1990. 'Jidō Fukushi Shisetsu no Unei' (The Management of Child Welfare Institutions), in Susumu Iida, Kyōji Ōshima, Kazumu Miyamoto, Yoshihito Toyofuku, and Kosaka Kazuo, *Yōgoshisetsu Naiyō Sōron* (An Outline of Practice in Children's Homes) (Kyoto: Minerva Shobō).

OZAWA, MAKIKO, 1996. *Kodomo no Kenri, Oya no Kenri: Kodomo no Kenri Jōyaku wo Yomu* (Children's Rights, Parents' Rights: Reading the Convention on the Rights of the Child) (Tokyo: Nichigai Kyōyō Sensho).

OZAWA, MARTHA N., 1991. 'Child Welfare Programmes in Japan', *Social Service Review*, 65/1, 1–21.

PALMORE, ERDMAN, and MAEDA, DAISAKU, 1985. *The Honorable Elders Revisited: A Revised Cross-Cultural Analysis of Aging in Japan* (Durham: Duke University Press).

PENG, ITO, 1995. 'Boshi Katei: A Theoretical and Case Analysis of Japanese Lone Mothers and their Relationships to the State, the Labour Market, and the Family, with Reference to Britain and Canada', Ph.D. thesis (London School of Economics).

—— 1997. 'Single Mothers in Japan: Unsupported Mothers who Work', in Simon Duncan and Rosalind Edwards (eds.), *Single Mothers in an International Context: Mothers or Workers?* (London: UCL Press).

PINGUET, MAURICE, 1993. *Voluntary Death in Japan*, trans. Rosemary Morris (London: Polity Press).

PRESTON, SAMUEL H., and KONO, SHIGEMI, 1988. 'Trends in Well-Being of Children and the Elderly in Japan', in J. Palmer, T. Smeeding and B. Torrey (eds.), *The Vulnerable* (Washington, DC: The Urban Institute Press).

PRINGLE, KEITH, 1998. *Children and Social Welfare in Europe* (Buckingham and Philadelphia: Open University Press).

PYLE, KENNETH B., 1974. 'Advantages of Followership: German Economics and Japanese Bureaucrats, 1890–1925', *Journal of Japanese Studies*, 1/1, 127–64.

RAYNER, MOIRA, 1995. 'Children's Rights in Australia', in Bob Franklin (ed.), *The Handbook of Children's Rights: Comparative Policy and Practice* (London: Routledge).

REDER, PETER, DUNCAN, SYLVIA, and GRAY, MOIRA, 1993. *Beyond Blame: Child Abuse Tragedies Revisited* (London and New York: Routledge).

REHABILITATION BUREAU, 1995. *The Community-Based Treatment of Offenders System in Japan* (Tokyo: Ministry of Justice, Japan).

RICHAN, WILLARD C., and MENDELSOHN, ALLAN R., 1973. *Social Work: The Unloved Profession* (New York: New Viewpoints).

ROBERTS, JOHN G., 1973. *Mitsui: Three Generations of Japanese Business* (New York and Tokyo: Weatherhill).

ROESGAARD, MARIE, 1998. *Moving Mountains: Japanese Education Reform* (Aarhus: Aarhus University Press).

ROHLEN, THOMAS, 1996. 'Building Character', in T. P. Rohlen and G. K. LeTendre (eds.), *Teaching and Learning in Japan* (Cambridge: Cambridge University Press).

ROSE, RICHARD, and SHIRATORI, REI (eds.), 1986. *The Welfare State: East and West* (Oxford: Oxford University Press).

ROWE, JANE, 1989. *Child Care Now: A Survey of Placement Patterns* (London: British Agencies for Adoption and Fostering).

RUDD, CHRISTOPHER, 1994. 'Japan's Welfare Mix', *The Japan Foundation Newsletter*, 22/3, 14–17.

SAIKŌ SAIBANSHO JIMU SŌKYOKU (ed.), 1988. *Yōshi Seido no Kaisei ni kansuru System Shiryō* (Documentation Concerning the Revision of the Adoption System) (Tokyo: Saikō Saibansho Jimu Sōkyoku).

SAITŌ, HIDE, 1985. 'Baby and Infant Homes: Past and Present', *Child Welfare: Quarterly News from Japan*, 6/2, 2–13.

SAKAMOTO, TAKESHI, 1993a. 'Chiiki Fukushi no Tenkai to Jidō Fukushi Shisetsu no Yakuwari' (The Role of Child Welfare Institutions and the Evolution of Community Welfare), *Kodomo Katei Fukushi Jōhō*, 7, 42–6.

—— 1993b. 'Hogo wo Yō suru Jidō no Fukushi' (Welfare for Children Who Need Protection), in Taneaki Takahashi, Susumu Sunaga, Keiko Takiguchi, Takeshi Sakamoto, and Eiko Uto, *Jidō Fukushi* (Child Welfare) (Tokyo: Asakura Shoten).

—— 1994. 'Yōgokei Shisetsu Nyūjo Jidō no Suii' (A Study of the Trends in Children Coming into Institutional Care), *Nihon Sōgō Aiiku Kenkyūjo Kiyō*, 31, 173–8.

SANSOM, G. B., 1962. *Japan: A Short Cultural History* (London: Cresset Press).

SARGEANT, HARRIET, 1994. 'A Child in Crime', *The Independent Magazine*, 325 (10 Dec.), 34–8.

SASAKI, MASATO, 1989. 'Stress and Coping among Divorced Single Women Living in Homes for Single Mothers and Children in Japan: A Descriptive Study', DSW thesis (Columbia University).

SATŌ, NANCY ELLEN, 1991. 'Ethnography of Japanese Elementary Schools: Quest for Equality', Ph.D. thesis (Stanford University).

SATO OYA KAI (ed.), 1990. *Sato Oya Kenshūkai Text* (Text of the Foster-Parents' Training Meeting) (Tokyo: Zenkoku Sato Oya Kai).

SEISHŌNEN TO TOMO NI AYUMUKAI (ed.), 1997. *Shizukanaru Tatakai: Hirooka Tomohiko to Ikoi no Ie no Sanjūnen* (Quiet Battle: Hirooka Tomohiko and Thirty Years of the *Ikoi no Ie* Home) (Tokyo: Asahi Shinbunsha).

SEKI, KOREKATSU, 1971. *Shūdan Yōgo to Kodomotachi: Fukushi to Kyōiku no Tōitsu no tame ni* (Group Protection and Children: Towards the Unification of Welfare and Education) (Kyoto: Minerva Shobō).

SHIINA, ATSUKO, 1993. *Oya ni Naru Hodo Muzukashii Koto wa Nai* (Nothing is More Difficult than Being a Parent) (Tokyo: Kōdansha).

SHIMAZU, YOSHIKO, 1994. 'Unmarried Mothers and their Children in Japan', trans. Miya E. M. Lippit, *US—Japan Women's Journal* (English supplement), 6, 83–110.

SHINAGAWA, MITSUNORI, 1999. 'Jidō Yōgo Hattatsushi ni okeru Shōshasei Yōgo no Ichizuke' (The Location of Small-Group Living in the History of the Development of Child Protection), in Shōshasei Yōiku Kenkyūkai (ed.), *Naze Shōshasei Yōgo ka* (Why Small-Group Living Should Be Supported) (Fukushima: Shōshasei Yōiku Kenkyūkai).

SHINKAWA, TOSHIMITSU, and PEMPEL, T. J., 1996. 'Occupational Welfare and the Japanese Experience', in Michael Shalev (ed.), *The Privatization of Social Policy? Occupational Welfare and the Welfare State in America, Scandinavia and Japan* (Basingstoke: Macmillan).

SHŌJI, YŌKO, 1984. 'A Breakdown in Family Relationships and the Problems for Children', *Child Welfare: Quarterly News from Japan*, 4/3, 2–16.

SHUGHART, WILLIAM F. II, and CHAPPELL, WILLIAM F., 1999. 'Fostering the Demand for Adoptions: An Empirical Analysis of the Impact of Orphanages and Foster Care on Adoption in the United States', in Richard B. McKenzie (ed.), *Rethinking Orphanages for the Twenty-First Century* (Thousand Oaks, London, and New Delhi: Sage Publications).

SINCLAIR, IAN, and GIBBS, IAN, 1998. *Children's Homes: A Study in Diversity* (Chichester: John Wiley).

Single Mothers' Forum (ed.), 1994. *Boshi Katei ni Kanpai: Rikon.Hikon wo Kodomo to tomi ni Ikiru Anata e* (Cheers to Single Mothers! Life as a Single or Divorced Mother) (Tokyo: Gendai Shokan).

SINGLETON, JOHN, 1967. *Nichū: A Japanese School* (New York: Holt, Rinehart & Winston).

SMITH, ROBERT, 1987. 'Gender Inequality in Contemporary Japan', *Journal of Japanese Studies*, 13/1, 1–25.

SOBUE, KIRSTIE, 1991. 'Otōsan to Okāsan ga Inai: A Study of Welfare Provision of Orphaned and Abandoned Children in Japan', BA thesis (Cambridge University).

SOEDA, YOSHIYA, 1990. 'The Development of the Public Assistance System in Japan, 1966–73', *Annals of the Institute of Social Science, the University of Tokyo*, 32, 31–65.

SŌMUCHO SEISHŌNEN TAISAKU HONBU (ed.), 1996. *Seishōnen Hakusho: Seishōnen Mondai no Genjo to Taisaku* (White Paper on Youth: The Situation of Youth Problems, and Policies for Dealing with Them) (Tokyo: Sōmuchō Seishōnen Taisaku Honbu).

STEVENS, CAROLYN S., 1997. *On the Margins of Japanese Society: Volunteers and the Welfare of the Urban Underclass* (London: Routledge).

SUZUKI, MASAJIRŌ, 1998. 'Revision of Child Care System', in *Child Welfare: Annual Report from Japan* (Tokyo: The Foundation for Children's Future).

TABATA, HIROKUNI, 1990. 'The Japanese Welfare State: Its Structure and Transformation', *Annals of the Institute of Social Science, the University of Tokyo*, 32, 1–29.

TACHIBANA, YŪKO, 1992. *Kodomo ni Te o Agetakunaru Toki* (Times When You Feel Like Hitting Your Children) (Tokyo: Gakuyō Shobō).

TAKAHASHI, MUTSUKO, 1997a. *The Emergence of Welfare Society in Japan* (Aldershot: Avebury).

—— 1997b. 'Ishi'i Jūji in Search of Utopia through Okayama Orphanage in Meiji Japan', unpublished paper delivered at the Eighth Conference of the European Association of Japanese Studies, Budapest, Hungary, 27–30 August.

—— and Hashimoto, Raija, 1997. 'Minsei i'in. Between Public and Private: A Local Network for Community Care in Japan', *International Social Work*, 40, 303–13.

TAKAHASHI, SHIGEHIRO, 1977. 'Child Murder/Mother Suicides in Japan', *PHP* 8/5, 61–76.

TAKAHASHI, TOSHIKAZU, 1987. 'Japanese Children's Homes in Recent Years', *Child Welfare: Quarterly News from Japan*, 7/4, 2–10.

—— 1998a. 'Advocate Katsudō: Toshi Katei Zaitaku Shien Jigyō' (The Activities of the Urban Child and Family Support Centres), in Nihon Kodomo no Gyakutai Bōshi Kenkyūkai (ed.), *Dai Yonkai Gakujutsu Shūkai Programme* (Programme of the Fourth Academic Meeting [of the Japan Study Group for the Prevention of Child Abuse]) (Wakayama: Nihon Kodomo no Gyakutai Bōshi Kenkyūkai).

—— 1998b. 'Reinforcement of Self-Supporting Capability of Children Requiring Care and Protection', in *Child Welfare: Annual Report from Japan* (Tokyo: The Foundation for Children's Future).

TAKAMI, YOSHIHIDE, 1996. 'Hogo wo Yō suru Jidō no Fukushi' (Welfare for Children Who Need Protection), in Katsuaki Hanawa, Katsumi Tokuda, and Kazuko Takatama (eds.), *Jidō Fukushi Gaku* (The Study of Child Welfare) (Tokyo: Bunka Shobō Hakubunsha).

TAKEGAWA, SHŌGO, 1988. ' "Fukushi Kokka no Kiki" sono Ato' (After the 'Crisis of the Welfare State'), in Shakai Hoshō Kenkyūjo (ed.), *Shakai Seisaku no Shakaigaku* (The Sociology of Social Policy) (Tokyo: Tokyo Daigaku Shūppansha).

TAKEI, EMIKO, 1999. 'Chien Kazoku to iu Gensō: Yōshi Sato Oya no Taiken kara' (The Blood Family as an Illusion: From the Experience of Fostering and Adoption), *Joseigaku Nenpō*, 20, 77–87.

TAKENAKA, TETSUO, 1988. *Jidō Shūdan Yōgo no Riron: Hattatsuron kara no Approach* (The Theory of Child Protection Group Work: The Approach from Developmental Theory) (Kyoto: Minerva Shobō).

—— 1995. *Gendai Jidō Yōgoron* (Current Child Protection Theory) (Kyoto: Minerva Shobō).

—— 1998. *Kodomo no Kenri Jōyaku: Jidai no Jidō Fukushi* (The UN Convention on the Rights of the Child: Child Welfare of this Era) (Kyoto: Bessatsu Shiryō, Minerva Shobō).

TAKIGUCHI, KEIKO, 1993. 'Jidō Fukushi no Rekishi' (The History of Child Welfare), in Sunaga Taneaki, Takiguchi Susumu, Takeshi Sakamoto and Eiko Uto, *Jidō Fukushi* (Child Welfare) (Tokyo: Asakura Shoten).

TAMAI, KINGO, forthcoming. 'Images of the Poor in an Official Survey of Osaka, 1923–26', in Richard Wall and Osamu Saitō (eds.), *Economic and Social Aspects of the Family Life Cycle* (Cambridge: Cambridge University Press).

TANAKA, NAOKI, 1996. *Shimin Shakai no Volunteer* (Volunteers in Civil Society) (Tokyo: Maruzen Kabushiki Gaisha).

TANIMURA, M., MATSUI, I., and KOBAYASHI, N., 1990. 'Child Abuse of One of a Pair of Twins in Japan', *The Lancet* (24 Nov.), 1298–9.

TANNO, KIKUKO, 1984. 'Yōgoshisetsujidō no Jinken to Oya no Kekkon ni tsuite no Chōsa Hōkoku' (Research Report on Parental Marriage and the Rights of Children in Children's Homes), in Shigeo Hasegawa (ed.), *Rikon to Kodomo no Jinken* (Divorce and the Rights of Children) (Tokyo: Zenshakyō Yōgoshisetsu Kyōgikai).

TATARA, TOSHIO, 1975. '1,400 Years of Japanese Social Work from its Origins through the Allied Occupation, 552–1952', Ph.D. thesis (Bryn Mawr College).

—— 1980. 'The Japanese Occupation and Japanese Public Welfare: An Overview of SCAP Activities during the Early Phase', in Thomas W. Burkman (ed.), *The Occupation of Japan: Educational and Social Reform* (Norfolk, V.: Gatling Press).

TENRIKYŌ SHAKAI FUKUSHISHISETSU RENMEI, 1989. *Kyōnai Shakai Fukushi Shisetsu Yōran* (An Outline of Tenri Social Welfare Facilities) (Tenri: Tenrikyō Shakai Fukushishisetsu Renmei).

THANG, LENG LENG, 1999. 'The Dancing Granny: Linking the Generations in a Japanese Age-Integrated Welfare Centre', *Japanese Studies*, 19/2, 151–62.

THOMPSON, LAWRANCE H., 1983. 'The Face of Christ in Japanese Welfare Activity', *Japan Christian Quarterly*, 49/1, 8–11.

TOCHIO, ISAO, 1991. 'Measures for Fatherless Families and Widows' Welfare', *Child Welfare: Quarterly News from Japan*, 11/3, 15–21.

—— 1998. 'Establishment of Child and Family Support Center', in *Child Welfare: Annual Report from Japan* (Tokyo: Foundation for Children's Future).

TOKUMASA, KŌJI, 1974. 'Shisetsu Yōgo kara Mita Konnichi no Jidō Mondai' (The Contemporary Problems of Children Viewed from Child Protection Institutions), undergraduate diss. (International Christian University, Tokyo).

TOKYO METROPOLITAN GOVERNMENT, 1995. *Tokyo Metropolitan Government in 1995* (Tokyo: Tokyo Metropolitan Government).

TOKYO-TO FUKUSHIKYOKU, 1998. *Aratana Kodomo no Kenri Hoshō no Shikumi Tsukuri ni tsuite* (On the Construction of a Fresh Plan to Protect the Rights of Children) (Tokyo: Tokyo-to Fukushikyoku).

TOKYO-TO FUKUSHIKYOKU JIDŌBU (ed.), 1990. *Jidō.Hitorioya.Fujin Fukushi Seisaku no Gaiyō* (Outline of Welfare Policy for Children, Single Parents, and Women) (Tokyo: Tokyo-to Fukushikyoku).

TOKYO-TO SHAKAI FUKUSHI KYŌGIKAI (ed.), 1986/7. *Jidō Fukushi Nenpō: Jidō Fukushihō Seitei 40-nen Kinnen* (Annual Report on Child Welfare: Fortieth Anniversary of the Enactment of the Child Welfare Law) (Tokyo: Tokyo-to Shakai Fukushi Kyōgikai).

—— 1996a. *Tomorrow (Tokyo no Yōgo)* (Tomorrow: Care in Tokyo) (Tokyo: Tokyo-to Shakai Fukushi Kyōgikai).

—— 1996b. *Kodomo no Kenri to Jidō Fukushi Shisetsu no Kodomotachi: Kenshūkai Part 2* (Children's Rights and Children in Child Welfare Institutions: Part 2) (Tokyo: Tokyo-to Shakai Fukushi Kyōgikai).

TOKYO-TO YŌIKU KATEI Centre, 1991. *Tokyo-to Yōiku Katei Seido 17-nenkan no Hōkoku* (Report on Seventeen Years of the Tokyo City Adoption and Fostering System) (Tokyo: Tokyo-to Yōiku Katei Centre).

TSUJI, YŌKO, 1982. 'Homicide Called Suicide: Mother–Child Double Suicide in Japan', unpublished paper.

TSUJI, ZENNOSUKE, 1934. *Social Welfare Work by the Imperial Household of Japan*, trans. Masao Nagasawa (Tokyo: Japanese Red Cross Society).

TSUTSUMI, MASARU, TAKAHASHI, TOSHIKAZU, NISHIZAWA, SATORU, and HARADA, KAZUYUKI, 1996.

'Higyakutaiji Chōsakenkyū: Yōgoshisestu ni okeru Kodomo no Nyūsho Izen no Keiken to Shisetsu de no Seikatsu Jōkyō ni kansuru Chōsa Kenkyū' (Research on the Abuse of Children in *Yōgoshisetsu*: Experience of Abuse Before Coming into Care and Behaviour While in Residential Settings), *Shakai Jigyō Kenkyūjo Nenpō*, 32, 213–42.

TSUZAKI, TETSUO, 1991. 'Fukushi Scandal to Shisaku.Jitsumu Kaizen Seiryoku: Eikoku Jidō Care wo Sōzai ni' (Welfare Scandals and the Power to Improve Policy: Cases from British Child Care), *Bukkyō Daigaku Shakai Fukushi Kiyō*, 25, 18–35.

—— 1996. 'Residential Child Care: Policy and Practice with Special Reference to Adolescents', unpublished paper presented at Kibble Education Care Centre, Scotland (25 Jan.).

—— 1997. 'Socio-cultural Causes of Institutional Abuse in Japan: The Issues of Leadership, Authority and Power Relations', *Early Child Development and Care*, 133, 87–99.

—— 1998. 'The System of Child Welfare without Fieldwork: The Japanese Way or Anachronism?', *Proceedings of the Second International Symposium on Child and Youth Welfare in Korea, Japan and China, October 1997* (Institute for Social Welfare, The Catholic University, Korea).

—— 1999. 'Shōshasei Yōgo wa Naze Fuenai no ka?' (Why Does Small-Group Living Not Increase?), in Shōshasei Yōiku Kenkyūkai (ed.), *Naze Shōshasei Yōgo ka* (Why Small-Group Living Should Be Supported) (Fukushima: Shōshasei Yōiku Kenkyūkai).

TSUZAKI, TETSURŌ, 1996. *Kodomo no Gyakutai: Sono Jittai to Enjō* (Child Abuse: The Situation and Support) (Osaka: Toki Shobō).

TSUZURA, MASAKO, 1990. 'Jidō Gyakutai no Jidōsōdanjo no Taiō' (The Response of Child Advisory Centres to Child Abuse), *Sekai no Jidō to Bosei*, 28, 37–41.

TURNER, VICTOR, 1969. *The Ritual Process* (London: Routledge & Kegan Paul).

UENO, KAYAKO, 1994. 'Jidō Gyakutai no Shakaiteki Kōsaku' (The Social Construction of Child Abuse), *Sociology*, 39/2, 3–18.

—— 1999. 'Shōshika Jidai no Survival: Jidō Gyakutai Mondai kara mita "Shakai Fukushi no Byōri" ' (Survival in a Time of Declining Fertility: Social Welfare Problems from the Perspective of Child Abuse Problems), *Gendai no Shakai Byōri*, 14, 5–23.

United Nations, 1998. *Concluding Observations of the Committee on the Rights of the Child: Japan* (Eighteenth Session: Consideration of Reports Submitted by States Parties under Article 44 of the Convention), UN Report CRC/C/15/Add.90 (June).

UTTING, WILLIAM, 1991. *Children in Public Care: A Review of Residential Care* (London: HMSO).

VOGEL, EZRA F., 1963. *Japan's New Middle Class: The Salary Man and his Family in a Tokyo Suburb* (Berkeley: University of California Press).

—— 1980. *Japan as Number One: Lessons for America* (Tokyo: Tuttle).

WAGATSUMA, HIROSHI, 1981. 'Child Abandonment and Infanticide: A Japanese Case', in Jill E. Korbin (ed.), *Child Abuse and Neglect: Cross-Cultural Perspectives* (Los Angeles and London: University of California Press).

WARNER, NORMAN, 1992. *Choosing with Care: The Report of the Committee of Inquiry into the Selection, Development and Management of Staff in Children's Homes* (London: HMSO).

WATANUKI, JŌJI, 1986. 'Is There a "Japanese-Type Welfare Society"?', *International Sociology*, 1/3, 259–69.

WATERHOUSE, RONALD, CLOUGH, MARGARET, and LE FLEMING, MORRIS, 2000. *Lost in Care— Report of the Tribunal of Inquiry into the Abuse of Children in Care in the Former County Councils of Gwynedd and Clwyd since 1974* (London: Stationery Office).

WEINER, MICHAEL (ed.), 1997. *Japan's Minorities: The Illusion of Homogeneity* (London and New York: Routledge).

WHITE, GORDON and GOODMAN, ROGER, 1998. 'Welfare Orientalism and the Search for an East Asian Welfare Model', in Roger Goodman, Gordon White, and Huck-ju Kwon (eds.), *The East Asian Welfare Model: Welfare Orientalism and the State* (London and New York: Routledge).

WHITE, MERRY, 1987. *The Japanese Educational Challenge: A Commitment to Children* (New York: Free Press).

—— 1993. *The Material Child: Coming of Age in Japan and America* (New York: Free Press).

WILSON, DONALD V., 1980. 'Social Welfare Personnel and Social Work Education during the Occupation of Japan, 1945–48', in Thomas W. Burkman (ed.), *The Occupation of Japan: Educational and Social Reform* (Norfolk, V.: Gatling Press).

WOO, DEBORAH, 1989. 'The People v. Fumiko Kimura: But Which People?', *International Journal of Sociology of Law*, 17, 403–28.

WORDSWORTH, JEAN, 1968. 'Impressions of a Canadian Social Worker in Japan', in Dorothy Dessau (ed.), *Glimpses of Social Work in Japan* (Kyoto: Social Workers' International Club of Japan).

YAMADA, NOBUHIRO, 1992. 'Volunteer Katsudō no Shinkyokumen to Yōgoshisetsu no Taiō ni tsuite' (On a New Phase in Volunteer Activity and the Response of *Yōgoshisetsu*), *Kikan Jidō Yōgo*, 23/4, 32–5.

YAMAMOTO, TADASHI (ed.), 1988. *The Nonprofit Sector in Japan* (Manchester: Manchester University Press).

YAMAMOTO, TAMOTSU, 1988. 'Revision of the Foster Care System', *Child Welfare: Quarterly News from Japan*, 8/3, 2–9.

—— 1989. 'New Measures for Support of Children Undergoing Treatment at Homes for Training and Education of Juvenile Delinquents', *Child Welfare: Quarterly News from Japan*, 10/1, 11–13.

YAMAMURA, YOSHIAKI, 1986. 'The Child in Japanese Society', in Harold Stevenson, Hiroshi Azuma, and Kenji Hakuta (eds.), *Child Development and Education in Japan* (New York: W. H. Freeman).

YAMANTA, TOKUJI, 1995. 'Okizari ni sareta Katei Yōiku Seikyūken: Kokusai Kateinen ni Idaita Kitai to Shitsubō' (The Right of Children Without Their Own Family to have Their Own Interests Respected in the International Year of the Family), *Atarashii Kazoku*, 27, 66–80.

YAMAOKA, YOSHINORI, 1988. 'On the History of the Nonprofit Sector in Japan', in Tadashi Yamamoto (ed.), *The Nonprofit Sector in Japan* (Manchester: Manchester University Press).

YŌGOSHISETSU KYŌGIKAI (ed.), 1977. *Nakumonoka* (I Am Not Going to Cry) (Tokyo: Kiyōshobō).

—— 1990. *Nakumonoka: Zokui* (I Am Not Going To Cry: Part 2) (Tokyo: Kiyōshobō).

—— 1996. *Yōgoshisetsu no Hanseiki to Aratana Hishō* (Fifty Years of *Yōgoshisetsu* and a New Take-Off) (Tokyo: Yōgoshisetsu Kyōgikai).

YOKOCHI, TAMAKI, 1994. 'A Comparison of Probation Work, Recruitment and Training in England and Wales and in Japan', M.Sc. thesis (University of Oxford).

YOKOGAWA, KAZUO [and others], 1985. *Kōhai no Karute: Shōnenkanbetsu Bangō 1589* (A Desolate Card: Juvenile Delinquent No. 1589) (Tokyo: Kyōdo Tsūshinsha).

YOKOSHIMA, AKIRA, 1977. 'Tenkōsei no Tekiō ni tsuite no Kangaekata' (Views on the Adjustment of Transfer Children), *Utsunomiya Daigaku Kyōiku Gakubu Kiyō*, 27/1, 139–53.

YONEKURA, AKIRA, 1984. 'Problems Involved in the Child Adoption and Foster-Parent Systems in Japan', *Child Welfare: Quarterly News from Japan*, 4/4, 2–10.

YONEYAMA, SHŌKO, 1999. *The Japanese High School: Silence and Resistance* (London and New York: Nissan Institute of Japanese Studies/Routledge).

YONEYAMA, TAKAHIRO, 1997. *Jidōfukushi no Enjo Gijutsu: Yōgo Katsudōron no Shiza to Jissen* (Skilful Support in Child Welfare: Practice and Viewpoints on Theories of Institutional Activities) (Tokyo: Bunkashobō Hakubunsha).

YOSHIDA, KYŪICHI, and UTO, EIKO, 1977. 'Nihon Shakai Jigyō to Yōgoshisetsu' (Japanese Social Welfare Work and Child Protection Institutions), in Yōgoshisetsu Kyōgikai (ed.), *Yōgoshisetsu Sanjūnen* (Thirty Years of Child Protection Institutions) (Tokyo: Yōgoshisetsu Kyōgikai).

YOSHIOKA, MUTUSKO, SAKŌ, TŌRU, KOJIMA, TAEKO, and ŌYAMA, MICHIKO, 1995. *Oyako no Trouble: Q and A* (Questions and Answers on Issues of Child–Parent Troubles) (Tokyo: Yūhikaku Sensho).

YUZAWA, YASUHIKO, 1983. 'Nihon ni okeru Yōshi Engumi no Tōkeiteki Ozei' (Current Statistical Trends in Japanese Adoption), *Atarashii Kazoku*, 3, 21–9.

—— 1994. *Japanese Families* (Tokyo: Foreign Press Center).

ZADANKAI, 1991. 'Yōgoshisetsu no Genjō to Kadai' (Themes and the Current Position of Children's Homes), *Kodomo to Katei* [Tokushū Yōgoshisetsu no Shōrai Tenbō], 28/7, 8–29.

ZENKOKU MINSEI.JIDŌIIN KYŌGIKAI, 1986. *Nihon no Minseiin* (The System of Community Volunteers in Japan) (Tokyo: Zenkoku Minsei.Jidōiin Kyōgikai).

ZENKOKU SHAKAI FUKUSHI KYŌGIKAI MINSEIBU, 1997. 'Minseiin Jidōiin no Katsudō to Rekishi' (The History and Activities of Minseiin Jidōiin), *Gekkan Fukushi* (Dec.), 30–7.

ZENSHAKYŌ (ZENKOKU SHAKAI FUKUSHI KYŌGIKAI) (eds.), 1991. *Yōgoshisetsu Handbook* (Tokyo: Zenshakyō).

Index